HUMAN COMMUNICATION THEORY

Second Edition

SARAH TRENHOLM

Ithaca College

PRENTICE HALL, Englewood Cliffs, New Jersey 07632

Library of Congress Cataloging in Publication Data

```
Trenholm, Sarah
    Human communication theory / Sarah Trenholm, -- 2nd ed.
      p.   cm.
    Includes bibliographical references and index.
    ISBN 0-13-446071-5
    1. Communication      I. Title
  P90.T7  1991
    302.2--dc20                                    90-46008
                                                      CIP
```

Editorial/production supervision and interior design:
   Ocean View Technical Publications/Jennifer Wenzel
Cover design: Lundgren Graphics, Ltd.
Manufacturing buyer: Ed O'Dougherty/Debbie Kesar/
   Mary Ann Gloriande

© 1991, 1986 by Prentice Hall, Inc.
A Division of Simon & Schuster
Englewood Cliffs, New Jersey 07632

Printed in the United States of America

10 9 8 7 6 5 4 3 2

ISBN   0-13-446071-5

Prentice Hall International (UK) Limited, *London*
Prentice Hall of Australia Pty., Limited, *Sydney*
Prentice Hall Canada, Inc., *Toronto*
Prentice Hall Hispanoamericana, S.A., *Mexico*
Prentice Hall of India Private Limited, *New Delhi*
Prentice Hall of Japan, Inc., *Tokyo*
Simon & Schuster Asia Pte. Ltd., *Singapore*
Editora Prentice Hall do Brasil, Ltda., *Rio de Janeiro*

CONTENTS

PREFACE

GOALS AND ASSUMPTIONS

This book is written for an undergraduate audience. Although it does not assume previous course work in communication theory, nor a high level of methodological sophistication, it is clearly not designed for the student looking for an easy A. Neither is it written for the student primarily concerned with developing communication skills. Rather, it assumes a student who wants to explore the hows and whys behind the skills, a student interested in theoretical issues.

An important concern of the text is to make the materials as easy to understand and as engaging as possible while at the same time being as true as possible to each theory's intent and complexity. To make the theories more understandable and more interesting to students, an attempt has been made to introduce practical examples that show how even the most "abstract" model can be used to explain real-life situations.

A strong organizational structure is used to help students make connections. One of the dangers of survey books is that they can easily become "shopping lists" of theories and isolated models. To help alleviate this problem, theory is conceptualized as a problem-solving activity, and the text focuses on a limited set of practical communication problems. In addition, numerous summaries and transitions are employed to help the student follow the flow of argument within the text.

Of course, ease of reading is not an end in itself. Two basic goals lie behind the writing of this text. The first is to provide the student with a survey of major social scientific theories of communication, theories that have generated research and discussion within the field. These are theories that any student of communication should be able to recognize and identify, either because they illuminate the nature of communication phenomena or because of their influence on subsequent theoretical formulations.

The second, and perhaps the more important, goal is to develop in the student a critical attitude toward theory, to drive toward the realization that theories are based on underlying assumptions that should not be accepted uncritically. It is important for students to see that theorists make choices, that theorizing is less a process of discovering an underlying concrete truth than of constructing a vision of reality. This necessitates including theories from various perspectives as well as discussing the nature of perspectives and ideological assumptions. While there is much to be said for a text based on a single perspective, the decision was made to present theories from a number of different approaches and, in this way, to open the door for critical debate. It also seems to be a truer representation of a field of study that, for better or worse, is an eclectic one.

While this eclecticism is a cause of concern to some, it may be viewed as one of the strengths of our field, for it means that we need not limit ourselves to a single body of literature for insights into human communication. This text is based on the belief that it is more important at the introductory level to stress similarities among the disciplines of the social sciences than to emphasize differences. A conscious effort has, therefore, been made to include not only the work of speech communication scholars but that of other social scientists as well.

The ultimate success of this project depends, of course, on what the instructor does with the material. Although this book is designed to lead the student in certain directions, whether or not this occurs depends largely on the instructor's guidance. Here there are several options. One option is to work though the materials as given, explaining the theories, leading the students toward critical debate, and emphasizing connections and applications. This can easily be done in a lecture or lecture-discussion format. The appendices on theory and research may or may not be included, depending on level and student interest.

A second option is to use a seminar format. One thing that is absolutely clear is that primary sources are always preferable to secondary ones (a difficult admission from the author of a sec-

ondary source). Student reports and papers on primary sources could form the basis of the course, with the text serving as an organizing framework. A final option might be to work rapidly through the text and then to introduce a coherent set of programmatic studies (for example, the research growing out of the constructivist framework, or cognitive schemata studies, or any of the attitude change programs), asking students to critique these studies in light of the theories included in the text.

The text itself is not a research review. It is designed for students who have not yet taken a methods course or who may be taking one concurrently. It does, however, include a lengthy appendix on research methods and, through the reseach abstracts, introduces students to representative kinds of research. The abstracts were chosen not so much for the research support they lend to the theories but rather as interesting examples of different methodologies. The goal is to present fairly simple studies that can familiarize students with research methods and motivate them to read additional journal articles.

The abstracts vary widely in approach and topic. Some were chosen because they are "classic," widely cited studies of historical interest or because they employ an unusual or creative approach to a given topic. Others were chosen because they illustrate a set of currently interesting programmatic studies. They are not all perfect examples of research nor are they all the "best" studies in the field. If students have a better than average grounding in research, the instructor may want to emphasize the appendices, asking students to abstract additional studies that exemplify current approaches to research.

Those of us who teach communication come from an array of backgrounds and hold a variety of interests. The text recognizes this diversity and provides the instructor with as much flexibility as possible in introducing the study of human communication.

ADDITIONS TO THE SECOND EDITION

New Trends in Theory

Theories come and go, and intellectual fashions alter with the years. Although there have not been dramatic changes since this text was first published, there has been a shift in emphasis, a revision of our view of human nature. The human being we seek to understand today is different in two ways from the one we previously described: He or she is much more clearly both a sense maker and a social actor. Today's theorists are no longer afraid to ask about what goes on inside the head of human actors. Thus, there is a continuing interest in cognitive operations such as goals, plans, and scripts, and a new interest in intentions and motivations. Where previous researchers shied away from questions of meaning, this topic is now seen as fundamental. Today's theorists are also not afraid to locate their subjects in a social context and to assert that reality is socially negotiated. Of course, these ideas are not new. The change is rather a matter of proportion. While previously these ideas were waiting in the wings, today they are begining to take center stage.

Humans as Sense Makers. The notion that people seek out information about the self and others is fundamental both to social comparison theory and to the consistency theories introduced in the 1950s and 1960s as well as to the attribution theories of the 1970s.

Today's models use different assumptions to understand how people make sense of action. Both the consistency and attribution models are extremely rational. They posit an individual who finds logical contradiction intolerable and who acts in everyday life as a naive scientist, an individual without needs, goals, or motivations that might get in the way of objective assessment of the world. Newer models put less emphasis on rational problem solving. They also posit individuals capable of formulating plans and intentions. We are no longer seen as creatures whose behavior is the product of external variables; instead, we are self-determining. As Rom Harre suggests, this view anthropomorphizes man. Finally, today's actor is much less isolated than before. Sense makers described in earlier models seemed to act alone; they were relatively impervious to the influence of others. Today's individual is fundamentally social.

Humans as Social Products. An insistence that human beings are embedded in social contexts is clearly nothing new. The symbolic interactionists introduced this idea as early as the 1930s, and theorists such as Erving Goffman developed a model of the human as an actor performing socially given scripts. Despite this, most models of communication have recognized social factors only peripherally, preferring to describe what people do to one another rather than what they do together. Today's social constructionists criticize earlier formulations for overlooking social/historical forces and for reifying social constructs. They maintain not only that humans are affected by cultural practices but that our most fundamental notions of reality, self, and other are socially created and maintained. What makes this view significant for our field is that it is through communication that our realities are negotiated and through talk that they are revealed.

We Live in a World of Significance. To the new generation of theorists, then, humans have a basic need to look for and create significance. We live in a world made up of (to use the vocabulary of the semioticians) an interlocking system of signifiers. As human actors we are compelled not only to talk but to talk about talk. As theorists we go one step farther, offering commentary on the way individuals comment on experience. Thus, we have a new interest not only in forms of talk and signification but in explanations, accounts, and narratives.

Critical Methodologies. If our model of human nature has changed, then so too has our orientation toward research. The recognition that reality is negotiated and maintained through talk leads logically to the realization that by controlling talk we control reality. Thus, a power dimension, a sense that all communication is political, has emerged, and this sense leads directly to the view that theory should not only explain and describe communication practices but that it should criticize them as well.

Changes in This Edition

Despite the fact that there are new currents in contemporary theory, I do not think it is time yet to abandon all our old models. The present edition retains most of the theories from the original but adds some new material. Chapter 1 remains essentially the same, although here and throughout the text the writing has been simplified and tightened and printing errors have been corrected. In chapter 2 the order of presentation has been reversed; we begin with a consideration of problems, and end with a consideration of context. In addition to an overview of situational contexts, a brief discussion of social, political, and historical contexts has also been added, with an emphasis on contributions made by feminist social critics.

In chapter 3 there are some major additions. A new perspective, based on that cluster of ideas that combines structuralism, semiotics, depth psychology, and literary theory has been added. Although this perspective, which I have labeled as semiotic, has been alive and well in Europe for

decades, it has only recently migrated to our shores. It is of particular importance in media criticism but can also be seen as an influence in general social theory. Chapter 3 also recognizes the decline of variable analytic methods and the emergence of interpretive and critical methods. Thus, the section on laws and rules has been revised and now compares deterministic, interpretive, and critical approaches to theory.

Interest in the structures people use to explain and justify their own and others' behavior are currently very important. Therefore, at the end of chapter 4, an overview of the social constructionist position has been added. Chapter 5 adds a very brief introduction to issues in conversation analysis. This area is growing rapidly and perhaps deserves more space than it has been given. Instructors for whom this is of special interest may wish to add materials of their own to those cited.

Chapter 6 outlines what is an essentially symbolic interactionist position. A very brief discussion of the relationship between narrative and identity has been added here. When chapter 7 was first written, the problem of evolution was given short shrift. Since then, there has been a renewed interest in developmental study, an area now referred to as life-span research. An introduction to some of these sources is now included in chapter 7. Finally, most of the original research abstracts have been retained. In addition, several have been added. Research Abstracts 4.3, 4.4, 6.2, 6.3, 8.3, and 10.3 are new to this edition.

OVERVIEW OF THE TEXT'S ORGANIZATION

PART I: INTRODUCTION TO THE STUDY OF HUMAN COMMUNICATION

This text consists of three parts. Part I presents a general introduction to the study of human communication. It examines some of the meanings that have been attached to the concept of communication and subdivides the subject matter of the field. The purpose of its three chapters is to provide the student with foundations for understanding subsequent theories. Chapter 1 begins with a brief history of our field and then examines definitions of communication. Chapter 2 introduces two concepts that serve as the basis of the organization of the remainder of the text: the concepts of communicative contexts and problems. Finally, in chapter 3, a discussion of basic perspectives toward theory and research is presented as a base for criticizing the models presented in Parts II and III.

PART II: COMMUNICATIVE PROBLEMS

In Part II we consider general theories of communication, using the framework developed in chapter 2. Discussion centers on five problems faced by all communicators: communicator acceptability, signification, social coordination and relational definition, communicative outcome achievement, and evolution.

Chapter 4 examines theories that explain the processes involved in choosing communicative partners. Chapter 5 discusses the nature of sign systems and reviews theories that explain how individuals encode and decode messages. In chapter 6, attention is given to models of identity formation and social coordination. Chapter 7 introduces two problems of communication. The first part of this chapter discusses general theories of motivation and influence; the second presents a brief overview of the importance of developmental theories of communication. The models presented in Part II are, for the most part, general in nature. They were chosen because they describe basic processes common to all instances of communication. Whether one's goal is to understand interpersonal relationships, group interactions, or public communication, the theories presented here should prove helpful.

PART III: CONTEXTS OF COMMUNICATION

Part II examines how communicative contexts serve to modify and constrain the ways the basic problems of communication are defined and solved. While theories in Part II focus on commonalities between contexts, the theories in Part III emphasize their differences. Here we discuss how communicators actually go about the day-to-day business of doing interpersonal, group, and public communication. In this section it should become clear that the five problems introduced in Part II are, in actual practice, overlapping and interconnected, and that, in real life situations, communicators must often go about solving all of these problems simultaneously.

chapter 1

THE HISTORY AND NATURE OF HUMAN COMMUNICATION

INTRODUCTION

For more than 25 centuries, people have sought to understand communication. Although they have taken many different approaches, their goal has always been to discover the processes by which human beings share ideas and influence one another. The field of speech communication, as we know it today, has a rich history, yet it has always been open to new discoveries and methods. It has changed in unanticipated ways and will undoubtedly continue to do so. In this text, we will examine some of the theory that has informed the study of communication. Focus will be on twentieth-century trends in communication inquiry, and the theories we examine will be drawn primarily from the social sciences.

Today the concept of communication has achieved overwhelming importance. Rapid development of new technologies for producing and transmitting information has foregrounded communication as a priviledged topic of inquiry. The control and management of communication systems is one of the central competences of our age.[1] Yet, as Lee Thayer has stated, despite the proliferation of communication technologies, "the human and 'organizational' communication problems we have today are not basically different from those Confucius pondered more than twenty centuries ago."[2] Thayer argues that a solution to these problems lies not in the mastery of technology, but instead in "a sound and comprehensive understanding of the phenomenon" of communication.[3] This book examines the state of this understanding in contemporary theories of communication.

HISTORICAL PERSPECTIVES

The Rhetorical Tradition

Classical and Medieval Rhetoric. Communication, as a subject of inquiry, is probably as old as civilization itself. We know that communication was a major area of interest to the ancient Greeks and Romans. In the fifth century B.C., Plato and Aristotle developed the first recorded communication theories in the West. They were followed by such major figures as Cicero, Seneca, Quintilian, and Longinus.[4] Thus, by the close of what has come to be known as the Classical period (A.D. 300–400) a substantial body of writing devoted to the study of communication existed.

The ancient Greeks focused their theories on persuasive argument and public communication. Their theories were essentially practical, for Greek society demanded a high degree of oral skill. In the Athenian legal system, for example, citizens were not allowed to hire lawyers to argue for them; consequently, they had to develop public speaking skills to plead cases before the several hundred jurors called on to judge them. Similarly, the democratic use of majority vote to determine public policy meant that public office seekers had to learn to present ideas clearly and persuasively.[5] Thus, early Greek theories focused on techniques for influencing others. The body of knowledge built around "the craft of persuasion" became known as *rhetoric*, and the theorists who wrote about it, *rhetoricians*.

One of the earliest and most influential models of rhetoric was developed sometime between the third and first centuries B.C. This model divided the process of rhetorical communication into five steps: invention, style, arrangement, memory, and delivery.[6] *Invention* referred to the process by which a rhetor chose message content. *Style* was the translation of content into appropriate words. *Arrangement* stood for the process of appropriately organizing a message. *Memory* meant storing content, style, and arrangement in the mind. *Delivery* was the production and dissemination of the message. During the Classical period a series of prescriptive guidelines were collected to provide the orator with a step-by-step guide to each part of the communication process.

At the same time that practitioners were using the canons as practical self-help guides, more serious rhetoricians were developing a body of theory about each canon. Thus, the canons can serve as a definition of the fields of inquiry that made up the Classical study of rhetoric. Rhetoricians interested in invention, for example, examined the nature of knowledge and knowing. Style involved the study of the nature of language. Arrangement included the study of processes by which information could be ordered and related. Memory encompassed processes of information storage and retrieval, while delivery focused on matters of message transmission. Many of these areas of theory are still important today and make up much of the subject matter of modern communication theory.

As Hellenic culture died out at the close of the Classical period, an interest in theory for theory's sake declined, and the Classical paradigm became fragmented, a state of affairs that continued into the Medieval and Renaissance periods (A.D. 400–1600).[7] Works became prescriptive and non-theoretical, consisting primarily of manuals on the art of letter writing and preaching, two processes of practical concern to medieval communicators.[8] Only with the secularization of thought that occurred in the seventeenth century did the theoretical study of human communication re-emerge.

"Modern" Rhetoric. Modern rhetoric is the body of communication study occurring roughly between 1600 and 1900. Douglas Ehninger iden-

Question #1

tifies four major trends during this time: classical, epistemological-psychological, belletristic, and elocutionist.[9] The classical approach to modern rhetoric reintroduced and elaborated on the classical paradigm, reversing previous prescriptive trends. Epistemological-psychological approaches focused on the mental processes involved in the act of communication and raised questions about how human beings "come to know, to believe, and to act."[10] Belletristic approaches emerged from an interest in the study of literature, poetry, and drama and a concern with the relationship between language arts and society. Finally, elocutionist approaches centered on aspects of delivery, prescribing detailed sets of verbal and nonverbal behaviors an orator could use to embellish his or her presentation. The first three approaches were essentially theoretical; the fourth was practical and atheoretical.

The Communication Theory Tradition

The Influence of Nineteenth-Century Science. Currently, it is common to divide our discipline into two ostensibly separate areas: (1) humanistic rhetorical study and (2) social-scientific communication theory. Both areas investigate the same question: How does the communicator impart ideas to the listener and with what effect? The methods used to answer this question, however, vary in fundamental ways.

The shift that was eventually to result in the communication theory approach began with nineteenth-century science. The "scientific method," which had its genesis in eighteenth-century philosophy and reached its height in the works of nineteenth-century natural and physical scientists, became immensely influential not only within the scientific community but within other disciplines as well. Rigorous control and manipulation, reliance on numerical measurement and mathematical models, and emphasis on empirical observation and inference that were characteristic of laboratory studies became the preferred model for

discovery. Students of human behavior sought ways to use these methods in their own work, and the social sciences emerged in response to demands for the discovery of scientific laws of human behavior.[11]

Contemporary Trends in the Social Sciences. Early in the twentieth century, behavioral psychologists led the way toward a scientific method for studying human behavior. Their aim was to discover the laws governing learning, and their approach was the behavioral experiment "in which the investigator manipulated a stimulus under controlled conditions in order to discover its effects on a response."[12] The goal of theory became the specification of invariant laws describing a mathematically functional relationship between variables, a goal that remains basic to much of the social-scientific work being done today.

Social-psychological theories, specifically the study of attitude change processes, also affected the emerging study of communication from a social-scientific point of view. Carl Hovland and his associates at Yale in the 1950s translated the classical paradigm of the ancients into a modern experimental framework in an attempt to understand the variables affecting persuasion. Examining factors such as "the order of arguments; use of evidence; emotional materials such as fear appeals, language intensity, and obscene language; source credibility variables; and audience variables such as sex, dogmatism, ego involvement in the subject of messages, and so forth," they forged new ways of investigating the classical canons through a science of communication.[13]

Another major influence on twentieth-century communication theories grew from engineering advances in machine technologies for transmitting information. Claude Shannon and Warren Weaver developed a mathematical communication theory known as *information* theory.[14] Their work led to the division of communication into source, encoder, message, channel, decoder, and

wordsely

→ *Scientific method*

Comm. theory Tradition   Question #2

Contempory Trends!

behavioral psychologist / Social - psychological / information Theory

- Social Context.

- 2nd Part Quest #2

destination. The human processes of transmitting messages and a machine analogy was incorporated into paradigms of the communication process.

Once again, the path of communication study appears to be changing. Just as dissatisfaction with the elocutionary movement led communication theory in a mathematical, scientific direction, so now a growing suspicion that human behavior cannot be understood from a mechanistic approach leads to a search for more productive models. In the 1980s and 1990s, a number of communication specialists are trying to forge a new approach based on rules theory and on advances in language philosophy, qualitative sociology, semiotic study, and critical theory. These theorists focus on the social context in which communication occurs, seeing communication not so much as a transmission of information but as a social construction, reevaluating many of our assumptions about human communication and raising important questions about being and knowing.[15]

EXPLORING THE CONCEPT OF HUMAN COMMUNICATION

The fact that communication has been an area of conjecture and study over the centuries does not necessarily mean it is well understood. Sometimes, the most popular and familiar concepts are the most confusing. This is especially true today when the popularity of communication as both a scientific and personal construct has reached unprecedented heights. There is actually a great deal of disagreement about what communication is and how it should be studied.

Communication has become a sort of "portmanteau" term. Like a piece of luggage, it is overstuffed with all manner of odd ideas and meanings. The fact that some of these do not fit, resulting in a conceptual suitcase much too heavy for anyone to carry, is often overlooked. What

follows will examine the current popularity of the concept of communication, review some of its divergent applications, and argue that communication, as currently thought of, runs the danger of being an overburdened concept. This section argues that uncritical use of the concept of communication often results in conceptual problems on both the scientific and individual levels.

The Popularity of Communication as an Explanatory Construct

It is easy to argue the need to study communication. It so pervades popular culture that we can hardly pass a day without encountering some statement of how important communication is. We are so often told that "all we need is more communication" that we view it as a kind of personal and social cure-all. On an individual level, we strive for better and more intimate interaction with friends and family, wonder whether our communication skills are adequate for professional advancement, and worry about what our "body language" is communicating to those around us. On a wider social level, we analyze social problems in terms of "communication gaps," style our politicians as good or bad communicators, and believe that solutions to international conflicts could be achieved if only world leaders were more willing to communicate.

The pervasiveness of the concept of communication can be seen in virtually every field of study. Geneticists, for example, often speak of the codes by which "directions" for development and growth are passed from one organism to another; information within the cell is seen as part of a communication system that allows inheritance and change. Biologists and neurophysiologists use communication models to describe processes within the bodies of living organisms.[16] They study the "language of the nerves," which allows the reception, integration, and conduction of sensory information along neural pathways as well as the internal "messages" organisms use to regulate temperature and oxygen content. They conceive of the body as a collection of mini-communication systems that allow an organism to adapt to its environment and regulate its metabolic processes.

Zoologists, too, study communication systems.[17] They try to unravel the distress signals of birds, the "language of courtship" in jumping spiders and crabs, and the use of threat displays by Siamese fighting fish. Even the process by which lowly slime molds emit chemical signals to attract each other has been studied as a form of communication. And communication systems of minor interest in protozoans achieve major importance in higher primates, as indicated by attempts to teach chimpanzees to use human "language."

Engineers and computer scientists are also concerned with communication, between man and machine and between machine and machine. They study how signals emanating in one part of a mechanical system are received by another part and work to regulate the system. For example, the process by which a floating buoy measures the gasoline level in an automobile and transfers that information to an accelerating arm on a control panel, causing the driver to stop for gas, has been described as communication as has the process by which a thermostat uses information about fluctuations in room temperature to activate a furnace. Scientists studying artificial intelligence also raise serious questions about the capacity of machines to engage in "intelligent" communicative behavior. Although HAL in *2001: A Space Odyssey* was only a fictional character, scientific advances in robotics make us wonder when a "real-life" HAL will be created.

These examples represent serious work on communication systems. If we also consider the pop-culture, talk-show notions of communication (reports of plants that "talk to" each other and of people who have experienced extraterrestrial communication), the concept becomes even more ubiquitous. It sometimes seems that there is no set of actions, human or otherwise, to which the label "communication" has not been applied.

Communication as an Overburdened Concept

The familiarity and popularity of communication is both a blessing and a curse for the serious student. Although human communication is recognized as an important field of study, too many meanings are attached to it. When a concept becomes as widely used as communication—when it borrows meanings from as many diverse fields—it becomes an *overburdened concept.*[18] The concept is asked to do too much work; it becomes overloaded with meaning, with the result that it eventually becomes meaningless. There are at least three dangers in overburdening a concept: conceptual confusion, conceptual oversimplification, and ideological masking.

Conceptual Confusion. One of the dangers of overburdening a concept is that it may be used to describe essentially dissimilar things. When this happens, our thinking about these things can become confused. Certainly, there are similarities among the instances of communication just reviewed, yet there also are differences. Applying a single concept to such different processes runs the risk of attaching inappropriate meanings to them. A meaning validly connected to the idea of a machine may cause confusion when it enters the semantic space reserved for humans. Meanings perfectly appropriate for describing people may cause contradictions when attached to animals. The problem is that the resulting confusion may not be immediately apparent or easily resolvable.

The use of the Shannon-Weaver model of electronic communication to describe human communication is a good example of *conceptual confusion.* To use this model in such a fashion is to view humans as analogous to electronic transmitter/receivers and, consequently, to attach a whole set of inappropriate meanings to them. Humans are like transmitters in some respects but, in others, they are very different. We humans are capable of considering our own actions, of actively processing information, of being both creative and malicious; radio transmitters are not. Linking human and machine in this way confuses the nature of both.

Frank Dance provides another example of this problem.[19] Language, he argues, has a particular meaning when used to describe human symbol using; in fact, it is intimately tied to notions of human cognition. To use the term language when describing mating signals emitted by the female stickleback fish is to attach new and contradictory meaning to both the ideas "human language" and "stickleback fish." The process engaged in by the stickleback is very different from the one engaged in by the human. We fail to understand human communication if we use a machine or animal model, and we risk imputing human characteristics to machines or animals if we work the other way.

Stephan Jay Gould gives us a final example of problems that arise when we borrow concepts originally used to explain one kind of phenomenon and apply them to another kind. Gould's example comes from the field of genetics and not only illustrates the problem of conceptual confusion but shows how the problem can be rectified by careful scientific thinking. In the 1950s, when Watson and Crick presented their Nobel Prize-winning model of the double helical structure of DNA, they explained the formation of organisms as the translation of a basic code made up of four units of information arrayed in various combinations. They argued that, using this "language," "DNA makes RNA and RNA makes protein, in a one-way flow of information, a unidirectional process of mechanical construction."[20]

The Watson-Crick model incorporated both machine-processing and language-coding analogies to describe the nature of DNA. Subsequent investigations have questioned the original analogy. What was once thought to be a one-way flow of information, such as that occurring in machine transmission, is now viewed differently. The genome (which carries the cell's genetic information) is now considered to be a fluid system capable of constant reorganization and change, a system that can turn back on itself and introduce new materials into DNA from the outside. While a modified communication analogy is still used to describe this system, the original machine-communication analogy led to misconceptions. The fact that contemporary genetic scientists could modify and build on Watson and Crick's work, however, underscores the original power of their model and "the fruitfulness of good science in general," which has methods for reevaluation and change built into it.[21]

Conceptual Oversimplification. A second danger in using an overburdened concept is that individual meaning may be set aside in favor of more general, oversimplified meaning. Formulating a concept involves a process of abstracting. A concept stands for a class of things, not for everything about those things, but merely for what they have in common. Meanings attached to a general concept are neither as varied nor as specific as meanings attached to the specific objects making up that general concept.

For example, when we observe a male scorpion making ritualized back and forth movements before a female, we observe a particular, concrete form of animal behavior. When we class those movements as a "mating dance," we put them into a more abstract category including all dance-like patterns of movement, whether found in scorpions or in other animals. Incorporating mating dances into the concept "tactile communication," we widen the category yet again. A description of tactile communication includes not only the dance of the scorpion but the actions of porpoises and whales nuzzling their mates, of orb web-spinning spiders emitting vibrations, of birds preening each other, and of humans shaking hands. As we include more diverse cases in the concept, statements about commonalities become more limited. We lose information about unique characteristics of the specific phenomena, favoring instead an oversimplified view of what they share in common. Each step up this "ladder of abstraction" takes us farther from concrete and unique behavioral descriptions and leads to more and more *conceptual oversimplification.*

The problems increase when we try to say something specific about the common behaviors of chimps, humans, computers, and thermostats. Certainly, all involve information processing. But as Edward Carterette and Donald Norman point out, "'Information processing' is an imprecise term that is quite empty apart from the meaning it is given in a particular discussion."[22] Thus, overburdening a concept, whether it be that of communication or of information processing, can lead to information loss through oversimplification. The effects of conceptual oversimplification and confusion lead to the third problem: *ideological masking.*

Ideological Masking. An ideology is a view of the world and a set of instructions for acting in it. Ideology need not be a political or economic philosophy such as socialism or capitalism, although these philosophies are ideological. There are also scientific and practical ideologies. A scientific ideology is a view of what science is and how it should be conducted. Whenever we engage in science, we tacitly accept a series of assumptions about the world and about how best to know that world.

Most ideologies are conservative; they tend to uphold the status quo. For example, the communication-theory approach to the study of human communication grew out of an acceptance of nineteenth-century scientific beliefs combined with elements of behaviorism and information theory. The approach incorporated an existing ideology based on linear cause and effect, reductionism, and quantification. It uncritically accepted a popular view of the world and of science; this view then began to dictate how research should be conducted and what questions communication scholars should ask. Although some scientists questioned the appropriateness of studying human interaction in a mechanistic way, they were caught in a bind: to question the pre-

vailing research method was to question an entire philosophical system. Most tried to explain away the difficulties they sensed. Others refused even to consider them. As William McGuire argues, "excessive preoccupation with and loyalty to [an] original insight blinds the thinker to other explanations."[23]

All concepts carry ideological meanings. Overburdened concepts are particularly troublesome because they tend to "imperialize" these meanings, or apply an ideology to the widest possible range of contexts, including those totally inappropriate. Only by carefully examining our assumptions can we avoid this problem. However, ideological assumptions appear so natural that we never think to question them. In chapter 3, we will explore the nature of ideological assumptions by examining different perspectives that can be used to study communication. It is enough to point out here that overburdened concepts involve us unknowingly in what Eco labels "ideological discourse"; discourse based on uncritical support of particular, and often contradictory, constructions of reality.[24]

This section has argued that the current concept of communication is an overburdened one suffering from three problems: conceptual confusion, conceptual oversimplification, and ideological masking. To avoid these problems, we need to sort out the meanings associated with the concept of communication and decide which ones we will accept.

Communication as a Family of Concepts

Given that communication is a confusing concept, how can we free it from ambiguity? One answer might be to stop using the term. Since our analysis shows the term to be overloaded with meaning, perhaps we could place a moritorium on its use. This, of course, is not a realistic solution. In both common and scientific usage, people will continue to speak of communication in a general way, and nothing can effectively stop this practice. Even if it were possible to erase the term, it is likely that a new one would simply be substituted for the old concept.

A related solution is for the scientific community to fix on a single meaning for the concept and to stick to that usage when discussing it. This, unfortunately, is equally unrealistic. In an early work, Dance reviewed attempts to provide a solitary definition for the concept and, instead, found many inherently antagonistic definitions.[25] He isolated 15 distinct conceptual components in these definitions. Communication, he found, was viewed as a process of symbol using, understanding, interaction, reduction of uncertainty, transference, and transmission of information. Its various functions included linking the individual to the environment, establishing commonality, exercising power, timebinding, and replicating memories. It was simultaneously seen as a process, a response, and a stimulus; and, while some defined it as an intentional phenomenon, others included nonintentional uses. Dance found that each conceptualization was based on a complicated series of assumptions.

While it is unrealistic to expect theorists to agree completely about the nature of communication, it is not unreasonable to propose that they recognize the overburdened nature of the concept and specify how they are referring to it when they use it. At the least, ideological assumptions would become apparent and a foundation for critical discussion would be provided. This solution necessitates two activities: (1) a recognition that communication refers to not one, but a collection of concepts and (2) a careful analysis of the nature of these related concepts. Dance has provided cogent arguments for this solution.[26] He believes communication is a family of related concepts, and he asks that the broader concept be subdivided into a collection of constructs with more limited meanings. He does this by presenting a taxonomy of related terms. Although Dance's taxonomy has not been entirely accepted, it does lead toward the solution being advocated. It also illustrates the analytic process at the heart of successful theory building. Theories are founded on concepts. A good theory begins with a careful examination of the domain it seeks to explain. Research Abstract 1.1 presents the Dance and Larson taxonomy.

The remainder of this chapter presents a slightly different subdivision of communication concepts. While departing somewhat from the Dance taxonomy, it employs the same strategy and many of the same ideological assumptions. It begins with the general and moves toward the specific. At the general level, *communication* refers to a process of acting on information. Within this broad concept are nested other, more specific, concepts. We will begin by distinguishing *human communication* (the process of sign production and exchange unique to humans as social beings) from communication as a whole. The concept of human communication will then be further subdivided into *symbolic human communication* (the process of creating, producing, and interpreting symbolic codes) and *spoken symbolic interaction* (the human use of spoken symbols to affect and influence others). Making conceptual distinctions is an essential step in theorizing about communication, for, in the process of defining and comparing concepts, theorists come to terms with basic questions about the nature of the domain they wish to study. In the present case, making distinctions between different forms of communication allows us to discuss important issues such as What makes human communication different from other forms of communication? How are symbolic codes different from nonsymbolic codes? What is the proper subject matter of the field of speech communication?

Figure 1.1 previews the forthcoming discussion of a family of communication concepts. Each solid circle in Fig. 1.1 represents a well-defined concept of communication. Broken circles indicate potential concepts, forms of communication that may exist but that have not as yet been clearly articulated. Circles within other circles stand for concepts embedded within other concepts. Forms of communication within the cir-

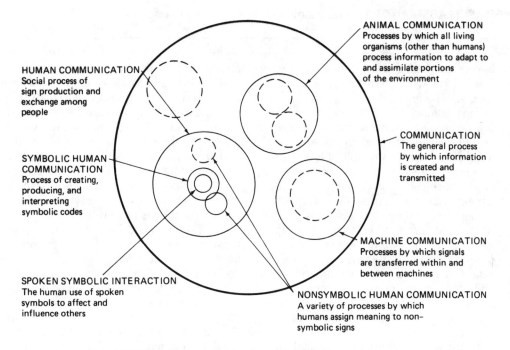

FIGURE 1.1: Communication: A family of concepts

cle designated "Human Communication" are of core importance, while forms of communication that fall outside this area are of more peripheral interest.

The Uniqueness of Human Communication

Developing a set of communication concepts involves an initial distinction between human communication and communication as a general process of information processing, for most agree that there is a qualitative difference between human and nonhuman communication. But what is it that makes humans unique from other living organisms?[27] In this section it will be argued that what makes humans different from all other living organisms is their nature as *sign producers* and *social beings*.

Let us begin by clarifying two terms: sign and code. Human communication occurs whenever individuals interact socially by using convention-

alized units of representation. Because humans are endowed with a particular cognitive structure, we create units of representation (words, gestures, visual configurations) by attaching units of expression (sights, sounds, movements) to units of content (ideas, concepts, physical "things"). The unit of representation created when an expression is connected to a content is called a *sign*. The term sign refers not only to symbolic units of expression, such as words, but also to naturally occurring stimuli, as long as they convey meaning by representing something other than themselves and can be conceptually manipulated. The system of rules connecting signs to one another and allowing shared meaning and exchange is called a *code*, the general term that encompasses both human language and other sign systems.

Although the term code is fairly easy to understand, the term sign is less clear because it has been used in the literature in two distinct ways.

RESEARCH ABSTRACT 1.1 A Taxonomy of Communication Concepts

In presenting their set of definitions, Dance and Larson work from the general to the specific. The first and most general element in their taxonomy is the concept of *stimulus*, any unit of sensory input capable of being received by an organism. Any potential sight or sound, any unit of touch, taste, or smell counts as a stimulus. When an organism selects a particular stimulus from among many and uses that stimulus to reduce uncertainty, the stimulus is converted into *information*. When the organism acts on the information by organizing or responding to it in some way, *communication* in its broadest sense has occurred. The concepts defined so far apply equally to all living organisms. Dance and Larson next consider uniquely human forms of communication.

Humans have two unique capabilities. First, they are endowed with *speech*, the ability to articulate discrete sounds. Second, they can create *symbols*, units of expression arbitrarily associated with units of content. When humans agree on the meanings of symbols and create systems governing their use, *language* is created, and when humans combine their ability to speak with their ability to use language, the result is *speech communication*. Finally, the intentional goal-directed use of speech communication is known as *rhetoric*.

For Dance and Larson, speech communication can and must be distinguished from communication in general, for the ability to engage in spoken language is that which makes humans unique and is part of what separates us from the lower animals. The relationship between elements in the Dance and Larson taxonomy is shown in the figure below:

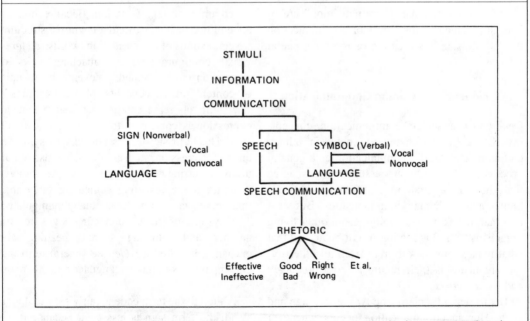

Source: Frank E.X. Dance and Carl E. Larson, *Speech Communication: Concepts and Behavior* (New York: Holt, Rinehart & Winston, 1972), pp. 1–16; copyright Frank E. X. Dance. For a more recent formulation, see Frank E.X. Dance, "What is Communication? Nailing Jello to the Wall," *ACA Journal*, Nov. 10, 1983.

Philosophers, linguists, and rhetoricians such as Pierce, Saussure, Barthes, Jakobson, Eco, and most modern semioticians use the term as described. Others, however, sometimes limit the term to refer only to "natural," nonarbitrary units of representation that are nonsymbolic. In this book, the term will be used in the first, more general sense, as it is used in most modern theories of language.

Humans Are Sign Producers. Let us now consider the unique attributes of human communication systems. How does the human ability to produce signs make a difference in our communication? Dance argues that nonhuman communication systems are physically and biologically constrained, reacting only to that which is temporally and spatially immediate. The emergence in humans of the ability to use language and other sign systems frees us from these constraints. It allows us to surmount immediacy and, consequently, to make and mark relationships.[28] Human languages (and human code systems in general) consist of interrelated signs that "on the ground of previously established social conventions, can be taken as...*standing for something else.*"[29] In other words, people, unlike lower animals, do not need to be in the presence of a thing in order to think about it: We can speak and think about things that have never "existed." Any study of human communication needs to include consideration of human code use and, in Eco's terms, an examination of *"everything which can be used in order to lie."*[30] Because humans have language, we are uniquely capable of creating a new kind of reality, one composed of signs and of "anything that can be and is talked about," whether or not those things exist in a physical sense.[31]

Humans Are Social Beings. This new kind of reality created through human communication is essentially social and cultural. Because humans are social animals, we live not only in a physical environment but in shared communicational environments.[32] Eco tells us that the codes comprising the human signifying system

set up a "cultural" world which is neither actual nor possible in the ontological sense; its existence is linked to a cultural order, which is the way in which a society thinks and speaks... . Since it is through thinking and speaking that a society develops, expands, collapses... a theory of codes is very much concerned with the format of such "cultural" worlds.[33]

This is similar to the *symbolic interactionist position* (see chapter 3) that the environment consists only of those objects that humans together recognize and know through social/cultural convention.[34] The symbolic interactionists argue that we can only understand human behavior if we understand the nature of humans as social beings. Together we create language and other code systems; the languages and codes we invent, in turn, make it possible for us to be together. Language is impossible without society, society is impossible without language, and human communication is impossible without both.[35]

The human communication system, then, is unique because of our language- and code-making capacity and its application in social interaction. We construct a social and symbolic world through a form of communication different and distinct from simple information exchange.

Symbolic and Nonsymbolic Communication Systems

Given that human communication is different in nature from communication produced by other living organisms, our next question is, Are there different kinds of human communication? If so, are these differences great enough to require additional subdivisions in our family of concepts? Below it is argued that there are indeed different forms of human communication, and the most important division is that between symbolic and nonsymbolic forms of communication.

Symbols: Arbitrary Intentional Signs. All signs are not alike. Although they all link content to expression and convey meaning to receivers through systematized codes, they differ in the way they establish these links and in the way the resulting codes are actually used. Some signs are based on arbitrary units of expression and are intentionally generated by their senders. These signs are called *symbols*, so defined because the relationship between their content and expression is arbitrary, rooted in convention rather than nature. When we refer to the green, leafy object growing in a forest as a "tree," we do so as a matter of cultural agreement. Use of the word "tree" is a matter of mutual choice. There is nothing inherently tree-like about the word; no natural rules dictate use of that word over others. People born in Germany call the same object "baum"; in France it is "arbre." Words are symbols, and human language is a symbolic code, just as the Morse Code, sign language, semaphore codes, and traffic lights are symbolic systems. The meanings of these codes are established through convention; their use is generally intentional.

Natural Nonintentional Signs. The link between expression and content that produces a sign is not always arbitrary. There are classes of signs that people use that do not depend on symbolic units of expression. In these kinds of signs, the relationship between content and expression is fixed and natural. The rash that allows a physician to diagnose measles is a good example. Society did not "decide" that the rash should be used to indicate measles as it did when it "decided" to use the word "measles" to describe the disease. A rash is a natural *symptom* of the measles, not a matter of choice. It is a sign to the physician, who, through inference and interpretation, assigns it a meaning. But the patient does not intentionally create the symptom to inform the doctor of the illness.

Few people would argue that a rash carries meaning in the same way as the word "measles." Both kinds of signs are meaningful to human

interpreters, yet most of us recognize that *having* measles is a different process than *talking about* measles. Different sets of rules govern each. Breaking out in a rash is neither a learned behavior not an intentional act. Talking about this process is both learned and intentional.

Expressive Behaviors. Although the concept of symptom can be clearly differentiated from that of symbol, other signs are not so easy to distinguish. Signs popularly known as "body language" fit this description. These signs exist halfway between symptoms and symbols and may be intentional or nonintentional, learned or natural.

Expression of emotion is a good example. Most people believe that emotional expressions such as shedding tears or smiling in joy are natural, universal signs like the rash in measles. In terms of their origin, these signs are natural, determined by physiology. The manner in which they are emitted, however, seems to be partially learned. Charlesworth and Kreutzer explain:

Both the environment and innate factors have effects on expressive behavior. The environmental may influence the time at which a behavior appears (many smiling individuals around a newborn may accelerate the appearance of the first social smile and may determine how often the behavior occurs once it first appears). The innate factors, on the other hand, seem to be mainly responsible for the morphological character of expressive behaviors (and hence the fact that they occur at all as such) and for the connections such behaviors have to emotional states associated with them.[36]

While in most cases symbols are used intentionally and symptoms unintentionally, expressive behaviors can be both intentional and unintentional. Although tears seem to be a sincere and "natural" reaction to sadness, it is possible to generate them intentionally, as when an actor cries on cue. People learn to control emotional expression and use it for essentially symbolic purposes. When a student discussing a grade with the teacher bursts into tears, it may be a symptomatic expression of emotion or a carefully planned symbolic communication. For the teacher, there is a practical reason for wanting to know exactly to what code system the tears belong. For the theoretician it is also important, because the theories designed to explain various code systems will be as different as the origins and uses of the codes themselves.

Most serious communication scholars recognize the error in classing all forms of human sign usage together and agree that conceptual distinctions are needed. For our present purposes, it is enough to say that symbolic sign systems should be differentiated from nonsymbolic systems and to point out that even finer distinctions can be made in the nonsymbolic area. Understanding symbolic codes is particularly important to understand human communication. Human beings are language users, and any study of our communication behavior that fails to account for the nature and uniqueness of spoken symbolic processes overlooks what it means to be human.

Some Notes on Speech Communication as an Area of Study

If intentional symbolic sign systems are the most important forms of human communication, it follows that symbolic processes should be the main focus of our field. There are many who agree with this view. They believe there is virtue in limiting the field and fear a loss of theoretical focus and identity if equal attention is given symbolic and nonsymbolic processes.

Other scholars disagree, believing that the process of assigning symbolic meaning is what makes human communication unique and that, while expressive behaviors may not begin as symbols, they end up as such when assigned conventionalized meaning. These scholars believe all signs processed by the human receiver are worth studying. They argue that limiting the field to symbolically produced and intentionally sent communication is unnecessarily restrictive.

The attitude adopted in this book is a compromise between the two views. The central focus of communication study should be spoken symbolic

interaction. To lose sight of this as a primary goal is to lose touch with our rhetorical traditions. Our field began as a study of how people influence each other through the spoken word, and this process is of continuing interest and importance.

This does not mean, however, that all other areas of study should be ignored. Any inquiry that allows us to understand the process of symbolic interchange is important. To explain how people communicate though use of symbols, we must also study related areas. Models of person perception and attribution, social theories of role construction, investigations of information processing and recall, motivational and cognitive structures, all can help us understand symbolic interaction. The ancients recognized these factors when they developed their model of the canons of rhetoric, and we should not turn our backs on this insight.

In what follows, we will examine theories that were specifically developed to describe human communication as well as theories whose original goal was to explain other, related forms of human and social behavior. The goal in each case will be to use these theories as a basis for understanding how humans communicate through spoken symbols and to discover what they have to say to us about human communication processes.

SUMMARY

In this chapter we have traced the study of human communication from ancient Greece to present day America. We have seen that, despite its long history, there is still disagreement over exactly what communication is. By dividing communication into a family of concepts, the chapter has offered its own answer to the question, What is communication? You and your instructor may agree or disagree with this answer, but I hope you will accept the idea that definitions are important and that making conceptual distinctions is the first step in understanding and explaining a phenomenon. Theorists actively engage themselves in a process of decision making and discovery, remaining open to new ideas and continually reevaluating existing concepts and models. By the time you finish this book, I hope you will be able to appreciate the creativity and excitement of this process.

REFERENCES

1. David K. Berlo, "The Context for Communication," in *Communication and Behavior*, eds. Gerhard J. Hanneman and William J. McEwen (Reading, Mass.: Addison-Wesley, 1975), p. 10.

2. Lee Thayer, "Communication: *Sine Qua Non* of the Behavioral Sciences," in *Interdisciplinary Approaches to Human Communication*, eds. Richard W. Budd and Brent D. Ruben (Rochelle Park, N. J.: Hayden, 1979), p. 9.

3. *Ibid.*, p. 9.

4. Nancy Harper, *Human Communication Theory: The History of a Paradigm* (Rochelle Park, N. J.: Hayden, 1979), p. 307. At the end of this work, Harper presents an historical chronology of major figures in the rhetorical tradition.

5. *Ibid.*, pp. 17–18.

6. *Ibid.*, pp. 26–27.

7. *Ibid.*, p. 70.

8. *Ibid.*, p. 71.

9. Douglas Ehninger, "Dominant Trends in English Rhetorical Thought, 1750–1800," *Southern Speech Journal*, 18 (Fall 1952), 3–11.

10. Harper, *History of a Paradigm*, p. 260.

11. Ernest G. Bormann, *Communication Theory* (New York: Holt, Rinehart & Winston, 1980), pp. 6–7.

12. *Ibid.*, p. 7.

13. *Ibid.*, p. 10.

14. Claude E. Shannon and Warren Weaver, *The Mathematical Theory of Communication* (Urbana: University of Illinois Press, 1949).

15. *Ibid.*, p. 14.

16. Theodore H. Bullock, "Neurons as Biological Transducers and Communication Channels," in *Concepts of Communication: Interpersonal, Intrapersonal and Mathematical*, eds. Edwin F. Beckenbach and Charles B. Thompkins (New York: John Wiley & Sons, 1971), pp. 33–56.

17. Herbert Frings, "Zoology," in Budd and Ruben, *Interdisciplinary Approaches*, pp. 33–56.

18. Frank E. X. Dance and Carl E. Larson, *The Functions of Human Communication: A Theoretical Approach* (New York: Holt, Rinehart & Winston, 1976), p. 30.

19. Frank E. X. Dance, "Swift, Slow, Sweet, Sour, Adazzle, Dim: What Makes Human Communication Human," *Western Journal of Speech Communication*, 44 (Winter 1980), 60–63.

20. Stephen Jay Gould, "Triumph of a Naturalist," *New York Review of Books*, 31, No. 5 (March 29, 1984), p. 3.

21. *Ibid.*, p. 3.

22. Edward C. Carterette and Donald A. Norman, "On the Uses of Sensory Information by Animals and Men," in *Concepts of Communication*, p. 361.

23. William J. McGuire, "A Contextualist Theory of Knowledge: Its Implications for Innovation and Reform in Psychological Research," in *Advances in Experimental Social Psychology*, vol. 16, ed. Leonard Berkowitz (New York: Academic, 1983), p. 14.

24. Umberto Eco, *A Theory of Semiotics* (Bloomington: Indiana University Press, 1976), p. 16.

25. Frank E. X. Dance, "The 'Concept' of Communication," *Journal of Communication*, 20 (June 1970), 201–10. See also Stephen W. Littlejohn, *Theories of Human Communication*, 3rd ed. (Belmont, Calif.: Wadsworth, 1989), pp. 4–6.

26. Frank E. X. Dance and Carl E. Larson, *Speech Communication: Concepts and Behavior* (New York: Holt, Rinehart & Winston, 1972); Dance and Larson, *Functions of Human Communication*; and Dance, "Swift, Slow."

27. Budd and Ruben, *Interdisciplinary Approaches*. See, in particular, articles by Lee Thayer, "Communication: *Sine Qua Non* of the Behavioral Sciences," Herbert Blumer, "Symbolic Interaction," and Peter L. Berger, "Sociology of Knowledge."

28. Dance, "Swift, Slow," p. 61.

29. Eco, *Theory of Semiotics*, p. 16.

30. *Ibid.*, p. 7.

31. Thayer, "Sine Qua Non," p. 12.

32. *Ibid.*, p. 21.

33. Eco, *Theory of Semiotics*, pp. 61–62.

34. Blumer, "Symbolic Interaction," in Budd and Ruben, *Interdisciplinary Approaches*, p. 143.

35. For a more detailed development, see Berger, "Sociology of Knowledge," in Budd and Ruben, *Interdisciplinary Approaches*, pp. 155–73.

36. W. R. Charlesworth and M. A. Kreutzer, "Facial Expressions of Infants and Children," in *Darwin and Facial Expression: A Century of Research in Review*, ed. Paul Ekman (New York: Academic, 1973), p. 160. For a general discussion of the genesis of nonverbal signs, see also Mark L. Knapp, *Essentials of Nonverbal Communication* (New York: Holt, Rinehart & Winston, 1980), pp. 26–35.

chapter 2

COMMUNICATION PROBLEMS AND CONTEXTS

INTRODUCTION

As we saw in chapter 1, communication is a popular concept that has been offered as a cure-all for most of society's ills. It is almost impossible to pick up a newspaper, or even take part in a conversation, without hearing the word communication. Every problem, personal or public, serious or trivial, has become a problem of communication, and everything we do, intentionally or not, is thought to communicate some hidden meaning. Even if we carefully limit our discussion to intentional, spoken communication, our field of study is still exceedingly broad.

To make studying the field more manageable, communication specialists often break communication into smaller parts. This chapter looks at two ways of dividing the domain. The first divides the communication process into five basic problems that all communicators must solve. The second separates communication into contexts.

There are two reasons to make these distinctions. The first is for purely organizational reasons. Communication is so vast a topic that it is impossible to study all of it at once. Consider the fact that each of the following people are engaging in communication: a husband and wife adjusting to one another over a period of years, a small group setting an agenda, a supervisor addressing a memo to newly hired workers, a salesperson trying to size up a potential customer, an evangelist exhorting sinners. The form communication takes, the way it functions, and the skills the communicators need are very different in each instance. For this reason, it is common practice to group similar forms of communication and study them as a unit. In fact, most large departments of communication offer separate courses in interpersonal, small group, public, persuasion, and so forth.

From the standpoint of theory, it is also important to break the field into smaller units. Theorists often prefer special to general theories. They often focus their attention on a single communication context, such as small group interaction, public speaking, or mediated communication; or they concentrate on a single aspect of communication, such as establishing credibility, adapting to receiver expectations, or formulating messages. Ernest Bormann believes that working on specific parts of the communication process may be the first step in generating larger, more all-inclusive theories.[1] In examining similar communication events, theorists can build detailed and specific theories. They can be aware of the special constraints that affect a given communication event. Of course, theorists must be careful not to overemphasize differences or overlook common elements shared by all forms of communication.

This chapter will present two ways of organizing communication study. We will begin by breaking the communication process into the general problems all communicators face in creating messages for one another. We will then consider how the context in which communication is embedded affects the way these problems are solved. At the same time we will keep in mind that these divisions are somewhat arbitrary and that communication is, after all, a unitary process.

FIVE COMMUNICATION PROBLEMS

In chapter 1 we briefly discussed the canons of rhetoric. The canons were a model of the basic processes communicators face in creating and sending messages. They broke the process of communication into identifiable parts. This chapter presents a similar model, one based on the idea that at some level a theory is a response to a problem. The model outlines five problems that all communicators must solve if they are to be effective: the problems of communicator acceptability and attribution, signification, social coordination and relational definition, outcome achievement, and evolution. As we shall see,

these problems occur in all situations, although their solutions may be context specific.

Problems and the Nature of Inquiry

In an early and influential article on the nature of inquiry in speech communication, Klaus Krippendorf argues that inquiry is always motivated by the posing of a problem.[2] Without the existence of a problem (that is, without the existence of some uncertainty), inquiry would be unnecessary. When we are confronted with a problem, we are prompted to answer the question contained in the problem. Thus, we engage in inquiry and theory building.

For Krippendorf, inquiry is the process of generating explicit knowledge. He distinguishes explicit knowledge (knowledge about) from implicit knowledge (knowledge of). The native speaker of a language has knowledge of the language in the sense of knowing implicitly how to speak it. This speaker, however, may not have knowledge about grammatical rules, may lack explicit knowledge. Possession of implicit knowledge does not imply possession of explicit knowledge; nor is the reverse true. As Krippendorf points out, "a kitten will surely land on its feet if dropped upside down, while the professor of physics who knows the laws of gravity and of the preservation of angular momentum will rarely be able to do the same."[3] The communication scientist's goal is to generate explicit knowledge about the workings of communication, and such inquiry will be prompted by problems framed as questions.

Five Communication Problems

There are certain points of uncertainty, or problems, that all communicators encounter. These problems reflect basic choices we make and basic tasks we accomplish during the process of communicating. Because the nature of the communication transaction depends on how each of these problems is resolved and because there is no one way to resolve each problem, the communicator is constantly forced to choose among alternatives.

What problems must each communicator solve to communicate appropriately with others? At a minimum, the communicator must be able to (1) choose a satisfactory communicative partner or partners, (2) construct meaningful signs capable of conveying information, (3) create and maintain satisfactory role relations through an exchange of messages, (4) control the interaction to achieve desired outcomes for self and others, and (5) exhibit the ability to adapt to changes over time.

These five problems occur in all contexts. Although they are listed separately, they are intimately interrelated. In many cases they occur simultaneously, and often the solution to one affects the solution to the others. The first problem is that of choosing a communicative partner, a process that involves the ability to attribute motives and characteristics. It is human nature to want to know what other people are like. We make judgments about people, and these judgments affect how we communicate with them.

Thus, the first problem is tied directly to the next, the problem of formulating messages. The words we use and the gestures we make are determined by the attributions we have made. We talk differently to different people, recognizing the necessity for adapting our messages. As we begin to send messages, we find ourselves confronting the third problem, deciding who to be and· what kind of relationship to construct. The way we talk helps form the relationship, but, at the same time, our expectations about the relationship determine the way we talk. Usually, we talk for some purpose, whether it be simply to pass the time or to gain some more specific end.

Thus, the fourth problem, that of outcome achievement, is never too far from our thoughts. It, too, interacts with the others, for our aims affect the ways we coordinate our relationships as well as the message strategies we choose. Finally, we must come to terms with the fifth problem, that of adaptation and evolution. Communication

is not static. As an interaction progresses, we must adapt to what has occurred; over time we must change our ways of dealing with one another. Finally, our experiences with all of these problems in one situation affect how we will solve them in the next situation. There is a dynamic interrelationship among the problems.

The Problem of Communicator Acceptability. The first problem confronting the communicator is that of choosing a communicative partner. This problem is called *the problem of communicator acceptability*. It involves a process of person perception and social judgment. In choosing to interact with others, each communicator gathers knowledge about the other and matches this knowledge with internalized criteria for successful interaction. This process is marked by uncertainty. The communicator must answer questions such as the following ones: What are the characteristics of my partner, group, or audience, and how will they respond to me? Can I trust the other? If I risk communicating in this instance, what rewards or punishments are likely and how successful will I be?

The problem of communicator acceptability is of practical import in the everyday lives of communicators. It is also important from a theoretical point of view. The theorist is interested in knowing how people go about solving this problem. Thus, he or she also asks questions, although these questions are at a meta level. The theorist tries to explain communication by asking, How and why do communicators choose to communicate with certain people and avoid communicating with others? How are motives and characteristics attributed to others, and how do these characteristics affect judgments about communicative transactions?

The Problem of Signification. A second task facing communicators is that of exchanging meaningful messages. This problem is called *the problem of signification*. Although the chief mode of communication individuals have at their disposal is their native natural language, communicators possess knowledge of other sign systems, both verbal and nonverbal. To create meaningful messages, they must choose from among these systems appropriate sets of signs. They must also be able to read the signs created by their partners. This problem is often experienced through the following questions: How can I explain myself to others? How can I convey my feelings to my partner? How can I interpret the meaning of a speaker's message? How can I make the greatest impact on my listener?

The theorist trying to explain this process goes well beyond these practical questions in an attempt to understand how language and other sign systems work. The communication scientist is likely to ask, What is language? How does it differ from other sign systems? How can its structure best be described? How do interactors coordinate their conversations to exchange meaningful messages?

The Problem of Social Coordination and Relational Definition. All signs, whether intentionally sent or accurately received, have message value. This is because all messages carry two types of information, content and relational.[4] Because messages carry relational information, they allow us to understand who we are as individuals. Through communication we define the nature of self and other, and we negotiate rules and roles to be followed throughout the course of the interaction. This is *the problem of social coordination and relational definition.* Each time we interact with one another, we engage in the process of constructing and sustaining a unique communicative culture.

While the average communicator may not be able to articulate the problem in these terms, he or she is usually aware of the uncertainties surrounding roles and rules and experiences this problem through the following kinds of questions: What is my partner telling me about who I am as a person? Am I being accepted or rejected? How am I expected to act in this situation? What is my role

in this relationship? If we are to continue interaction, how shall we proceed?

The observer trying to understand this process is concerned with mechanisms used to define self and other and asks, How does communication lead to the concept of self, and how does the concept of self constrain communicative interactions? What process is involved in role presentation and negotiation? How do interactors send relational messages and agree on interactional rules? What factors signal social competence, and what factors impede such a process?

The Problem of Achieving Communicative Outcomes. The fourth problem is *the problem of communicative outcomes*, which can be classified in two ways: consciously articulated goals and purposes and unexpected outcomes that inevitably result from communicating. Communicators are probably most concerned about the first type, since people often communicate with a purpose in mind and need to know how they can best achieve it. This problem is often experienced through the following types of questions: How can I best gain my ends in this situation? How can I construct a message to persuade, inform, or entertain my audience? How can I influence and control those around me?

The theorist also wants to know how intended effects are achieved and may begin by asking, How does a communicator effect a change in the attitude or behavior of another? What communicative strategies can lead to success in a given situation? How do communicators successfully influence one another? The theorist may also examine unintended results by asking questions such as, What unexpected outcomes are associated with the process of communication? How does engaging in communication change the interactors? Are there basic functions fulfilled by all communicative events?

The Problem of Evolution and Change. Communication occurs in time. It is not static but continuous and progressive. It evolves from one state to another. What works at the beginning of a transaction may not work later on because, throughout the course of a transaction, new messages are exchanged, roles are developed, and outcomes are achieved. The problem communicators face here is how to respond to this change. The communicator coming to terms with *the problem of evolution and change* asks, What do I do now? How can I maintain a desired relationship over the course of time? Are old strategies enhancing or inhibiting current communication?

Many theoreticians have been intrigued with progressive patterns of behavior. They have generally addressed questions such as, How do communication systems move from one state to another? What factors signal a change or realignment within the communication system? Are there identifiable stages in the communicative event in which I am interested? If so, what are the hallmarks of each stage, and what factors affect progression through these stages? Some theoreticians may experience this problem in a more general way. They may be aware that social and historical factors affect communication systems and that the ways we communicate are often the products of social forces. These theoreticians may, therefore, ask, How do communication practices reflect and reinforce cultural practices? How have communication rules and norms changed historically? How are interactants constrained by social pressures of which they are often unaware?

We are confronted by all of these problems whenever we communicate. They are as relevant to us when we work out an interpersonal relationship as they are when we communicate with coworkers or design a persuasive campaign. Thus, these problems cut across communication contexts. Still, the context in which they occur has an effect upon them. The way we approach each of these problems depends on the context in which we find ourselves. The language we use with a close friend is different from that which we use when addressing an audience. Group roles are different from public roles. Thus, to understand the problems more fully, we should look at the

contexts in which they occur. In the rest of this chapter, we will investigate the idea of context.

THE NATURE AND FORM OF COMMUNICATION CONTEXTS

As C. David Mortensen tells us, "Communication never takes place in a vacuum; it is not a 'pure' process, devoid of background or situational overtones."[5] Communication always takes place somewhere. Where it takes place is its *context*. If you were to ask most people to name the contexts of communication they would probably answer, interpersonal, small group, public, and so on. They would define context in terms of the number of people involved, their physical distance from one another, and their purposes for interacting. Most of our discussion in this chapter will be on this kind of situationally based context, for that is the most common way of thinking about context in our field. But we should also keep in mind that context can mean something more. Context refers to all the elements that surround and shape interaction and not just those that are physical. Situational contexts are embedded within wider cultural and historical contexts as well. Once we have looked at some of the standard ways communication contexts have been defined, we will look at the relationship between these and wider social contexts.

Situational Contexts and Communication

Communication is constrained by a variety of situational factors: the number of interactors, their physical distance from each other, the channels open for use, and the frequency and duration of a typical transaction. Clearly, we communicate in different ways when conversing with a friend in a quiet restaurant than when delivering a public lecture in an auditorium. In the first case, since interaction is direct and face-to-face, feedback is immediate, time limitations are flexible, and a spontaneous, individual, and unstructured transaction develops. In the second, because the number of participants is large and the feedback limited, a different type of communication is required, one characterized by formal role relationships and a preplanned, prepackaged message strategy. Because the situations differ, the forms of communication also differ.

One way to distinguish context involves the identification of situational characteristics affecting communication. Several authors have outlined these characteristics. Gerald Miller centers his discussion on four: "*number of communicators, degree of physical proximity, number of sensory channels available for the communicator's use, and immediacy of feedback* [italics added]."[6] Miller argues that these dimensions are interrelated and that of the four the first is most important. "Indeed, it could be argued that number of communicators is *the* key situational dimension, since any substantial change in that variable is almost certain to produce changes in the other three."[7]

David Swanson and Jesse Delia also discuss characteristics of contexts, adding additional factors to the analysis. They mention *ability of interactors to adapt messages* to specific needs of others, *formalization of communicative roles*, and *specificity of purpose.*[8] As the number of communicators and the distance between them varies, there will be accompanying changes in the nature of both the message being constructed and the cognitive skills necessary for successful interaction. These authors feel that as communicators move from the focused interaction of interpersonal communication toward more distanced, more heterogeneous, and less immediate forms, such as mass communication, increasingly strong demands are placed on them to preplan messages and to see the world from the perspective of more generalized audience members. As we move from context to context:

We must become *increasingly reflective.* That is, we must make increasingly determined efforts to put aside our own interpretations and attempt to see the world

from varied perspectives of the individuals with whom we are interacting.[9]

Swanson and Delia and Miller view contexts as lying along a continuum, from interpersonal communication to mass communication (see Fig. 2.1). There is no exact point at which we switch from one context to another. As Miller tells us, "the dividing point between situational contexts is highly arbitrary and subject to the whim of the individual researcher."[10]

While it is useful to subdivide communication in this way, the theorist should not lose sight of the commonalities that cut across all contexts. David Swanson and Jesse Delia caution us:

It is important to dispel the notion that each context requires understandings and skills that are unique to it and useful in no other context. There is one basic process of communication.... *The basic process of communication operates in every context in fundamentally the same way, even though each context requires slightly different skills or special applications of general communicative principles.*[11]

Interpersonal Communication. The first context identified in the situational approach is face-to-face *interpersonal communication.* Although number of communicators is one of the most important criteria affecting context, there is disagreement about the exact number of persons in interpersonal interactions. Some authors believe that as long as the individuals involved are close (relationally as well as physically) and focused on one another, the exact number is unimportant and can range from two to three or even more.

Others, in particular William Wilmot, argue that interpersonal communication should be restricted to two-person exchanges because important qualitative changes occur as soon as a third party joins a transaction. "In a dyad," says Wilmot, "the two members can fully focus on one another, exchange freely, and become finely tuned."[12] He believes, however, that it is rare for equality of exchange and empathy to occur between three people. When three individuals interact

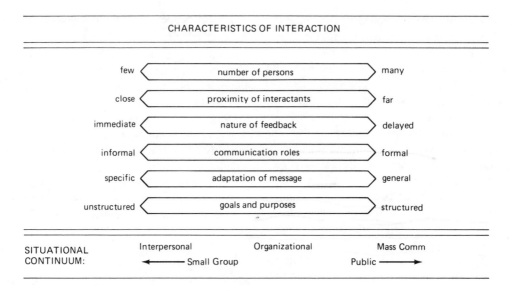

FIGURE 2.1: Situational characteristics and the continuum of contexts

the basic properties of all larger groups begin to emerge. Leadership functions become more identifiable, communication networks are established, and coalitions or subsystems are formed. And importantly, majority opinion can be appealed to as a tactic to change another participant's point of view. The addition of new members to a face-to-face transaction dramatically changes the nature of the system.[13]

The interpersonal context differs from others because it is focused, and the number of sensory channels is maximal; that is, participants can see, hear, touch, smell, and (perhaps) even taste one another. Because of this immediacy, nonverbal acts have a strong impact on the nature of the communication, providing both intentional and unintentional feedback. Also, because of the availability of verbal and nonverbal feedback, communicators feel no need to prepackage messages. The content is relatively spontaneous; communicative partners can interrupt, ask questions, and similarly direct the flow of the conversation. Accompanying this spontaneity in message content and organization is an informality in the roles of speaker and listener. It is unnecessary to make a sharp distinction between roles in this context, for they are reciprocal.

Another difference between this and other contexts is "the typical absence of clearly defined purposes and goals on the part of the interactants."[14] The key words here are "clearly defined." Many interpersonal interactions just seem to happen; they have a casual, time-passing flavor. This is not to say that when we converse casually we are not accomplishing an end, but we may not be consciously aware of that end. Indeed, in the interpersonal context, believing that someone is trying to make a good impression or to influence us generally leads to a negative reaction.[15]

Small-Group Communication. The next context is *small-group communication.* Here, as in interpersonal communication, we can disagree about number of participants. John Brilhart and B. Aubrey Fisher argue that "the group be small enough so that each member knows, and is able to react to, every other member." Fisher refuses to place an upper limit on groups, although he stipulates that a group must include at least three people.[16] Others have argued that the optimal size for small task groups is around five to seven.

Although group feedback is similar to feedback in interpersonal situations in that it uses maximal sensory channels and is generally immediate, there are important differences between these two contexts. One of the major differences is that in a group we have some choice in whom to address. Messages can be relayed to a particular member through different networks. The simple, direct link between communicators in the interpersonal context becomes more complicated in the group context.

Wilmot notes that communication in groups is more psychologically complicated than communication in dyads or pairs. In a pair there is only one potential relationship. In a threesome, six possible relationships exist: a-b, a-c, b-c, ab-c, ac-b, and bc-a. Add a fourth person, and there are 25 possible relationships. This number increases dramatically as more members are added, creating difficult problems of coordination and alignment. Networks and leadership are ways of coping with this confusion. Wilmot believes "leadership emerges because it can reduce the psychologically complicated relationships. Group transactions can be reduced to a series of pair relationships of each member with the leader... ."[17]

In groups, there is a tendency for roles to become well defined, particularly the role of leader. Although role differentiation occurs in dyads, roles are more overt and permanent in groups. Group members are aware of their roles and use group conformity pressures to maintain them. In a group, the potential also exists for isolates or deviants to emerge. This is impossible in a dyad, for if one party becomes isolated, the dyad is broken and ceases to exist. This is why groups are more stable than dyads. As Fisher suggests, "In a 3-member group, interaction does not cease because of the whims or the actions of only a single person. That is, no one person has the power to destroy or disrupt completely the entire social system."[18]

The size of the small group allows members to tailor specific messages to one another, so this characteristic barely changes as we move from the interpersonal to the group context. In terms of goal specificity, however, we do find changes. Swanson and Delia say that, especially in problem solving groups, members

typically have rather clearly defined goals and purposes... . While communication may wander, the range of topics discussed will tend to be restricted by their perceived relevance to the task at hand... . This implies, further, that *in problem-solving groups the individual must suppress his own goals and purposes to facilitate the functioning of the group as a whole and the attainment of group goals.*[19]

Fisher also stresses this point, saying that "perhaps the most significant difference between the dyad and the group is the feeling of identification with the larger system... ."[20]

Organizational Communication. As we proceed along the continuum, we encounter the next situation, *organizational communication.* According to Everett Rogers and Rekha Agarwala-Rogers, an organization is a "stable system of individuals who work together to achieve, through a hierarchy of ranks and division of labor, common goals."[21] Situationally, the organizational context differs from the group both in number of interactors and in the hierarchical structure developed to respond to increased membership. As Richard Farace says, "Organizations, in general, are typically *larger* than groups (organizations are sometimes called 'groups of groups'), have a much more extensive *hierarchy* (to control and coordinate their members), and have much greater *specialization* and differentiation (so that their members can perform a wide range of tasks)."[22] As Daniel Katz and Robert Kahn indicate, "The behavior of people in organizations is still the behavior of individuals, but it has a different set of determinants than behavior outside organizational roles."[23]

Feedback in an organization is less spontaneous and direct than in previously discussed contexts. Members are no longer always in face-to-face interaction; thus, the number of sensory channels diminishes. Because members have limited access to one another, feedback systems are more structured. Indeed, network analysis is a major area of study in the organizational context. Roles, too, are more formalized. As positions and titles change, so do rules about communicative relationships. Different modes of address, message content, and communicator style are associated with different organization positions.

Finally, formal organizational communication is highly goal-oriented, involving preplanned and carefully structured messages. Communication within the organization involves a higher degree of strategic planning than it does with a dyad or small group.

Face-to-Face Public Communication. The most important factor affecting *public communication* is the fact that the speaker must communicate with a large number of people at once. This means the speaker cannot know each member of the audience as can the leader of a small group, and it often means a heterogeneous collection of listeners whose background and experiences may differ markedly from that of the speaker. In addition, the speaker is placed in the situation of addressing these diverse audience members simultaneously. Because the communicative event occurs before an assembly, intra-audience influence also has a potent effect on the success of the message.

Although the public speaker does receive direct feedback, it is often nonverbal, since it may be impossible for audience members to stop the flow of communication to ask questions or make verbal comments. Because nonverbal cues are notoriously hard to interpret, the quality of feedback the speaker receives is more limited than in interpersonal or group contexts.

Communicative roles are also more formal, and use of the terms sender and receiver to describe interactors is appropriate in this context. Both speaker and audience have clearly articulated expectations about each other's behavior. Public speaking situations are also carefully structured and planned in advance. An audience does not generally drop in to pass the time of day with the speaker, nor does the speaker assemble the audience just to get to know them.

Because of the heterogeneity of the average audience, the speaker cannot tailor his or her speech to specific others but must gauge audience attitudes and adapt the speech to appeal to the common denominator within the audience. He or she must also preplan the message in light of audience characteristics. The ability to empathize with audience members, to choose appealing ideas, images, and examples, to organize the presentation, and to deliver the message so that it overcomes intra-audience effects are important skills within this communication context.

Mediated Mass Communication. The context of *mediated mass communication* is similar to the public context; however, instead of being in direct contact with the audience, the communicator must transmit the message though some mechanical or electronic medium. Because the communicator is separated from the audience, there is no instantaneous feedback nor any immediate and direct way of knowing how well-received the message is. Feedback is available, but it is generally delayed. The wealth of nonverbal cues available in smaller face-to-face interactions is missing.

Communicative roles in the mass communication context are highly defined. The audience plays the role of consumer rather than producer of messages. The speaker is the source of the message and operates under fairly stringent expectations, carefully and strategically planning and producing the message.

Swanson and Delia cite some advantages and disadvantages of this form of communication:

To summarize, use of the mass media of communication seems to offer distinct *advantages* to the communicator: (1) potentially large audiences; (2) media well-suited to particular responses the communicator seeks; (3) auditors that are not influenced much by other people during reception of the message. At the same time, serious *disadvantages* are present in the mass media: (1) voluntary attention allows audiences to 'turn off' exposure; (2) media expectations may be impossible for a communicator to fulfill; (3) the diversity and anonymity of the audience make the task of audience analyses and adaptation extremely difficult.[24]

The traditional contexts presented show a situational approach to examining the field of speech communication. As the number of communicators increases and spatial arrangements between them become more distant, certain adjustments are needed for effective communication to occur. The nature and method of achieving feedback, role expectations, and message organization and content assume different forms in response to these changes.

The Styles Approach
to Communication Contexts

The situational approach is not the only way to differentiate among contexts. An understanding of physical constraints helps explain various forms of communication but does not paint a complete picture. One of the most interesting of the alternative approaches to context is provided by Ernest Bormann. Bormann is more interested in the rules and customs that shape the way individuals communicate with one another than he is with the physical constraints under which communication occurs. His view is more rhetorical and more social and so will provide us with a bridge between communication contexts and wider social and historical contexts.

Bormann believes that we are embedded in *rhetorical communities* and that we share with others in our communities certain rules, customs, and conventions that allow us to engage in significant discourse.[25] We share a common language as well as common norms and rules for behavior. In addition, we share a sense of the kinds of communication transactions that are appropriate and suitable and the kinds of relationships we can have with others. Bormann tells us that "rhetorical communities can be studied in much the same manner as ethnographers study cultural communities."[26]

The usages common to a rhetorical community becomes its *style*. New styles arise when old norms, customs, and rules of communication become inadequate. For example, the political and social upheaval of the the 1960s emphasized the need to communicate in an authentic "humanistic" way. New standards for effective communication emerged, and sensitivity and encounter sessions were established to instruct communicators in these new standards. Eventually, critical theories were developed to refine our understanding of communication in the resulting rhetorical community, and concepts such as openness, trust, and self-disclosure were used to judge the adequacy of communication within that rhetorical community. Over time, new generations came to accept these communication values and to see the world from inside the predominant discourse.

Bormann tells us that new rhetorical styles emerge in a trial-and-error way as participants try to find ways of communicating that will allow them to adapt to social and cultural forces. As the style becomes stable, it becomes reified. "Experts" in that communication style arise to coach others in the appropriate ways of speaking and behaving in the community, and models of ideal communication practices are written.

Members of rhetorical communities accept communication practices with very little thought about the inherent assumptions that are embedded in them, although these assumptions have powerful effects. In fact, members eventually come to share a common *rhetorical vision*. The vision includes a consensus on what is or is not "good" communication. It also includes common values and philosophic beliefs. People who join a religious community, for example, share not only a sense of how to talk to one another and to their God, they also share common values such as "that miracles are a likely occurrence, God is the ultimate source of true knowledge, the supernatural makes its presence felt in visible fashion and communicates directly with human beings, and the only true avenue to knowledge is the direct experience of communion with God."[27]

A rhetorical style is a context for communication because it surrounds and affects the way people communicate, and it constrains their actions and beliefs. It is clear that the way we solve communication problems, and perhaps the way we define them, is a product of our rhetorical vision. This approach to context is of great interest to theoreticians, who may try to understand communication by examining the nature of a given style and its effects on those who use it. Theorists with an ethnographic or historical/critical bent find this approach to subdividing the field of communication very useful. Bormann lists a few examples of the kinds of theoretical questions a styles theorist might ask:

Why do some rhetorical communities put such great emphasis upon informal two-person transactions? some upon emotional small group communication? some upon larger group meetings in which several people deliver long uninterrupted speeches? Why do some rhetorical communities put such emphasis upon music as a component of the transactions, such as the televised commercial message of the 1960s and 1970s or the Methodist camp meeting of the early nineteenth century, while others use very little music at all?[28]

What is of particular interest in Bormann's approach is that he recognizes that we do not communicate in isolation, that there are wider social and historical forces that determine our communication actions. While it is certainly true that communication situations are important contexts, they are embedded within society and thus sensitive to social norms and rules. The interpersonal, small group, and public contexts are themselves contextualized by social rules and norms. Thus, Bormann sets the stage for some final thoughts about the effects of cultural forces on communication practices.

Culture and History as Context

Feminist Criticism. As we have seen, the standard definition of context seldom looks beyond the immediate physical surroundings when trying to explain the factors that affect communication. It sometimes appears that when people form relationships, whether interpersonal, group, or public, they become autonomous agents affected only by one another and the physical limitations that separate or join them. Current critical theorists point out, however, that communication situations are part of larger political, cultural, and historical contexts that have immense effects on the way we construct relationships.

While the feminist critics are by no means the only scholars who emphasize the contextualizing effects of social/political structures, they have clearly shown us that we are affected by social contexts. Feminist critics recognize that communication practices are constrained from outside by social conventions (ideas of what it is to be a male or female, the way power is distributed within a given culture, the amount of economic resources available to men and women) and that the ways we communicate maintain and reinforce these conventions. They believe that the dominant discourse (or rhetorical vision, in Bormann's terms) limits women's abilities to express their own unique experiences and to determine their destinies.[29] Thus, feminist critics study the ways women internalize "those representational structures that govern their material conditions"[30] as well as the ways women come to "use cultural forms to analyze their own situation" and how women find ways to express "their anger, discontent, and sarcasm in relation to their positioning within the patriarchy."[31]

Feminist scholars have raised a number of important questions about gender construction and communication, including the following: How are women's and men's experiences affected by patriarchal structures? How are these structures linked to economic and political realities, and how do they lead to subjugation and oppression? How is gender-identity constructed and maintained through communication? What is the relationship of women to language and symbolic practices?[32]

Feminist scholarship has not only made us more aware of gender and politics as context, it has also expanded the notion of the theorist's project; for not only is the goal of feminist studies to understand the relationship between gender and communication, it also involves envisioning ways of changing this relationship. Many of the feminist scholars talk about the possibility of developing a "feminist discourse," a language that will allow feminists to express meanings excluded or dismissed by dominant language practices. This discourse would allow individuals to assert the feminist perspective and also to transform social practices that are oppressive.[33] This view of theory as political action will be taken up in the next chapter when we contrast different ideas of what theory is for.

Historical Contexts. Not only do we often overlook the effects of social and political contexts, but we also tend to believe that the ways we communicate are invariant across time. Although we may recognize that language style has changed over the years and that if we were suddenly transported to Colonial times then we might have some difficulty in understanding those around us, we seldom consider the fact that, across time, the functions of communication may change as radically as its form. Currently, a number of theorists are recognizing that the basic social practices we take for granted (the kinds of communication relationships we form as well as the ways we conceive of the self and the purposes for which we talk) have changed dramatically over the years in response to technological, economic, and political structures.

While a full development of how communication practices have changed over the years is not yet available, a number of interesting studies point the way to a fuller understanding of transhistorical communication studies.[34]

It is important to keep in mind that this text samples theories from one particular point in time: It gives examples of the ways American social scientists (many of them men) living in the twentieth century have sought to understand communication. These theories subscribe to a certain type of rhetorical vision that affects the kinds of questions they ask and the way they seek to answer them. The problems and situational contexts used to organize this book can themselves be contextualized. They are products of current perspectives and paradigms. Communication study in the twenty-first century may look very different than it does today, but for now we must content ourselves with viewing communication from current standpoints and recognizing that we are doing so.

ORGANIZING THEORY BY PROBLEM AND CONTEXT

The theories presented in the remainder of this text are organized around an intersection of problem and situational context. Figure 2.2 illustrates this intersection. In the next part of this book, we will study general theories that apply to all situational contexts. These theories will be discussed according to the communication problems they address. Thus, we will examine theories of communicator acceptability in chapter 4, theories of signification in chapter 5, theories of social coordination in chapter 6, and theories of outcome achievement and evolution in chapter 7. These chapters focus on human communication as a unitary process involving the solving of common problems.

While it is important to recognize commonalities, we need to remember that answers to these five problems are also affected by the situational and functional demands of context. The final part of this text examines the unique constraints that situation and function place on communication theory. Here, concepts and models are more specifically bound to situation. Chapter 8 looks at models of interpersonal communication, chapter 9 investigates small-group theory, and chapter 10 focuses on explanations of public communication.

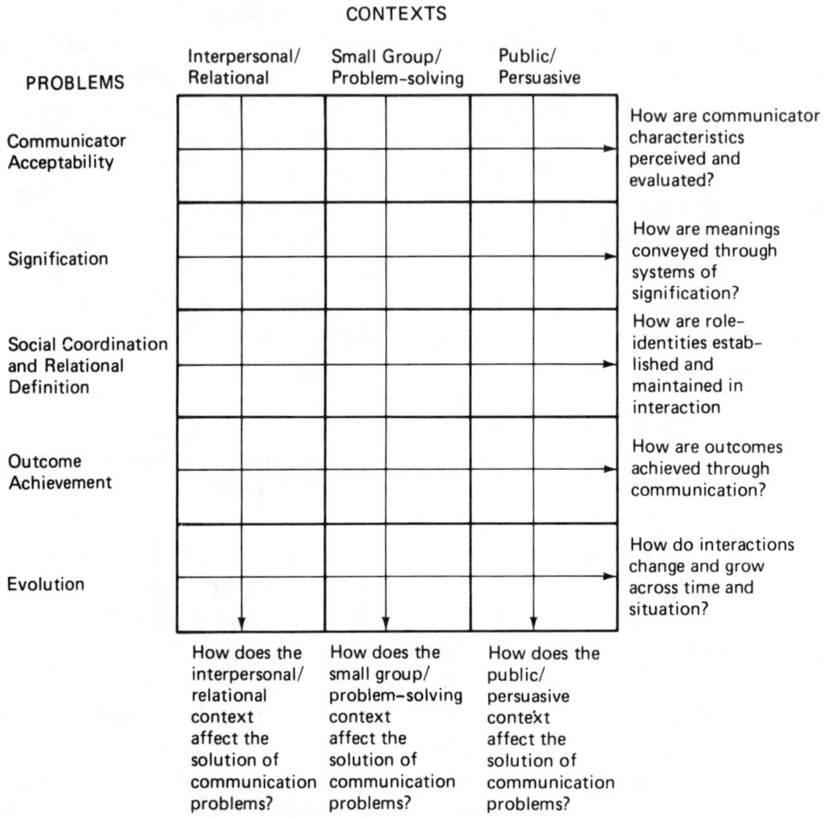

CONTEXTS

PROBLEMS	Interpersonal/ Relational	Small Group/ Problem-solving	Public/ Persuasive	
Communicator Acceptability				How are communicator characteristics perceived and evaluated?
Signification				How are meanings conveyed through systems of signification?
Social Coordination and Relational Definition				How are role-identities estab-lished and maintained in interaction
Outcome Achievement				How are outcomes achieved through communication?
Evolution				How do interactions change and grow across time and situation?
	How does the interpersonal/ relational context affect the solution of communication problems?	How does the small group/ problem-solving context affect the solution of communication problems?	How does the public/ persuasive context affect the solution of communication problems?	

FIGURE 2.2: The problem–context matrix

Before we begin our examination of communication theories, we will have one more introductory chapter. Chapter 3 discusses the topic of ideology raised in chapter 1 and hinted at in our discussion of alternate ideas of context. This chapter examines the philosophic perspectives and research methods that affect how we conduct inquiry and answer the problems just discussed. Once introduced to the various philosophical and methodological approaches of speech communication theories and to the assumptions behind each approach, you will be better able to evaluate the theories in the rest of the text.

REFERENCES

1. Ernest G. Bormann, *Communication Theory* (New York: Holt, Rinehart & Winston, 1980), p. 73.

2. Klaus Krippendorf, "Values, Modes, and Domains of Inquiry into Communication," *The Journal of Communication*, 19 (June 1969), 105–33.

3. *Ibid.*, p. 109.

4. See Paul Watzlawick, Janet Beavin Bavelas, and Don D. Jackson, *Pragmatics of Human Communication* (New York: W. W. Norton, 1967).

5. C. David Mortensen, "Communication Postulates," in *Contexts*, ed. Jean M. Civikly (New York: Holt, Rinehart & Winston, 1981), p. 21.

6. Gerald R. Miller, "The Current Status of Theory and Research in Interpersonal Communication," *Human Communication Research*, 4 (Winter 1978), 165.

7. *Ibid.*, p. 165.

8. David L. Swanson and Jesse G. Delia, "The Nature of Human Communication," in *Modules in Speech Communication* (Chicago: Science Research Associates, 1976), pp. 37–38.

9. *Ibid.*, p. 37.

10. Miller, "Current Status of Theory," p. 165.

11. Swanson and Delia, "Nature of Human Communication," p. 36.

12. William W. Wilmot, *Dyadic Communication* (Reading, Mass.: Addison-Wesley, 1979), pp. 18–19.

13. *Ibid.*, p. 18.

14. Swanson and Delia, "Nature of Human Communication," p. 40.

15. Jack R. Gibb, "Defensive Communication," in *Messages*, 3rd ed., ed. Sanford B. Weinberg (New York: Random House, 1980).

16. B. Aubrey Fisher, *Small-Group Decision Making*, 2nd ed. (New York: McGraw-Hill, 1980), p. 25. See also, John K. Brilhart, *Effective Group Discussion*, 3rd ed. (Dubuque, Iowa: William C. Brown, 1978).

17. Wilmot, *Dyadic Communication*, p. 19.

18. Fisher, *Small-Group Decision Making*, p. 26.

19. Swanson and Delia, "Nature of Human Communication," p. 40.

20. Fisher, *Small-Group Decision Making*, p. 26.

21. Everett M. Rogers and Rekha Agarwala-Rogers, *Communication in Organizations* (New York: The Free Press, 1976), p. 6.

22. Cassandra L. Book and others, *Human Communication: Principles, Contexts, and Skills* (New York: St. Martin's Press, 1980), p. 170.

23. Daniel Katz and Robert L. Kahn, *The Social Psychology of Organizations* (New York: John Wiley & Sons, 1966), p. 391.

24. Swanson and Delia, "Nature of Human Communication," p. 45.

25. Bormann, *Communication Theory*, p. 60.

26. *Ibid.*, p. 62.

27. *Ibid.*, p. 67.

28. *Ibid.*, p. 64.

29. Cheris Kramarae, *Women and Men Speaking: Frameworks for Analysis* (Rowley, Mass.: Newbury House, 1981), p. 3.

30. Cathy Schwichtenberg, "Feminist Cultural Studies," *Critical Studies in Mass Communication*, 6 (June 1989), 202–208, p. 205.

31. *Ibid.*, p. 204. See also, Janice Radway, "Identifying Ideological Seams: Mass Culture, Analytical Method, and Political Practice," *Communication*, 9 (1986), 93–123.

32. Paula A. Treichler and Ellen Wartella, "Interventions: Feminist Theory and Communication Studies, *Communication*, 9 (1986), 1–18.

33. Lana Rakow, "Feminist Studies: The Next Stage," *Critical Studies in Mass Communication*, 6 (June 1989), 209–14.

34. Paul Secord, "Love, Misogyny, and Feminism in Selected Historical Periods: A Social-Psychological Explanation," and Jan E. Dizard and Howard Gadlin, "Family Life and the Marketplace: Diversity and Change in the American Family," in *Historical Social Psychology*, eds. Kenneth J. Gergen and Mary M. Gergen (Hillsdale, N. J.: Lawrence Erlbaum Associates, 1984); Howard Gadlin, "Private Lives and Public Order: A Critical View of the History of Intimate Relations in the United States," in *Close Relationships: Perspectives on the Meaning of Intimacy*, eds. George Levinger and Harold L. Raush (Amherst, Mass.: University of Massachusetts Press, 1977).

chapter 3

PERSPECTIVES, ASSUMPTIONS, AND METHODOLOGICAL APPROACHES

INTRODUCTION

The theme of this chapter can be found in the story of the hypothetical meeting between two of the greatest of early astronomers, Tycho Brahe and Johannes Kepler.[1] Both wanted to explain the movements of the planets, but their theories differed. Brahe held the traditional belief that the solar system was earth-centered, while the more revolutionary Kepler assumed that the sun, not the earth, formed the center of the universe. In the story, the two meet at dawn to resolve their problem. As the sun appears, both turn to each other and say, "See, I am right!" Barnett Pearce, Vernon Cronen, and Linda Harris ask an important question about this story: Did the two astronomers see the same thing?[2]

In one sense, they did; we assume the images they saw were identical. In a more important sense, however, they did not see the same thing. "One 'saw' the sun rise above an immobile earth, and the other 'saw' the earth rotate to expose an immobile sun."[3] Their assumptions about the solar system caused them to see the "same" thing differently.

If something as straightforward as a sunrise depends so heavily on underlying assumptions for its meaning, you can imagine how essential assumptions are to an abstract construct like communication. In this chapter, we will review five different philosophic perspectives, each of which sheds a different light on what communication is. We will also examine three different methodological approaches to theory and research.

Why begin our discussion of communication theory on such an abstract level? Because theories depend on underlying assumptions that are often difficult to uncover. To the people of

Brahe's day, the "fact" that the earth was the center of the universe was so obvious (and any other alternative so blasphemous) that it was never questioned or even viewed as an assumption. Only when this idea was examined and questioned could the science of astronomy move in new and more productive directions.

Theories are the products of human beings who have been taught a particular view of the world and are, therefore, at the mercy of that view's unquestioned assumptions. Only by questioning their assumptions can theorists step outside the familiar and test their own views. The upcoming discussion of perspectives will explain how underlying systems of thought determine what we see when we view a social phenomenon. It will also challenge some common assumptions about communication.

PERSPECTIVES ON HUMAN COMMUNICATION

A *perspective* is a coherent set of assumptions or beliefs about some phenomenon. As we shall see, a single act of communication may be viewed in a variety of ways, depending on the perspective we take. According to one view, communication is the transmission of a message through a channel; according to another it is a subjective process whereby a receiver mentally filters incoming stimuli. Some scientists believe communication is the creation of self through social interaction. Others define it as a series of highly patterned redundant behaviors, and still others see communication as discourse, as a system of meanings produced by invisible social and cultural forces. Each of these ways of viewing communication originates in a different perspective.

Perspectives help us determine the relevant parts of a phenomenon and help us in the "selection of concepts to load the system."[4] The five perspectives to be discussed originate in different academic areas, focus on separate key concepts, differ about where communication occurs, and

prompt different questions about the communication process. Our discussion of the first four perspectives draws (with modifications and additions) on ideas presented by B. Aubrey Fisher in *Perspectives on Human Communication.*[5] Although Fisher's system is not the only taxonomy of perspectives on communication, it serves as a solid introduction to the variety of viewpoints in our field.

The Mechanistic Perspective

The first perspective Fisher discusses is the *mechanistic perspective.* This perspective follows the philosophic assumptions of nineteenth-century physical scientists. These scientists studied mechanics, a branch of physical science that describes how energy is transferred between physical objects. Much of our current thinking about human communication can be traced to these physicists and to the work of twentieth-century information scientists who followed them. Although modern physical scientists repudiate many of their assumptions, a mechanistic perspective is still evident in the social sciences.

As a way of describing the movement of physical objects, the mechanistic view says the world can be broken down into independently existing parts governed by universal laws. It implies that if we know all the laws governing physical relationships, we can predict all future states of affairs. Under this view, the future is determined by its past, and objects follow the laws of cause and effect. For example:

If the foot of a walking man hits a pebble, energy is transferred from the foot to the stone; the latter will be displaced and will eventually come to rest again in a position which is fully determined by such factors as the amount of energy transferred, the shape and weight of the pebble, and the nature of the surface on which it rolls.[6]

Pool players will recognize the applicability of mechanistic laws. Theoretically, it is possible to predict the path of a ball by using knowledge of the angle at and force with which it is struck, the surface of the pool table, and so forth. In both examples, a necessary relationship exists between antecedents (the force with which an object is hit) and consequents (the trajectory it follows), which can be explained by universal laws of cause and effect.

Karl Deutsch sums up ideas implied in classical mechanics:

The classical concept or model of mechanism implied the notion of a whole which was completely equal to the sum of its parts...which would behave in exactly identical fashion no matter how often those parts were disassembled and put together again, and irrespective of the sequence in which the disassembling or reassembling would take place. It implied consequently the notion that the parts were never significantly modified by each other, nor by their own past, that each part once placed into its appropriate position with its appropriate momentum, would stay exactly there and continue to fulfill its completely and uniquely determined function.[7]

Assumptions of the Mechanistic Perspective. We can see that the mechanistic perspective contains several implications. First, mechanistic functioning is linear and one-directional. Subparts in a mechanistic system have specific functions that are transferred forward in a direct line to the next part of the sequence. The pool cue hits the cue ball, which directs the eight ball into the corner pocket. "Each component is like a link in a chain—each link connected to the next link and connected to other links only through the intervening links. Taken together all links form a complete chain."[8]

In addition, each component has a preordained function and affects only the component that is next in line. A component cannot "decide" to change its effects or skip a step. If one component wears out or breaks down, the system ceases functioning until the faulty component is replaced or repaired. A affects B, B affects C, and so forth. If B does not occur, the entire system grinds to a halt: A cannot directly cause C. The first assumption of the mechanistic perspective, then, is that *the subparts of a mechanical system transfer their functions in a linear, sequential fashion.*

This perspective also implies that the elements of a mechanistic system are material entities that exist in time and space. "The behavior of a material object is conceptualized as a movement or flow across space—a movement from one place to another."[9] Since material objects take up space, two objects cannot occupy the same space at the same time. Thus, a second assumption of the mechanistic view is that *the world can be viewed as a series of collisions between material objects, as a sequence of actions and reactions, of causes and effects.*

Third, the mechanistic perspective assumes that an effective way to study an object is to isolate and examine each of its subunits. Reduction of an object or process into subunits does not destroy the object's or process's reality. Physical objects may be reduced to molecules, atoms, and subatomic particles. Behaviors can be reduced to kinesic or microkinesic units. Language can be broken down into phonemes and morphemes. A final assumption of this perspective is that *a whole can be reduced to a collection of parts, and the sum of the parts is equal to the whole.* In the next section, we will see how these assumptions apply to the study of communication.

Components of the Mechanistic Perspective. The mechanistic view is not merely a product of nineteenth-century scientific thinking. Scientific developments in the twentieth-century are also incorporated in the mechanistic model. During and following World War II, advances in weapons technology and telecommunications led to quantification and measurement of electronically transmitted signals. Claude Shannon and Warren Weaver developed the new science of information theory. While nineteenth-century physics dealt with the transmission of energy, twentieth-century theories focused on the transfer of electronically transmitted information. An adaptation of the Shannon-Weaver model is illustrated in Fig. 3.1. According to this model, a source encodes or transmits a message that travels along a channel until it reaches its destination where it is decoded

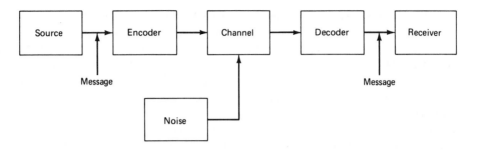

FIGURE 3.1: A mechanistic model of communication

by a receiver.[10] This model is thought to work in essentially the same way whether the source is a human communicator using spoken language or a radio transmitter generating electronic signals.

Of course, information theory is more sophisticated than the simple model shown in Fig. 3.1. Its goal is precise mathematical measurement and description of concepts such as channel capacity and units of information.[11] Still, the concepts in the diagram are key components of the Shannon-Weaver mechanistic model.

We can apply the diagram to face-to-face spoken communication between two people. The two people become sender and receiver. The sender encodes the message into units of spoken language that are conveyed by sound waves to the receiver, who decodes the message. Any feature not intended by the sender but inadvertently included in the message is called noise. The goal of communication under this model is the transfer of a message from source to receiver with as little noise as possible. The extent to which the message retains its integrity at various points along the channel is called fidelity. Thus, according to this perspective, the important components that describe communication are *source, message, channel, noise, receiver, encoding-decoding,* and *fidelity.*

The Shannon-Weaver model illustrates all the tenants of mechanistic thinking. First, it views the communication process as linear and sequential; the message flows along the channel in a straight line from sender to receiver. If interference occurs

somewhere along its path, the system will stop, unable to forward its message. According to the Shannon-Weaver model, communication can break down if the connection between sequential parts is destroyed.

Second, this model views communication as a process composed of material objects. The message is a "thing" traveling between sender and receiver and separate from them. During message transmission, the laws of cause and effect are obeyed. A receiver's communicative response is an effect caused by several factors including the sender's ability to construct an intelligible message, the capacity of the channel to handle the message, and the amount of noise in the system. Finally, this view of communication is reductionist because the process is broken down into separate components that can be studied in isolation. The three implications of the mechanistic perspective apply to the model in Fig. 3.1.

The Locus of Mechanistic Communication. One of Fisher's most interesting contributions to our understanding of perspectives is his belief that each perspective locates communication in a slightly different place. In the mechanistic perspective, communication occurs in the channel. Under this perspective, "communication study... focuses on the channel, and events or functions occurring on the channel become fodder for research and theorizing."[12]

The locus of communication can affect the kind of questions a researcher will ask. Because, in the mechanistic perspective, communication originates with a sender who creates a message, the following questions are typical: How do source characteristics affect transmission and reception of a message? and What effects will a particular kind of message have? The notion that the channel directly affects the message leads to other questions such as Are multiple channels more effective than single channels? or How does a particular kind of channel affect communication? Since channels can break down or be blocked, questions such as What happens when the amount of information in a message exceeds channel capacity? or How does the presence of an intermediary filter information? lead to further investigation.

The mechanistic perspective has been one of the most influential in communication theory. We assume that one person can "send" a message to another as though the message could exist apart from sender and receiver and could be directed across space. We believe in communication breakdowns and barriers as though some physical obstruction could block out a message and as though the presence of this obstruction is not a message in its own right. We talk about message effects as though communication is something a sender "does to" a receiver.

These assumptions are so ingrained that it is hard to believe communication can be viewed in any other way. Discussion of the next four perspectives, however, will show that there are other ways to think of communication, other components that describe communication, and different sets of questions about how communication works.

The Psychological Perspective

The *psychological perspective* is less a unique perspective than a modification of the mechanistic perspective that assumes that all information is filtered through individual subjects. It recognizes that messages do not exist outside the human mind and suggests that any information processed by the human mind is a message. The psychological perspective relocates communication within the mental processes of senders and receivers.

The psychological perspective is a synthesis of many scientific views, particularly those represented in behavioral and cognitive psychology. Fisher describes this perspective as a form of "post-Skinnerian behaviorism with a strong flavor of cognitive explanation."[13] It views human beings as organisms who actively seek out and process incoming stimuli and whose behaviors are the result of learned responses.

Barnlund, in describing communication as meaning, takes a psychological view:

The word "communication" stands for those acts in which meaning develops within human beings as neuro-motor responses are acquired or modified. It arises out of the need to reduce uncertainty, to act effectively, to defend or strengthen the ego. Its aim is to increase the number and consistency of meanings within the limits set by attitudes and action patterns that have proven successful in the past, emerging needs and drives, and the demands of the physical and social setting of the moment.... It should be stressed that meaning is something "invented," "assigned," "given," rather than something "received."[14]

Assumptions of the Psychological Perspective. The psychological perspective draws heavily on learning theory, which views human behavior as a series of stimulus-response ($S \rightarrow R$) chains. Human beings are constantly bombarded by *stimuli* (units of sensory input). What individuals do as a result of processing these stimuli are *responses* (units of behavior). For example, when a father hears his baby's cry (stimulus), he checks to see if the child is in trouble (response). When a neighbor sees smoke rising from a nearby roof (stimulus), she calls the fire department (response). Responses in turn can become stimuli when processed as units of sensory input. For example, the response of calling the fire department may become a stimulus for fire fighters whose response is the complex set of behaviors involved in answering an alarm. All responses are elicited by stimuli, and all stimuli lead to responses. Human beings are both senders and receivers because we simultaneously react to and produce stimuli. The first assumption of the psychological perspective is that *human subjects exist independently within stimulus fields that they both process and produce.*

Behavior was first described as a simple S→R chain, but as Fisher points out, this scheme was soon modified with greater emphasis on the organism (O). The behavioral equation was rewritten as S→O→R when scientists recognized that the organism is an active agent, not merely a passive receptor. This discovery led to a concern with describing the mental processing or conceptual filtering that occurs within the human organism. Fisher offers an example that illustrates this process:

To observe a shark's dorsal fin in the water and the subsequent behavior of a swimmer heading post haste to shore will lead us to infer that the stimulus (the fin) activated the mediational process internal to the organism (the swimmer experienced fear), which then led to a behavioral response (flight behavior). Responses, then, do not emanate directly from the stimuli but are mediated through internal states within the organism, the human being.[15]

How does the swimmer know that the fin signals danger and that flight is an appropriate response? By recognizing that this stimulus is similar to past stimuli that signaled danger. The mechanism that allows an individual to recognize similarities among S→R situations is called a *mental set*, "a collection of criteria or expectations based on prior experiences that are inherently applied to each new experience as a means for determining the similarity or difference between the new situation and past experiences."[16] A set is the mental structure we use to filter information conceptually. Because sets are products of experience, organisms constantly evolve as a result of prior stimulus/response relationships. A second assumption of the psychological perspective is that *subjects are modified by the stimuli they receive.* Within the human actor there exist conceptual structures that are the products of experience built up over time.

The psychological perspective assumes that the perception of incoming stimuli is selective and that the organism has a choice in how it responds to a selected stimulus. This occurs because the organism is aware that different responses have different consequences. If we rewrite the behavioral equation one more time, incorporating the consequences (C) resulting from a response, we have something like this: S→O→R→C.

Fisher notes that the addition of consequences (or reinforcements) subtly changes the concept of causality provided by this perspective. Now, not only the past, but also the future can affect behavior. By anticipating the outcome of a response (for example, imagining staying in the water as the shark approaches), an organism chooses its actions. The psychological perspective suggests that human beings, unlike simple mechanical systems, can control their responses. A third assumption of this perspective is that *the human subject can selectively attend to incoming stimuli and can choose future responses* on the basis of both past experience and anticipation of the future.

The psychological perspective, while grounded in a behaviorist model, exceeds it by viewing the human actor as an active information processor capable of making choices and being guided by goals and needs. A cognitive, humanistic component is added to what began as a straight behaviorist model.

Components of the Psychological Perspective. The psychological perspective is most often combined with the mechanistic to explain communication. Figure 3.2 typifies the way communicologists integrate psychological and mechanistic concepts to describe the communication process.

In this model, the concepts of channel, noise, and message are retained. Sender and receiver are combined into joint sender-receivers, and stimuli are internally interpreted. Almost the entire process occurs within the individual. Although this

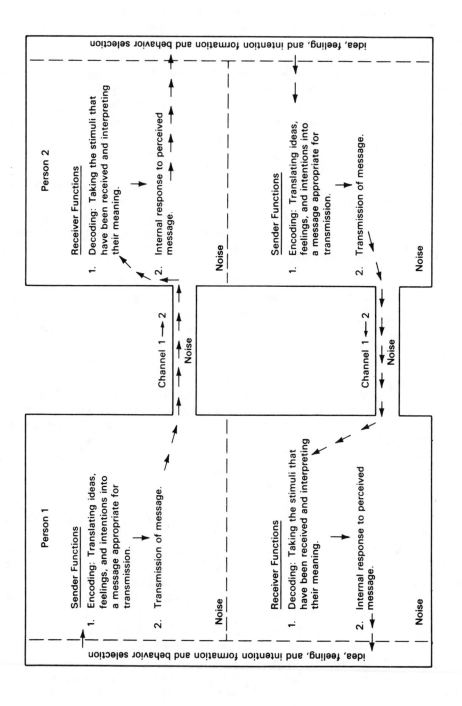

FIGURE 3.2: A psychological model of communication. (From David W. Johnson, Reaching Out [Englewood Cliffs, N.J.: Prentice Hall, 1972] p. 63.)

model is not very clear about the nature of internal filtering and the evolution of mental sets, it does include most of the typical components of the psychological perspective: *individuals who are simultaneously sender-receivers, channel, message stimuli, internalized responses*, and *noise*. If we add the idea of evolving mental set, or what Fisher calls *conceptual filters*, we then have the most important parts of communication. "Human communication in a psychological model is thus a continuous production and reception of stimuli added to and selected from the stimuli available in the informational environment."[17] As communicators, we actively choose to attend to certain stimuli, interpret them by means of our own unique mental structures, and respond by emitting certain behaviors capable of stimulating others.

Locus of Psychological Communication. According to Fisher, "The psychological perspective of human communication clearly focuses on the individual as the primary 'place' to look for communication to take place."[18] More particularly, psychological communication occurs in the conceptual filters of the individual.

What happens when we locate communication within conceptual filters? First, the distinction between sender and receiver blurs. Theorists view communication not as something a sender does to a receiver, but as something a sender-receiver does with a message. Research tries to determine why the sender-receiver responds to a message in certain ways, creating mental constructs to explain the nature of communicator responses. The sender-receiver is endowed with enduring psychological properties that affect behavior. Questions such as, How do an individual's personality traits affect the production and reception of messages? are common. Drives, needs, goals, and attitudes are studies as they affect message construction and reception.

Second, under this perspective, a successful communicative relationship requires that two people share experiences and goals. To communicate effectively, the sender-receivers must share meanings: Their internalized conceptual filters must be similar. Perceived similarity becomes an important variable in interpersonal attraction and satisfaction. While this idea is more fully developed in the interactionist perspective, it has its beginning in the psychological view.

This ultimately leads to the emergence of intrapersonal communication as an area of study in its own right. Researchers become interested in describing general methods of processing information. Thus, questions such as, How are motives attributed? How do separate cognitions influence one another? and How are cognitive schema constructed? become important under this perspective.

Until recently, almost all communication research has been based on a combination of mechanistic and psychological reasoning. Certainly, psychological constructs have greatly affected how we think about communication. The old saw, "Meanings are in people, not in words," illustrates the psychological view, as does a general emphasis on individual human subjects whose personalities and value systems affect their interactions. To most people, the assumptions of the psychological perspective are unquestionable. But, as we shall see, the interactionist view reverses the psychological, suggesting that individuals exist not as subjects but as objects of society and that communication instead of being created by the self is something that creates the self.

The Interactionist Perspective

The *interactionist perspective* stems from a body of theory and research known as symbolic interactionism. This term designates a sociological theory first developed by Charles Horton Cooley, George Herbert Mead, and later by Herbert Blumer.[19] The major difference between the psychological and the interactionist perspective is that interactionism locates all human action within society, recognizing that while society is based on individual actions, individuals act as they do because they are members of society. The individual cannot be thought of in isolation from interactions with others.

Symbolic interactionism suggests the world exists as it does because human beings can act toward objects within their worlds and can designate these actions through symbolic activity. According to the interactionist perspective, the world can be broken down into objects, but these objects are neither material entities (as in the mechanistic view) nor stimuli (in the psychological sense). Rather, they are action plans. "An object doesn't exist for the individual in some preestablished form. Perception of an object has telescoped in it a series of experiences which one would have if he carried out the plan of action toward the object."[20] An object, whether a simple physical "thing," such as a cup of coffee, or an abstract concept, such as responsibility, has significance because it is a goal of human action and because people act toward it by designating it with a socially created symbol.[21] A deadline, for example, is not a material entity, "but exists because a newspaper editor and...reporters coordinate their activities toward it and act as if it must be met."[22] In this sense, all the "things" that make up our world, including ourselves, are products of symbolic actions, constituted and created through the communication process.

Assumptions of the Interactionist Perspective. The concept of the symbol is basic to this perspective. An object becomes significant when it is named, that is, when an arbitrary sign or symbol is attached to it. Hewitt explains the importance of the symbol:

The capacity to use and respond to symbols has revolutionary consequences for the species that develops it. The framework of space and time within which action occurs is further expanded and complicated. At the same time, the actions of individual members of the species become more intricately linked together, since the existence of symbols to represent the world makes it possible not only to experience the environment in more complex ways, but, crucially, to share that experience with others. And, finally, the very character of the

environment itself—of what is or may be environmental to the organism—is expanded, so that it becomes necessary to think of the environment not as a given reality, but as a reality subject to symbolic definition.[23]

Symbols are essentially social. They have meaning because they are used by members of a group in similar ways. The term "danger" becomes socially significant because the community agrees on its meaning. When a person shouts "danger," he "calls forth the response of flight in himself as well as others. Not only does he designate...action for himself but he does so for others as well."[24] Symbols are significant because they are shared. The first assumption of the interactionist perspective is that *communication occurs through the creation of shared significant symbols*.

Symbols also allow individuals to designate themselves as objects, to become conscious of their own existence. "The organism that minds itself—is aware of itself as part of the world—has gained an important capacity for control over its own acts. For just as it can anticipate the behavior of others of its species, it anticipates (imaginatively) its own acts as well."[25]

According to Mead, the self is both subject and object, both "I" and "me." The "I" is the active ego, the part of the self that initiates actions. The "me" is the self as object, the "I" observed by itself. The self acts as an "I" and consciously observes its own actions as a "me." This process of acting while simultaneously observing is called self-indication. Self-indication allows the self to see itself as others do. It allows the individual to internalize social processes.

Mead's concept of self differs from the psychological concept of self as an independent subject filtering experience through enduring mental structures. In Mead's view, "the individual constructs the experiences of self" by acting toward the self as though it were a social object and by designating it symbolically.[26] The second assumption of this perspective is that *the self is constructed through communication*. A self not designated symbolically is not communicated about and does not exist.

Meanings are created when two or more individuals regard an object in similar ways. When you and I communicate about an object, I indicate to you both my interpretation of the object (my action plan) and my expectations of your interpretation (my view of your action plan). You do likewise. Communication implies coorientation. It necessitates role-taking, the process of assuming the perspectives of others and seeing things as they do. For Mead, the highest stage of role-taking occurs when the concept of "generalized other" is attained. "The generalized other represents typical members of a society or culture with which the individual identifies herself."[27] To interact socially, the individual must see the world as the generalized other might. Effective communication involves the ability to create messages understandable not only to self but to undifferentiated others as well. It implies the ability to assume another's viewpoint and code messages from this viewpoint. A third assumption of the interactionist perspective is that *social activity becomes possible through the role-taking process*.

According to the interactionist perspective, self and society are created though the communication process. Using symbols to designate self and others is necessary for coordinated social action. Humans exist in and through communication; human action can be understood through the shared symbol systems that make action possible.

Components of the Interactionist Perspective. Figure 3.3 represents David Swanson and Jesse Delia's model of the concept of shared orientation that lies at the core of the interactionist perspective. In the Swanson and Delia model, two individuals create shared meaning by exchanging significant symbols. Through a process of role-taking, they take on the perspectives of self and other. Their ability to share individual perspectives is, in part, a product of their common culture, shared knowledge, and language. They are situated in a social context that is simultaneously a product of their individuality and a force determining their individuality. Many of the basic components of the interactionist perspective are included: *self, society, significant symbols, shared meaning, coorientation,* and *role-taking*.

The Locus of Interactional Communication. According to this perspective, communication is not centered in a structure such as a channel or conceptual filter but rather in the role-taking process. Communication occurs not as a product of sequential actions and interactions between two separate individuals but as individuals simultaneously experience each other. It is collective rather than individual. Fisher quotes the existentialist Marcel who states, "The fact is that we can understand ourselves by starting from the other, or from others, and only by starting from them."[28]

The interactionist perspective has influenced our thinking mainly by stressing the importance of roles as they affect human communication and by emphasizing the creation of shared meaning. Individuals have not one self (as implied by the psychological perspective) but multiple selves depending on those around them. In a real sense, we are the products of others. The concept of self-fulfilling prophecy arises because we often behave on the basis of expectations internalized from others. The concept of self-concept, as a product of past symbolic interactions, is also interactionist. (Chapter 6 presents several interactionist theories.)

The interactionist view of communication effectiveness differs from other views. Mechanistically, effectiveness is an attempt to minimize information loss by increasing fidelity. Psychologically, it is a product of similarity of mental structure. In the interactionist perspective, it becomes a process of sharing emergent meanings.

Although the interactionist view has not been as influential as the psychological, its validity is growing, particularly among those interested in language development and social/cognitive processing. The recognition of communication as "an emergent, creative activity through which

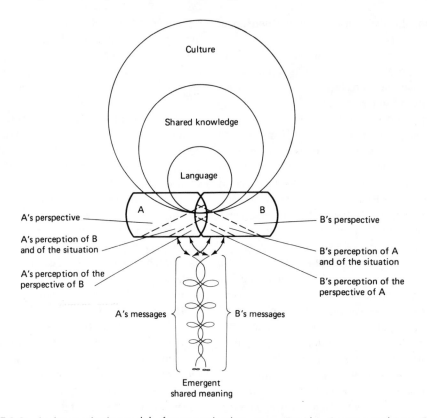

FIGURE 3.3: An interactionist model of communication. (From David L. Swanson and Jesse G. Delia, "The Nature of Human Communication," in *Modules in Speech Communication*, eds. Ronald L. Applbaum and Roderick P. Hart [Chicago: Science Research Associates, 1972], p. 38.)

social reality is constantly being recreated, affirmed, repaired, and changed" is clearly based on interactionist principles.[29]

The Pragmatic Perspective

The term pragmatics originates with Charles Morris, a language philosopher who divided the study of language into three parts: syntactics (the study of grammatical structure), semantics (the study of meaning), and pragmatics (the study of language in action). The *pragmatic perspective* concerns itself with behavioral patterns that people use while interacting. Although Morris originally coined the term, a group of psychotherapists

known as the Palo Alto Group developed the basic ideas that establish the pragmatic perspective. Chief among them were Paul Watzlawick, Janet Bavelas, and Don Jackson, whose classic work directly applied this perspective to communication theory.[30]

The therapists of the Palo Alto Group described disturbed communication not as "the incurable and progressive disease of an individual mind" but as "the only possible reaction to an absurd or untenable communicational context."[31] They argued that disturbed, like normal, behaviors simply were reactions to particular interactive situations. In developing their approach, they relied heavily on general systems theory, for they believed that interaction is best understood as a system of behaviors.

Hall and Fagan, two general systems theorists, define system as "a set of objects together with the relationships between the objects and between their attributes."[32] Anatol Rapoport defines a system as a "whole which functions as a whole by virtue of the interdependence of its parts."[33] Both definitions imply that a system's parts depend on one another for proper functioning. The Palo Alto Group argued that communication should not be considered as the acts or utterances of single individuals but rather as a system and that during communication each individual's actions are understandable only in relation to one another.

A *system* is any interrelated set of elements acting together as a unit (an automotive electrical system, the human circulatory system, an ecological system, or a family interaction system). When any collection of objects or actions work as a whole because they are interrelated, they are a system. Systems can be open or closed. An open system can exchange energy or information with its environment; it is oriented toward change and growth. A closed system lacks such an interchange and is not self-correcting. Mechanical or physical systems are generally closed, while human systems are open to the extent that they import new information from the environment.

Of course, all collections of people are not systems. For example, all persons wearing red sweaters on a certain day are a "heap" or "aggregate," not a system, since they do not interact interdependently. Many collections of people do act as systems, however, especially people who share common goals and communicate with one another. Labor union members are part of a system; member relatedness rather than individuality determines collective behavior. The acts of individual members on a picket line are explainable only when placed in the context of the system (the union). From the pragmatic perspective it is less instructive to view members of a system as individual psychological entities than it is to view their interrelated sequences of behaviors.

Consider the following example:

The fox population of a certain area of northern Canada shows a remarkable periodicity in the increase and decrease of its numbers. In a cycle of four years it reaches a peak, declines to near extinction, and finally starts rising again. If the attention of the biologist were limited to the foxes, these cycles would remain unexplainable, for there is nothing in the nature of the fox or of the whole species that could account for these changes. However, once it is realized that the foxes prey almost exclusively on wild rabbits, and that these rabbits have almost no other natural enemy, this *relation between* the two species provides a satisfactory explanation for an otherwise mysterious phenomenon. For it can then be seen that the rabbits exhibit an identical cycle, but with increase and decrease reversed: the more foxes there are, the more rabbits are killed by them, so that eventually food becomes very scarce for the foxes. Their number decreases, giving the surviving rabbits a chance to multiply and thrive again in the virtual absence of their enemies, the foxes. The fresh abundance of rabbits favors the survival and increase of foxes, etc.[34]

Unless we view the system as a whole, the behaviors of each species are meaningless. Once we see that they belong to a system, however, the relations between their behaviors becomes clear. What holds for foxes and rabbits holds for human communicators as well.

Assumptions of the Pragmatic Perspective. Although the pragmatic perspective is not identical to general systems theory, it is closely aligned; therefore, to understand this perspective, it is first necessary to understand the properties of systems. Several properties characterize open systems. The first is *wholeness*. A change in any part of a system changes all parts and the system as a whole. For example, the serious illness of one family member affects every member of the family and the family's behavior as a unit. Kathleen Galvin and Bernard Brommel suggest that families develop a certain degree of cohesion and adaptability that characterizes their behavior as a system.[35] In this example, the family may either bond more tightly together and engage in more rigidly determined patterns of coping, or it may experience disintegration, loss of solidarity, and a high level of unpredictability. Regardless of which path it follows, the system as a whole experiences change.

A corollary of wholeness is that of _non-summativity_, meaning that a system is more than the sum of its parts. When group members work together to solve a problem, their solution is usually of a higher quality than that which could be achieved by the individuals working separately. When people form a system, something happens that enhances and changes individual inputs. Similarly, the outcome of interaction between two people cannot be predicted outside the interaction, because their behavior is partly determined by the way the other acts.

The principles stated so far imply a third characteristic of systems, _equifinality_. Just as a system is greater than its separate parts, so its output is greater than the sum of its initial inputs. Because an open system can import information from its environment and use it to regulate itself, the system's operation is not determined by its initial conditions. Different causes may lead to the same effect, and different effects may be achieved by the same cause. "Stated in another way, open systems are purposeful...and possess the ability of self-regulation. They can make assessments of the structure and functioning of their own systems as well as the state of the environment and act accordingly."[36] Watzlawick, Bavelas, and Jackson point out:

In the case of the open system...organizational characteristics of the system can operate to achieve even the extreme case of total independence of initial conditions: _the system is then its own best explanation,_ and the study of its present organization the appropriate methodology.[37]

The pragmatic perspective borrows ideas from general systems theory and applies them to human communication. But, what exactly does a communication system consist of? To those who follow the pragmatic view, interactive systems consist not of individuals but of behaviors. The pragmatic researcher is not interested in an indi-

vidual self within whom communication occurs but in what occurs between people, and what goes on between people is actual patterns of behaviors.[38] Fisher even suggests that a group can be understood, not as a collection of people, but as a collection of actions, each constrained by the system as a whole.[39] The pragmatic perspective first assumes, therefore, that _communicative exchanges, not individual members, are the ingredients of the system._

Once we accept that the pragmatic scientist is interested not in people but in their behaviors, other ideas follow. It is meaningless to try to explain behaviors in terms of individual motivations. Under the psychological perspective, we explain why a person acts in a particular way, for example, why a wife nagged her husband, by referring to some process inside the wife herself. Pragmatically speaking, however, what motivates the individual is unimportant. We are not interested in why she acts the way she does; instead, we want to know how the wife's behavior affects other behaviors in the system and how they proceed from previous behaviors. Rather than ask _why_ about a person, we ask _what for_ about a behavior.[40]

Under the pragmatic view, the wife's nagging behavior is understandable only in terms of the behaviors that precede and follow it. Let us assume that every time the wife nags, her husband withdraws, and every time he withdraws, she responds with more nagging. Why does she nag? Because he withdrew. Why does he withdraw? Because she nagged. Her behavior is a response to his, and pragmatically this is explanation enough. It is unnecessary to posit complicated intrapsychic processes or to explain either behavior. We only need to know that the couple is locked in a repetitive pattern, that each of their actions constrains the next. Albert Scheflen expressed this idea when he says the goal of communication study should lie in "asking what behavior means rather than asking what people mean by their behavior."[41] The second assumption of the pragmatic view is that _behaviors are_

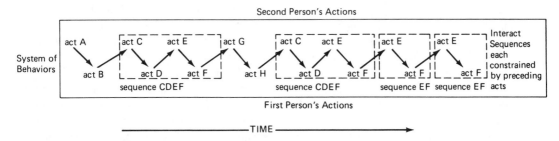

FIGURE 3.4: A pragmatic model of communication. Each letter represents a particular kind of communicative act. Over time, an EF (or FE) sequence emerges. Whenever person 1 engages in act E, person 2 responds with act F. Whenever person 2 engages in act F, person 1 feels compelled to respond with act E. Their interaction becomes repetitive and predictable. Larger and more complex sequences, or phases, occur if we examine a large segment of interaction. Acts E and F may be content or relational messages.

not the result of people; they are the result of other behaviors.

The goal of the observer of communication, then, is to uncover redundant behavior patterns. Any single behavior is meaningless. The smallest meaningful unit is the interact (A's behavior followed by B's). An interaction can only be explained when a pattern of behavior is identified. As two people interact, they define their relationship, and their behavior becomes patterned. The job of the researcher is to discover this pattern.

The early work of the anthropologist Gregory Bateson offers further explanation. In the 1930s, Bateson worked with the Iatmul tribe of New Guinea. To describe their social system, he created a construct labeled *schismogenesis*, which is an escalation resulting from repeated interaction. When A's behavior leads B to increase his or her behavior, which in turn leads A to a further increase, we have schismogenesis. Bateson identified two types: complementary and symmetrical. The former occurs whenever two individuals or groups, A and B, engage in unequal but complementary behaviors. For example, when A indulges in assertive behavior and B responds with submissive behavior, it is likely that B's submission "will encourage a further assertion, and that this assertion will demand still further sub-

mission."[42] Unless the pattern is restrained, the system will spiral out of control. The example of the nagging wife and the withdrawn husband illustrates this complementary pattern.

The second configuration, symmetrical schismogenesis, occurs when A's and B's behaviors are identical. "If, for example, we find boasting as the cultural pattern of behavior in one group, and that the other group replies to this with boasting, a competitive situation may develop in which boasting leads to more boasting, and so on."[43] When these patterns are overlaid on a communication system, they explain how the system works. The third assumption of the pragmatic approach is that *in order to understand a communication system, we must examine sequences of behaviors and look for the redundant patterns that characterize the system.* In this sense, the system is its own best explanation.

Components of the Pragmatic Perspective.
Figure 3.4 represents the pragmatic perspective. It illustrates a simple two-person system. The sequential acts of each individual are indicated by uppercase letters. The arrows bind acts together and indicate interactions. As interaction progresses, a number of sequences (punctuated by the broken lines) emerge, ending with E-F-E sequences. The nature of E and F are unspecified,

but, if we think of E as nagging and F as withdrawing, then we have a representation of the nag-withdraw interact just discussed. More complex patterns can be identified by using this model. The components identified here are *act, interact, constraints, redundancy* (resulting in *patterns* of interacts such as *phases* and *cycles*) and *system*.

Unlike previous models, we do not focus on individual senders and receivers. The mechanistic, psychological, and interactionist models center on the individual self. In this perspective, however, the self virtually disappears. The pragmatic scientist examines behaviors in and of themselves, believing identification of recurrent patterns will more efficiently explain the system than any complicated intrapsychic concepts possibly could. The self is treated as a "black box," a box that cannot and need not be opened for study. Watzlawick, Bavelas, and Jackson explain that the black box concept means "it is sometimes more expedient to disregard the internal structure of a device and concentrate on the study of its specific input-output relations. While it is true that these relations may permit inferences into what 'really' goes on inside the box, this knowledge is not essential for the study of the function of the device in the greater system of which it is a part."[44]

Locus of Pragmatic Communication. Communication in the pragmatic perspective lies in the sequence of behaviors composing the system. Minimally, it resides in the interaction; more often, it lies in larger patterns such as episodes, phases, or cycles. How does this affect theorizing about communication? First, it removes attention from internal processes and focuses it on behaviors. Research questions about attitudinal or personality variables are not part of pragmatic inquiry. Instead, attention is on interaction. Less emphasis is placed on searching for causal variables. More emphasis is placed on tracing system states. The property of equifinality exemplifies this reasoning. If "the same behavior in two peo-

ple can spring from quite different interactional causes," and if behavior is multidetermined, then it follows that "searching for any generalizable list of reasons is quite fruitless."[45]

What kinds of questions might a pragmatic scientist ask? Fisher characterizes them as "what," "how," and "how come" questions.[46] Typical ones include What are the stages in leadership emergence? What phases commonly occur in discussion groups? Given stage A, is it likely that another state, phase B, will occur? How do communication relationships develop over time and what mechanisms are involved? Focus is on identifying patterns and mapping emerging system states.[47]

The Semiotic Perspective

The term *semiotics* first appears in the works of the great Swiss linguist Ferdinand de Saussure. Saussure spent most of his life describing the system of meanings found in natural language, but he was also aware that there were other, nonlinguistic, ways to convey meaning, and that these modes of communication were also systemic in nature. Saussure foresaw a time when scholars would turn their attention to describing a general theory of signs. "One can thus conceive," he wrote, "*of a science which studies the life of signs in the heart of social life... . It would teach us of what signs consist, what laws rule them.*"[48]

Although Saussure himself never investigated the full impact of semiotics, it was not long before others took up the call, taking as their task examination of the many meaning systems that surround us. The first semioticians were European literary critics and language theorists, many of whom had been influenced by a system of thought known as *structuralism*. Structuralists believed that beneath the surface of human thought and action, there is a discoverable structure, that this structure is systemic, and that meaning is created by a series of contrasts and oppositions among the elements of this system. The task of the structuralist was to explain this system, in much the same way that Saussure had laid bare the structure of the language system. Thus, anthropologist Claude Levi-Strauss tried to uncover the structure of myth, Jean Piaget explored the structure of children's thought, and Roland Barthes looked for structure in literary meaning.[49]

Structuralism was not the only influence on the early semioticians. They were also influenced by Freudian psychoanalytic theory and by Marxism. In his seminal work on the interpretation of dreams, Freud had uncovered within the human being a language of the unconscious, a language at once opposed and connected to the language of rational thought. Elements of this "language" often emerged in disguised and complex forms in dreams and fantasies. The goal of the psychoanalyst was to uncover and interpret the latent or hidden meanings manifested in surface images. Thus, Freud described a hidden language of the mind in which signs carried multiple, overdetermined meanings.[50]

Marxism added a political element to the semiotic project. Having become aware that we live in a world where meanings are often disguised and symbols may take on several levels of significance, it was a short step to the discovery that one of these levels of meaning was ideological. According to Marxist scholars, the sign systems that surround us act on behalf of the status quo, reinforcing dominant political and economic relations.[51]

In a sense, the semiotic enterprise is distantly related to both the interactionist and the pragmatic perspectives, although its origins are quite different from either of these American empiricist approaches. Like the interactionist approach, the semiotic perspective recognizes the importance of symbolic social forces in shaping the individual. Like the pragmatic approach, it suggests that meanings are systemic and that human subjects are less important that the system itself. Its emphasis on the ubiquity of nonlinguistic systems of signification, its rejection of the self, and its overtly political nature, however, make it different from both.

Assumptions of the Semiotic Perspective. Perhaps the most important insight Saussure gave to modern language study was the idea that signs do not carry meaning by referring to objects in the physical world. Their meaning comes instead from the way they are used in conjunction with and in opposition to other signs in the system. The word "dog" carries meaning not because it refers to a hairy four-legged mammal but because it can be used with words like "bark" and "chase" and in opposition to words like "cat." The word "satyr" means what it does not because it points to an existing thing but because it is neither a "man" nor a "goat." Signs gain meaning because they are different from other signs within a signifying system. That is why the task of translating from one language to another is often so difficult. The system of contrasts that gives meaning to a word in one signifying system will be different in another. The first assumption of the semiotic perspective, then, is that *language and other semiotic codes are self-contained systems of differences.*

Another important point made by semioticians is that sign systems are not individual but social constructions. Signifying systems exist because groups of people agree to use them, and just as there are many different groups of language users, so there are many different ways of signifying. The particular ways of talking and writing and thinking adopted by a group is called a *discourse.* It is a domain of language use that embodies the views and values of a particular group. There is thus a discourse of science and a discourse of common sense. Capitalism has its own language, as does Marxism. And the feminist and the masculinist differ in part because they work out of different discourses. People are born into a predominant discourse which serves to define their world and which determines their communication practices. Although it is possible to invent new discourses, it is a difficult process,

Metaphors for Communication in the Semiotic Perspective

THE MASK. Signifying systems are masks behind which lies a disguised ideology.

THE MIRROR. Our sense of ourselves as independent human actors is largely a product of discourse. Language is the mirror which allows us to glimpse a reflected self.

THE MIRAGE. The relationship between signs and an independent reality is essentially imaginary. Signs have meaning only within the signifying system itself.

FIGURE 3.5: A semiotic view of communication

for dominant practices blind people to other ways of constructing meaning. Thus, the second assumption of the semiotic approach is *meaning is not created by individuals but by the discourses that surround and constitute them.*

Modern semiotic theory recognizes that there is a power dimension to language. To a large extent, dominant discourses control us by supporting ideologies. An *ideology* can be defined as "the sum of the ways in which people both live and represent to themselves their relationship to the conditions of their existence."[52] Ideology is what people believe is true about their lives, and ideologies are essentially conservative systems of thought. They operate to resign people to the way things are. Thus, dominant discourses have inscribed within them the ideology of dominance. The third assumption of the semiotic approach is that *discourses have ideological import, working to support the status quo.*

Although ideology is always present in a signifying system, it is often present in a disguised form. In the discourse employed by semioticians, "it is transparent; it strives to efface its own effects." Most people are simply not aware that when they use a particular discourse they are accepting a value system, that no act of communication is apolitical. Given their strong belief in the hidden political power of discourses, semioticians often take as their task the decoding of ideology. In the words of Marshall Blonsky, "mingling Saussure with Marx and Sartre, they discovered the power to grasp unassertive objects as signs, as the bearers of accepted opinion and

ideological trickery. The first semiology was a vast project of ideological criticism aimed at spying out the wheel works of idea and content production."[53] Because only by decoding discourse can people control their lives; a final assumption of the semiotic perspective holds that to *understand communication it is necessary to uncover the latent ideological meanings hidden beneath the surface of communication.*

Components of the Semiotic Perspective. For each of the other perspectives, a graphic model has been provided, a model that visualizes the components of the perspective and their relationship to one another. While it is probably possible to draw a model of semiotic assumptions, perhaps by showing human subjects embedded within a hierarchy of controlling discourses behind which lies an invisible ideology, our semiotic model will take another form. Models do not have to be visual; they can be verbal as well. Metaphors can sometimes be models, if they provide an explanation of how a process operates. In the case of the semiotic model, three metaphors seem particularly relevant: the metaphor of the mask, the mirror, and the mirage (see Fig. 3.5).

The metaphor of the mask shows the disguised nature of ideology that hides behind and speaks through a dominant discourse. The individual communicator may not realize that in using a given discourse he or she dons the mask and "speaks the ideology." The metaphor of the mirror shows the relationship between perceptions of individual autonomy and signifying systems.

Individuals are constituted in language, and our sense of self, our belief that we originate meaning, is reflected in language use. The mirror of language and other signifying practices, however, does not give an accurate reflection of reality. It is like a fun house mirror that throws out a distorted image. In the case of the semiotic mirror, the distortion lies in an image of the human subject as an autonomous actor. Finally, the metaphor of the mirage points out the illusory nature of the reality constructed by sign systems. The mirage is not "really" there. Its validity comes from its self-contained logic.

Regardless of which metaphor we use, the basic components of the semiotic perspective can be seen. They consist of *sign, signifying system, discourse, and ideology.*

Locus of Semiotic Communication. According to the semiotic perspective, communication lies not within the independent subject but within the socially shared discourse. The semiotic perspective completes a process begun with the interactionists and continued by the pragmatists: the decentering of the human subject. It is not people who communicate, it is systems of meaning.

The semiotic approach widens our understanding of meaning production. It is not just language that means; there are many signifying systems. Images, movements, social behavior, codes of conduct, clothing, all are systems of meaning. Semioticians see signs everywhere. They examine the language and grammar of such diverse cultural products as film, photography, fashion, architecture, advertising, food, traffic signs, and a variety of other objects and practices. Thus, those who take a semiotic perspective ask questions such as the following ones: What systems of meaning are present in a given literary form (like the novel or the comic book)? What is the ideology of the American TV sit-com and what are its effects? What is the message of post-modernist architecture? How do magazine advertisements tell a story visually? The world of the semiotician is a world in which things as well as people com-municate. The job of the semiotician is to decode this communication.

METATHEORY: LAWS, RULES, AND CRITICAL THEORY

The perspectives examined so far differ in the assumptions they make about underlying communication processes. We will conclude this chapter by reviewing three more approaches to communication theory, approaches that focus not on the question, What is communication? but on What is theory? In addressing this question, we will look at three metatheories: the positivist or laws approach, the interpretive or rules approach, and the critical approach. Positivist theorists believe that theory's goal is to generate statements of cause, to uncover the factors causing a phenomenon, to explain why it occurs. Interpretive theorists, on the other hand, do not believe that human action is determined. They believe humans make choices when they act and that theory should focus on uncovering the mechanisms by which such choices are made. Finally, critical theorists believe that the role of the theorist is to criticize the social structures that govern human action. The theorist should not stop at explaining the rules that govern human action but should make evident the costs involved in following those rules.

Assumptions of the Positivist (Laws) Approach

The *positivist approach* assumes that regularities govern life. Events are not random; they have causes and are contingent on each other. Theory's purpose is to describe these regularities or contingencies. Adherents of the laws approach believe we can describe human behavior the same way we describe the movements of physical objects: by uncovering actions and reactions, causes and effects. People act as they do because some antecedent condition causes them to. We can explain classes of actions, then, by discovering the forces that acted on them. Humans are not uniquely exempt from the contingencies governing all physical objects. In this sense, the model of man underlying this approach is mechanistic and deterministic.

Positivist theory takes the form of *laws*, causal statements that link variables together. According to positivists, the generative mechanism for human action is causation, but a special kind, one that is probabilistic. To understand this, we need to distinguish between two kinds of cause. The first is *absolute*. It implies that there is a universal, invariable connection between a cause and its effect. For example, if we believe that X causes Y, then, under the absolute view of causation, we would express their connection by saying, "If and only if X, then Y." This means we can make exact predictions about specific actions, for every time X occurs, Y follows, and Y never occurs without X. There are no exceptions to absolute laws.

Most social scientists in the communication field view causation less stringently, taking a *probabilistic* view. According to this view, X and Y's relationship is expressed, "If X occurs, Y will occur with a certain probability (P)." X and Y need not always occur together, although in most cases they do. Laws, then, are general statements about how humans will probably respond to given conditions. Although laws do not allow the prediction of specific events, they allow the prediction of classes of responses. Most laws theorists in communication accept the probabilistic view of causation as the basic generative mechanism for human action.

What does a law actually look like? It generally takes the form, "If X, then Y, under conditions C_1, C_2, C_3"; or "X and Y tend to go together in the presence of C." Mary John Smith gives examples of laws used to explain persuasive effects:

"If factual information is used in a persuasive message, it will probably produce greater attitude change than a message without evidence, if the source lacks credibility with recipients, the evidence is unfamiliar to receivers, and so forth"; "If viewers are exposed to televised violence, then they are likely to behave aggressively, provided latent aggression is already present in the viewers"; and, finally, to use one of Berger's examples, "Perceived similarity of attitudes between persons has a high probability of producing a high level of attraction between two persons."[54]

All three examples involve explanation by cause, all assume a connection between variables, and all try to answer "why" questions. Because the laws approach is traditionally used for theory construction in the social sciences, it is probably more familiar to us. Most of the theories presented in Part II of this text consist of laws-based explanations; Appendix A, on evaluating theories, is also based on positivist metatheory.

Assumptions of the Interpretive (Rules) Approach

The human model assumed by the *interpretive approach* contrasts with that of the positivists. Rom Harre states, "In new paradigm studies, a human being is treated as a person, that is, as a plan-making, self-monitoring agent, aware of goals, and deliberately considering the best ways of achieving them."[55] According to the positivist approach, human behavior is generated by environmental contingencies; in the interpretive approach, the human being generates his or her own behavior. In this sense, the interpretive approach "anthropomorphizes" people.

Instead of a mechanistic model we have an actional model of the human being. Smith summarizes four principal assumptions that she believes form the basis for this view. First, humans are active rather than passive agents; they exercise control over their environments. Second, humans are intentional; they have goals that they try to accomplish. Third, humans exercise choice; in meeting goals they select among alternative actions. Finally, humans use cognitive schematic structures to assign meaning to reality; reality is not given, it is constructed.[56]

Interpretive theorists often use rules to build theory. A rule is an explanation of how human subjects make sense of their worlds and go about accomplishing their goals. Rules are answers to questions such as, What does he think he is doing? How did she know how to act in that situation? or What kind of conventions did they follow to accomplish their ends? Rules follow the formula, "In order to accomplish X, engage in behaviors Y_1, Y_2."

Interpretive theorists use the concept of rule in a special sense. Rules are not explicitly stated, written guides to behavior, nor are they like the rules of a game described in an instruction book. The rules interpretive theorists talk about are implicit rules, rules held unconsciously. Consider the way the term rules is used in rules of grammar. While most of us follow grammatical rules when writing or speaking, we would be hard pressed to state these rules explicitly. As Dan Slobin points out, "since no complete and adequate grammar of English (or any language) has yet been written, in fact none of us *knows* the rules of English according to this criterion. We can follow them and use them implicitly, but we can state them only rarely, imperfectly, and with uncertainty."[57]

There is some controversy about the locus of rules. Some theorist believe that rules are cognitive structures located within the individual being observed. They believe rules are "means-end generalizations, specifying those actions people believe they *should* take to maximize personal goals."[58] They exist within the individual either as socially learned conventions or as individually generated action plans. Susan Shimanoff's view of rules follows this line, which is also reflected in the works of many communication theorists such as Reardon, Pearce, Cronen, and Conklin.[59]

Authors who take a sociolinguistic, ethnographic, or pragmatic approach such as Birdwhistell, Hymes, or Scheflen[60] view rules as "investigator-generated postulates" about perceived regularities in human action.[61] For these writers, rules do not necessarily exist as such within communicators but are statements generated by researchers who want to know what kind of

knowledge a communicator needs to communicate competently within a given community. According to Jackson, "the rule is an inference, an abstraction—more precisely, a metaphor coined by the observer to cover the redundancy he observes."[62]

Stuart Sigman also believes that rules are attempts by researchers "to uncover the organization and logic which provide for patterned and meaningful behavioral production,"[63] although he assumes that rules are not totally external to individual communicators, for "interpersonal actors act as if they knew these rules."[64] The logic the scientist uncovers is the kind an individual needs in order to be an active and competent member of a culture.

What does a rule look like? Smith gives the following examples of persuasion rules: "'If you wish to be an accepted member of a social group, you must (are obligated to) conform to group attitudes and behavior patterns,' and 'If you wish to defend your ego against attack, you must avoid (prohibit yourself from) threatening persuasive messages.'"[65] Our discussion of the coordinated management of meaning in chapter 5 gives further examples of rules.

Choosing Between Rules and Laws

While advocates of each approach argue that their approach is better, many theorists believe that both forms of theory are useful. They suggest that certain kinds of behaviors are best described by laws while others are best studied by using rules. Pearce, for example, discusses two kinds of behavior: controlled and influenced. Controlled behaviors are caused and therefore can best be described by laws. "A person's meanings or volition have no effect on controlled behavior; if a person steps from a curb and is hit by a speeding Mack truck, none of these will change the distance, direction, and trajectory of his body."[66] Influenced behavior, on the other hand, is "structured by socialization and is appropriately explained by describing the rules which persons follow as they conduct purposive action."[67] Influenced behavior is willful; for example, following norms of politeness at a funeral or employing turn-taking cues in conversation.

Pearce, a rules theorist, says we can determine whether a behavior is rule-governed by asking five questions: (1) "Is there a logically or empirically necessary relationship between antecedents and consequences?" (2) "Is the observed pattern a recurring one?" (3) "Can the communicators themselves generate identical or functionally equivalent behaviors?" (4) "Can the communicators perceive alternative sequences of messages which are inappropriate?" and (5) "Are sanctions (positive or negative) applied to deviations from the pattern?"[68] The answer to question one must be no, and the answer to the rest, yes, if behaviors are rule-governed. These criteria are similar to those of Shimanoff who says rule-related behaviors must be controllable (must involve an element of choice), contextual (must occur in particular situations), and "critiqueable" (must be subject to evaluation and sanction if inappropriate).[69] Behaviors that do not meet these criteria are best explained by some concept other than rules.

Assumptions of the Critical Approach

The interpretive scientist's major concern is in understanding the intentions and desires of individuals and uncovering the ways social actors go about achieving these intentions. The interpretive scientist "reveals *what* the agents are doing by seeing what they are up to and how and why they would be up to that."[70] In the process, the interpretive scientist tried hard to describe subjects' choices without making value judgments. Critical theorists, on the other hand, believe that it is necessary to make value judgments, to analyze those features of a social situation that frustrate human actors and should therefore be altered.

Critical theory is based on the assumption "that a great many of the actions people perform are caused by social conditions over which they

have no control.... . A critical social science is one which seeks to uncover those systems of social relationships which determine the actions of individuals and the unanticipated, though not accidental, consequences of these actions."[71]

Social scientists who take a critical stance often use historical accounts to show why the social system is as it is and why it has failed its members. Often it takes the form of what is called *ideological-critique*, an attempt to show that the beliefs and ideologies held by individuals are illusory and destructive.

To understand how radically critical theory differs from either positivist or interpretive thought, we can compare the kinds of theory each would generate around the topic of gender differences. A positivist would either try to explain the variables that lead to gender differences or, using gender as an independent variable, investigate how men and women are differentially affected by common communication strategies. Thus, a positivist might ask, "Will persuasive strategies based on social modeling rather than on rational argument be more effective with women than with men?"[72]

An interpretive theorist will be less concerned with effects and more concerned with describing how female (or male) communicators go about achieving their ends. Thus, the interpretive theorist may ask questions such as, What kind of talk do women engage in? or How do women understand their place in the social structure, and what communication strategies do they use to fulfill their roles?

Critical theorists are not satisfied with these kind of descriptions of gender differences. According to Brian Fay, a critical theory of woman's experience should do a number of things. First, it should articulate the dissatisfactions felt by women under a given social structure. It might, for example, show that during the 1950s and 1960s the rule that a woman's place was in the home often led to feelings of frustration, boredom, and uselessness, that common definitions of fulfillment meant that many women could never be fulfilled. In addition, a critical theory of women's experience should try to explain why women's lives are now changing, perhaps by pointing to changes in economic forces that now require that increasing numbers of women work outside the home. Finally, a true critical theory would point out the sorts of actions women might take to achieve satisfaction (i.e., how they might alter the political structure, how they might use consciousness-raising groups for support, or how the development of a feminist discourse could change women's conceptions of themselves).[73]

Critical researchers in communication address themselves to questions such as the following ones: How does language serve to define women in derogatory ways, and how can this language be reformed? Do portrayals of women in the media reinforce destructive stereotypes? and What role can communication play in empowering women?

REFERENCES

1. Norwood R. Hanson, *Patterns of Discovery* (Cambridge: Cambridge University Press, 1958).

2. W. Barnett Pearce, Vernon E. Cronen, and Linda M. Harris, "Methodological Considerations in Building Human Communication Theory," in *Human Communication Theory*, ed. Frank E. X. Dance (New York: Harper & Row, 1982), p. 3.

3. *Ibid.*, p. 3.

4. Eugene J. Meehan, *Value Judgment and Social Science: Structures and Processes* (Homewood, Ill.: Dorsey, 1968), p. 83.

5. B. Aubrey Fisher, *Perspectives on Human Communication* (New York: MacMillan, 1978).

6. Paul Watzlawick, Janet Beavin Bavelas, and Don D. Jackson, *Pragmatics of Human Communication* (New York: W. W. Norton, 1967), p. 29.

7. Karl W. Deutsch, "Some Notes on Research on the Role of Models in Natural and Social Science," *Synthese*, 7 (1948–49), 506–33.

8. Fisher, *Perspectives*, p. 102.

9. *Ibid.*, p. 103.

10. For a schematic of the model as originally developed see Warren Weaver, "The Mathematics of Communication," in *Basic Readings in Communication Theory*, 2nd ed., ed. C. David Mortensen (New York: Harper & Row, 1979), p. 29.

11. The classic work in the field is Claude Shannon and Warren Weaver, *The Mathematical Theory of Communication* (Urbana: University of Illinois Press, 1949).

12. Fisher, *Perspectives*, p. 112.

13. *Ibid.*, p. 137.

14. Dean C. Barnlund, "A Transactional Model of Communication," in *Foundations of Communication Theory*, eds. Kenneth K. Sereno and C. David Mortensen (New York: Harper & Row, 1970), p. 88.

15. Fisher, *Perspectives*, p. 140.

16. *Ibid.*, p. 141.

17. *Ibid.*, p. 146.

18. *Ibid.*, p. 147.

19. Charles Horton Cooley, *Human Nature and the Social Order* (New York: Charles Scribner's Sons, 1902); George Herbert Mead, *Mind, Self and Society*, ed. C. W. Morris (Chicago: University of Chicago Press, 1934, 1962); Herbert Blumer, *Symbolic Interactionism: Perspective and Method* (Englewood Cliffs, N. J.: Prentice Hall, 1969).

20. Bernard N. Meltzer, "Mead's Social Psychology," in *Symbolic Interaction: A Reading in Social Psychology*, 2nd ed., eds. Jerome G. Manis and Bernard Meltzer (Boston: Allyn & Bacon, 1972), p. 15.

21. John P. Hewitt, *Self and Society: A Symbolic Interactionist Social Psychology* (Boston: Allyn & Bacon, 1976), p. 44.

22. *Ibid.*, p. 45.

23. *Ibid.*, p. 28.

24. *Ibid.*, p. 30.

25. *Ibid.*, p. 33.

26. Fisher, *Perspectives*, p. 168.

27. *Ibid.*, p. 171.

28. Gabriel Marcel, *The Mystery of Being* (Chicago: Henry Regnery, 1960) I, p. 9; quoted in Fisher, *Perspectives*, p. 179.

29. Jesse G. Delia and Lawrence Grossberg, "Interpretation and Evidence," *Western Journal of Speech Communication*, 41 (Winter 1977), 36.

30. Watzlawick, Bavelas, and Jackson, *Pragmatics*; Gregory Bateson, *Steps to an Ecology of Mind* (New York: Ballantine, 1972); C. Wilder-Mott and John H. Weakland, *Rigor and Imagination: Essays from the Legacy of Gregory Bateson* (New York: Holt, Rinehart & Winston, 1981); Carol Wilder, "The Palo Alto Group: Difficulties and Direction of the Interactional View for Human Communication Research," *Human Communication Research*, 5 (Winter 1979), 171–86.

31. Watzlawick, Bavelas, and Jackson, *Pragmatics*, p. 47.

32. A. D. Hall and R. E. Fagen, "Definition of System," *General Systems Yearbook*, 1 (1956), 18.

33. Anatol Rapoport, "Foreword," in *Modern Systems Research for the Behavioral Scientist*, ed. Walter Buckley (Chicago: Aldine, 1968), p. xvii.

34. Watzlawick, Bavelas, and Jackson, *Pragmatics*, p. 19.

35. Kathleen M. Galvin and Bernard J. Brommel, *Family Communication: Cohesion and Change* (Glenview, Ill.: Scott, Foresman, 1982), pp. 13–14.

36. Fisher, *Perspectives*, p. 202.

37. Watzlawick, Bavelas, and Jackson, *Pragmatics*, p. 129.

38. Fisher paraphrases a remark by Janet Beavin Bavelas, "The interactional view is not difficult to understand. Communication occurs *between* people and not *within* them. It's as simple as that." B. Aubrey Fisher, "The Pragmatic Perspective of Human Communication: A View from System Theory," in *Human Communication Theory: Comparative Essays*, ed. Frank E. X. Dance (New York: Harper & Row, 1982), p. 202.

39. B. Aubrey Fisher, *Small-Group Decision Making: Communication and the Group Process* (New York: McGraw-Hill, 1980).

40. Watzlawick, Bavelas, and Jackson, *Pragmatics*, p. 45.

41. Albert E. Scheflen, *How Behavior Means* (Garden City, N. Y.: Doubleday, 1974), p. 183.

42. Gregory Bateson, *Naven*, 2nd ed. (Stanford, Calif.: Stanford University Press), p. 176.

43. *Ibid.*, p. 177.

44. Watzlawick, Bavelas, and Jackson, *Pragmatics*, pp. 43–44.

45. Fisher, "A View from System Theory," p. 206.

46. *Ibid.*, p. 207.

47. Wilder, "The Palo Alto Group," pp. 171–86.

48. Ferdinand de Saussure, *Cours de Linguistique Generale*, ed. T. de Mauro (Paris: Payot, 1974) p. 33. Quoted and translated by Marshall Blonsky, ed., *On Signs* (Baltimore: The Johns Hopkins University Press, 1985), p. xvi.

49. For a general introduction, see Terence Hawkes, *Structuralism and Semiotics*, (Los Angeles: University of California Press, 1977). See also Claude Levi-Strauss, *From Honey to Ashes: Introduction to a Science of Mythology: 2* (New York: Harper & Row, 1973); Sarah F. Campbell, ed. *Piaget Sampler: An Introduction to Jean Piaget through his Own Words* (New York: John Wiley & Sons, 1976); Jean Piaget, *Biology and Knowledge*, trans. Beatrix Walsh (Chicago: University of Chicago Press, 1971) and *The Construction of Reality in the Child*, trans. Margaret Cook (New York: Ballantine, 1971); Roland Barthes, *Mythologies*, trans. Annette Lavers (London: Cape, 1972).

50. Freud, Sigmund, *The Interpretation of Dreams*, trans. James Strachey (New York: Avon, 1965).

51. See, for example, Louis Althusser, *For Marx*, trans. Ben Brewster (Harmondsworth: Penguin, 1969) and "Ideology and Ideological State Apparatuses," in *Lenin and Philosophy and Other Essays*, trans. Ben Brewster (London: New Left Books, 1971).

52. Catharine Belsey, *Critical Practice* (New York: Methuen, 1980), p. 42.

53. Blonsky, *On Signs*, p. xvii.

54. Mary John Smith, *Persuasion and Human Action* (Belmont, Calif.: Wadsworth, 1982), p. 61.

55. Rom Harre, "Some Remarks on 'Rule' as a Scientific Concept," in *Understanding Other Persons*, ed. Theodore Mischel (Oxford: Basil Blackwell, 1974), p. 148.

56. Smith, *Persuasion*, p. 59.

57. Dan I. Slobin, *Psycholinguistics* (Glenview, Ill.: Scott, Foresman, 1971), p. 55.

58. Smith, *Persuasion*, p. 63.

59. Susan B. Shimanoff, *Communication Rules: Theory and Research* (Beverly Hills: Sage, 1980); Kathleen Kelley Reardon, *Persuasion: Theory and Context* (Beverly Hills: Sage, 1981). For citations on Pearce, Conklin, and Cronen see the section on coordinated management of meaning in chapter 5.

60. See Ray L. Birdwhistell, *Kinesics and Context* (Philadelphia: University of Pennsylvania Press, 1970); Dell Hymes, *Foundations in Socio-Linguistics* (Philadelphia: University of Pennsylvania Press, 1974); Scheflen, *How Behavior Means*.

61. Stuart J. Sigman, "On Communication Rules from a Social Perspective," *Human Communication Research*, 7 (Fall 1980), 37–51, p. 40.

62. Don D. Jackson, "The Study of the Family," in *The Interactional View*, eds. Paul Watzlawick and John H. Weakland (New York: W. W. Norton, 1977), p. 11.

63. Sigman, "Communication Rules," p. 39.

64. *Ibid.*, p. 38.

65. Smith, *Persuasion*, p. 63.

66. W. Barnett Pearce, "The Coordinated Management of Meaning: A Rules-Based Theory of Interpersonal Communication," in *Explorations in Interpersonal Communication*, ed. Gerald R. Miller (Beverly Hills: Sage, 1976), p. 19.

67. *Ibid.*, p. 19.

68. *Ibid.*, pp. 26–27.

69. Shimanoff, *Communication Rules*, pp. 126–27.

70. Brian Fay, *Social Theory and Political Practice* (New York: Holmes and Meier, 1975), p. 79.

71. *Ibid.*, p. 94.

72. McGuire, William J. "Attitude and Attitude Change," in *Handbook of Social Psychology*, vol 2, 3rd ed., eds. Gardner Lindzey and Elliot Aronson (New York: Random House, 1985); Sarah Trenholm, *Persuasion and Social Influence* (Englewood Cliffs, N. J.: Prentice Hall, 1989).

73. Fay, *Social Theory*, p. 101.

chapter 4

THE PROBLEM OF COMMUNICATOR ACCEPTABILITY AND ATTRIBUTION

INTRODUCTION

Think about it. When you meet strangers, how do you decide whether they will become friends? What makes you confide in one roommate but not the other? Why do you believe one speaker is telling the truth while another is lying? These questions illustrate a fundamental human problem, the problem of deciding on the acceptability of potential communicative partners. In this chapter we will examine how people size up other people. We will break this process down into its constituent parts, review relevant theories, and synthesize these theories into an overall model of the process of communicator acceptability.

Choosing to communicate with a specific person or group of people is essentially a problem of perception and judgment, a process of matching. We must match the perceived characteristics of a potential communicator to general characteristics we believe are desirable in communicative partners. To accomplish this matching we must, first of all, understand our own goals and needs. We then observe others and determine their characteristics. Finally, we decide whether we have found a match. Although the process appears simple, understanding how it is achieved takes us into the realm of person perception, attribution theory, information processing, and interpersonal judgment.[1]

In what follows, we will examine several theories that help explain how we judge the characteristics and worth of other people. As you read about these theories, remember that they do not completely solve the problem of communicator acceptability. Furthermore, many of them conflict with each other. You should, therefore, be critical, examining each theory for its strengths and weaknesses and its basic assumptions.

This chapter begins with the question, How do we perceive the characteristics of other people? Related questions follow: How do we decide on a person's intentions? How do we determine outcomes of an interaction? and How do we decide on criteria of acceptability? These questions are interrelated so that it is difficult to determine which comes first. Still, the process of person perception seems a good point of departure. If we are to understand how people choose communicative partners, we must understand the process we use to attribute characteristics to one another.

PERSON PERCEPTION: HOW DO WE PERCEIVE OTHERS' CHARACTERISTICS?

The Perception of Natural Objects

Perceiving other people is similar to perceiving any natural object. It is an active, not a passive process, and it is naive to believe there is a world out there that is immediately understood and directly accessible. Imagine, for example, that you are seated at your desk, writing. You are relatively unaware of the temperature of the room, the pressure of your fingers on the keys of your word processor, the hum of an air conditioning unit, or the color of the books on your shelf. You are only aware of the screen in front of you, the motion of the cursor as it moves across the screen, and the cup of coffee cooling on your desk. You tune out certain stimuli, and select others. In perceiving the natural objects around you, you choose and process stimuli that lead to *structure, stability*, and *meaning*.[2]

The fact that attention is selective is easy to verify. The next time you are out with friends, pick a scene. After you pass it, ask each friend to describe what he or she saw. Chances are they

will provide different descriptions. People not only attend to different aspects of objects, they also characterize and code what they see in unique ways. People *structure* their perceptions.

People also act as though objects around them have *stability*. As you walk toward an object, its image on your retina gets larger. As you pass in or out of shadows, the amount of light increases or decreases. You do not experience constantly changing stimuli. Instead, you experience objects of stable size and color. To produce this state of constancy, you must actively process information.

Finally, you perceive the stimuli that you receive daily as related in meaningful ways. Events follow events in an orderly fashion. A vehicle is driven down a street, turns a corner, and is gone. Another follows, and you wait until it too has disappeared before crossing the street. You recognize the vehicles as cars, you experience their diminishing size as an indication that they are moving away from you, but you know that they continue to exist even though they are no longer in your visual field. You divide the stream of ongoing sensations into a series of events that have *meaning* for one another.

In summary, "past experiences and purposes play an absolutely necessary role in providing us with knowledge of the world that has structure, stability, and meaning. Without them, events would not make sense; with them, our perceptions define a predictable world, an orderly stage for us to act on."[3]

The Process of Person Perception

People are just as much the focus of perception as natural objects. David Schneider, Albert Hastorf, and Phoebe Ellsworth give an overview of the complex processes involved in making sense of people as perceptual objects (see Fig. 4.1). They divide person perception into six separate but related processes, emphasizing that "any and all of the processes of person perception can go on simultaneously and that often the perceiver is very active in moving back and forth among the various stages to check conclusions."[4]

Person Perception Processes

	I Attention	II Snap judgment	III Attribution		IV Trait implications	V Impression formation	VI The prediction of future behavior
			Reactive	Purposive			
Stimulus:	Appearance, context, behavior stream.	Categorized appearance and behavior.	Behavior units where the perceiver is dominated by the hypothesis that the actor has responded to a powerful internal or external stimulus.	Behavior units where the experience is dominated by intentionality on the part of the actor.	The attribution of a trait.	Perceiver's hypothesis that a group of traits are attributed to the actor.	Behavior units, snap judgments, traits, general impressions.
Output:	Selecting and categorizing.	Immediate affective reactions (attraction or withdrawal) and stereotyped judgments.	A causal hypothesis as to why the behavior occurred, pointing to the effects of particular stimuli and inferences about why the person responded to the stimuli.	The attribution of a trait, intention, attitude, or ability.	The hypothesis that certain other traits also exist.	The formation of a general judgment, often likeability. Organization of the stimuli.	Prediction as to how a person will behave in certain classes of situations.

FIGURE 4.1: A model of person perception. (From David J. Schneider, Albert H. Hastorf, Phoebe C. Ellsworth, Person Perception, 2nd ed. [Reading, Mass.: Addison-Wesley, 1979], p. 16.)

The first process is labeled *attention*. In this process, individuals observe the behaviors and appearances of others by attending to certain details and ignoring others. Just as with physical objects, individuals select stimuli and process them in ways that create structure, stability, and meaning. This selection process is partly due to the salience of a feature or behavior of the stimulus and partly to the observer's purposes.

For example, as you sit studying in the library, you do not consciously notice everyone who passes by, although you are probably aware you are not alone. At some level, you monitor your environment. You occasionally glance up as someone passes, but if they appear normal then you dismiss them and return to your work. From time to time, however, you do allow someone's features or behavior to capture your attention. You experience what Frank Dance and Carl Larson describe as an "orientation shift"; instead of reading your book, you "orient" toward the other.[5] As long as stimuli stay within the normal range, you probably do not attend to them. When the range of normal expectancy is violated, however, your attention shifts and you categorize and code the stimulus. Schneider and his colleagues explain, "We do not suggest that the perceiver must give an explicit verbal label to every behavior or context, but we do claim that the perceiver always performs some classification activity, if nothing more than deciding that behavior, appearance, and contexts appear normal."[6]

The next step in the person perception process involves making so-called *snap judgments*, which are perceptions of liking. They may arise from experiences with people who emitted similar cues or more often from cultural stereotypes. Either way, they provide an immediate handle on the person being judged. Snap judgments help us decide whether to proceed further in the person perception process or to dismiss the person as an object of perception. Once we make a positive snap judgment we are ready to do more serious perceptual work by engaging in the next process, attribution. *Attribution* is the process of seeking causal explanations for people's behaviors, of asking the question, Why do people act the way they do?

You ask attribution questions all the time. If friends say they hold political opinions close to yours, you may wonder if they are being honest or merely trying to create a good impression. If you fail your next exam, it is important to determine whether you failed because of low ability or because the test was too hard. If a loved one vows eternal devotion, it is vital to know if the vow is sincere. All these situations involve attributions of cause.

Schneider and others describe two kinds of attribution situations. In the first, the observer simply assumes an act was due to an unintentional response to a stimulus. For example, as a result of stubbing a toe, a person may unintentionally cry out. An observer's task is not to determine the actor's intention but to determine what caused the reaction. Nonverbal and expressive behaviors are usually classed as reactive; the process of determining their meaning is one form of attribution.[7]

In the second situation, the observer assumes an act was intentional and sets out to determine what external or internal motivations provoked an actor's response. For example, if a friend offers to lend you $20 till payday, you may want to know if your friend is being helpful (is motivated by an internal cause) or expects something in return (is motivated by an external cause). Situations in which we try to determine someone's internal or external motivations are the most commonly studied form of attribution.

The fourth and fifth processes that Schneider and his associates describe are closely related. The first is labeled *trait implications*. Here, the observer goes beyond asking what causes a person's actions and asks instead, What kind of person am I dealing with? Having observed a single trait or made a single attribution, observers infer other traits. If you decide your friend is being helpful in lending you money, you may assume he is sincere, tolerant, honest, and modest, rather than dishonest, unreliable, superficial, or irresponsible.[8] Certain traits imply others. Most of us have theories about the relationship between traits, although we often have very little evidence to support our theories. Walter Mischel argues that there is very little evidence that "traits exist anywhere but in the cognitive structure of observers."[9]

Once we attribute traits, we organize our perceptions around a central trait description. This process is known as *impression formation*. Having decided that your friend possesses a number of positive traits, you organize your perceptions around a central impression, "kind hearted." You can now classify your friend with other kind hearted people. You have answered the question, What is my friend like?

The final process in person perception is *prediction*. A major reason we engage in attributions and impression formation is that they allow us to predict an individual's subsequent behaviors. You may want to know whether or not your friend is kind hearted simply out of curiosity, or you may feel the need to know how your friend will respond to future situations. To get along in the world, we need to predict what the people around us will do.

Schneider and his colleagues point out that, while we may use trait information to predict, the process of drawing inferences about the probability of particular behaviors goes beyond attribution. Kind-hearted people are expected to perform more kind than cruel acts; yet, it is foolish to believe that every act they perform will be kind. Our knowledge of the attitude-behavior problem tells us that predicting specific actions from knowledge of generalized attitudes is risky at best.[10] In attribution, perceivers argue from a particular act to a general disposition. Yet, in prediction, "the perceiver goes from a general disposition to a concrete act. The perceiver says, in effect that this, and no other act will be performed. If [this] seems intuitively like a more risky cognitive activity, it is."[11] There is reason to believe that, in making predictions, we simultaneously

use several different types of information in some weighted combination.[12] The information may be based on past behaviors, the nature of the situation, dispositions, or traits.

Person perception involves a series of interrelated and highly complex processes. The most useful of these in explaining communicator acceptability are attribution and impression formation, which we examine next.[13]

ATTRIBUTION MODELS: HOW DO WE DECIDE ON OTHERS' INTENTIONS?

The attribution models we will examine were all derived from the early work of Fritz Heider.[14] Heider believed people perceive behavior as being caused. The locus of this cause is either internal (a property of the actor, such as helpfulness) or external (a property of the environment, such as pressure to act normally). The central question addressed by *attribution theory* is, How can we decide whether others' actions are internally motivated (and thus true indicators of who they are) or externally motivated (i.e., merely responses to the demands of a particular situation)? While attribution theory was not originally developed to explain communication, it addresses an important issue. To communicate with others successfully we need to know what they are like. Making attributions is a natural part of the communication process.

In what follows, we will briefly review three attribution models. Each accounts for a slightly different situation, each uses slightly different concepts and principles, yet each specifies the conditions that allow human actors to make internal attributions to others.

Jones and Davis' Correspondent Inference Theory

The Jones and Davis model applies to a specific type of situation, one in which we observe a choice.[15] Edward Jones and Keith Davis believed that choice making is a very useful source of information. For example, if we observe someone giving money to charity rather than spending it on a night on the town, we will probably decide that the person is motivated by a concern for others. We are likely to feel that we know about the person.

Jones and Davis' model specifies two conditions under which observing choice-making behavior leads to stable internal attributions: when the choice alternatives are distinct (when they share a single *non-common effect*) and when the choice arrived at is not socially acceptable (when it is *non-normative*). When these conditions do not hold, when people choose between similar alternatives or their behavior is standard, then attributions will be unstable.

Let us assume, for example, that we want to determine how serious someone is. Knowing that this person's favorite old movie is *Return of the Jedi* rather than *Raiders of the Lost Ark* does not help us decide, because the alternatives (both popular action adventure movies) are so similar. Knowing, however, that the individual we are observing chose to see a documentary on Chinese peasant farmers rather than a rerun of *Raiders* tells us something, for these two alternatives have dissimilar effects. The rewards they offer are quite different. The presence of non-common effects, then, may be used as the basis of attributional inference.

While entertainment value seems to be the big difference between them, it may not be the only one. Perhaps the documentary movie costs less to see, plays in a theatre closer to home, is more aesthetically or politically appealing, or is required viewing for a class in documentary film. What happens when a number of non-common effects distinguish alternatives? We feel uncertainty. If the documentary film is not only more serious but it costs less, we cannot tell whether our actor is intellectual or cheap. To find out, we need to observe further choices.

From an attributional point of view, the fewer the non-common effects the more stable our attributions will be. If there is only one plausible non-common effect between two alternatives, then we can easily make attributional inferences. If both movies cost the same, if both are convenient and aesthetically pleasing, if neither is required viewing, if, in short, the only difference is seriousness of content, then we can more safely use this difference to make an internal attribution.

A second kind of information also leads to internal attributions, the degree to which results of a choice are non-normative. If two alternatives are equally normative, then we have little basis for attribution. If they differ in social acceptability, however, we can make inferences. In fact, we tend to believe that non-normative behavior is a truer indication of a person's nature than normative behavior.

Let us assume that we want to determine how considerate a teenager really is, and we do so by observing this teenager in the process of deciding whether to offer a seat on a bus to an elderly passenger. If we live in a part of the country where respect for elders is normative, we learn little by seeing the teenager give the seat up. We are more likely to make an internal attribution if we see the teenager steal the seat than offer to stand. Conversely, if we live in an area where the norm for teenagers is to act tough and cool, we will learn more if the teenager offers the seat.

The Jones and Davis model implies that we judge others by observing their choices, and choices contrary to norms are indicative of a person's true nature. This model explains why some communicators are judged to be credible and trustworthy while others are not.

Kelley's Covariation Model

Non-normativity is not the only way we judge communicator acceptability. Harold Kelley, in his covariation model, describes other kinds of information we use in making attributions.[16] While the Jones and Davis model was based on observing an actor choose between a single set of alternatives at a specific point in time, Kelley's covariation model assumes there are situations where we can observe an individual engaging in many activities across an extended period. In such situations, other kinds of information are used to form inferences: the *consistency* of an actor's behavior, the degree to which the actor *differentiates* between stimuli, and the extent to which an

actor's behavior shows *consensus* with the behavior of others.

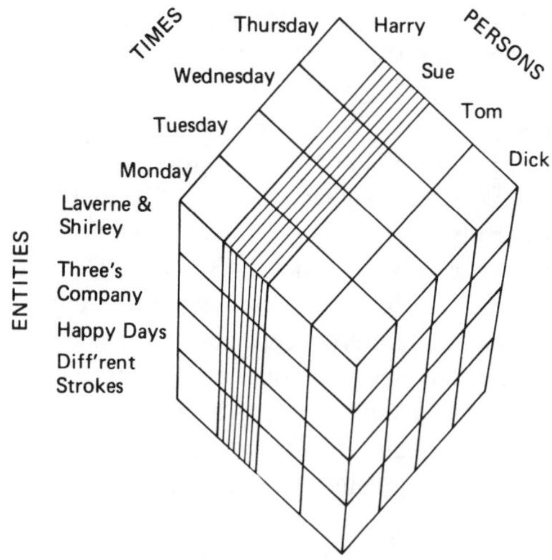

Kelley believes the causes for any particular action can be viewed as (1) lying within the person performing the action, (2) lying within the entity or thing the person is responding to, or (3) arising from situational variables such as time or manner of presentation. The first leads to an internal attribution and the second two to external attributions.

Assume you observe a friend, Sue, laughing at reruns of the television situation comedy *Laverne and Shirley.* You may wonder if Sue is easily amused, if the sit-com is genuinely funny, or if her behavior is due to a particular set of external circumstances. To decide, you make additional observations. If no one else watching the show laughs at it (low consensus), if Sue laughs every time she tunes in (high consistency), and if she laughs at other comedies (low differentiation), then we assume it is something in Sue rather than in the show or the situation that caused the original effect. We attribute an internal cause to Sue: She is easily amused (see Fig. 4.2A).

On the other hand, if almost everyone who watches the show laughs at it (high consensus), if Sue and others do not laugh at other television comedies (high differentiation), and if every time Sue and her friends tune in to *Laverne and Shirley* they laugh (high consistency), then we will attribute the effect to an external cause: The show is a comedy classic (see Fig. 4.2B). Finally, if Sue laughs at the show only once and fails to laugh at other times, then we can interpret her behavior as situationally bound. Perhaps she was in a giddy mood the first time you observed her, but she is generally not easily amused.

Kelley sums up the covariation principle in this way: "An effect is attributed to the one of its possible causes with which, over time, it covaries."[17] In the first example, the effect of laughter covaried with Sue's behavior rather than with other entities or with specific situations. We were, therefore, justified in attributing a personal cause.

A. Data pattern indicating attribution to person

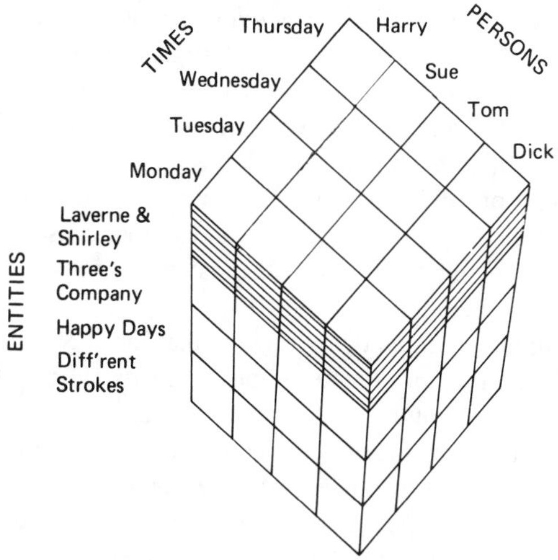

B. Data pattern indicating attribution to entity

FIGURE 4.2: Kelley's ANOVA cubes

In the second, the effect covaried with the show itself and was thus due to an external cause.

In summary, internal attributions are based on three principles: consistency, differentiation, and consensus. As another example, assume Sue has just asked her teacher for permission to turn in a late paper. Her teacher will probably blame her more if this is the third time she has asked for an extension. If the teacher also discovers that Sue has failed to complete work in other classes, and if all other students except Sue manage to do the work, then the teacher will look to Sue's disposition as the cause of her behavior.

Kelley's Discounting and Augmenting Effects

When dealing with close friends or associates, we can use the information outlined in the covariation model because we are in a position to make detailed observations over time. In other situations, however, we deal with strangers whom we observe only once. Kelley recognized that in these cases we also make attributions of intent and asked, How can attributions be made when only a single instance of behavior is observed? In response, he suggested two principles: the *discounting principle* and the *augmentation principle*.[18] Both involve choosing which of two or more causes should be given the greater weight.

The discounting principle states, "The role of a given cause in producing a given effect is discounted if other plausible causes are also present."[19] In other words, if there is only one plausible cause for an action, it will be given more weight than if there were another, equally plausible cause that could explain the event. This general principle predicts the same attributions as the Jones and Davis model, but it approaches the process from a slightly different point of view.

For example, assume we observe a dinner guest complimenting a hostess. There are at least two plausible causes for the compliment: The actor may have actually enjoyed the meal, or the actor is being polite. We will feel less certain that the first explanation is the case because of the

possibility of the second. However, if the dinner guest tells the hostess the meal was mediocre, then we assume the guest really feels that way, since the politeness explanation has clearly been ruled out. In such a case, we have confidence in our attribution.

Or, assume that an employee makes a request of two coworkers, one of whom is his subordinate and the other is his superior. Assume also that both comply. Our employee would probably think that the superior complied because of an internal motivation. Our employee might be less certain in the case of the subordinate. In this case, there are two possible explanations: (1) the subordinate may truly want to help or (2) the subordinate may be trying to be ingratiatng. Because of the presence of a plausible external cause (ingratiation), the internal cause (sincere desire to help) is partially discounted.[20] In both examples, the possibility that the actor is trying to be ingratiating facilitates the effects we observe (the compliment and the compliance) and thus leads to the *discounting* of internal motivations.

Kelley recognized there are cases in which external causes do not facilitate effects but rather inhibit them. These cases may be explained by the *augmentation principles*. Assume that we want to judge the relative intelligence of two students on the basis of their chemistry grades. Both get A's, but Linda's A was in Advanced Organic Chemistry, while Gerry's A was in the nonmajor's version of Chemistry and Society. The difficulty of the respective courses is an external cause that affects our estimation of Linda and Gerry's internal intelligence. A difficult course generally inhibits high grades. Knowing that Linda excelled in a situation where people normally do poorly increases our estimate of her internal intelligence: It augments the effect. According to the augmentation principle, "When there are known to be constraints, costs, sacrifices, or risks involved in taking an action, the action once taken is attributed more to the actor than it would be otherwise."[21]

Criticism of Attribution Models

A successful attribution model must predict the behaviors of actual interpreters. Unfortunately, actual observers depart somewhat from the rational behaviors predicted by these models. They do so by showing what are known as *attributional biases.* To the extent that these biases are systematic, consistent, and predictable, they indicate areas where theories need to be strengthened.

Jones and Nisbett have pointed out one attributional bias, the tendency for observers to underestimate external situational causes in favor of internal ones. This effect is especially strong regarding other people. They hypothesize that "there is a pervasive tendency for actors to attribute their actions to situational requirements, whereas observers tend to attribute the same actions to stable person dispositions."[22] If *you* cheat, you do so because you are dishonest; if *I* cheat, I do so because I am forced to. Jones and Nisbett believe this effect occurs because an actor has more precise information about his or her own circumstances and intentions than he or she has of another's actions; data are processed differently in the two cases.

There are several other biases at odds with attribution model assumptions. There is evidence that subjects tend to underutilize consensus information.[23] In addition, information that is personally salient may be given more weight than it actually deserves.[24] Finally, people act egotistically, taking more credit for good effects and less for bad ones than they should according to theory.[25] Research Abstract 4.1 supports the presence of attributional biases and illustrates the impact such biases have on the success or failure of day-to-day communicative interactions.

Attribution biases question the assumptions of the models we have discussed, particularly those of the covariation model, which is based on a view of people as naive scientists who systematically test hypotheses by objectively looking at data patterns. Actually, the average person's ability to judge covariation is quite weak.[26] People's

tendency to overlook certain kinds of information only adds to the evidence that the average person is less objective than the model suggests.

Person perception does not stop with attributions. Once they are made, individuals use them to form impressions of the other. Next, we look at theories that describe the impression formation process.

IMPRESSION FORMATION: HOW ARE OUR IMPRESSIONS ORGANIZED?

The Asch Paradigm

Impression formation research owes much to the early work of Solomon Asch, who explored the ways knowledge of specific traits is combined into a general impression.[27]

Each person confronts us with a large number of diverse characteristics. This man is courageous, intelligent, with a ready sense of humor, quick in his movements, but he is also serious, energetic, patient under stress, not to mention his politeness and punctuality. These characteristics and many others enter into the formation of our view. Yet our impression is from the start unified; it is the impression of one person. We ask: How do the several characteristics function together to produce an impression of one person? What principles regulate this process?[28]

Asch suggested that this impression can be formed in two basic ways: (1) we can look at each trait separately and independently, our general impression being the sum of each of these separate impressions, or (2) as the result of seeing the entire person as a whole we can view separate traits in relation to each other in the context of a given personality. Asch favored the latter view.

The method he developed to investigate impression formation is known as the Asch paradigm. Briefly, Asch presented subjects with lists of terms, for example, "intelligent, skillful, industrious, cold, determined, practical, cautious," and asked them to describe the person to whom the terms applied.[29] Asch observed that some qualities appeared to be more important than others.

RESEARCH ABSTRACT 4.1 On Getting Along With One's Roommate

Sillars' *purpose* was to determine the relationship between how people make attributions and how they manage conflicts. He believed that attributional biases (the tendency to attribute the responsibility for a problem to others rather than to self and the tendency to see partners as internally motivated and self as externally motivated) adversely affect conflict resolution. Those who make internal attributions about a partner will choose less effective methods of conflict resolution than those who make external attributions or who blame themselves.

Sillars identified three kinds of conflict resolution techniques: passive-indirect, distributive, and integrative. The first involved suppressing, ignoring, or communicating indirectly about conflict. The second included seeking concessions and expressing negative evaluations of partners. The third included information exchange, positive affect, and mutual action. Sillars hypothesized that people choose conflict strategies based on the attributions they make about their partners, that attributional biases discourage integrative ways of dealing with conflict; and that one's choice of strategy affects probability of resolution.

To test these propositions, Sillars used a common situation: conflict between college roommates. The *methods* he used included content analysis of open-ended responses to a questionnaire. Sillars gave a questionnaire to a random sample of 140 first-year dormitory residents at a large midwestern university. The questionnaire asked respondents to write in detail about a recent roommate conflict and to answer closed-ended questions about the conflict and the strategies used to resolve it. Also measured were satisfaction with roommate, duration and importance of the conflict, overall frequency of conflicts, and the degree of responsibility attributed to self and roommate. Written descriptions were submitted to content analysis. Each strategy described was coded as passive-indirect, distributive, or integrative. Interrater agreement between independent coders was approximately 80 percent.

The results were as follows: Analysis indicated that, on the average, respondents attributed more responsibility for the conflict to their roommates than to themselves. Correlations between attributions and strategies revealed that those who made stable attributions and attributed responsibility to their partners were more likely to use passive than integrative strategies. Analysis of the relationship between strategy selection and satisfactory resolution showed that integrative techniques more frequently led to conflict resolution and generated more positive feelings about the relationship. The analyses supported Sillars' contention that people who attribute conflict to their own unstable characteristics will be more communicative and less competitive than those who attribute conflict to the stable characteristics of their partners. The results also indicated the presence of strong attributional biases and supported the notion that integrative strategies are more productive than passive or distributive strategies.

This study demonstrates the negative effects that result from attributional biases. Sillars shows that the way we attribute responsibility to others affects our ability to communicate effectively and productively.

Source: Alan L. Sillars, "Attributions and Communication in Roommate Conflicts," *Communication Monographs*, 47 (August 1980), 180–200.

For example, changing a central trait such as "cold" into its opposite "warm" reorganized the entire impression. In addition, omitting the central trait or replacing it with a less central one also changed the impression. Finally, Asch found that traits central in one context may change their importance and meaning in other contexts. "Warm," for example, in the context of "obedient, weak, shallow, unambitious, vain," has a different meaning than "warm" in the context of "vain, shrewd, unscrupulous, shallow, envious."[30] In the first case, subjects described the person's warmth as a result of "dog-like devotion" and in the second as insincerity.

Asch suggests "the characteristics forming the basis of an impression do not contribute each a fixed, independent meaning but...their content is itself partially a function of the environment of the other characteristics, of the mutual relations."[31] And later he says, "To know a person is to have a grasp of a particular structure."[32] For Asch it is not individual traits considered separately but the system of traits that give meaning. Research Abstract 4.2 presents a study that reinforces Asch's view. It takes Asch's thinking and makes an unobvious prediction, employing the Asch paradigm in a more sophisticated manner than many trait impression studies.

The Social Schemata Approach

Impression formation theory has recently returned to the position hinted at by Asch when he said knowing a person is a process of grasping

RESEARCH ABSTRACT 4.2   Can a Person Have Too Much of a Good Thing?

Delia agreed with Asch that when separate personality traits are combined into an overall evaluation they are not simply added or averaged. He felt people integrate the meanings of individual traits into unique general impressions by using context to define a trait's meaning.

Delia used this reasoning to develop a surprising hypothesis: that a person whose positive traits all reflect a single personality dimension may end up being devalued. He argued that this person may be seen as having too much of a good thing and be considered narrow and inflexible. In comparison, a person who possesses a variety of positive traits is seen as having a multi-faceted personality. Delia's *purpose* was to verify Asch's idea that meanings are a function of context by seeing whether a person can have too much of a good thing.

The *method* he used was a variation on the Asch paradigm. Because he wanted to see whether a person described by highly positive unidimensional traits appears less attractive than a person described by multi-dimensional traits, he chose traits located along a single tautness-looseness continuum. From a list of 20 such traits, he chose eight highly positive ones that represented tautness: intelligent, clean, efficient, level-headed, punctual, neat, ambitious, and self-disciplined.

Two other positive traits, easy-going and sensitive, were chosen from the looseness end. Two experimental conditions were prepared. In condition 1, the first eight traits described a stimulus person. In condition 2, intelligent and clean were deleted and replaced by easy-going and sensitive. Traits used to describe the condition 1 stimulus person were highly consistent and unidimensional, while the traits describing the condition 2 stimulus person showed more variation and were multidimensional.

Before the study began, Delia had subjects rate each trait on a seven-point scale from least favorable to most favorable.

continued...

RESEARCH ABSTRACT 4.2 (*continued*)

This provided out-of-context ratings. Then the two stimulus descriptions were presented to a group of 48 subjects. They were told that as part of a class project a student named Howard had volunteered to let others form a second-hand impression of him, and the traits were actual descriptions written by people who knew him well. Subjects in both conditions wrote a description of Howard after reading the traits. In addition, they rated him on general likability and task and social attraction scales and indicated whether Howard had too little or too much self-discipline. Subjects also rated each trait separately. These were the in-context ratings.

The *results* supported Delia's hypothesis. When Howard was described by condition 1 traits, he was perceived as less likable and socially attractive than when described by condition 2 traits. The hypothesis that in condition 1 Howard would have too much of a good thing was confirmed: A larger percentage of subjects saw Howard as "excessively self-disciplined" in the first condition. Subjects also described Howard more negatively in their written essays in condition 1, indicating that positive traits in context may result in negative evaluations.

Delia compared out-of-context trait ratings with those done in context and found their meaning changed. These changes were highly correlated to overall ratings of likability. The results clearly supported the "change of meaning" hypothesis. Delia interpreted these findings to mean that during impression formation people gather stimulus information, organize it around a central evaluation, use this evaluation to assign meanings to individual traits, and infer further traits. Impression formation is an active "effort after meaning" and not a passive integration of preexisting information.

Source: Jesse G. Delia, "Change in Meaning Processes in Impression Formation," *Communication Monographs*, 43 (June 1976), 142–57.

---

structure. Current studies specify how a holistic impression is formed by using the concept of the *social schema*. In their review of schema research, Shelley Taylor and Jennifer Crocker discuss not only what a schema is but more generally, what schemata do for us.[33] In our previous discussion of person and object perception, we noted that perception involves active selection. To make selections and process them efficiently, the perceiver needs selection criteria and guidelines for processing. Taylor and Crocker believe schemata provide these processing aides.[34] A schema contains knowledge that allows us to recognize an object or situation. "For example, if we do not have a conception of a chair, we do not recognize a chair when one is before us; we recognize it only if we have a schema or theory about what a chair is."[35] Schemata describe an object's attributes, specify the relationship among these attributes, and represent specific examples of the object. As such, one of the chief functions of a schema is to provide an answer to the question, What is it?[36]

Schemata allow us to complete several cognitive tasks. First, they help us structure our perceptual worlds. When we see an object or event, we match it with the closest possible schema. We then use the knowledge contained in the schema to structure our perception of the event. To borrow an example from Taylor and Crocker, when we go to the circus, we use the "circus schema" to relate the ring-master, high-wire acts, clowns, and animals into a meaningful whole. We know the purpose and structure of what is happening because these are contained in our schema.

Besides allowing us to decode and classify information, schemata let us fill in missing data. If, during the circus parade, we do not see any elephants, we look around until we find them; our schema tells us that there must be elephants if it is a real circus. Our schema also provides default options, or typical representations of an object, that we can plug in for missing information.[37] Even if we miss this year's circus and depend on another's description, our guesses about events will be accurate if our schema is well defined. "Did the clowns have white faces, orange hair, loud-colored jackets, and big, floppy shoes; and did about 10 of them jump out of a very tiny car?" we might ask. The answer to our question will probably be yes.

Finally, schemata help us judge how well a particular event or object fits in.[38] A clown in street clothes is not a pure instance of a clown and will seem out of place in a circus. Objects or events that depart from a schema are confusing and are hard to process. A schema, in short, is "a cognitive structure that represents some stimulus domain. It is organized through experience; it consists of a knowledge structure (a representation of the attributes of that stimulus domain); and it also includes plans for interpreting and gathering schema-related information."[39] Different types of social schemata include person schemata (what is an extrovert like?), role schemata (what is a fireman or a politician like?), and event schemata (what happens at a cocktail party or a football game?). Next, we will consider one specific person schema model, that of Cantor and Mischel.

Cantor and Mischel's Prototype Model

Nancy Cantor and Walter Mischel see the impression formation process as one of categorization. They believe we have a natural tendency to group people according to their similarities, place them in categories, label these categories, and then use these labels to communicate about similarities and differences.[40] Although Canter and Mischel prefer to use the terms "category," "fuzzy category," or "set" to describe the groupings people use to guide their perceptions, their model corresponds to other social schemata models.

First, they believe we organize our perceptions around categories that contain representations or prototypes of the objects belonging to the category. In categorizing a real-life object, people judge how well the object fits into (is prototypical of) the category. A category, however differentiating, does not have clear-cut boundaries. Instead, it is defined by its most representative case, its prototype. That is, to determine whether someone belongs to a certain category of individuals we compare him or her to the prototype, or perfect example, of that category. We determine whether someone is a "real go-getter" by comparing that person to an abstract image of what a real go-getter is like.

Categories exist at many levels and can be divided into subcategories. Like other schemata, they are hierarchical. The category "real go-getter" may be one part of a wider category "ambitious people," which, in turn, may belong to an even wider category. Similarly, there may be several different types of "go-getters," each of which may be exemplified by a more specific prototype. "While consistent, coherent descriptions, capturing the gist of another's behavior, are achieved by moving to more abstract levels of person categorization, more vivid, salient person images require less inclusive slots."[41]

Cantor and Mischel identify two sets of rules people follow to identify prototypes. In the first, the observer is able to evaluate several attributes of an actor. Evaluation is made in three ways: by *breadth* (the total number of category-consistent attributes), *dominance* (whether category-consistent attributes stand out when compared to the total number of observed attributes), and *differentiation* (the relative absence of attributes incompatible to the category). For example, we class someone as a "real go-getter" only if he or she has a sufficient number of related traits (assertiveness, ambition, energy, and so forth), if these traits dominate the actor's personality, and if he or she exhibits few incompatible traits (such as shyness, self-effacement, or submission).

The second set of rules involves situations where an observer has only partial knowledge of someone's behavior. Here, an individual is judged to be prototypical if he or she exhibits "the most central (highly associated) category attribute(s) consistently and intensely across many situations, and particularly in situations where such behavior is not routinely observed (…non-normative situations)."[42]

Cantor and Mischel offer an alternative to Asch's model. They subscribe to Asch's belief that to grasp the characteristics of another we must view a set of traits as a unified whole. Where Asch is unclear about the mechanism used to accomplish this, however, Cantor and Mischel posit the existence of hierarchically organized categories (person schemata) containing information about the prototypical instance in a particular category. In organizing our perceptions about someone, we call up an appropriate category and compare the individual's traits with the prototype.

Criticisms of the Social Schemata Models

The social schemata approach is a promising development in the person perception area, chiefly because the schema construct explains how we code information about others. However, a major difficulty lies in our inability to test the existence of schemata. Taylor and Crocker suggest that few studies have been able to falsify the existence of schemata. They argue that a good theory must do more than demonstrate the possible existence of a construct. It needs to set up a test that can verify either the existence or the nonexistence of a construct. "The concept of schema and its processing functions currently provide the basis for nothing more than demonstration studies. Though predictions can be generated by schema theory, failure to show a hypothesized

effect will likely be attributed to failing to specify the right schema or measurement error, rather than a failure of the theory itself."[43] Until we find better ways to test whether schemata exist, their value will be suspect.

EXCHANGE THEORIES: WHY DO WE CHOOSE TO ASSOCIATE WITH PARTICULAR OTHERS?

So far, we have considered how we perceive others and form impressions of them, but we have not yet addressed the question of how these perceptions and impressions lead to judgments of acceptability. In this section we address ourselves to the question, Given a potential communicative partner with specific characteristics, what determines whether we will choose to have a relationship with that person? Two theories are related to this question. Homans' Social Exchange Model, and Thibaut and Kelley's Comparison Level Model. Once we examine these theories, we will look at a simple model that unifies all of the processes discussed.

Homans' Social Exchange Theory

George Homans' work combines principles from two areas: learning theory and elementary economics. Briefly, Homans believes all social interactions involve some form of exchange or anticipated exchange.[44] Just as, economically, people exchange goods and services, socially they barter sentiments and activities. For example, we offer help (an activity) in exchange for gratitude (a sentiment), talk in exchange for friendship, or love in exchange for security. In making this kind of bargain, we calculate the rewards we are likely to receive, the costs we will incur, and the investments we have made. In essence, we determine the value of a particular relationship and are more likely to form relationships in which we stand to make a profit.

According to Homans, a reward is any positive outcome resulting from a particular activity. In a dating relationship the reward may be the excitement and fun of being with a particular individual, an increase in social standing resulting from dating someone popular, or freedom from loneliness or boredom. But rewards always imply costs. If Sheila decides to date Brian, she foregoes the pleasure of being with Mark. If she goes to the movies with Charles, she gives up a chance to stay home and read a good book. Some costs are so minimal, and some rewards so positive, that the decision is comparatively easy. When rewards and costs are nearly equivalent, however, the decision is difficult, for the profit (rewards minus costs) will be small. Homans believes people try to maximize profits, although they may sometimes forgo short-term profits in exchange for long-term gains.

In dyadic interactions, both parties calculate their profits. According to Homans, no exchange continues for very long unless both partners think they are making a profit. Cases in which one partner's profits overshadow another's are perceived as unjust and lead to feelings of resentment and anger. Distributive justice occurs to the extent that

$$\frac{A\text{'s reward} - A\text{'s costs}}{A\text{'s investments}} = \frac{B\text{'s rewards} - B\text{'s costs}}{B\text{'s investments}}$$

Investments consist of the attributes each party brings to the exchange such as skill, effort, credibility, or experience. Profits may be balanced by investments. If you have more experience and skill than I, I may feel that you deserve a greater profit than I do. In such a case the relationship may be perceived as just, even though my profit is less than yours.

What does this tell us about an individual's choice of communicative partners? It implies that we use information about others' characteristics to predict the likelihood that they will provide rewards, and we choose the relationship that best maximizes profit. We use both verbal and nonverbal cues to make these judgments. Research Abstract 4.3 uses an experimental methodology to test hypotheses about the kinds of cues we use

to determine whether associating with someone will be rewarding to us.

Thibaut and Kelley's Comparison Levels Model

John Thibaut and Harold Kelley's model also explains why we enter some relationships and refuse to enter others. Their model, however, accounts for the interdependent dyadic nature of interactions more fully than Homans'.[45]

Thibaut and Kelley suggest that all interactive partners have a repertoire of behaviors they may use in a given situation. During an interaction, A and B may enact any number of behaviors. Because A and B are interdependent, the consequences of their actions depend on their joint behaviors. For A to determine how to act in a given instance, A must review his or her choices, try to predict what B's most likely choices are, and compute the results of possible combinations of their behaviors.

We can conceptualize the relationship between any two people as a matrix. Along the top are all possible behaviors that A may enact. Along the side are B's choices. Within the matrix are the payoffs that will accrue to each. Figure 4.3 shows a situation from Game Theory that illustrates mutual outcome dependence. It is called the Prisoner's Dilemma. Here A and B are two prisoners who jointly commit a crime. Both are separately interrogated and offered a deal by the district attorney. Each is told that if she confesses and turns state's evidence, she will go free while her partner will go to jail. The dilemma arises because the prisoners realize that if both confess, both will be punished. Their problem is second-guessing what their partner will do. They must compute the consequences of their joint actions.

The consequences of an action may either be rewards (gratifications or the "means whereby a drive is reduced or a need fulfilled") or costs ("any factors that operate to inhibit or deter the performance of a sequence of behavior").[46] The rewards in the prisoner's dilemma example are the chance to go free after committing a crime.

RESEARCH ABSTRACT 4.3   Nonverbal Behaviors and Social Rewards

Most of us have expectancies about appropriate nonverbal behavior. When people deviate from expected norms, we generally devalue them, feel discomfort, and compensate in some way. If, on the other hand, people keep a polite distance and show normal interest levels, they will be seen as rewarding. Burgoon and Hale wondered if there are times when it is more rewarding to have our expectations violated than to have them confirmed. They argued that violations of expectations lead to arousal, which in turn leads us to attend to our partners more fully. If our partners are rewarding and their violation is in a positive direction, we may interpret and evaluate their violation positively, and our communication patterns and outcomes will improve. If, on the other hand, they are not very rewarding and their violation is a negative one, then we should experience negative outcomes.

Burgoon and Hale designed a study to investigate what would happen when communicators violated or conformed to their own preestablished levels of nonverbal immediacy with friends and strangers. They hypothesized that interactions with friends would be more rewarding than with strangers. They also predicted that, in interactions with friends, increases in nonverbal immediacy would lead to increased attraction and credibility and relational messages of intimacy, involvement, similarity, and equality; while, in interactions with strangers, increases in nonverbal immediacy would lead to decreases in attraction and credibility and a sense of detachment and distance. Finally, they believed that decreases in immediacy would decrease rewards regardless of whether the interactors were strangers or friends.

The *method* was experimental. Participants were pairs of friends, who interacted with one another and with strangers. One member of each pair acted as a confederate for the manipulation of immediacy. In the

continued...

The costs are the possibility that your partner will turn you in. Every relationship has potential costs and rewards that depend on both partners' actions.

Thibaut and Kelley believe that rewards and costs are determined both exogenously and endogenously. *Exogenous determinants* refer to the skills, values, and needs that the interactants have outside a particular situation. If, for example, A is shy or easily embarrassed, while B is bold and self-confident, then many behaviors will be more costly for A than for B. *Endogenous determinants* are the specific results of pairing A's action with B's. Both interact to determine rewards and costs.

In choosing among preferred consequences, A and B must have some standard of acceptability.

Thibaut and Kelley present such standards. The first, called *comparison level*, or CL, is used to evaluate the attraction of a particular relationship. It is "Some modal or average value of all known outcomes, each outcome weighted by its 'salience,' or strength of instigation... ."[47] The second, called *comparison level for alternatives*, or CL_{alt}, is used to decide whether to remain in or leave a relationship. CL_{alt} is defined as "the lowest level of outcomes a member will accept in light of available alternative opportunities."[48] As soon as CL falls below CL_{alt}, a member will leave a relationship.

For example, assume you are now a member of a social group. The group provides you with a number of outcomes resulting jointly from your behaviors and those of other group members. Per-

RESEARCH ABSTRACT 4.3 (*continued*)

normal immediacy condition, the confederate acted normally. In the nonimmediacy condition, the confederate increased the physical distance between self and partner and communicated in a distant and unreceptive way. In the high immediacy condition, the confederate moved closer and seemed more involved than normal.

Following discussion, the participants rated the credibility, attraction, and relational messages of the confederates. A factorial design was used, with three levels of immediacy (high, medium, and low) and two levels of communicator reward (stranger or friend.)

The *results* of an analysis of variance showed that friends were indeed seen as more rewarding (in terms of attraction, credibility, and expression of intimacy and similarity) than strangers. Results also indicated that nonimmediacy violations produced negative ratings with both friends and strangers. The immediacy violation was less clear. While it did not increase rat-

ings as Burgoon and Hale had thought it might, it did not decrease them markedly, either with friends or with strangers. There appeared to be no significant cost to violating immediacy in a positive direction, but there was no gain either. Overall, the results also showed that decreased nonverbal immediacy communicated detachment, dissimilarity, and dominance, while increased immediacy communicated more involvement, intimacy, similarity, and moderate dominance. Although not all of their hypotheses were confirmed, the direction of the results were promising and showed partial support for their model of nonverbal expectancy violations. The study helped the researchers learn more about how we evaluate others on the basis of their nonverbal behaviors.

Source: Judee K. Burgoon and Jerold L. Hale, "Nonverbal Expectancy Violations: Model Elaboration and Application to Immediacy Behaviors," *Communication Monographs*, 55 (March 1988), 58–79.

haps you are only moderately happy with the group. It provides you with a certain amount of social status, you have a reasonably good time attending social functions, and you enjoy many of the members. There are headaches as well, however. The business meetings are tedious, some members are difficult to get along with, and it is expensive to belong. Your CL is your perception of the average outcomes or consequences the group provides for you. CL$_{alt}$ is the average outcomes provided by other groups. You remain in the original group only so long as the perceived CL does not fall below CL$_{alt}$. If it does, you are likely to leave the group and join another that is more advantageous.

What is true of the group is also true of the dyad. When two people decide to continue being

roommates, both compute CLs and CL$_{alt}$s. Only if both feel there are more rewards in staying together than in leaving will they continue their relationship. Sometimes, one person will have better alternatives than the other. In such a case, that roommate may decide to leave the relationship. Attraction to and dependence on a dyad is a function of "(1) the matrix of the possible outcomes of interaction; (2) the process of exploring or sampling the possibilities; and *ultimately* (3) whether or not the *jointly* experienced outcomes are above each member's CL$_{alt}$."[49]

Criticism of Social Exchange Models

Exchange models are based on the concept of rewards and costs, a concept borrowed from

	Confess	Don't Confess
Confess	Both receive maximum term in jail	A goes to jail; B turns state's evidence
Don't Confess	B goes to jail; A turns state's evidence	Both get off; D.A. has no case

B's Choices

A's Choices

(Note: Here both A and B have identical choices; in many actual matrices this is not the case.

FIGURE 4.3: Modified inter-action matrix (zero-sum)

learning theory. In most learning theories, no objective attempt is made to define rewards. No lists of objectively rewarding behaviors are given. Homans, for example, follows other learning theorists in defining rewards as anything that increases the occurrence of a behavior. If you continually seek an alternative, even if it objectively seems to be a poor one, that alternative is, by definition, rewarding. Some critics of learning theories believe this is circular reasoning and reject the theories accordingly.

Another problem with exchange models, particularly with the CL formulation, is the model's inability to specify exactly how CL is computed: It fails to specify how we assign values to outcomes and how we average and weigh these assignments.

A final facet of exchange models that bothers some critics is their image of man as a profit seeker. If you believe that people are primarily motivated by the rewards and costs in a relationship, then you probably accept exchange models. If you think this inadequately explains why people interact, then you will be less satisfied with the exchange theory models.

THE CRONKHITE-LISKA MODEL: HOW ARE COMMUNICATIVE PARTNERS CHOSEN?

Although we began with a straightforward question involving choice of communicative partners,

our discussion has led us to a number of complex theoretical considerations, and we seem to have strayed from our original problem. The goal of this section is to summarize what we have learned and return to our original concern. Consideration of the Cronkhite and Liska model will allow us to do so.

For Gary Cronkhite and Jo Liska, choice of communicative partner is a process of matching derived criteria with attributed characteristics. Figure 4.4 diagrams this process. An attractive feature of the model is that you can enter it at any point. It can be read from left to right or right to left. For this discussion, we will begin at the far right and work back toward the left.

Cronkhite and Liska assume that whenever we encounter a potential communicative partner we encounter that person in a particular situation, and we enter the situation with particular needs and goals.[50] Goals and situations affect each other. At a cocktail party certain goals can be met (meeting others and indulging in polite chit-chat), but others (self disclosure) are totally inappropriate.

In light of your needs and your grasp of a situation, you derive certain criteria that govern your choice of a communicative partner. In choosing a professor, for example (assuming your goal is intellectual stimulation and your definition of the situation is formal classroom learning), you may look for qualities such as intellectual honesty, clarity of expression, objectivity, and expertise. In choosing someone to give you personal advice,

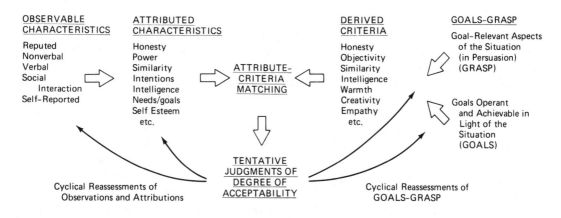

FIGURE 4.4:   The process one individual uses to judge the acceptability of another. (Adapted from Gary Cronkhite and Jo R. Liska, "The Judgment of Communicant Acceptability," in *Persuasion: New Directions in Theory and Research*, Vol. 8: Sage Annual Reviews of Communication Research, eds. Michael E. Roloff and Gerald R. Miller [Beverly Hills: Sage, 1980].)

you derive other criteria, perhaps warmth, empathy, understanding, and willingness to listen. These criteria are, in a sense, a measure of the outcomes or consequences you hope to receive as a result of an interaction. In the Thibaut and Kelley model, they are the outcomes that determine your CL.

Once you determine derived criteria, you match them with attributed criteria. You do this by observing the characteristics of potential partners and by using attribution and impression formation processes to decide on attributed characteristics. Assume you need help with a problem. Your derived criteria are experience in dealing with similar problems, warmth, willingness to help, and trustworthiness. You observe several people including Anne. You ask friends about Anne's ability to help others, observe her verbal and nonverbal behaviors, and recall past offers of help. You infer she is warm, responsive, and analytic. Your only other choice is Tom, but you believe that, although he is kind, he tends to be impatient and to gossip. While Anne is not a perfect match, her attributed characteristics meet your derived characteristics fairly closely, and you choose her as an acceptable partner.

The same process occurs whenever we judge another's ability to meet our communication needs. Whether we are judging the trustworthiness of a speaker or the attractiveness of a group, person perception, attributions, and exchange considerations are used to match our needs with the characteristics of others. In doing this perceptual and judgmental work, we solve a major problem faced by all communicators: how to determine the communication acceptability of another person.

SOCIAL CONSTRUCTIONISM: WHERE DO JUDGMENTAL CATEGORIES COME FROM?

The theories in this chapter all suggest that humans have a deep need to understand their social worlds. We may seek information about others to achieve rewards and avoid punishments as the exchange theories suggest, or we may do so simply because as a species we are essentially curious and creative. Whatever the reason, we spend a great deal of time and effort in making sense of physical events, of other people, and even of ourselves. But what determines the understandings we arrive at and why do we categorize people as we do? There are three approaches to this question. The first, called the *realist position*, answers that we categorize others as we do because that is the way they are. According to this view we are fairly passive receivers of a directly accessible reality. The second, called the *innatist position*, replies that we categorize others as we do because that is the way we are. Humans are physiologically "wired up" to view the world in certain ways. The third approach, called the *social constructionist position*, holds that we see the world as we do because we "have participated in social practices, institutions, and other forms of symbolic action (e.g., language) that presuppose or in some way make salient those categorizations."[51]

The basic tenets of the social constructionist position are evident in its name. It argues that we construct our realities and that these constructions are social products. To the social constructionist, human processors are not passive receivers, but active creators. Jerome Bruner tells us that social constructionism is "a view that takes as its central premise that 'world making' is the principal function of mind."[52]

Most of the models in this chapter assume that communication originates in individuals, that communication starts with "an intending and competent" individual intent on transmitting and receiving information.[53] Social constructionists questions this assumption, locating communication not in individuals but in social structures. When social constructionists say that communication is located in society, they mean that communication is a product of social structure: The rules that govern and constrain communication are to be found in the economic forces, class structures, community traditions, epistemological assumptions, and language practices that surround us. As Stuart Sigman points out, we are governed by historical patterns and hierarchical structures "that transcend single face-to-face moments, and are not well formulated by views of the world as locally managed and lived."[54]

One of the most important external forces affecting our perceptions of self and other is language. While language occurs only through the utterances of individual humans, the language system as such transcends individuals. We are born into a language community and presented with a means of communicating that is more likely to affect us than we are to affect it. Or, as Pittinger, Hackett, and Kanehy say, "It is treacherously misleading to think of language and other communication systems as cloaks donned by the ego when it ventures into the interpersonal world; rather we think of ego (or 'mind') as arising from the internalization of interpersonal communicative processes."[55] Rom Harre goes even further: "For me, a person is not a natural object, but a cultural artifact."[56]

The social constructionist position challenges some of our most basic beliefs. An interesting example can be found in Suzanne Kessler and Wendy McKenna's book on the social construction of gender.[57] Here, the authors show how difficult it is to defend the view that there are two and only two sexes and demonstrate the contradictions that emerge when we try to account for all gender classification on the basis of biological differences. They point to alternative ways of describing gender and discuss the lengths to which people go to preserve basic beliefs about sex. For these authors and for other social constructionists, meaning is not found in the objective world but in a system of beliefs maintained by social consensus.[58] If we share social beliefs with others, we will interpret the world as they do; if we do not, however, our interpretations will be very different. Research Abstract 4.4 shows the kind of misunderstandings that occur when people construct different views of a single occurrence. This study is interesting not only because it illustrates the social construction of reality but also because it is a good example of interpretive methodology.

An important part of the social constructionist project is the necessity of historicizing "lan-

RESEARCH ABSTRACT 4.4   Sexist Jokes and Male Bonding

One night, 45 fraternity brothers burst into a sorority dining hall and forced the 30 women there to listen to a speech on penis envy and watch a demonstration of methods of masturbation using a rubber penis. Normally, the women tolerated and even enjoyed sexual banter and jokes, but this time their reaction was different. They ordered the men from the house and reported the incident. To avoid disciplinary action, the men agreed to meet with the women to discuss the incident, and Lyman acted as discussion facilitator.

Clearly, the men and women perceived the "joke" differently.

The women saw the incident not as sexual but as sexist. They perceived the action as aggressive and threatening. As one woman said, "…it went too far, and I felt afraid to say anything. Why do men always think about women in terms of violating them, in sexual imagery? You have to understand that the combination of a sexual topic with the physical threat of all of you standing around terrified me."

The men defended their act by arguing that it created a special kind of male intimacy. For them this kind of rule-governed aggression was an integral part of their lives in the fraternity. They were surprised at the women's reactions, because this joke was mild compared to the dirty talk and insults that were normal at the frat. Part of living in the fraternity involved learning to take the worst kind of insults without losing one's cool. The men reported it was common for them to make sexually explicit remarks about each other's mothers and to describe in detail each other's girlfriends' bodies. What the women saw as aggression, they saw as a test of strength.

Lyman suggests that jokes are often outlets for aggression. "The joke form expresses emotions and tensions that might endanger the order of the organization, but that must be spoken lest they damage the social order." Through this kind of joke the fraternity members were able to express and share aggression, sexual feeling, and the desire to break the rules without being punished. What kinds of tensions and fears were being expressed by jokes targeting women? Lyman believes two kinds: fear that an intimate relationship with a women would trap them and break up the group ("I think that being in a frat, having close friendships with men is a replacement for having close relationships with women") and fear that they would soon have to enter the work force and lose their independence ("College is a stage in my life to do crazy and humorous things. In 10 years when I'm in the business world I won't be able to carry on like this"). Both these fears could be expressed by displacing their anger onto women.

By carefully listening to the comments of both the men and women, and by incorporating theories about the psychological functions of jokes, Lyman was able to describe the different ways the participants constructed the reality of this incident. His was an interpretive study with critical overtones. Lyman concludes, "Men are allowed to direct anger and aggression toward women because social norms governing the expression of anger or humor generally replicate the power order of the group… . These men had so internalized the governing of male emotions by rules that their anger itself could emerge only indirectly through rule-governed forms such as jokes and joking relationships."

Source: Peter Lyman, "The Fraternal Bond as a Joking Relationship: A Case Study of the Role of Sexist Jokes in Male Group Bonding," in *Changing Men: New Directions in Research on Men and Masculinity* (Beverly Hills: Sage, 1987), 148–63.

guages of understanding." Thus, social constructionists draw heavily on cross cultural and historical studies, recognizing that across time and culture our understandings of entities and
relationships are likely to undergo dramatic
changes. A case in point is Howard Gadlin's study
of the nature of the self. Starting with colonial
America, he maps changing notions of privacy
and individuality against changing economic and
social conditions. Gadlin's work is of special
interest as it addresses corresponding changes in
communication norms throughout this period.[59]

Social constructionism is more than an
abstract epistemological position. The socially
constructed meanings we use to judge ourselves
and others have real world effects:

Thus to construct persons in such a way that they possess inherent sin is to invite certain lines of action and
not others. Or, to treat depression, anxiety, or fear as
emotions from which people suffer is to have far different implications than to treat them as chosen, selected,
or played out as on a stage. Conventions of discourse
are important, then, because they are so closely connected to other activities in which we engage.[60]

The social constructionists remind us that the
categories we use to understand and evaluate others have real implications for the quality of our
lives.

REFERENCES

1. Gary Cronkhite and Jo R. Liska, "The Judgment
of Communicant Acceptability," in *Persuasion:
New Directions in Theory and Research*, eds.
Michael E. Roloff and Gerald R. Miller (Beverly
Hills: Sage, 1980).

2. David J. Schneider, Albert H. Hastorf, and Phoebe
C. Ellsworth, *Person Perception*, 2nd ed. (Reading, Mass.: Addison-Wesley, 1979), pp. 2–7.

3. *Ibid.*, p. 7.

4. *Ibid.*, p. 248.

5. Frank E. X. Dance and Carl E. Larson, *The Functions of Human Communication: A Theoretical
Approach* (New York: Holt, Rinehart & Winston,
1976), p. 78.

6. Schneider, Hastorf, and Ellsworth, *Person Perception*, p. 249.

7. *Ibid.*, p. 30.

8. *Ibid.*, p. 160.

9. Quoted in Edward E. Jones and Richard E.
Nisbett, "The Actor and the Observer: Divergent
Perceptions of the Causes of Behavior," in *Attri-
bution: Perceiving the Causes of Behavior*, 2nd
ed., eds. Edward E. Jones and others (Morristown,
N. J.: General Learning Press, 1972).

10. Martin Fishbein and Icek Ajzen, *Belief, Attitude,
Intention, and Behavior* (Reading, Mass.: Addison-Wesley, 1975).

11. Schneider, Hastorf, and Ellsworth, *Person Perception*, p. 200.

12. *Ibid.*, p. 197.

13. *Ibid.*, p. 200.

14. Fritz Heider, "Social Perception and Phenomenal
Causality," *Psychological Review*, 51 (1944),
358–74.

15. Edward E. Jones and Keith E. Davis, "From Acts
to Dispositions: The Attribution Process in Person
Perception," in *Advances in Experimental Social
Psychology*, vol. 2, ed. Leonard Berkowitz (New
York: Academic, 1965).

16. Harold H. Kelley, "Attribution Theory in Social
Psychology," *Nebraska Symposium on Motivation*
(Lincoln: University of Nebraska Press, 1967).

17. Harold H. Kelley, "The Processes of Causal Attribution," *American Psychologist*, 28 (1973), 107–
28, p. 108.

18. Kelley, "Processes of Causal Attribution," p. 108.

19. *Ibid.*, p. 108.

20. *Ibid.*, p. 113.

21. *Ibid.*, p. 114.

22. Jones and Nisbett, "Actor and Observer," p. 80.

23. Schneider, Hastorff, and Ellsworth, *Person Perception*, p. 236.

24. *Ibid.*, p. 233.

25. *Ibid.*, p. 239. See also Alan J. Sillars, "Attribution
and Communication: Are People 'Naive
Scientists' or Just Naive?" in *Social Cognition and
Communication*, eds. Michael E. Roloff and
Charles R. Berger (Beverly Hills: Sage, 1982), p.
83.

26. Sillars, "Attribution and Communication," p. 79.

27. Solomon E. Asch, "Forming Impressions of Personality," *Journal of Abnormal and Social Psychology*, 41 (1946), 258–90.

28. *Ibid.*, p. 258.

29. *Ibid.*, p. 262.

30. *Ibid.*, p. 267.

31. *Ibid.*, p. 268.

32. *Ibid.*, p. 283.

33. Shelley E. Taylor and Jennifer Crocker, "Schematic Bases of Social Information Processing," in *Social Cognition: The Ontario Symposium*, vol. 1, eds. E. Tory Higgins, C. Peter Herman, and Mark P. Zanna (Hillsdale, N. J.: Lawrence Erlbaum Associates, 1981).

34. *Ibid.*, p. 90.

35. *Ibid.*, p. 91.

36. *Ibid.*, p. 91.

37. *Ibid.*, pp. 103–04.

38. *Ibid.*, p. 111.

39. *Ibid.*, p. 124.

40. Nancy Cantor and Walter Mischel, "Prototypes in Person Perception," in *Advances in Experimental Social Psychology*, vol. 12, ed. Leonard Berkowitz (New York: Academic, 1979), p. 4.

41. *Ibid.*, p. 26.

42. *Ibid.*, p. 36.

43. Taylor and Crocker, "Social Information Processing," p. 127.

44. George Caspar Homans, *Social Behavior: Its Elementary Forms* (New York: Harcourt Brace Jovanovich, 1959).

45. John W. Thibaut and Harold H. Kelley, *The Social Psychology of Groups* (New York: John Wiley & Sons, 1959).

46. *Ibid.*, p. 12.

47. *Ibid.*, p. 21.

48. *Ibid.*, p. 21.

49. *Ibid.*, p. 23.

50. Cronkhite and Liska, "The Judgment of Communicant Acceptability."

51. Richard A. Schweder and Joan G. Miller, "The Social Construction of the Person: How Is It Possible?" chap. 3, in *The Social Construction of the Person*, eds. Kenneth J. Gergen and Keith E. Davis (New York: Springer-Verlag, l985), p. 41.

52. Jerome Bruner, "Life As Narrative," *Social Research*, 54 (Spring l987), 11–32, p. 11.

53. Stuart J. Sigman, *A Perspective on Social Communication* (Lexington, Mass.: D. C. Heath, 1987), p. xii.

54. *Ibid.*, p. xii.

55. Robert Everett Pittinger and others, *The First Five Minutes: A Sample of Microscopic Interview Analysis* (Ithaca, N. Y.: Paul Martineau, 1960), p. 223.

56. Rom Harre, *Personal Being: A Theory for Individual Psychology* (Cambridge, Mass.: Harvard University Press, 1984), p. 20. See also Rom Harre, ed., *Life Sentences: Aspects of the Social Role of Language* (New York: John Wiley & Sons, 1976); Rom Harre, *Social Being* (Oxford: Basil Blackwell, 1979); Rom Harre, David Clarke, and Nicola de Carlo, *Motives and Mechanisms: An Introduction to the Psychology of Action* (New York: Methuen, l985); Rom Harre, ed., *The Social Construction of Emotions* (New York: Blackwell, 1986); and Peter Muhlhausler and Rom Harre, *Pronouns and People: The Linguistic Construction of Social and Personal Identity* (Cambridge, Mass.: Blackwell, 1990).

57. Suzanne J. Kessler and Wendy McKenna, *Gender: An Ethnomethodological Approach* (New York: John Wiley & Sons, 1978).

58. Kenneth J. Gergen, "Social Constructionist Inquiry: Context and Implications," in *The Social Construction of the Person*, eds. Kenneth J. Gergen and Keith E. Davis (New York: Springer-Verlag, 1985).

59. Howard Gadlin, "Private Lives and Public Order: A Critical View of the History of Intimate Relations in the United States," in *Close Relationships: Perspectives on the Meaning of Intimacy*, eds. George Levinger and Harold L. Raush (Amherst, Mass.: University of Massachusetts Press, 1977), pp. 33–72.

60. Gergen, "Social Constuctionist Inquiry," p. 7.

chapter 5

THE PROBLEM OF SIGNIFICATION

INTRODUCTION

This chapter considers the second problem faced by communicators: using available signs and codes to produce meaningful messages. The ability to engage in this task—to take part in the process of *signification*—is, of course, one of the defining characteristics of being human. It is also one of the most remarkable and complex feats any of us ever faces.

To get a sense of its complexity, think about the process of engaging in a simple conversation. How do you translate your intentions into gestures and phrases? Why are certain words used, and how are they transformed into a series of phonated, articulated sounds that others can understand? How do you create meaningful grammatical utterances, and how do you ensure that they are appropriate for the social situation and interpretive abilities of others? These are but a few of the questions posed by the problem of signification.

When we consider that each utterance we create is unique and creative, that much of what we say we have never said or heard before, and that, on a day-to-day basis, we comprehend statements totally new to us, then we begin to realize how remarkable this process is. Our discussion will begin with an overview of the nature of signs, an examination of how signs represent meaning, and a description of nonverbal code systems. We will then focus on the verbal code, examining how sounds are combined into words and how words are strung together to make sentences. Finally, we will consider pragmatic aspects of language.

SIGNS AND CODES: WHAT ARE THE ELEMENTS OF MESSAGE SYSTEMS?

Every message system, whether linguistic or nonlinguistic, verbal or nonverbal, is a system of signs. As we saw in chapter 1, a *sign* unites an idea or concept with its representation. There are many kinds of signs. Words are signs that unite sounds and concepts; pictures and gestures are signs that use visual representations to convey meaning. Although we often think the word, drawing, or gesture is, itself, the sign, strictly speaking the sign is the *relationship* between concept and representation.

We live in a world saturated with signs. In every act of speech, both linguistic and non-linguistic signs are created and exchanged. As Terence Hawkes points out:

Every speech act includes the transmission of messages through the "languages" of gesture, posture, clothing, hairstyle, perfume, accent, social context, etc., over and above, under and beneath, even at cross-purposes with what words actually *say*. And even when we are not speaking or being spoken to, messages from other "languages" crowd in upon us: horns hoot, lights flash, laws restrain, hoardings proclaim, smells attract or repel, tastes delight or disgust, even the "feel" of objects systematically communicates something meaningful to us.[1]

Humans, then, are immersed in a world of signs: To be human is to be a creator, disseminator, and consumer of signs.

Saussure's Analysis of Signs

The Swiss linguist Saussure was one of the first to analyze the nature of sign systems.[2] As a linguist, he was naturally interested in verbal signs. For Saussure, a sign is that which unites a "sound image" with a concept. The sound component, for example, the auditory stimulus made by uttering the word "tree," he called the *signifier.* The concept—the idea of the physical object tree—was labeled the *signified.* The *sign* was the relationship between the two. Saussure realized that neither the signified nor the signifier could stand alone. A sound without a concept would be meaningless; a concept without a sound would be mute. In describing the relationship between the two, Saussure used the analogy of a piece of paper. One side, he said, was the signified; the other, the signifier. These two parts cannot be separated, for each gives substance and support to the other. Creating a word is like cutting a shape

from this paper. We simultaneously cut into both the conceptual and representational sides.

Saussure emphasized that the relationship between signified and signifier is arbitrary. By arbitrary, he did not mean we are free to create signs in any way we see fit; language cannot exist without a collective contract between members of a society about the meaning and use of signs. "Arbitrary" means there is no natural relationship between the sound image, or signifier, and the object it signifies.

The word "tree," in short, has no "natural" or "tree-like" qualities, and there is no appeal open to a "reality" beyond the structure of the language in order to underwrite it... . The word "tree" means the physical leafy object growing in the earth because the *structure of the language* makes it mean that, and only validates it when it does so.[3]

Peirce's Typology of Sign Types

Saussure's discussion of the arbitrary sign focused on only one kind of sign, the verbal sign, or symbol. For Saussure, a *symbol* is an arbitrary sign that, through conventional agreement, represents an object but bears no natural relationship to it. But not all signs are symbols. Charles Sanders Peirce identified two other ways signs convey meaning: iconically and indexically.[4]

According to Peirce, some signs are *icons*, signs that represent objects by being similar to them. A portrait indicates its subject by resembling it. It is iconic because it is like the object it represents. When we mime a situation we also use iconic signs. Most nonverbal signs belong either to the iconic classification or to Peirce's second class, the index. The *index* is a sign that represents an object by creating an "existential bond" or causal connection with it. A footprint in the sand is an index that someone has been there. Clues are indices of a crime. A blush caused by embarrassment or a smile caused by happiness are both examples of Peirce's second type of sign.

Peirce recognized that signs sometimes hold overlapping membership in different categories. A photograph of a model, for example, is iconic in that it recreates the model's image. It is also an index of the model's presence before the camera. It is a remnant of her being at a particular place on a particular day. It may also contain symbolic elements, if, for example, the model wears a flowing white gown to represent innocence. According to Peirce, we should think of signs as simultaneously being symbolic, iconic, and indexical, rather than as belonging absolutely to one of these classes. Peirce's taxonomy broadens our understanding of meaning systems and shows that nonlinguistic nonintentional signs share equal place with symbols as means of creating information. Modern students of language have pursued this idea, and now there is an entire field of study devoted to understanding the nature of all kinds of signs. Called *semiology*, this field combines the study of language, nonverbal communication, art, literary texts, and cultural and political artifacts.

Digital and Analogic Codes

Signs do not exist in isolation. They exist within systems or *codes* that determine their meaning and uses. Just as signs may differ in structure and purpose, so too may codes. One common category system divides codes into two classes: digital and analogic.[5] To understand how they differ, think about the difference between a picture and a verbal description of an object. A picture is an icon, a "self-explanatory likeness."[6] Through its continuously flowing lines and spatial forms, it indicates an object by resembling it. Although social conventions are used in drawing, objects portrayed iconically usually cross cultural lines. For example, ancient Japanese drawings of animals can be appreciated by modern Westerners, even though the two cultures involved are separated by centuries. A verbal description does not cross cultural lines so readily. Most of us could not pick up a Japanese book and read its words. This is because words are symbolic and carry meaning only in reference to other words. The word "cat" differs from the word "hat" not

because "cat" resembles the soft furry animal or "hat" looks like the head covering, but because the /c/ and /h/ sounds are systematically different from one another. To understand a verbal description of an object we must understand the code system and its distinctions. Words belong to the *digital* code while drawings are part of an *analogic code*.

Another way to see the differences between these two codes is to compare an old-fashioned wristwatch with a digital watch. The old-fashioned watch uses an analogic code; the movement of the hands is analogous to the passage of time. The digital watch, on the other hand, indicates time by presenting a series of discrete numbers. Or consider the thermometer. Thermometers give us both analogic and digital information. The fever thermometer indicates the magnitude of the fever analogically, by showing the degree to which mercury moves up a capillary tube. At the same time, it translates this information into numbers. The numbers 98.6 represent a temperature in digital form, while the mercury is more like a picture of the fever.

Humans have the unique ability to utilize both analogic and digital communication simultaneously. The nonverbal gestures we use are analogic, while the words we use are digital. The distinction is important because, as Paul Watzlawick and his colleagues argue, each code is suited to a different kind of communication. Digital codes best convey information about objects (content information), while analogic codes best convey information about our feelings toward those objects (relational information). "Digital message material is of a much higher degree of complexity, versatility, and abstraction than is analogic material."[7] As such, it is well suited to logical construction and abstract thought. Analogic message materials, on the other hand, always invoke relationships; they are useful for communicating feelings.

Judee Burgoon and Thomas Saine nicely summarize the distinctions between the two codes.[8] Verbal language, they tell us, has several important characteristics not fully shared by the nonverbal code system. First, verbal language (the digital code) is governed by rules for interpreting, ordering, and combining verbal signs. Although efforts have been made to find similar rule structures in nonverbal codes, these attempts have met with little success.[9] Second, digital codes allow a degree of self-reflexiveness that is absent in analogic codes. Language can comment on itself; we can talk about what we have just talked about. Although a nonverbal sign can comment on a verbal message (a wink can invalidate one's words), analogic codes rarely comment on themselves.[10]

Another difference is that nonverbal codes are limited to the present tense, while digital codes allow discussion of past and future as well. Try, for example, to indicate without words or nonverbal emblems that something occurred in the past. You will probably find this impossible. Finally, verbal language lets us reference the negative; it allows us to refer to the absence of something, to talk about something that does not exist. This is impossible in a purely analogical code.[11]

The digital code expresses certain kinds of information that cannot be indicated analogically. The opposite is also true. Analogic codes are more emotionally powerful than digital codes. We therefore often find ourselves at a loss when we try to express feelings and emotions in words. When a person needs comforting, a touch or smile is much more effective than words. Attempts to digitalize analogic communication often fail.

NONVERBAL CODES: HOW CAN NONVERBAL SIGNS BE CLASSIFIED?

A Taxonomy of Nonverbal Behaviors

Mark Knapp, drawing on the work of Paul Ekman and W. V. Friesen, G. L. Trager, and others, offers a comprehensive classification system for the nonverbal dimensions of human communication.[12] Figure 5.1 outlines his taxonomy. As you

I. BODY MOTION OR KINESIC BEHAVIOR
   A. Emblems
   B. Illustrators
   C. Affect Displays
   D. Regulators
   E. Adaptors
II. PHYSICAL CHARACTERISTICS
III. TOUCHING BEHAVIOR
IV. PARALANGUAGE
   A. Voice Qualities
   B. Vocalizations
V. PROXEMICS
VI. ARTIFACTS
VII. ENVIRONMENTAL FACTORS

FIGURE 5.1: Nonverbal dimensions of human communication. (Source: Mark L. Knapp, *Essentials of Nonverbal Communication* [New York: Holt, Rinehart & Winston, 1980].)

can see, Knapp divides the nonverbal domain into seven categories. The first is *kinesic behavior*, which includes body movement, eye behavior, and posture. Nonverbal acts in this category vary a great deal. Some are highly intentional and planned; for example, an obscene gesture or a movement indicating direction or size. Others are expressive and less controlled; for instance, a sigh, a smile, or a friendly glance. Some nonverbal behaviors convey information in a language-like way. Others are purely expressive. Because there are so many different types of kinesic behavior, it helps to subdivide them into emblems, illustrators, affect displays, regulators, and adaptors.

Emblems are nonverbal acts that are symbolic rather than truly analogic. They are arbitrarily determined and tied to specific concepts. "The sign language of the deaf, nonverbal gestures used by television production personnel, signals used by two underwater swimmers, or motions made by two people who are too far apart to make audible signals practical—all these are emblems."[13] Emblems are highly intentional and preplanned and are most often used when verbal channels are blocked or impractical. *Illustrators* are more truly analogic than emblems. They are nonverbal acts that illustrate what is being said. Gestures that indicate the size or shape of an object are examples of illustrators, as are movements that "accent or emphasize a word or phrase; movements which sketch a path of thought."[14] These signs may not be preplanned; however, if they are pointed out to us, then we become aware of using them. They often occur in situations where the verbal code alone is unable to convey meaning efficiently and accurately. Aids to speech, they enhance our use of words.

Affect displays are analogic acts indicating emotional states. Most often they take the form of facial expressions, although the droop of a shoulder or an exuberant stance can convey emotion as readily as a smile or grimace. Affect displays are often outside our awareness, as when we frown or roll our eyes without realizing it. However, they can be intentional, as when we hide our feelings from others. In either case, they are culturally patterned and learned. *Regulators* are "nonverbal acts which maintain and regulate the back and forth nature of speaking and listening between two or more interactants."[15] They indicate what we want the speaker to do, whether it be to continue talking, elaborate or clarify what has been said, or give others a chance to speak. Shifts of posture, head nods, puzzled facial expressions, and averted gaze are all used in this way. Like traffic signals, these signs regulate the flow of talk, allowing smooth turn-taking and indicating the beginnings or endings of talk. "They are like overlearned habits and are almost always involuntary, but we are very much aware of these signals when they are sent by others."[16]

Adaptors are acts that originate in response to some physical or emotional need. They often occur in fragmented form and may arise in situations bearing only a slight resemblance to the situations in which they were originally learned. For example, clenching our fists may have originally been part of an aggressive display; later, we use it whenever we feel angry, even if we do not intend to follow through by hitting or punching. Grooming behaviors (straightening clothes, patting our

hair) are adaptors used when we feel self conscious. Next time you are in a social situation, watch for grooming. You will be amazed how often it occurs. Adaptors are usually not meant to have communicative value but may be triggered by events similar to those in which they were originally learned.

Physical characteristics, such as height, weight, body type, skin and hair color, are the next type of nonverbal sign. Physical attractiveness is an important source of evaluation as Knapp points out:

Physical attractiveness may be influential in determining whether you are sought out; it may have a bearing on whether you are able to persuade or manipulate others; it is often an important factor in the selection of dates and marriage partners; it may determine whether a defendant is deemed guilty or innocent.... it may be a major factor contributing to how others judge your personality, your sexuality, your popularity, your success, and often your happiness.[17]

Touching behavior is another category of nonverbal behavior. How and how often we touch one another is a major source of relational messages. Studies show that many different meanings are conveyed through touch. *Paralanguage* refers to how something is said rather than to the actual verbal content of what is said. Voice qualities such as pitch, rhythm, articulation, and resonance affect the meaning of an utterance and the characteristics we attribute to its sender. Vocalizations such as sighs, groans, and whines are also examples of paralanguage and add to the meaning conveyed by a verbal utterance.

Proxemics refers to our use of social and personal space. How we position ourselves vis-a-vis one another has great communicative value. As an experiment, try moving closer to someone as you talk. Chances are the individual will become uncomfortable and will move backward in order to adjust the amount of personal space being used. If you do this repeatedly and subtly, you can back someone around an entire room.

Artifacts are the objects we own and control that give others information about us. Articles of dress, cosmetics, or status symbols such as cars, watches, and jewelry make strong statements about who and what we are. Finally, the nature of our *environments* and the objects within them affect the nature of our communicative behaviors. We act differently in a cathedral than in a country-western bar. What we say in one place is different from what we say in another.

Dimensions of Nonverbal Meaning: Liking, Dominance, and Responsiveness

Albert Mehrabian suggests that three types of meaning are conveyed nonverbally: liking, dominance and power, and responsiveness.[18] *Liking* is generally conveyed by the degree of immediacy we show others. By leaning forward, touching, making eye contact, and the like, we increase nonverbal immediacy, and thus liking. Power or *dominance* is also signaled by nonverbal actions. Individuals who feel in command generally use relaxed body posture and expansive gestures, while individuals who feel subservient show body tension and tend to take up less space.

Finally, a general level of *responsiveness* can be read from nonverbal behavior. The amount of facial expressiveness, the rate at which you speak, and the volume of speech indicate to another your level of emotional arousal. You can test this by observing people in conversation. It should be easy to tell, simply from observation, whether or not they like each other, who is in charge, and how much enthusiasm and arousal they generate.

The Relationship of Verbal and Nonverbal Codes

Although nonverbal behaviors may be unaccompanied by verbal utterances, they often occur together. Burgoon and Saine present six ways that the two codes work in conjunction: redundancy, substitution, complementation, emphasis, contradiction, and regulation.[19]

Redundancy, or message repetition, is one way the nonverbal code is used in conjunction with the verbal. For example, in giving directions we may repeat part of the verbal message by using an illustrator to point the way. Nonverbal signs may also *substitute* for certain parts of the verbal message. When someone asks us how our day was, we can simply sigh and roll our eyes, substituting these affect displays for verbal descriptions.

Complementation occurs when we include nonverbal cues in a verbal message. Responsiveness cues, for example, complement a verbal message by indicating how we feel about what we say. *Emphasis* is a kind of nonverbal underlining. Using vocal emphasis, we italicize parts of the verbal message that are particularly important.

Another relationship between verbal and nonverbal codes is that of *contradiction*. By saying, "I love you," in a bored or exasperated tone, we negate the verbal meaning of the statement. Finally, regulators can be used to control and *regulate* ongoing action. These are a few ways that nonverbal cues enhance or negate verbal messages. Without them, verbal messages would be stilted and unemotional; with them, they are rich in feeling and meaning.

Some argue that most of the social meaning of communicative messages is carried through nonverbal channels. Mehrabian has assigned weights to the verbal, vocal, and facial aspects of communication, arguing that verbal channels account for only .07 of social meaning, while the vocal and facial channels account for .38 and .55, respectively. This research has been widely quoted and as widely misinterpreted. Research Abstract 5.1 presents the results of two studies that led to this claim. The figures arose in a highly artificial, experimental context. In actual interaction we can expect the verbal element to play a larger role, and, certainly, when we want to convey abstract, logical information, the verbal code is the most useful. Still, much information is conveyed nonverbally. Rather than specifying percentages, it is probably safer to assume that certain kinds of information are conveyed verbally and other kinds nonverbally. To test this yourself, watch

RESEARCH ABSTRACT 5.1 How Much Social Meaning Is Nonverbal?

In 1967, Mehrabian published two highly influential studies. His *purpose* was to determine the relative impact of verbal and nonverbal channels when used together and to see how much meaning is due to vocal, facial, or verbal cues. He hypothesized that nonverbal channels would convey more meaning than verbal channels, under certain conditions.

In the first study, Mehrabian compared content meaning with meaning based on vocal tone. His *method* was to present three kinds of words (words with positive, neutral, and negative verbal meanings) in three different tones (indicating liking, neutrality, or disliking). All possible combinations were presented so that, in most of the conditions, the verbal and vocal channels were inconsistent with one another. By asking subjects to rate the speaker's attitude toward a hypothetical receiver, he felt he could determine if subjects responded primarily to the verbal or the vocal meaning.

His first task was to choose the words. On the basis of pretest ratings he chose as positive the words: honey, thanks, and dear; as neutral: maybe, really, and oh; and as negative: don't, brute, and terrible. He then recorded two speakers saying each word three times using positive, neutral, or negative tones. One third of the subjects were asked to attend only to word meanings, one third, only to vocal meanings, and one third to all of the information.

The *results* were as follows. In the first condition (attend to word meanings), the verbal channel had the largest effect. In the second (attend to tone), the vocal channel was most important, although content also played a part. In the third condition (attend to both), the effects of tone were primary.

Mehrabian concluded that attitude judgments of single word inconsistent messages are based primarily on vocal tone.

In the second study, Mehrabian added a third channel, the face. Here he chose one word: maybe. He recorded two speakers saying the word positively, neutrally, or negatively. He accompanied their tape with photographs displaying positive, neutral, or negative facial expressions. Subjects were exposed to all combinations of vocal tone and facial expression. They then estimated speaker's attitude. The effects of the facial component were significantly greater than those of the vocal.

Mehrabian concluded, from these studies, that "the combined effect of simultaneous verbal, vocal, and facial attitude communications is a weighted sum of their independent effects—with the coefficients of .07, .38, and .55, respectively." Although it is unclear how he arrived at these numbers, they have been widely accepted and interpreted as indicating that 93 percent of all communicative meaning is nonverbal. This interpretation is not warranted by the studies, which used one-word messages in a laboratory setting.

To conclude that in all cases vocal and facial cues provide more information than verbal cues is an odd conclusion, one that illustrates how careful we should be in extrapolating from experimental research.

Source: Study 1: Albert Mehrabian and Morton Wiener, "Decoding of Inconsistent Communications," *Journal of Personality and Social Psychology*, 6 (1967), 109–14. Study 2: Albert Mehrabian and Susan R. Ferris, "Influence of Attitudes from Nonverbal Communication in Two Channels," *Journal of Consulting Psychology*, 31 (1967), 248–52.

Communicative intentions: People form intentions toward one another			
Language Level	*Description of Level*	*Unit of Analysis*	*Theoretical Approach*
Pragmatic level of language	Coherent discourse with communicative purpose is created by combining individual utterances according to pragmatic rules	Basic unit is the text or (in conversation) the turn	Theoretical approach is Functional–Actional
Syntactic level of language	Propositional meaning is conveyed by combining and ordering individual units of meaning according to grammatical	Basic unit is the sentence or utterance	Theoretical approach is Transformational– Generative
Morphemic level of language	Discrete units capable of conveying meaning are created by combining individual classes of sounds according to morphemic rules	Basic unit is the morpheme	Theoretical approach is Structural– Descriptive
Phonemic level of language	Classes of sounds which are identical for the purpose of conveying meaning are created by combining sound variants according to phonemic rules	Basic unit is	
Undifferentiated stream of sounds: People engage in linguistic sound–making behavior			

FIGURE 5.2:   Levels of linguistic analysis: Conveying intentions through linguistic behavior

television with the sound turned off or observe people who are conversing out of earshot. Try to determine how much and what kind of information is conveyed and how much and what kind is missing.

THE VERBAL CODE: WHAT ARE THE COMPONENTS OF LANGUAGE?

Despite the importance of the nonverbal code, we can agree that most intentional communication is conveyed through spoken language. It is hard to imagine how we could communicate in a fully human way without using the verbal code. While study of the nonverbal code has only recently become popular, theoretical examination of the verbal code began centuries ago. A full examination of classical theories of language could fill volumes; this section will present only a small sample of language theories. Figure 5.2 provides a framework for this discussion.

Spoken language is highly complex and may be analyzed in different ways. At the most basic and molecular level (indicated at the bottom of Fig. 5.2), spoken language exists as a stream of sounds. The nature of these sounds, features that distinguish them from one another, and rules for correctly combining them into larger units form a level of language theory called the *phonemic level*. Theorists consider classes of sounds to be the building blocks of language. These classes of sounds are called *phonemes*. Phonemes do not exist in isolation, nor are they independently capable of carrying meaning. Only when assigned conventionalized meanings and combined into larger units (words, or, more technically, *morphemes*) do they function as signs. Thus, the next highest level of theoretical analysis is the *morphemic level*. Here, theorists try to understand the structure of the basic units of meaning in language. The approach that theorists use most frequently at both the morphemic and phonemic levels is *structural-descriptive*. Their goal is to describe the features that distinguish each unit and to discover the structure of relationships between them. This approach is like the one used by physical scientists. The physicist or chemist who analyzes a physical object into discrete elements, who describes the unique features of each element, and who then tries to understand the laws governing the combination of these elements is essentially using a structural approach.

Though the structuralist approach allows a great deal of precision in describing the phonemic and morphemic levels of language, it falls short of explaining how meaningful sentences are generated. If our interest lies not with isolated words or classes of sounds but with grammatical sentences, then we move up to the next level, the *syntactic level*. Here, the basic unit is the sentence or utterance. For syntactic theorists, or grammarians, the goal of language theory is to understand how sentences are generated, to establish the rules governing sentence construction. The approach most often used is *transformational-generative*. Generative linguists are less concerned with how sentences are used than in how they are formed, for they see language as an ideal system of grammatical rules, rules only imperfectly realized in speech communication.

To understand the use of language in communicative interaction, we move to the next highest level, the *pragmatic level*. The basic units are units of communicative intent. Coherent and purposeful discourse is analyzed by looking at units such as the text, the turn, or the move. The general approach is *functional-actional*. John Searle argues that this is the most appropriate level for studying language, since a study of the formal features of language apart from their use in communication would be like a "formal study of the currency and credit system of economies without a study of the role of currency and credit in economic transactions."[20] The pragmatic level is concerned with language in coordinated communicative interaction. In the rest of this chapter, we will examine these three levels of analysis and their corresponding theoretical approaches.

THE MORPHO-PHONEMIC LEVEL: WHAT ARE THE COMPONENTS OF SOUNDS AND WORDS?

The Structuralist-Descriptive Approach to Language

Theorists interested in studying language at the level of individual sounds and signs view language as an idealized system of relationships. Although they recognize that in actual practice languages change over time, they believe that underlying these changes there is a stable discoverable structure that remains constant. It is this structure that Saussure labeled *langue*.

Language has two aspects: *langue*, the underlying stable structure, and *parole*, the manifestation of langue that occurs in actual speech. As Hawkes suggests, "The nature of the *langue* lies beyond, and determines, the nature of each manifestation of *parole*, yet it has no concrete existence of its own, except in the piecemeal manifestation that speech affords."[21] Saussure, and the structural linguists who followed him, believe language theory should focus on the nature of the langue. They are less interested in actual speech behavior or communicative interactions. Instead, they are primarily interested in the structure of an ideal language system itself.

A major tenet of structuralist theory is that each element in an idealized language system acquires its unique identity and meaning through its relationship to other elements within the system rather than to an outside reference. A word, for example, is meaningful not because it is like something in the real world of objects but rather because of its place within the language system. A sound is identifiable simply because it is systematically different from other sounds. The only way to understand the elements of langue is to understand their relationship to each other and to the system as a whole.

Saussure believed two kinds of relationships exist among elements of the language system: *paradigmatic* and *syntagmatic*. Paradigmatic relationships are based on patterns of contrasts or differences. For example, sounds are distinguishable only because they contrast with one another; words have their meanings because they are different from other words. A syntagmatic relationship is based on the kinds of combinations the system allows. Certain sounds can be combined, while others cannot. Certain words follow one another, while other sequences do not. To understand the language system's structure, we must understand how the elements within it differ from one another, and we must also understand the rules governing their combinations.

The Sound System of Language

The first step in studying the sound and meaning systems of language is to identify the smallest unit of sound. What is this unit? The average person would probably answer, "A letter of the alphabet." This answer would be close to the mark but incorrect, because letters are mere graphic representations for classes of sounds, and writing systems do not scientifically represent sounds. Although the English writing system is designed to represent our language's sound system, it does so very imperfectly. For example, a single letter can represent several different sound classes (compare the "c" in century and in car-

nal), and different letters can represent the same sounds (compare the "k" in karat with the "c" in carrot). Our system of representing sounds by letters is so inexact that the word fish could be spelled *ghoti*, if we use the "*gh* sound in cou*gh*, the *o* in w*o*men, and the *ti* in na*ti*onal."[22]

The phoneme, and not the letter, is identified as the minimal unit of the sound system. *Phonemes* are classes of sound identical in terms of their ability to signal differences in content within the system. In English, "cat" and "hat" carry different meanings. What makes the difference is the /c/ and /h/ sounds; /c/ and /h/ are therefore different phonemes. One way to identify phonemes is to look for words like cat and hat, or pin and bin. These words differ by a single sound and are called minimal pairs. When we find a minimal pair, we know the sounds that differentiate them are phonemes.

Phonemes like /c/ and /h/ and /p/ and /b/ are referred to as classes of sounds because each time we say a phoneme we pronounce it slightly differently. These variations in production, however, are unimportant for all practical purposes. So, we class all the slightly different ways of saying a given sound together as a single phoneme. The structuralist linguist faces the task of hunting for all the sound classes within the language.

While identifying all of the phonemes in the language is the theorist's first task, the second task is to analyze the features that define them. Distinctive features analysis describes how one phoneme differs from another. For example, the major difference between the /p/ and /b/ phonemes is the amount of vocal cord vibration that occurs when these sounds are made. When we say /b/, our vocal cords vibrate; when we say /p/, they do not. You can feel this difference by placing your hand on your throat and making both sounds. This distinctive feature is called voicing.

A feature like voicing is one of the distinctive features of English. Each language uses a slightly different set of distinctive features. Some examples of distinctive features include whether a sound is a vowel or consonant, where the tongue is placed when the sound is made, or whether the sound is nasalized. Although there is no space here to describe the definitions of each feature, any introductory phonology text should discuss them in more detail.

Paradigmatic contrasts such as those described in distinctive features analysis are not the only kind of relationship existing between sounds. Sounds are not isolated; they are combined with one another. Yet, within any particular language, only certain combinations are permissible. Another task of phonemic theory is "to formulate the syntagmatic laws governing phonemic combination: roughly, laws of the form, phonemes with certain features do not occur in a certain position in the neighborhood of phonemes with certain other features."[23] For example, in English, a word beginning with "ft" is unlikely to occur. A structural description of language's sound system, then, involves the isolation of basic units, their description in terms of paradigmatic differences, and the discovery of syntagmatic rules of combination.

The Morphemic System of Language

Morphemic analysis uses methods and concepts similar to phonemic analysis. Its goal is to find the minimal unit of meaning within the language, "the smallest units in the expression system that can be correlated with specific meanings in the content system."[24] Such a unit is the *morpheme*. Just as /c/ and /r/ are separate phonemes, so "cat" and "rat" are separate morphemes. Individual words are morphemes because they have different meanings, but smaller units such as prefixes and suffixes are also morphemes. For example, adding an "s" to the end of "cat" changes its meaning significantly. The "s" is a morpheme that signals plurality. Just as a single phoneme is a class of sounds, so a morpheme is also a class of individual variants. The plurality morpheme [Z] can be made in a number of different ways. It includes the [-s] that distinguishes cat and cats, the [-z] in dogs, and the [-iz] in foxes.

Syntagmatic relationships also exist between morphemes, with rules governing their permissible combinations and contexts. Nouns and verbs, for example, occur in different contexts. A noun can precede a verb ("the cat caught the rat"), but verbs do not combine with other verbs in the same way. "The caught ran after the jumped" is nonsensical.

The contribution of structural-descriptive theory to an understanding of the sound and sign systems of language cannot be overemphasized. We have only scratched the surface in this brief overview of phonemic and morphemic theory. However, for most of us whose major interest is communication, language is not interesting until words and sounds are combined into sentences and are used in actual interaction. The next theory we will discuss brings us closer to this level. We begin with a consideration of the works of Noam Chomsky who tried to describe the cognitive processes by which individuals produce sentences.

THE SYNTACTIC LEVEL: HOW ARE SENTENCES PRODUCED?

In 1957, when Noam Chomsky introduced his theory of syntactic structures, he revolutionized our way of thinking about language. Although the structuralist approach resulted in an exact description of language's components, Chomsky argued it could not be the basis of a complete language theory because it failed to describe the cognitive processes used to generate sentences. He believed the goal of language theory is to explain a person's ability to produce and understand meaning at the level of the sentence. For Chomsky, language must be viewed against the backdrop of the individual's total mental life.[25]

Chomsky's inquiry was prompted by the question, "How can new sentences, sentences we have never seen or heard before, be produced and understood?" For example, you can understand the sentences that make up this paragraph, although you probably have never seen these words in exactly this order before. How is this possible? Because these sentences are new, it cannot be a matter of rote learning. According to Chomsky, if we do not learn sentences by rote, then there must be another internal mechanism allowing their creation and recognition. He suggested that we have internalized rules that let us generate sentences and that these rules are somehow innate.

Chomsky saw language theory's goal as the construction of *grammars*: theories about the rules of language that allow its users to distinguish sentences from nonsentences. The linguist's grammar is an explanation of what a native speaker must "know" in order to generate all and only well-formed utterances, a scientific theory of what goes on in the speaker's head as he or she produces grammatical sentences. Chomsky sums up this notion as follows:

My own view is this. We may imagine an ideal homogeneous speech community in which there is no variation in style or dialect. We may suppose further that knowledge of the language of this speech community is uniformly represented in the mind of each of its members, as one element in a system of cognitive structures. Let us refer to this representation of the knowledge of these ideal speaker-hearers as the grammar of language. We must be careful to distinguish the grammar, regarded as the structure postulated in the mind, from the linguist's grammar which is an explicit articulated theory that attempts to express precisely the rules and principles of the grammar in the mind of the ideal speaker-hearer... . The [speaker's] grammar of the language determines the properties of each of the sentences of the language... . To introduce a technical term, we say that the grammar "generates" the sentences it describes and their structural descriptions.[26]

Several points are important. First, Chomsky realized that speakers in different communities follow slightly different grammars and, within a single community, not all show the same amount of language mastery. Does this mean that the linguist must create an individual grammar for each person or group? Chomsky answers this question in the negative by hypothesizing an ideal speaker-listener in a homogeneous speech community. It

is the knowledge of this hypothetical individual that a grammar describes.

Second, we know that when a person speaks factors such as memory or attention span, fatigue, emotional involvement, and physiological state affect linguistic performance.[27] The utterances that occur (speech *performance*) may deviate from the underlying grammar (linguistic *competence*). Although actual speech performance is the only clue we have to the speaker's grammatical competence, it must be distinguished from it, for the sentences we mean to say are not always the ones we manage to say. The distinction between performance and competence is similar to that made by Saussure between langue and parole.

There is one final and controversial point about Chomsky's theory. He believes that the ability to use grammar involves innate cognitive structures that are part of our biological endowment. Chomsky calls this fundamental cognitive state "universal grammar." It is "a system that is genetically determined at the initial state and is specified, sharpened, articulated, and refined under the conditions set by experience, to yield the particular grammars that are represented in the steady state attainment."[28] For Chomsky, language learning, and learning in general, is the growth of genetically programmed cognitive structures under the triggering and shaping influences of the environment.[29] He uses an analogy to physical development. The organism does not learn to reach puberty; it does so because it is so programmed. Environmental factors such as nutrition, however, can markedly affect the onset of puberty. In the same way, humans have the potential for language, but the environment in which we are reared specifies the nature and manner of language learned. The innateness hypothesis has been criticized by many theorists, especially behavioral learning theorists, who think it neglects the effects of environmental and societal influences and limits human individuality. For Chomsky, however, the innate endowment does not limit us, but allows us the possibility of a rich

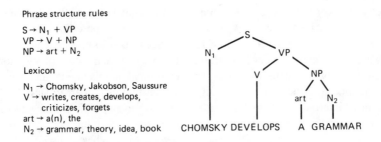

Phrase structure rules

$S \rightarrow N_1 + VP$
$VP \rightarrow V + NP$
$NP \rightarrow art + N_2$

Lexicon

$N_1 \rightarrow$ Chomsky, Jakobson, Saussure
$V \rightarrow$ writes, creates, develops,
    criticizes, forgets
$art \rightarrow$ a(n), the
$N_2 \rightarrow$ grammar, theory, idea, book

FIGURE 5.3:   A simple phrase-structure grammar

and creative mental life and gives us the ability to develop as individuals capable of free choice.

In what follows, we will examine Chomsky's ideas about the innate cognitive structures that allow language processing, and we will study the grammatical rules that he hypothesized make up linguistic competence. Because Chomsky is one of the most important theorists of the twentieth century, his work, although somewhat technical, merits attention.

A Structural Analysis of the Sentence

Although Chomsky went beyond a structural description to a generative one, he did not abandon consideration of structure. He recognized, as traditional grammarians had, that to understand a sentence we must understand its structure. Every sentence can be broken down into its constituents: nouns, verbs, clauses, and phrases. The simple sentence, "Chomsky develops a grammar," is a combination of subparts. Some parts are more closely related than others. To use Saussure's term, some have a stronger syntagmatic relationship than others. Intuitively, we know that, if we divide this sentence into two units, the noun "Chomsky" will be one and the verb phrase "develops a grammar" will be the other. We know this because each part can be replaced by a single word and yet leave a meaningful sentence. For example, we can substitute "He" for "Chomsky" and "theorized" for "developed a theory," and we

still retain the original meaning. If we divide the sentence in another way, say between "Chomsky developed a" and "grammar," then we will be hard pressed to find single word substitutes.[30]

The sentence can be further subdivided. The verb phrase can be divided into the constituents "develops" and "a grammar," and the latter can be separated into "a" and "grammar." These divisions show us the sentence's underlying structure, which consists of a hierarchical ordering of parts. One way to indicate sentence structure is to use a tree diagram. Figure 5.3 gives an example. Look at the right side of the figure. The S stands for the sentence as a whole. NP means "noun phrase," N means "noun," VP means "verb phrase," and art means "article." The diagram is called a phrase-structure diagram. The grammar resulting from this analysis is a *phrase-structure grammar*.

Knowing the meaning of a sentence involves knowing its structure. This becomes more evident if we turn to another sentence, "Chomsky and Jakobson are visiting linguists." This sentence has two possible meanings. It could be telling us who Chomsky and Jakobson are: linguists from out-of-town. On the other hand, it could be telling us what they are doing: visiting some of their linguist friends. The meaning we assign to this sentence depends on the structure we believe it has. Because this sentence is ambiguous, it can have two different phrase structures. Figure 5.4 illustrates the tree diagrams for both meanings of the sentence. The fact that we recognize this sentence

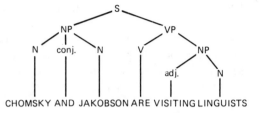 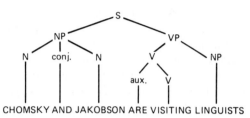

FIGURE 5.4: Two tree diagrams for the same ambiguous sentence

as ambiguous means that we "know" at some deeper level the structures of its meanings.

Generative Mechanisms in Grammar

The tree diagrams in Figs. 5.3 and 5.4 allow us to identify underlying sentence structures. A grammar that does no more than this, however, is rather weak. According to Chomsky, a grammar should generate new sentences in addition to analyzing old ones. A true grammar should specify *generative rules* that can create grammatical structures and fill them in with actual words. Chomsky hypothesized that we use what he called "rewrite rules" to produce sentences. If you refer back to the left side of Fig. 5.3, you will see a simplified generative grammar that lets us produce several sentences including the familiar "Chomsky develops a grammar." The arrows should be read as "may be rewritten as." Thus, the first rule says a sentence (S) may be rewritten as a noun (N_1) and a verb phrase (VP). The VP may then be rewritten as a verb (V) and a noun phrase (NP); the noun phrase can be rewritten as an article (art) and an object (N_2). Finally, we can substitute words for each grammatical part; for example, the word "Chomsky" for N_1, "develops" for V, "a" for the article, and "grammar" for N_2. The grammar in Fig. 5.3 lets us create sentences such as "Saussure criticizes the book" and "Jakobson forgets the ideas" as well as "Chomsky develops a grammar." As a grammar's vocabulary

grows and as its rewrite rules become more complex, more elaborately structured sentences can be generated. Chomsky believed we use rewrite rules to create structures, and we plug in words to these structures. We are not consciously aware of these rules, yet we "know" them; otherwise, we could neither create grammatical sentences nor recognize ambiguous ones.

Transformational Aspects of Grammar

Phrase-structure grammar only allows the generation of simple present tense declarative sentences. How do we produce more complex constructions? To account for additional grammatical forms, Chomsky introduces another set of rules: *transformational rules*. A transformational rule lets us rearrange or transform the elements in a basic declarative sentence to ask questions, construct passives, change tenses, and so on. Chomsky believes humans begin by generating a basic declarative sentence and then rearrange the elements to make other kinds of sentences.

How do transformation rules work? Take, for example, the sentence, "Chomsky develops a grammar," and consider how it can be transformed into the question, "What did Chomsky develop?" As Dan Slobin explains, "In transformational terms, a question of this sort is formed by replacing the object noun phrase by an appropriate question word and moving that question word to the front of the sentence."[31] The following mental processes occur in the individual formulating the question. First, "Chomsky develops a grammar" is generated. Then, the object "grammar" is changed into a question marker, yielding "Chomsky develops what?" Through displacement, the word order is then changed to "What Chomsky develops?" By adding the auxiliary "did," we get the final form, "What did Chomsky develop?" Of course, we do not puzzle all of this out consciously. The process is instantaneous and outside our awareness.

The final form of the sentence, ready for utterance, is what Chomsky calls a *surface structure*. These structures are derived from the simpler structures originally formed by phrase-structure rules. These he calls *deep structures*. The deep structure contains the meaning of the sentence. The surface structure contains the actual words and constructions we use. The ambiguity found in the sentence "Chomsky and Jakobson are visiting linguists" exists partly because a single surface structure may come from two different deep structures. The only way to know what this sentence means is to consider which deep structure is intended.

Chomsky believed that three subsystems must be used to generate sentences: the syntactic system, the semantic system, and the phonological system. So far, we have been discussing the grammatical or syntactic component that can be summarized as follows. We start with a base that consists of phrase structure rewrite rules and a word list or lexicon. The rewrite rules produce "preterminal strings" into which we insert words from the lexicon. The lexicon includes words and enough semantic information so that we can avoid producing syntactically correct but meaningless strings such as "colorless green ideas sleep furiously." The result of this initial process is the deep structure. Transformational rules are then applied to create the surface structure form of the sentence. To produce actual sound, we run the surface structure though the phonological component, applying phonological rules to translate grammatical structure into strings of sounds.

Most of Chomsky's attention was focused on the syntactic component. The phonological component was of only peripheral interest, and the semantic component was not well defined. In later versions, Chomsky modified his theory by introducing trace-grammar, an attempt to deal with some of the problems of meaning and logical form.

Summary of Chomsky's Theory

We can sum up Chomsky's thought in four principles. First, humans have an innate capacity for language. Language behavior is not achieved through rote learning. Instead, humans have a built in potential to use language, a capacity enhanced by direct experience but existing apart from it. Second, actual linguistic performance is based on linguistic competence. Chomsky believes that there are underlying structures in the human mind that allow linguistic behavior, and these structures he calls linguistic competence. Third, to understand language competence, we must understand the mental rules governing language production and reception. A theory of language is a description of the rules that generate well-formed utterances. Finally, in the actual production of linguistic forms, speakers move from deep-structure meanings to surface-structure forms. If we keep these principles in mind, we can understand and appreciate the originality of Chomsky's approach. Although technically complex, transformational-generative grammar is an interesting and creative example of theory building.

Chomsky was very clear that he wanted to describe language, not communication. As students of communication, however, we want to understand not only how sentences are generated but how they are used. For this we turn to the pragmatic level of language and to functional-actional theories.

PRAGMATICS: HOW IS LANGUAGE USED IN COMMUNICATION?

The pragmatic investigation of language use is a growing field of study. Many pragmatic theories are being proposed, addressing questions such as the following: How do people affect each other through words? How can we understand a sentence's communicative implications? and How do we create and sustain coordinated meanings?

The last section of this chapter presents three theories that address these questions: John Searle's theory of the speech act, Barnett Pearce and Vernon Cronen's theory of the coordinated management of meaning, and H. P. Grice's theory of conversational maxims. It also introduces some of the questions addressed by a field of study known as conversation analysis.

Searle's Speech Act Theory

Searle believes that a theory of language must be a theory of communication. Since linguistic communication is always an intentional act, language theory must analyze utterances in terms of their intentions. For Searle, every utterance contains two kinds of content: propositional and intentional. To explain the difference, he examines four sentences: (1) Sam smokes habitually. (2) Does Sam smoke habitually? (3) Sam, smoke habitually. (4) Would that Sam smoked habitually.[32] In Chomsky's terms, each is a transformation of a single deep structure. In Searle's analysis, what distinguishes each of these surface structures is that each accomplishes a different *speech act*. In the first case, the speaker makes an assertion or, perhaps, criticism of Sam. In the second, the speaker asks a question. In the third, the speaker issues a command and, in the fourth, expresses a wish. A complete speech act includes, in addition to the proposition made on the content level, the speaker's intention as well. Examples of speech acts are requesting, asserting, questioning, thanking, warning, promising, and so on.

For Searle, all speech acts are governed by conventional rules called *constitutive rules*. These rules define the conditions under which a particular utterance counts as a particular speech act.[33] Speakers must know these rules to create and interpret speech acts. This knowledge, however, is implicit rather than explicit. According to Searle, language theory should concern itself with uncovering the implicit rules of the language game. For example, take the speech act of promising. Searle sets down five rules to illuminate what it means to promise. These rules are examples of language theory at the speech act level.[34] In reading them, remember that Pr stands for promise, T for a sentence or larger text, S indicates the speaker, H indicates the hearer, and A is an act of the speaker.

The first rule may be expressed as follows: "Pr is to be uttered only in the context of a sentence (or larger stretch of discourse), the utterance of which predicates some future act A of the speaker S." This rule is called the *propositional content rule*. It describes the content of a promise. For example, if I promise to return a book I borrowed from you, I do so by generating a sentence that tells you about a future act I will perform (returning the book).

Preparatory rules specify the conditions under which a given speech act (in this case a promise) is made. The first preparatory rule is: "Pr is to be uttered only if the hearer H would prefer S's doing A to his not doing A, and S believes H would prefer S's doing A to his not doing A." If I promise to return your book, I must believe that you want it back. Generally, we do not promise to do things others dislike. It is unlikely I would promise to ruin or lose your book or to return it if you clearly no longer wanted it. Although we sometimes hear, "You'll be sorry, I promise you," such utterances are threats not promises.

The third rule outlined by Searle is also preparatory and may be stated, "Pr is to be uttered only if it is not obvious to both S and H that S will do A in the normal course of events." Promises are generally made only when it is possible the action may not be completed. I promise to return the book because we both know that sometimes books are lost or kept. It is nonsensical for me to promise to continue breathing; in the normal course of events, I will do so anyway.

The next kind of rule is called a *sincerity rule*. Such a rule specifies the speaker's intentions when making a promise. This rule may be stated, "Pr is to be uttered only if S intends to do A." If I do never intend to return your book, saying I will return it is not a promise but a lie. The fifth and final rule is the *essential rule*. It can be stated, "The utterance of Pr counts as the undertaking of an obligation to do A." Whenever I make a promise, I obligate myself.

For every speech act, similar rules exist. Communicating is like playing a game in which each speech act is a move and the rules dictate each permissible move. If we make inappropriate moves, then we violate the rules of the game. Speech act theory writes the manual describing how the game of communication is played. At some level we "know" the rules of the communication game, just as we "know" the rules of grammar and phonology. We know how to promise, and we know what it entails. We can interact with one another because these rules exist as matters of convention. Without them, coordinated and meaningful social activity would be impossible. (Fig. 5.5 lists the rules for requesting, asserting, questioning, greeting, and congratulating.)

When we communicate we succeed only to the extent that we recognize each others' intentions. For example, when you utter the words, "Have you got the time?" I must recognize this not merely as a question but as a request. If I interpret it as a question, I simply answer, "Yes," and go about my business. My response fails to account for your intention, and our interaction leads to frustration. But, if I correctly interpret your utterance as a request, and I know the rules of making requests, then I will give you the time. Similarly, if I tell you, "You look great today," you need to know if my comment was an assertion, a compliment, or a joke. Only when the meaning of the

speech act is uncovered will communication succeed.

Criticism of Searle's Theory

Searle's analysis is valuable because it tells us that syntactic meaning is not the only kind carried by a unit of discourse. An interaction's full meaning must include recognition of the speech act contained in the utterances exchanged. Searle also enlarges our understanding of the nature of rules. He sees human communication as a rule-governed activity and attempts to specify the nature of these rules. Finally, he defines language study as interactional rather than individual. Although he emphasizes the importance of speech acts, he does not describe how we interpret speech acts nor how we, as speakers, choose one speech act over another. The next theory, coordinated management of meaning, investigates how meanings are assigned to speech acts and how speakers coordinate these acts as they communicate.

The Coordinated Management of Meaning

The coordinated management of meaning (CMM) is a theory developed over a number of years by several communication scholars. Its chief architects are Barnett Pearce, Vernon Cronen, and Forrest Conklin, although other researchers have added their contributions. Because this theory has grown since Pearce's original work in the mid-1970s, it's a particularly interesting example of the process of theory building.[35] Although it is beyond the scope of this text to highlight all the recent changes, anyone interested in seeing the theory evolve can find more information in articles listed in the endnotes.[36]

As the name suggests, CMM describes how we create and sustain meanings during interaction. It explains how communicators "transform raw sensory data into meanings and meanings into actions."[37] CMM is about two separate but

		Request	*Assert, state (that), affirm*	*Question*[1]
Types of rule	Propositional content	Future act *A* of *H*.	Any proposition *p*.	Any proposition or propositional function.
	Preparatory	1. *H* is able to do *A*. *S* believes *H* is able to do *A*. 2. It is not obvious to both *S* and *H* that *H* will do *A* in the normal course of events of his own accord.	1. *S* has evidence (reasons, etc.) for the truth of *p*. 2. It is not obvious to both *S* and *H* that *H* knows (does not need to be reminded of, etc.) *p*.	1. *S* does not know 'the answer', i.e., does not know if the proposition is true, or, in the case of the propositional function, does not know the information needed to complete the proposition truly (but see comment below). 2. It is not obvious to both *S* and *H* that *H* will provide the information at that time without being asked.
	Sincerity	*S* wants *H* to do *A*.	S believes *p*.	S wants this information.
	Essential	Counts as an attempt to get *H* to do *A*.	Counts as an undertaking to the effect that *p* represents an actual state of affairs.	Counts as an attempt to elicit this information from *H*.
	Comment:	*Order* and *command* have the additional preparatory rule that *S* must be in a position of authority over *H*. *Command* probably does not have the 'pragmatic' condition requiring non-obviousness. Furthermore in both, the authority relationship infects the essential condition because the utterance counts as an attempt to get *H* to do *A in virtue of the authority of S over H.*	Unlike *argue* these do not seem to be essentially tied to attempting to convince. Thus, "I am simply stating that *p* and not attempting to convince you" is acceptable, but "I am arguing that *p* and not attempting to convince you" sounds inconsistent.	There are two kinds of questions, (*a*) real questions, (*b*) exam questions. In real questions *S* wants to know (find out) the answer; in exam questions, *S* wants to know if *H* knows.

FIGURE 5.5: Some common types of speech acts. (From John R. Searle, *Speech Acts: An Essay in the Philosophy of Language* [Cambridge: Cambridge University Press, 1969].)

related problems: how individuals organize and manage meanings and how they coordinate their meanings with one another. CMM offers the following propositions: (1) Individual meanings are organized into hierarchical systems. (2) Individual meaning systems consist of sets of interlocking rules. (3) Through interaction, individual rule systems become intermeshed to form coordinated interpersonal systems. We will examine each of these propositions in turn.

CULTURAL PATTERNS
↕
LIFE SCRIPTS
↕
CONTRACTS
↕
EPISODES
↕
SPEECH ACTS
↕
CONTENT
↑
RAW SENSORY DATA

FIGURE 5.6: The CMM hierarchy of meaning

The Hierarchical Organization of Meaning. According to CMM, communication is influenced by several levels of meaning, each differing in degree of abstraction. Each level is hierarchically embedded within another, so higher levels help us interpret meaning at lower levels. Figure 5.6 lists seven levels of meaning.

At level 1, communication behaviors occur as *raw sensory data*, or uninterpreted visual and auditory stimuli. At this level, the stimuli have no meaning because they have not yet been interpreted by another. You can understand the nature of level 1 data if you have ever visited a country where the people speak an unfamiliar language. In this situation you have no way of punctuating the sounds you hear into meaningful chunks.[38] Pearce and others remind us that "regardless of the loftiness of an idea or the subtlety of the style, the only commodity exchanged by communicators are physical disturbances in the environment (e.g., soundwaves, light waves, etc.) transmitted to the brain by a physiochemical process."[39]

At level 2, communication takes on *content* meaning. Raw sensory data are converted into information, often in the form of predications about "things" and their relations. The statement "You're looking good," for example, conveys content information about your physical state but conveys as yet no instructions about the intentions of the speaker. To understand content fully we need level 3 information. Level 3 adds additional meaning by specifying the *speech acts*

being performed. Speech acts tell us about the intention of the speaker. The statement "You're looking good" may accomplish different acts: it may convey information, compliment, comfort, condescend, or even insult. To understand communication fully, we must know the meaning of the speech act being performed. At level 3, content gains significance "as an act done by the speaker to the hearer."[40]

Level 4 meanings help us to interpret a speech act by telling us the *episode* in which it occurs. The sociologist John Gumperz suggests that conversations can be divided into episodic units or "discourse stages."

Members of all societies recognize certain communicative routines which they view as distinct wholes, separate from other types of discourse, characterized by special rules of speech and nonverbal behavior and often distinguishable by clearly recognized opening and closing sequences.[41]

Episodes are sequences of messages that exist as units and have an end. Episodes may "vary widely in scope (from 'having coffee with' to 'having an affair with')... . A description of an episode answers the question, 'What does he think he is doing?'"[42] Examples of episodes might include having a fight, studying for a test, taking part in a business conference, joking around, or picking someone up. The nature of the episode gives meaning to the particular speech act. Thus, "You're looking good" can be a compliment in an episode of friendly greeting or a diagnosis in an episode of medical examination. The statement "Your mother's a duck" is an instance of gamesmanship when said in the episode of sounding (a form of ritual insult practiced by urban youth). In almost any other context, it is either a serious insult or a nonsensical statement. Research Abstract 5.2 outlines the nature and rules for the episode called sounding.

Level 5 is composed of *master contracts* that add further meaning to communicative behaviors. "A master contract is made up of patterns of episodes comprising the person's expectations for the kinds of communicative events which should occur between self and other."[43] The master contract tells communicators who they are to one another: friends, lovers, enemies, etc. Each master contract implies certain episodes. For example, we expect neighbors to enact certain episodes such as borrowing a lawn mower, having a backyard barbeque, or chatting about the weather. We do not expect them to engage in episodes such as taking part in a brawl, stealing each other's possessions, or giving psychiatric advice. Problems in meaning occur if an episode contradicts master contract expectations.

At level 6, lower levels are constrained by *life scripts*. The term, borrowed from psychologist Eric Berne, refers to "the person's expectations for the kind of communicative events which can and 'should' occur to her/him."[44] Your life script is your sense of self. The person who defines self as a loyal husband forms different master contracts and engages in different episodes from the

RESEARCH ABSTRACT 5.2   A Discourse Analysis of Sounding

Labov contends that to produce meaningful discourse actors must follow implicit discourse rules that outline "the roles of speaker, addressee, and audience, their rights and obligations, and other constraints." He begins with a three-turn conversation that illustrates the social meaning of talk. The conversation involves sounding, a culturally patterned interaction ritual consisting of impersonal insults directed to an opponent's relatives. It is often engaged in by urban ghetto youth. In the following example, Rel sounds on Stanley. Rel: "Shut up please!" Stanley: "...'ey you tellin' *me?*" Rel: "Yes. Your mother's a duck."

To an outsider this exchange is meaningless. Only by uncovering the work of each utterance and the rules of the interaction can we understand what is occurring. Labov's general *purpose* is to describe rules for the episode called sounding. His *method* is observational. He and his researchers contacted groups of pre-adolescent and adolescent boys from Harlem. Audio tapes were made of their interactions on trips and in group sessions; these tapes were analyzed to establish the form and function of sounding. Results were as follows:

Attributes and Persons Sounded On. Sounds are generally directed toward an opponent's mother, although other relations

(father, uncle, grandmother, and aunt) can be targets. The target's age, weight, ugliness, skin color, smell, food preferences, poverty, and sexual activity may be insulted. Sounds often include reference to brand names or media figures. "They say your mother eat Gainesburgers," "Your mother look like Flipper," and "Your mother Pussy Galore," are examples.

The Shape of Sounds. Sounds have identifiable structures. *Your mother is like* is perhaps the most frequent, but there are other forms: "*Your mother wear* high-heeled sneakers to church," "*Your mother so* skinny she ice skate on a razor blade," "*Your mother eat* Dog Yummies," "*Your mother raised you on* ugly milk," and "*I went to your house and saw* roaches walkin' round in combat boots." Although sounds do not always use obscene words, their intent is usually obscene. "Many sounds are 'good' because they are 'bad'— because the speakers know that they would arouse disgust and revulsion among those committed to the 'good' standards of middle-class society."

The Activity of Sounding and Its Evaluation. Sounds take the form of a contest. One wins by "topping" a previous sound.

continued...

RESEARCH ABSTRACT 5.2 (*continued*)

Sounds are presented to an audience that responds with laughter and approval. The member who has the best sound dominates the group and gains respect. Sounds are ritual, not personal, insults. They are a game or art form allowing individuals to show verbal dexterity and creativity.

Applied Sounding. Sounding may be used instrumentally. A sounder may, for example, use a sound to "cool out" potential conflict by defining the interaction as ritual. This is what Rel did in the example above. His sound said, in effect, "Calm down. This is just a game, unless, of course, your mother really is a duck." Rel used a sound to depersonalize the situation, to allow a retreat into the sanctuary of ritual.

The Rules for Sounding. Labov identified three rules. Through a rule of interpretation, members learn to recognize a sound's form and know when it has taken place. A rule of response tells members that the expected response to a sound is another sound. A third rule instructs them to relate new insults to earlier ones. By following these rules, participants produce meaningful ritualized discourse.

Source: William Labov, "Rules for Ritual Insults," in *Studies in Social Interaction,* ed. David Sudnow (New York: The Free Press, 1971).

---

person who styles himself as a carefree bachelor. Finally, level 7 adds *cultural patterns* to the hierarchy. These are "very broad images of world order and man's relationship to that order."[45] These emerge as mythologies, ideologies, or metatheoretical perspectives and locate all lower levels within a culturally based framework that legitimizes certain ways of acting and responding to the world.

Individuals differ in the complexity of their meaning systems and in the degree to which they are locked into a given level. For example, persons with very strong life scripts may feel compelled to engage in certain relationships and to avoid certain episodes. Furthermore, they may be unable to understand episodes that do not fit their life script. Others may show more flexibility and be able to assign multiple meanings to the messages they encounter. Research Abstract 5.3 illustrates one way cultural patterns determine life scripts and episodic interpretations.

Intrapersonal Rules. How do individuals use these seven levels of meaning to communicate? CMM suggests that we employ two types of rules to assign meaning and coordinate action: constitutive and regulative rules. *Constitutive rules* specify how meanings at one level determine meanings at another. For example, when we decide that "You're looking good" is a compliment, we follow the rule that states, "Given the contract friend and the episode polite conversation, the content 'You're looking good' is a compliment and is to be evaluated as a friendly overture."

The following two examples of constitutive rules are taken from Research Abstracts 5.2 and 5.3 and are illustrated in Fig. 5.7. In the first, the constitutive rule is as follows: In the cultural milieu of southside Chicago, an adult male who has the life script of being a real man and who wishes to be perceived as a respected member of his peer group will, in the episode of a bar room argument, interpret a comment about his mother as a challenge to fight. The second example shows another constitutive rule for interpreting a similar content level message. Here, because the definitions of culture, life script, master contract, and episode differ, the interpretation also differs. The culture is the urban ghetto, the life script is

RESEARCH ABSTRACT 5.3 The Nature of Talk in Teamsterville

Philipsen investigates the meaning of speech for members of a southside Chicago community labeled Teamsterville, a neighborhood of predominantly white, blue-collar, low-income workers who share sharply defined cultural understandings about the value of speaking. Philipsen tries to uncover these understandings and, in the first article, focuses on "the appropriateness of speaking versus other actional strategies (silence, violence, or nonverbal threats) in male role enactment or self-presentation." In the second article, he investigates the occasions for talk existing for the Teamsterville male. He shows that different cultures make different assumptions about "the value, purposes, and significance of speaking as a mode of human experience." The major *methods* used were participant observation and interviewing. Philipsen entered the community twice, once working as social group worker, later conducting field research.

For the Teamsterville male, there are three types of speaking situations. The first type occurs in symmetrical role relationships. When with other men of the same age, ethnicity, occupational status, and residence, Teamsterville men are allowed to talk freely. This activity occurs, for boys, at the street corner; for men, at the corner bar. The living room or backyard (middle class locations for talk) are seldom used for this purpose in Teamsterville.

The second situation involves asymmetrical role relationships. Interactions with wife, child, boss, outsider, or men of a dif-ferent ethnicity are considered "unnatural" situations for talk. Although talk may occur with these people, it is generally of minimal duration and low quality. The last situation includes responses to insults, attempts to influence inferiors, and meetings with authority figures. Here, talk is proscribed. If a male responds to an insult or disciplines his wife or child by talking, he violates social expectations. For example, if a Teamsterville boy "talks back" to an adult male, the adult must respond with nonverbal threats or physical punishment. When a Teamsterville man deals with outsiders in matters of employment, law, politics, or welfare, he uses an intermediary, often a local precinct captain, Catholic parish priest, or union steward to talk for him. On such occasions, the Teamsterville man relies on his relationships with recognized intermediaries and uses what Philipsen calls a "rhetoric of connections."

Philipsen concludes that the meaning of speech in Teamsterville differs from that in other communities. Here, "speech is seen as an instrument of sociability with one's fellows, as a medium for asserting communal ties and loyalties to a group, and serves—by its use or disuse, or by the particular manner of its use—to signal that one knows one's place in the world."

Source: Gerry Philipsen, "Speaking 'Like a Man' in Teamsterville: Cultural Patterns of Role Enactment in an Urban Neighborhood," *The Quarterly Journal of Speech*, 61 (February, 1975), 13–22; and "Places for Speaking in Teamsterville," *The Quarterly Journal of Speech*, 62 (February, 1976), 15–25.

that of a member of the community, the contract is that of peer group, and the episode is that of sounding. The comment about one's mother in this case will be interpreted as a form of gamesmanship, however, not a challenge to fight. The New York City youth engaged in sounding has a different set of rules from the southside Chicago adult engaged in an argument.

Although constitutive rules help us interpret meaning through contextualization, they do not

A Simple Example of Two Constitutive and Two Regulative Rules of Communication						
EXAMPLE 1:		In the culture of Southside Chicago				
		if one's life script is that of a "Real Man"				
		and one's master contract is that of group member				
		and an episode of bar room argument is being enacted				
Constitutive Rule₁	= *If*	another adult male speaks	*then*	an insult to one's mother	*counts as*	a challenge to fight
Regulative Rule₁	= *if*	one encounters a challenge to fight	*then*	one is obliged to fight and prohibited from talking	*in order to*	maintain one's status with the group
EXAMPLE 2:		In the culture of the New York City ghetto				
		if one's life script is that of "Brother"				
		and one's master contract is that of group member				
		and an episode of sounding is being enacted				
Constitutive Rule₂	= *If*	it is the opponent's turn	*then*	an insult to one's mother	*counts as*	gamesman-ship
Regulative Rule₂	= *If*	a young other initiates sounding	*then*	it is legitimate either to engage in sounding or to scoff at that kid's game	*in order to*	maintain one's status with the group

FIGURE 5.7: A simplified diagram of the general form of constitutive and regulative rules and their relationship to hierarchical meanings. The constitutive rule tells us how to interpret a given behavior; a regulative rule tells us what response to make. Both are determined by context. The brackets above the rules show different levels of meaning which provide contextual information. (Adapted from W. Barnett Pearce and others, "The Structure of Communication Rules and the Form of Conversation: An Experimenal Simulation," *Western Journal of Speech Communication*, 44 [Winter 1980], 23–24.)

show us how to respond to others nor how to choose the most appropriate speech act for a given episode. *Regulative rules* perform this function, specifying that "in the context of certain social actions, if given antecedent conditions pertain, then there exists some degree of force for or against the performance of subsequent actions."[46] They tell us what we should or should not do during interaction. Figure 5.8 also contains examples of regulative rules.

In example one, the Teamsterville man is in the same situation as before. He has heard an insult to his mother and has used a constitutive rule to interpret it as a challenge. He now consults

a regulative rule to decide how to proceed. This rule lists possible responses to the given situation. His regulative rule is likely to be as follows: Given a challenge to fight by a member of one's peer group, and given all of the contextualizing levels of meaning, the real man is obliged to fight back if he is to maintain his status and identity.

Interpersonal Systems of Rules. So far we have looked at individual meaning systems. Communication, however, does not take place in isolation. When two people interact in social contexts, "important parts of their regulative rules are controlled by the actions of others. The process of communication thus reflects a logical force produced by the nonsummative combination of two or more persons."[47]

As an example of how rules are coordinated, let us imagine a hypothetical interaction between a (highly stereotyped) construction worker and a (highly stereotyped) liberated woman.[48] The construction worker is taking part in a male ritual that involves rating the appearance of female passersby. As he sees the woman approach, he searches for a regulative rule telling him how to behave. This rule tells him it is obligatory to comment overtly about her appearance. He therefore yells out his appraisal of her. To process his comment she must search for a constitutive rule that tells her how to interpret his remark and a regulative rule indicating how she should respond. Let us assume that she interprets his remark as a chauvinistic putdown and decides that the only appropriate response is to call him a male chauvinist. They have entered an episode of mutual insults. If they decide to continue, both must search for more rules to indicate their next moves.

Of course, other episodes are possible. If the liberated woman felt it legitimate to engage the worker in a serious discussion of women's rights, she might decide to enact an episode of consciousness raising instead of exchange of insults. The construction worker would then have to search his meaning structure for a different set of regulative and constitutive rules. As the conversation progressed, new episodes would appear, each constrained by the actions of both parties. In interaction, the nature of the system rather than the nature of each individual determines what happens.

Criticism of CMM Theory. Currently, CMM theorists are involved in examining the constraints that determine the nature of interactions, questioning how our actions are determined by antecedent conditions, anticipated consequences, and by the logical force resulting from system interaction. They are also looking at relationships between various levels in the hierarchy. It is clear that CMM is not a completed theory, but rather one that is in progress. The scope of CMM is very broad. It seeks not only to explain how individuals interpret others' behavior but also how these interpretations determine future behavior. It accounts not only for the individual's meaning system but also for the interpersonal system resulting from interaction. It recognizes that individuals do not exist in isolation and that meanings are mutually negotiated. In addition, it is one of the most fully developed of the current rules approaches to interaction. In all respects, CMM provides a valuable theoretical framework for understanding the pragmatics of language.

Grice's Cooperative Principle

The final theory we will review extends the idea of coordination of communication by assuming that we cannot engage in rational, meaningful communication with others without ground rules for effective use of language. Language use is a social activity, implying some degree of cooperation. When two or more people talk, they adhere to basic principles allowing them to exchange information in significant and logical ways. Without such principles of cooperation, interaction would be chaotic. There would simply be no reason to communicate. What Grice has done in developing a set of conversational maxims is to indicate the minimal agreements that people must make in order to engage in cooperative interaction.

Cooperation and Coordination. Grice argues that when we converse with others we are bound by the common purpose of exchanging information. If we are to achieve that purpose, we must cooperate with one another. Certain conversational moves must be placed off limits (for example, lying or deliberately trying to confuse one another). The basic principle that Grice believes lies at the heart of rational interaction is what he calls the *cooperative principle*. This principle states, "Make your conversational contribution

---

The maxim of QUANTITY

Make your contribution neither more nor less than is required.

    a. Make your contribution as informative as is required for the current purposes of the exchange.

    b. Do not make your contribution more informative than is required.

The maxim of QUALITY

Try to make your contribution one that is true.

    a. Do not say what you believe to be false.

    b. Do not say that for which you lack adequate evidence.

The maxim of RELATION

Be relevant.

The maxim of MANNER

Be perspicuous.

    a. Avoid obscurity of expression.

    b. Avoid ambiguity.

    c. Be brief (avoid unnecessary prolixity).

    d. Be orderly.

FIGURE 5.8: Grice's conversational maxims. (From H.P. Grice, "Logic and Conversation," in *Syntax and Semantics*, Volume 3: Speech Acts, eds. Peter Cole and Jerry L. Morgan [New York: Academic Press, 1975], pp. 41–58.)

such as is required, at the stage at which it occurs, by the accepted purpose or direction of the talk exchange in which you are engaged."[49] While the cooperative principle may seem obvious, it is fundamental. To communicate we must recognize and accept the direction talk is to take. If we refuse, we are at cross purposes, unable to connect with one another. If I want to ask you directions, you must either attempt to fill my request or refuse it. If, instead, you launch into a discussion of the French Revolution or some other equally irrelevant topic, normal meaning exchange becomes impossible.

Grice believes that the cooperative principle can be broken down into four conversational maxims. These are presented in Fig. 5.8. If one of the maxims is violated, then meanings will be disrupted. Usually, the listener will search for an explanation to account for the violation. He will try to determine what the implications of the violation are. For example, if I request information about an individual and you abruptly change the topic, I assume you are implying (making an *implicature*) that my question was unsuitable. Implicatures point out two things. The first is that we know, and take very seriously, the conversational maxims. The second is that implied meanings exist, that we can mean more than we actually say. The first point shows the validity of the maxims; it illustrates that we follow unwritten conversational rules. The second helps to explain how we convey information without directly stating it. It draws our attention to the fact that syntactic and semantic rules are not enough to explain how sentences convey meanings, that there is a pragmatic aspect to meaning.

Conversational implicature often arises in situations where one of the conversational maxims is deliberately flouted. In such situations, we assume the speaker is able to fulfill the maxim but for some reason has decided not to.[50] Grice gives several examples. Assume we receive a letter of recommendation for a candidate seeking a job in philosophy. The letter, in its entirety, reads, "Dear

Sir, Mr. X's command of English is excellent, and his attendance at tutorials has been regular. Yours, etc."[51] The writer has clearly violated the *maxim of quantity*; letters of recommendation usually give more information. Most people would assume the writer is implying something about the candidate that he prefers not to say in so many words: that Mr. X is not very good at philosophy.

In irony or sarcasm, the *maxim of quality* is flouted. If you and I both know that X's job performance is dismal and I say, "I wish I had more workers like X," you will probably conclude that I mean the opposite of what I say. Abrupt topic changes violate the *maxim of relation*. If, for example, you start gossiping about a mutual friend, and I respond with "nice weather," you realize I am implying that I do not wish to gossip. Finally, using complicated constructions when simple ones will do is a violation of the *maxim of manner*. Grice compares two remarks that might describe a singer's performance: (1) "Miss X sang 'Home, Sweet Home'" and (2) "Miss X produced a series of sounds that corresponded closely with the score of 'Home, Sweet Home.'"[52] The second statement implies that Miss X's performance was far from satisfactory.

Criticism of Grice's Theory. Grice's analysis is impressive in its simplicity. He shows us that we often convey more by an utterance than what we actually say. He also convinces us that communication simply cannot exist without basic cooperative rules and guidelines, that one cannot understand ordinary communication without understanding the social agreements that make rational interaction possible.

All three pragmatic theories reviewed in this chapter investigate language in use. Searle tells us that to understand an utterance, we must know what the speaker is trying to do. CMM theory outlines the kinds of context information that let us assign meaning to speech acts. Grice takes a general view, showing that interaction is meaningless unless human actors agree to abide by certain cooperative principles.

Analyzing Talk: A Brief Overview of Research on Conversation

Each of the pragmatic theories has argued that, to understand language, we must understand that communicators are social beings with goals and purposes who do things with language. Clearly, one of the primary things we do with language is talk. Recently, scholars have turned their attention to the study of how people understand and manage conversations. They have found that conversation is not as simple as it appears, that to carry on a conversation participants must master a variety of knowledge structures. In addition to knowing the phonology and morphology of a language, conversants must also know rules of grammar, must adhere to conversational maxims, must understand the social rules governing speech acts, and must follow conversational rules as well.

According to Margaret McLaughlin, conversation is a "relatively informal social interaction in which the rules of speaker and hearer are exchanged in a nonautomatic fashion under the collaborative management of all parties."[53] What makes conversations a particularly intriguing form of communication is the nonautomatic character of member contributions. In some forms of communication (for example, debates), the order of talk as well as the length and nature of each turn is firmly fixed. In conversations, however, members decide together, most often tacitly, how to proceed. Together they decide what the conversation is about, where it is going, and whose turn it is to lead it there. This is not to suggest, however, that conversations are unstructured, random events. Most conversation analysts believe that conversation is a "highly organized activity whose structure may best be understood by recourse to the notion of *rule*."[54] Thus, the goal of much conversation research is to uncover the rules that govern coherent, well-managed interactions. In striving to develop these rules, conversation analysts have asked a variety of questions of which the following are just a small sample: How do participants keep track of the subject under discussion as a conversation continues, and how do they ensure that their contributions make sense? How do people manage their conversations so that awkward gaps and overlaps do not occur? When conversations go awry, how do interactants repair the resulting misunderstandings? Do people exhibit differing conversational styles?

Providing answers to these questions is well beyond the scope of this book. However, it is possible to provide a taxonomy of research areas and to offer citations of relevant research for those of you who wish to explore this area more fully. Next we will focus on four major categories of research: conversational coherence; conversational management; facilitatives, preventatives, and repairs; and conversational style.

Conversational Coherence. We have all experienced it: thinking we understand exactly what our partner is talking about, we find to our dismay that we are on totally different wavelengths. During talk we often use ambiguous referents, comment on multiple stimuli in quick succession, jump from topic to topic, and even insinuate plans and strategies into seemingly "innocent" talk. All of this makes it difficult to follow the thread of a conversation and easy to get lost during talk. Analysts interested in the general problem of *coherence* try to determine how we keep track of what is going on during conversations, how we determine "the relevance of...successive utterances both to those that precede them and to the global concerns of the discourse as a whole."[55]

The problem of coherence may concern itself with very specific questions (e.g., how do we keep track of pronoun referents from one utterance to another?), in which case we call it *cohesion*, or it may concern itself with larger sequences such as *topic changes* (e.g., how do people move smoothly from one topic to the next?). Theories seem either to be very local or very global. Local theories concern themselves with identifying the linguistic markers that allow people to chain together utterances.[56] Global theories, on the other hand, posit general schemata that provide overall cognitive maps of a conversation, schemata that participants use to understand, plan, and report on conversations.[57]

Conversational Management. Not all conversations run smoothly. Sometimes our talk is plagued by awkward and seemingly endless pauses or by embarrassing interruptions. Often we do not know how to enter a conversation or end it gracefully. From time to time we have trouble getting a word in edgewise. All of this is due to the relative freedom of exchange characterizing conversation. Participants must negotiate turns, and research on *turn-taking* seeks to catalogue the subtle verbal and nonverbal cues occurring at or near points of speaker exchange. Studies show that speakers use a variety of intonational, syntactic, and gestural cues to signal the end of a turn: changes in intonation at the end of clauses, change in frequency and duration of gestures, change in volume, relocation of gaze, or the use of sociocentric sequences such as "so," "anyway," "but, uh," and so forth.[58] There is a large literature on the cues and rules we use to share the floor with one another.

Facilitatives, Preventatives, and Repairs. Learning to make sense of conversations and take turns smoothly is obviously not all it takes to carry on a successful conversation. There are appropriate and inappropriate ways to talk. *Facilitatives* are ways of making sure our contributions support ongoing relationships. As Catherine Garvey points out, "Talk could not operate without a facilitation system to reduce friction and minimize the potential conflicts and embarrassments that can arise in social contact. This system reflects the speakers' ritual concerns and their pervasive awareness of interpersonal status in the transactions of daily life."[59] Garvey catalogues the following mechanisms as facilitatives: markers of courtesy and concern, displays of support during another's turn, selection of forms of address, the use of appropriate forms of request, and politeness norms.[60]

Sometimes facilitation does not work and a speaker realizes that what he or she is about to say will give offense. In this case there are ways of warding off attack by using verbal formulae called *preventatives*. If a speaker feels it is necessary to make a comment that might be disruptive, he or she may preface the remark with a *disclaimer*. Thus, a speaker may appeal for suspension of judgment by saying, "Now, don't get mad before I explain," or may hedge by saying, "I'm new to all this, so I may not have my facts straight, but…" A number of scholars have written on the power of disclaimers to help us avoid conversational misunderstandings.[61]

When preventatives do not work and offense is given, there must be some mechanism through which interactants can set things right. There appear to be a number of verbal routines, called *repairs*, which the individual can use to correct violations of "grammar, syntactical, conversational, and societal rules."[62] (See Research Abstract 6.2 in the next chapter for a discussion of some of these methods.) In response to a problematic action, individuals may attempt to explain their side of the story by offering *accounts*.[63] They may either *excuse* their actions by showing that they were in fact not responsible for the unfortunate act ("My dog ate my paper") or they may try to *justify* their action by showing that it had positive outcomes ("I just did it for your own good"). Another form of repair is the *apology*, whereby an individual, unable to explain away the offense through an account, expresses regret.[64] In each case, the utterance of a verbal sequence, if done according to social expectation, has the power to repair errors and offenses. Conversations are essentially risky; we can say the wrong thing at the wrong time and hurt others. Without mechanisms for correcting the errors that naturally occur during interaction, we would have a difficult if not impossible time communicating clearly and effectively.

Conversational Style. Everything we say must be said in some way: in a certain tone of voice, at a certain speed, with a certain enthusiasm or lack thereof. As speakers we make choices, and these choices are our style. Deborah Tannen explains, "I use style to refer to no more nor less than a way of doing something. It is crucial to make clear that *style* does not refer to a special way of speaking, as if one could choose between speaking plainly or speaking with style. Plain is as much a style as fancy."[65] Style is important because it usually results in evaluation of the speaker's personality and because when styles conflict, effective conversation becomes impossible.

There are obviously many ways style could be analyzed.[66] Tannen's discussion is a useful introduction to the topic because it takes a pragmatic perspective, showing how problems in style become problems in communication. Tannen believes that we do not develop our style randomly. We make strategic decisions about how we will relate to others, and these strategies determine style.

Tannen uses the work of Robin Lakoff on the logic of politeness as a basis for her discussion of relational strategies.[67] Whereas Grice believes communicators are essentially rational information processors for whom a lack of clarity or the use of indirectness is problematic, Lakoff observes that speakers often intentionally refrain from saying what they mean, following three *rules of politeness*. They are (1) do not impose, (2) give options, and (3) be friendly.[68] According to Lakoff, all speakers must decide the extent to which they will abide by each rule. People who follow the first rule try their best to avoid being intrusive. Their language strategy is that of *distance*, and their talk will be depersonalized, formal, and indirect. Thus, someone using this strategy may suggest a future meeting by saying, "I'd welcome the opportunity to interact with you at a future date." An individual who follows the second rule attempts the strategy of *deference*. His or her language may be hesitant, apologetic, and euphemistic. When making an appointment, this individual might say, "I know you're terribly busy, but if you're sure you have the time, perhaps we could get together." Finally, the speaker who follows rule three will try to establish *camaraderie*. Such an individual will be direct and blunt, assuming a relationship of equality. This person might make a date by saying, "I'll be by tomorrow at 8. You can cook dinner, and we'll talk."

Each strategy results in a different style of talk. Not only will word choices vary, but so too will factors such as pacing, tone of voice, management of topic shifts, and narrative strategies. Thus, the individual who wants to show considerateness and distance may speak more slowly and calmly, use less pitch variability, pause more, and use fewer personal details than will the individual who wants to establish personal involvement. While we may vary our strategies according to the situation, Tannen argues that many of us develop an overall style that pervades our conversations regardless of context, affecting both our sense of self and the attributions others make about us. Style is an important determinant of conversational success. Tannen tells us that "whenever style is shared, there is a metamessage of rapport" and that differences in style lead to discontent and dissonance.[69] When an individual who prides himself or herself on being open and friendly interacts with an individual who values considerateness and politeness, it is likely the former will consider the latter aloof, pompous, and rigid, while the latter will see the former as excessively informal, presumptuous, and intrusive. Thus style contributes to the success or failure of our talk, and conversations depend on stylistic strategies.

REFERENCES

1. Terence Hawkes, *Structuralism and Semiotics* (Los Angeles: University of California Press, 1977), p. 125.

2. Ferdinand de Saussure, *Course in General Linguistics* (London: McGraw-Hill, 1966).

3. Hawkes, *Structuralism*, pp. 25–26.

4. Charles Sanders Peirce, *Collected Papers*, ed. Charles Hartshorne, Paul Weiss, and Arthur W. Burks (Cambridge, Mass.: Harvard University Press, 1931–1958).

5. Paul Watzlawick, Janet Beavin Bavelas, and Don D. Jackson, *Pragmatics of Human Communication* (New York: W. W. Norton, 1967).

6. *Ibid.*, p. 61.

7. *Ibid.*, p. 65.

8. Judee K. Burgoon and Thomas Saine, *The Unspoken Dialogue: An Introduction to Nonverbal Communication* (Boston: Houghton Mifflin, 1978), pp. 18–20.

9. See, for example, Ray L. Birdwhistell, *Introduction to Kinesics* (Louisville: University of Kentucky Press, 1952), for a discussion of the linguistic-kinesic analogy.

10. Burgoon and Saine, *The Unspoken Dialogue*, p. 19.

11. *Ibid.*, p. 22.

12. Mark L. Knapp, *Essentials of Nonverbal Communication* (New York: Holt, Rinehart & Winston, 1980); Paul Ekman and W. V. Friesen, "The Repertoire of Nonverbal Behavior: Categories, Origins, Usage, and Coding," *Semiotica*, 1 (1969), 49–98; G. L. Trager, "Paralanguage: A First Approximation," *Studies in Linguistics*, 13 (1958), 1–12.

13. Knapp, *Essentials of Nonverbal Communication*, p. 5.

14. *Ibid.*, p. 5.

15. *Ibid.*, p. 6.

16. *Ibid.*, pp. 7–8.

17. *Ibid.*, p. 119.

18. Albert Mehrabian, "A Semantic Space for Nonverbal Behavior," *Journal of Counseling and Clinical Psychology*, 35 (1970), 248–57.

19. Burgoon and Saine, *Unspoken Dialogue*, pp. 11–12.

20. John R. Searle, *Speech Acts: An Essay in the Philosophy of Language* (Cambridge: Cambridge University Press, 1969), p. 17.

21. Hawkes, *Structuralism*, p. 21.

22. Harold J. Vetter, *Language Behavior and Communication: An Introduction* (Itasca, Ill.: F. E. Peacock, 1969), p. 20.

23. Philip Pettit, *The Concept of Structuralism: A Critical Analysis* (Berkeley and Los Angeles: University of California Press, 1977), p. 12.

24. Frederick Williams, *Language and Speech: Introductory Perspectives* (Englewood Cliffs, N. J.: Prentice Hall, 1972), p. 60.

25. Noam Chomsky, *Language and Mind* (New York: Harcourt Brace Jovanovich, 1968), p. 84.

26. Noam Chomsky, *Rules and Representations* (New York: Columbia University Press, 1980), pp. 219–20.

27. Dan I. Slobin, *Psycholinguistics* (Glenview, Ill.: Scott, Foresman, 1971), p. 7.

28. Chomsky, *Rules and Representations*, p. 234.

29. *Ibid.*, p. 33.

30. See Slobin, *Psycholinguistics*, pp. 12–13 for a discussion of this method of determining constituent parts.

31. *Ibid.*, p. 16.

32. Searle, *Speech Acts*, p. 22.

33. *Ibid.*, p. 33.

34. *Ibid.*, p. 63.

35. W. Barnett Pearce, "The Coordinated Management of Meaning: A Rules-Based Theory of Interpersonal Communication," in *Explorations in Interpersonal Communication*, ed. Gerald R. Miller (Beverly Hills: Sage, 1976), pp. 17–35.

36. Donald P. Cushman and W. Barnett Pearce, "Generality and Necessity in Three Types of Theory about Human Communication with Special Attention to Rules Theory," *Human Communication Research*, 3 (Summer 1977), 244–53; Vernon E. Cronen, W. Barnett Pearce, and Lonna M. Snavely, "A Theory of Rule-Structure and Types of Episodes and a Study of Perceived Enmeshment in Undesired Repetitive Patterns ('URPS')," in *Communication Yearbook 3*, ed. Dan Nimmo (New Brunswick, N. J.: Transaction Books, 1979), pp. 225–39; W. Barnett Pearce and Forrest Conklin, "A Model of Hierarchical Meanings in Coherent Conversation and a Study of 'Indirect Responses,'" *Communication Monographs*, 46

(June 1979), 75–87; W. Barnett Pearce, Vernon E. Cronen, and Forrest Conklin, "On What to Look at When Analyzing Communication: A Hierarchical Model of Actors' Meanings," *Communication*, 4 (1979), 195–220; W. Barnett Pearce and others, "The Structure of Communication Rules and the Form of Conversation: An Experimental Simulation," *Western Journal of Speech Communication*, 44 (Winter, 1980), 20–34; Vernon E. Cronen and W. Barnett Pearce, "Logical Force in Interpersonal Communication: A New Concept of the 'Necessity' in Social Behaviors," *Communication*, 6 (1981), 5–67; W. Barnett Pearce, Linda M. Harris, and Vernon E. Cronen, "Communication Theory in a New Key," in *Rigor and Imagination*, eds. C. Wilder-Mott and John H. Weakland (New York: Holt, Rinehart & Winston, 1981); W. Barnett Pearce and Vernon E. Cronen, *Communication, Action and Meaning: The Creation of Social Realities* (New York: Holt, Rinehart & Winston, 1982); Vernon E. Cronen, W. Barnett Pearce, and Linda M. Harris, "The Coordinated Management of Meaning: A Theory of Communication," in *Human Communication Theory: Comparative Essays*, ed. Frank E. X. Dance (New York: Harper & Row, 1982).

37. Cronen and Pearce, "Logical Force," p. 19.

38. Pearce and Conklin, "A Model of Hierarchical Meanings," p. 76.

39. Pearce, Cronen, and Conklin, "On What to Look At," p. 209.

40. *Ibid.*, p. 204.

41. John J. Gumperz, "Introduction," in *Directions in Sociolinguistics*, eds. John J. Gumperz and Dell Hymes (New York: Holt, Rinehart & Winston, 1972).

42. Pearce, "The Coordinated Management of Meaning," p. 21.

43. Cronen and Pearce, "Logical Force," p. 21.

44. *Ibid.* See also Eric Berne, *What Do You Say After You Say, "Hello?"* (New York: Bantam, 1972).

45. Cronen and Pearce, "Logical Force," p. 21.

46. *Ibid.*, p. 25.

47. *Ibid.*, p. 34.

48. Cronen, Pearce, and Snavely, "Perceived Enmeshment in Undesired Repetitive Patterns," p. 229.

49. H. P. Grice, "Logic and Conversation," in *Syntax and Semantics*, vol. 3, eds. Peter Cole and Jerry L. Morgan (New York: Academic, 1975), p. 45.

50. *Ibid.*, p. 49.

51. *Ibid.*, p. 52.

52. *Ibid.*, p. 55.

53. Margaret McLaughlin, *Conversation: How Talk Is Organized* (Beverly Hills: Sage, 1984), p. 271. Our brief discussion of the topics undertaken by conversation analysts owes a great deal to this excellent introduction to a complex and difficult area of study.

54. *Ibid.*, p. 14.

55. *Ibid.*, p. 270.

56. See, for example, M. A. K. Halliday and R. Hasan, *Cohesion in English* (London: Longman, 1976). For a general discussion of topic change, see Sally Planalp and Karen Tracy, "Not to Change the Topic but...: A Cognitive Approach to the Study of Conversation" in *Communication Yearbook 4*, ed. Dan Nimmo (New Brunswick, N. J.: Transaction Books, 1980).

57. See, for example, van Dijk, T. A., *Studies in the Pragmatics of Discourse* (The Hague: Mouton, 1981), and *Macrostructures: An Interdisciplinary Study of Global Structures in Discourse, Interaction, and Cognition* (Hillsdale, N. J.: Lawrence Erlbaum Associates, 1980.)

58. Margaret McLaughlin, *Conversation*, p. 100. For a classic discussion of turn-taking, see Harvey Sacks, Emanuel A. Schegloff, and Gail Jefferson, "A Simplest Systematics for the Organization of Turn-taking for Conversation," in *Studies in the Organization of Conversational Interaction*, ed. Jim Schenkein (New York: Academic, 1978). See also S. Duncan, Jr. and D. W. Fiske, *Face to Face Interaction: Research, Methods, and Theory* (New York: John Wiley & Sons, 1977). For a discussion of the problematics of beginnings and endings, see Paul Krivonos and Mark L. Knapp, "Initiating Communication: What Do You Say When You Say Hello?" *Central States Speech Journal*, 26

(1975), 115–25; Mark L. Knapp and others, "The Rhetoric of Goodbye: Verbal and Nonverbal Correlates of Human Leave-Taking," *Speech Monographs*, 40 (1973), 182–98.

59. Catherine Garvey, *Children's Talk* (Cambridge, Mass.: Harvard University Press, 1984), p. 2.

60. Penelope Brown and Stephen Levenson, "Universals in Language Usage: Politeness Phenomena," in *Questions and Politeness: Strategies in Social Interaction*, ed. E. Goody (Cambridge: Cambridge University Press, 1978).

61. John P. Hewitt and Randall Stokes, "Disclaimers," *American Sociological Review*, 40 (1975), 1–11. For sources on responses to disclaimers, see Robert A. Bell, Christopher J. Zahn, and Robert Hopper, "Disclaiming: A Test of Two Competing Views," *Communication Quarterly*, 32 (Winter 1984), 28–36

62. Margaret McLaughlin, "Preventatives and Repairs," chap. 6 in *Conversation*.

63. Marvin B. Scott and Stanford M. Lyman, "Accounts," *American Sociological Review*, 33 (1968), 46–62, provides a classic discussion of account sequences. For a later version, see Peter A. Schonbach, "A Category System for Account Phases," *European Journal of Social Psychology*, 10 (1980), 195–200.

64. Barry R. Schlenker and Bruce W. Darby, "The Use of Apologies in Social Predicaments," *Social Psychology Quarterly*, 44 (1981), 271–78.

65. Deborah Tannen, *Conversational Style: Analyzing Talk Among Friends* (Norwood, N. J.: Ablex, 1984), p. 8. See also, Deborah Tannen, *That's Not What I Meant!* (New York: William Morrow, 1986).

66. Robert Norton, *Communicator Style: Theory, Application, and Measures* (Beverly Hills: Sage, 1983).

67. Robin Lakoff, *Language and Woman's Place* (New York: Harper & Row, 1975).

68. Tannen, *Conversational Style*, p. 11

69. *Ibid.*, p. 27.

chapter 6

THE PROBLEM OF SOCIAL COORDINATION AND RELATIONAL DEFINTION

INTRODUCTION

In social settings, how do we know what is expected of us? How do we act out social roles and create satisfactory identities? What means do we use to assure others that we are socially competent individuals? In short, how do we coordinate our actions in order to build rewarding relationships? These questions are central to the third problem facing communicators: the problem of social coordination and relational definition.

In chapter 1 it was argued that language and society are so intimately connected that one cannot exist without the other, that to communicate we must not only master language but also a system of social relations. This chapter focuses on the social needs of communicators. The theories we will examine argue that there is a circular relationship between communication and culture.

Cultural identities and meanings determine the nature of our communication, while at the same time communication allows the negotiation of new cultural identities and meanings. We talk and act as we do because our culture says this is how someone in our position should act and talk, yet it is through talk that cultural understandings are maintained and sometimes changed.

We will begin by considering how role identites affect interaction, reviewing several theories that suggest that we act as we do to present and maintain socially approved definitions of self. Next, we will consider how communication allows the construction of self and social reality, how we choose between different identities and manage to create a unique sense of self. We will then examine how people coordinate their behaviors during interaction and look at what it takes to be a socially competent communicator. Finally, we will consider the relationship between communication, self, and society.

CLASSICAL ROLE THEORY: WHAT ARE ROLES?

Classical role theory shows how societies are ordered and how these orderings affect individual behavior. Because role theory assumes that society constrains its members, endowing them with rights and obligations and teaching them appropriate behavior, it bears directly on the nature of communication. Inherent in the expectations that make up roles are instructions for communicating.

Most role theories begin with the notion of *social hierarchy*; that is, they assume that members of a society are neither identical nor equal but can be differentiated from one another and ranked in terms of status. An ordered ranking of the groups that exist within a society is called a hierarchy, and one's place or status in that hierarchy is called a *position*.[1] Societies can thus be regarded as consisting "of a complex organization of positions."[2] Although each position is filled by a number of individuals, structurally speaking, the positions, not the individuals, are of prime importance. "When the people are subtracted... from a society, what is left is a great network of positions, all the elements of which are more or less related to and consistent with one another."[3]

Societies vary in the number and complexity of the positional heirarchies they recognize; however, even the simplest society provides the following positions: (1) age-sex; (2) occupational; (3) prestige; (4) family, clan, or household; and (5) associational groupings.[4] American society, for example, includes positions such as infant, teacher, president, husband, and Rotarian, each belonging to a different organizing hierarchy. Members of different positions fulfill different functions. Each position carries "shared assumptions on the part of group members concerning the contributions (to be) made by the occupant of

a position."[5] The function of parent is to nurture the young of the group, while the function of priest is to provide spiritual leadership for the community. Groups or societies expect the functions of each position to be carried out in socially appropriate ways. The holder of a position has certain rights and in turn is expected to perform certain duties.

The pattern of expected behavior associated with a given position is called a *role*. "Role consists of the activity the incumbent would engage in were he to act solely in terms of the normative demands upon someone in his position."[6] A role is a generalized guideline that indicates required, permitted, and forbidden behaviors for the holder of a position. It does not spell out all the behaviors to be enacted by the role incumbent; actors are given some choices in how they go about fulfilling their roles. The actual way a person fulfills a role during interaction is termed *role enactment* or *role performance* and contains many behaviors irrelevant or supplementary to the role. For example, while "treating ill patients is a necessary part of the physician's prescribed role," and "poisoning patients is forbidden, and thus totally excluded from the role prescription," physicians can choose the cars they drive, the clothes they wear, and the bedside manner they affect.[7] Most performances are flexible, only rough approximations of the idealized role.

An individual's role performance occurs through interaction with *role others* who are referred to as a *role-set*. Thus, the role-set of the surgeon includes colleagues, patients, nurses, interns, orderlies, and the like. The role-set of parent includes the presence of at least one child.[8] This means the role incumbent must know not only his or her own role prescriptions but those of others as well. We thus share understandings about one another's expected behaviors, understandings that help our interactions take place in relatively predictable ways.

Although every member of society fulfills at least one position and is bound by at least one set of role prescriptions, most of us fulfill many roles. During a typical day, an individual is expected to be many different kinds of people. Ralph Linton gives a classic example:

Let us suppose that a man spends the day working as a clerk in a store. While he is behind the counter, his active status is that of a clerk, established by his position in our society's system of specialized occupations... . When he retires to the rest room for a smoke and meets other employees here, his clerk status becomes latent and he assumes another active status based upon position in the association group composed of the store's employees as a whole... . When closing time comes he lays aside both his clerk and store association statuses and, while on the way home, operates simply in terms of his status with respect to the society's age-sex system... . As soon as he arrives at his home, a new set of statuses will be activated. These statuses derive from the kinship ties which relate him to various members of the family group... . If it happens to be lodge night all his familiar statuses will become latent at about eight o'clock. As soon as he enters the lodge room...he assumes a new status, one which has been latent since the last lodge meeting, and performs in terms of this role until it is time for him to take off his uniform and go home.[9]

The way an individual fulfills the demands of different roles is called *role versatility*, the movement between roles *role transition* and the number of roles competently performed *role repertoire*.[10]

We are all enmeshed in a network of interrelated and, occasionally, conflicting obligations. To be competent and fully socialized members of society, we learn to fulfill a variety of expectations and to move skillfully from one role to another. As Erving Goffman suggests:

We do not take on items of conduct one at a time but rather a whole harness load of them and may anticipate learning to be a horse even while being pulled like a wagon. Role, then, is the basic unit of socialization. It is through roles that tasks in society are allocated and arrangements made to enforce their performance.[11]

Although role theory concentrates more on the structural nature of social organization than on interaction, it still has many implications for communication. If, as members of society, we are bound by rights and obligations inherent in our positions, then our communicative behaviors become constrained by these structures. The way we talk, the people we talk to, and the situations in which we talk are at least partially determined by the social structure. We are not fully constrained by roles—we can each negotiate our identity within interactions—yet the concept of role is crucial for understanding social communication.

Role Identity: How Do Individuals View Themselves?

We spend much of our time imagining how we will perform in various roles. We may imagine ourselves achieving fame, praise, and popularity, picturing others' reactions to our triumphs. We may fantasize about the look of envy on a rival's face, the applause and acclaim after a successful performance. These imaginary rehearsals lead to what McCall and Simmons call role identity, one's "imaginative view of himself *as he likes to think of himself being and acting* as an occupant of a position."[12]

Role identities are heavily idealized conceptions of self. Because they grow out of role, they are conventionalized and socially given, but because they involve individual idealizations, they may also be idiosyncratic. In a sense, they are individual variations on cultural themes. Role identities serve as action plans and as criteria for evaluating performances. We work hard to maintain and legitimize them.[13] George McCall and J. L. Simmons argue that "one of man's most distinctive motives is the compelling and perpetual drive to acquire support for his idealized conceptions of himself."[14] Humans are thus like actors, engaged in playing roles that will bring them credit.

Goffman's Dramaturgical Model

Of the many theories that view communicative interactions as "dramatic" performances, one of the earliest and most interesting is provided by

Erving Goffman. This model is most fully developed in *The Presentation of Self in Everyday Life*,[15] but elements can be found in his articles "Face Work" and "Role Distance."[16] In what follows we will examine Goffman's treatment of interaction as a dramatic performance.

Role Identity and the Concept of Face. In "Face Work," Goffman develops the concepts of face and line, suggesting that interactions are motivated by actors' efforts to maintain socially approved identities. Goffman tells us that all human actors are concerned with maintaining their own and others' faces. A *face* is a socially approved identity, a view of the nature of self. To "lose face," or to be "out of face," is to present aspects of self that conflict with approved social values.

Social actors claim face by taking a *line* during interaction. Line is the pattern of verbal and nonverbal acts by which actors express their view of situations and their evaluations of themselves and others.[17] The lines we take allow us either to maintain or lose face. After all, an actor's social face "is on loan to him from society; it will be withdrawn unless he conducts himself in a way that is worthy of it. Approved attributes and their relationship to face make of every man his own jailer even though each may like his cell."[18]

For Goffman, social interaction involves a careful coordination of face and line. The methods by which this is achieved are known as *face work*. To study face work "is to study the traffic rules of social interaction."[19] Appropriate face work depends on the communicators' skill and knowledge. First, interactors must be aware of the rules of face work; this is known as "tact, *saviorfaire*, diplomacy, or social skill."[20] To exercise this skill, actors must first show *perceptiveness*: They must be aware of the interpretations others will place on their lines and the meanings they should place on others'. Second, actors must be willing to enact appropriate lines in two ways: by being *prideful* and *considerate*.

To be prideful is to care enough about the self to present an appropriate face. Each individual "will be required to show self-respect, abjuring certain actions because they are above or beneath him, while forcing himself to perform others even though they cost him dearly... . He must ensure that a particular expressive order is sustained—an order that regulates the flow of events, large or small, so that anything that appears to be expressed by them will be consistent with his face."[21]

To show considerateness, "he is expected to go to certain lengths to save the feelings and the face of others present, and he is expected to do this willingly and spontaneously because of emotional identification with the others and with their feelings."[22] Social actors defend not only their own faces but also those of others.

Goffman outlines two basic kinds of face work that stave off social embarrassment. First is the *avoidance process*, whereby individuals avoid or diffuse potentially threatening situations. Actors try to avoid interactions that may lead to problems. If that is impossible, and they must take part in potentially risky interactions, they steer away from topics or activities that might demand inconsistent lines either from themselves or others. If unforseen incidents occur, the actor takes pains to redefine them as unimportant and nonthreatening. The second type of face work involves the *corrective process*. If an indiviudal is trapped in a situation incompatible with face, he or she will be forced into corrective work. Goffman sees this process as a game with four basic moves: challenge, offering, acceptance, and thanks.

The first move is a *challenge*, by which the party whose face is threatened recognizes the slight and indicates that "the threatening event itself will have to be brought into line."[23] A challenge like "Just what did you mean by that remark?" shows that the offended individual is unwilling to ignore a threat to face. The *offering* is normally the second move. Here the offending individual (the one who caused the disruption) is given a chance to correct the offense. This may be done by indicating the offense was meaningless or trivial, or it may be done by offering an excuse or engaging in self-disparagement. "I was only joking" or "I'm sorry. I always seem to put my foot in my mouth," serve as offerings. *Acceptance*, the third move, allows the first party to acknowledge the offering. "Oh that's alright. I guess I was overreacting" or "OK, but don't let it happen again" show acceptance. *Thanks* is the final move. Here, the offender conveys gratitude for the acceptance. "Thanks, I'm glad you're not mad" might be a terminal move used to reestablish the expressive order.

Of course, there are variations on these moves. The offender may refuse to make an offering, thus throwing play back to the challenger who must then decide whether to withdraw the challenge or escalate the contest. Because the cost of escalation is generally high for both players, the offender usually offers an apology.[24] Unless the offender deliberately wants to cause trouble (a process known as *aggressive face work*), he or she will make every effort to avoid escalation.[25]

Human actors are especially vulnerable to threats to face during interaction. "An unguarded glance, a momentary change in tone of voice, an ecological position taken or not taken, can drench a talk with judgmental significance…there is no occasion of talk so trivial as not to require each participant to show serious concern with the way in which he handles himself and the others present."[26] Because of the inherent dangers to face that can occur in interaction, talk is generally guided by conventions and procedural rules. Interactors are expected to demand only the amount of attention to which they are socially entitled. They must modify expressions of interest and concern according to their partner's status. Too much or too little emotional involvement will disrupt the interaction. Interruptions and pauses must also be avoided and surface agreements must be maintained.

Entering and leaving a conversation are particularly risky. For example, we generally hesitate to join others if we are unsure of our welcome, and we often ask permission to enter a conversation. If we decide not to join people we know, then we usually feel the necessity of offering an explanation. Leaving conversations also requires rhetorical and social skills. (See Research Abstract 6.1 for an analysis of leave-taking rules.) We are expected to sum up the conversation, indicate why we are leaving, and make plans to renew the acquaintance at a future date. Even after a disastrous interaction, we must act as though we look forward to future encounters. "It was great. I'll call you next week" is offered by most competent communicators, even when the probability of their voluntarily communicating again is close to zero.

Interaction involves a delicate balance. The person who disregards social conventions is "a real threat to society; there is nothing much that can be done with him, and often he gets his way."[27] On the other hand, the person with too much perceptiveness and pride "must be treated with kid gloves, requiring more care on the part of others than he may be worth to them."[28] And the person with too much savoire-faire and considerateness appears overly socialized and "leaves the others with the feeling that they do not know how they really stand with him." The competent communicator strikes just the right note; smooth and orderly interactions depend on face work skills.[29]

The Communicator as Performer. In *Presentation of Self in Everyday Life*, Goffman further develops his view of the communicator as social performer. He uses an extended dramatic metaphor to explain how communicators manage social interactions. In his view, interactors are always involved in staging dramas, dramas that let them project their definitions of a situation and display their concepts of self.

For Goffman, the individual is both actor and audience. Both roles constrain his or her behavior. In presenting self to others (in taking the role of actor) the individual is at once two people. As a *character*, he or she is "a figure, typically a fine

RESEARCH ABSTRACT 6.1 On Saying "Goodbye"

The *purpose* of this study was to describe leave-taking norms, in particular, to look at verbal and nonverbal behaviors associated with departures and to determine the effects of status and acquaintance on these behaviors. Knapp and his colleagues argue there are three functions of leave-taking: to signal inaccessibility, to signal supportiveness, and to summarize the interaction. They wanted to see how each is shown verbally and nonverbally.

Their *method* was to videotape students as they interviewed familiar or unfamiliar people of either the same status or higher. Subjects' concluding remarks and behaviors were coded. Two types of categories were used: verbal and nonverbal. Some of the verbal categories coded the function of the concluding remarks (justifications or legitimizations of the leave-taking, appreciation or concern for the other's welfare, expressions of desire for future contact). Others recorded the forms of the utterance (whether it was a filler, a reinforcement, or a buffer such as "uh" or "well"). Nonverbal categories included changes in body position, movements of the limbs, eye contact, smiling, and so on.

The *results* indicated that status and acquaintance had little effect on leave-taking. In general, leave-taking was shown verbally by increases in professional inquiry (How long have you been a major?), reinforcement (Yeah), buffing (Well), and appreciation (I really want to thank you). Nonverbally, leave-taking was signalled by breaking eye contact, left-positioning, forward lean, and head nodding. The major status difference was that the low-status partner did more reinforcement and buffing. More reinforcements also occurred between those previously acquainted than between strangers.

Nonverbal behaviors peaked during the 15 seconds prior to standing. The authors suggest, "In the light of such patterns, it is easy to see why we often become frustrated if we are not 'released' after rising. Such an interpersonal denial means that we must go through the whole routine again!"

Analysis showed the presence of only two of the leave-taking functions: signalling inaccessibility and support for the relationship. Little summarizing took place, although this could have been due to the college atmosphere. While the majority of nonverbal cues signalled inaccessibility, indications of warmth, approval, and affiliation were either directly verbalized or indicated nonverbally. The authors conclude: "Perhaps because we feel that the termination of an interaction may be perceived as a threat to terminate the relationship, we humans go through a veritable song-and-dance when taking leave of our fellows."

Source: Mark L. Knapp and others, "The Rhetoric of Goodbye: Verbal and Nonverbal Correlates of Human Leave-Taking," *Speech Monographs*, 40 (August 1973), 182–98.

one, whose spirit, strength, and other sterling qualities the performance was designed to evoke."[30] As a *performer*, however, he or she is a "harried fabricator of impressions involved in the all-too-human task of staging a performance."[31] The individual as performer is actively involved in a process of impression management. Like the stage actor, the social actor presents to others a character—a self he or she hopes they will accept and approve.

Although we generally believe that character and self are equivalent, for Goffman, the self is a *product* of a scene that comes off, and is not a *cause* of it. The self, then, as a performed character, is not an organic thing that has a specific location, whose fundamental fate is to be born, to mature, and to die; it is a dramatic effect arising diffusely from a scene that is presented; and the characteristic issue, the crucial concern, is whether it will be credited or discredited.[32]

Like a stage actor, the performer relies on proper staging. The performance must occur in an appropriate setting. During the performance, the performer must maintain an illusion of truth, must avoid breaking out of role, and must rely on reactions and support from fellow actors. In a sense, the individual is not only an actor but a director, stage manager, and set designer as well. The part of an individual's performance that normally occurs before an audience is called *front*. It includes all the expressive equipment necessary to stage a performance.[33] Front involves both *setting* ("furniture, decor, physical layout, and other background items which supply the scenery and stage props for the spate of human action played out before, within, or upon it") and *personal front* (all other items of expressive equipment such as "insignia of office or rank; clothing; sex, age and racial characteristics; size and looks; posture; speech patterns; facial expressions; bodily gestures and the like").[34]

Without a proper front, it is difficult for the performer to present a believable character. An audience will reject a performance without an appropriate front. Assume, for example, that you need to consult an attorney. You expect a competent lawyer to exhibit professional appearance and demeanor and to command an appropriate setting. If you were to enter the lawyer's office and find a dingy paint-chipped room with folding chairs instead of a spacious, well-appointed waiting room with book-lined walls, you would no doubt be taken aback. If, instead of finding receptionists, secretaries, and earnest-looking law clerks, you found a sign saying "ring bell for service," you would begin to retreat. Finally, if when the lawyer appeared he or she were wearing jeans and a rumpled shirt, it is unlikely you would wait around to discuss fees. The would-be professional, who cannot afford an appropriate setting

or who fails to fit stereotyped expectations, will have a difficult time establishing a professional self.

Even if an individual has an appropriate front, he or she must maintain *expressive control* during interaction. Any discrepancy, any unmeant gesture, can undo the performance. The lawyer who appears too anxious for our business or not anxious enough, too stuffy or too familiar, may put us off. It is not enough for an actor to worry about his or her own behavior; concern must be given to that of supporting players. Thus, lawyers rely on their office staff, rock stars on their entourage, and politicans on their families to provide them with an appropriate image. While these team members help in staging, they can also give the act away. The performer depends on their cooperation and good will.

Goffman outlines three qualities necessary for successful peformance: loyalty, discipline, and circumspection. Performers must display *dramaturgical loyalty* to team members. They must not betray the team's secrets, must not up-stage one another, and must maintain proper distance from those outside the team.[35] Second, they must be *dramaturgically disciplined*, controlling their expressive equipment, staying in character, avoiding unmeant gestures, and not getting carried away by their own performance.[36] Finally, they must show *dramaturgical circumspection*. They must use foresight and design in staging. They must choose loyal and disciplined team members, select an appropriate audience, gather all necessary sign equipment, limit the amount of knowledge the audience has about their plans, and prepare in advance for all contingencies.[37] This involves careful scheduling and audience segregation. It will never do, for example, to allow the person to whom you vowed eternal devotion last night to overhear you play the same scene today with someone else.

An actor needs a place where this act can be prepared, rehearsed, or escaped from. This place Goffman calls the *back region*, an area where no member of the audience is allowed. The faculty lounge and the rehearsal studio are examples of back regions, as is the closet in a private home into which rumpled laundry and old newpapers are thrown just before the guests arrive. Actors depend on their back regions for privacy and carefully protect them from intrusion.

Presenting an appropriate self image through interaction with others is a difficult and risky business. Luckily, most audiences exhibit considerateness and tact and will help performers stage their show. They stay away from back regions or give warning coughs or knocks if forced to intrude. If they inadvertently encounter back region behaviors, then they often pretend not to hear or see it. When in the front region, they properly attend to the performance, pretending interest and enjoyment whether or not they feel it. In addition, they restrain their own behavior in order not to detract from the performance currently being staged. Not only are expectations placed on the performer but on the audience member, too. Both are committed to ensuring smooth social performances.

For Goffman, being onself is not a simple matter:

To *be* a given kind of person, then, is not merely to possess the required attributes, but also to sustain the standards of conduct and appearance that one's social grouping attaches thereto... . A status, a position, a social place is not a material thing to be possessed and then displayed; it is a pattern of appropriate conduct, coherent, embellished, and well-articulated.[38]

Maintaining Role Distance. Goffman paints a portrait of an actor trapped within the confines of a socially given role, constrained by the demands of a scripted self. In "Role Distance," he modifies this view. He discusses how the actor fights to keep from disappearing completely into the "virtual self available in the situation."[39] While actual situations (*situated activity systems* in Goffman's terms) inevitably express something about the individual (result in a *situated self*), it is possible for the individual to deny aspects of this self by actively manipulating the situation.[40] He or she can drive a wedge between self and role.

"This 'effectively' expressed pointed separateness between the individual and his putative role" is called *role distance.*[41]

The need for role distance arises in part because each person is a "multiple-role performer rather than a person with a particular role."[42] A particular situated activity can never fully define all aspects of the self. Individuals often need to indicate to others, "I do not dispute the direction in which things are going and I will go along with them, but at the same time I want you to know that you haven't fully contained me in the state of affairs."[43] Role performances often use expressive nonverbal gestures to display this distance. Consider the case of a surgical intern. She must portray a very humble role, one that does not give much scope to her self image as a competent medical practitioner and one that does not allow her to express other aspects of her identity. To combat the situated self, our intern may affect "a careful bemused look" implying "this is not the real me."[44] She may allow her attention to wander so that her contributions to the ongoing activity do not quite fit, necessitating recall by nurse or chief surgeon. When this happens, she is careful not to show chagrin. She may assume a joking attitude that reminds others of "less exalted worlds" in which their superior position is undermined. By these means, our intern sends a message to those present that "there are other places I can be and other identities I can assume that are counter to the self you are asking me to be here and now."[45]

Of course, a communicator cannot go too far in signaling role distance. He or she cannot be too much of a deviant. Yet society does not expect communicators to invest themselves totally in every role. We cannot find every role equally attractive. Goffman argues that human actors are given a certain amount of leeway by society. People in new roles, for example, are given a sort of "learner's grace period" in which to make mistakes. Apologies and excuses allow deviations from role to be accepted. Extenuating circumstances are recognized and accepted because society views each member as a multiple role taker who should "compartmentalize himself within limits but who cannot, according to our conception of him, be asked to go too far in this compartmentalization."[46] Although we play roles, there are mechanisms available to excuse role deviations and other problematic behaviors. (See Research Abstract 6.2 for a discussion of some of these mechanisms.)

Criticism of the Dramaturgical Model. Goffman's insights into the social meaning of common everyday occurrences are unequaled. He illuminates social behavior and sheds new light on interaction. Nevertheless, he is not above criticism. He can be difficult to follow, for he introduces new terms and concepts without showing how they are connected to older formulations. His analogies are illuminating, but, like all analogies, they break down. While interaction is in many ways dramatic, it is probably closer to improvisational theater than it is to scripted performance. Many of our role performances must be negotiated as we go along in life. We are not handed a fully developed script. Goffman also overemphasizes the social constraints placed on human activity and underemphasizes human creativity. In "Role Distance," Goffman implies that we have some choice about whether or not to accept a given script, but he does not say why we choose to play some roles rather than others. It is probably unfair to criticize a theorist for not saying everything there is to say about a given process. Others have tried to outline some of the factors determining how participants choose roles. We will consider their efforts next.

McCall and Simmons' Role-Identity Model

McCall and Simmons begin their discussion of role identity by acknowledging that we each have many roles to play and arguing that our basic task in life is to juggle the demands of these roles and "to negotiate a 'safe' and 'meaningful' passage through life."[47] For McCall and Simmons, role identities are hierarchically organized. Each identity is connected to others and ordered in terms of importance and salience. The prominence of a particular identity is related to a number of factors: "its degree of self- and social support, one's degree of commitment to and investment in it, and the extrinsic and intrinsic gratifications associated with it."[48]

Choosing Roles. Our identities vary in terms of *self and other support*. Assume an individual views himself as a great artist. This identity will dominate other identities if it is supported by self perceptions. As long as the individual is pleased with his artistic work, he sees himself as an artist; if, however, his work falls short of his own standards, he may give up his art. In addition to self support, the amount of support received from others helps determine role prominence. If the appraisals and evaluations of significant others—family, friends, or art experts—conflict with the idealized role of artist, he will have a difficult time maintaining this aspect of identity.

Social support is not the only factor affecting role identity. Many artists struggle for years despite negative reviews. *Commitment and investment* in the role also determine its overall salience. If our artist has "gambled his regard for himself" on becoming an artist, if our artist has staked "his entire fortune or life's work" on this aspect of self, then it may be impossible for him to give up the dream, even in the face of universal discouragement from others.[49]

Extrinsic and intrinsic rewards must also be taken into account. Extrinsic rewards, such as "money, labor, goods, favors, prestige, and the necessities of life itself," enter into the equation.[50] Should our artist finally manage to sell a painting and pay the rent, this extrinsic reward reinforces self image. Even without extrinsic gratifications, intrinsic rewards may be enough to keep the artist going. The sheer pleasure of creative work, of performing competently in a chosen field, must be considered.

RESEARCH ABSTRACT 6.2   How Do We Try to Save Face?

According to Metts and Cupach, embarrassment occurs "when there is some public violation of a taken-for-granted rule which is part of the actor's repertoire." Their *purpose* was to study the kinds of communication strategies people use to cope with embarrassing events. In particular, they wanted to see what kinds of strategies actors would use in a variety of predicaments and what strategies observers would use to help others save face.

Their *method* was as follows. One hundred twenty students enrolled in a large introductory course in interpersonal communication served as respondents. They filled out questionnaires that asked them to describe an embarrassing situation, explain why it was distressing, and rank the degree of embarrassment they felt on a seven-point scale. They then described what they said or did to reduce embarrassment as well as what others present did to help.

Open-ended responses were coded for type of situation, actor's remedial strategies, and others' remedial strategies. Four types of situations were identified: faux pas (an intentional act that turns out to be inappropriate, such as wearing informal clothes when others are dressed formally), mistake (an intentional act that is appropriate but executed incorrectly, such as trying to use an expired credit card), accident (an unintentional act that is inappropriate, such as spilling something), and recipient (an embarrassment caused by unexpected attention of another person, for example, having one's parents appear when one's boyfriend is spending the night).

The categories used to code actors' remedial strategies were simple apology ("Excuse me"), excuse ("I was too sick to come"), justification ("This really isn't what

it seems"), humor (laughing it off), remediation (cleaning up a spill), escape (leaving the scene), avoidance (acting as though nothing has happened), and aggression (attacking so that the embarrassment looks like justified anger). The same basic categories were used for other remediation strategies with the addition of empathy ("Don't worry, it happens to everyone") and support (giving verbal or nonverbal assurance). Categorizing reliability for the three category sets was between 90 and 100 percent agreement.

Two hierarchical log-linear analyses were performed to find if some strategies were used more than others and if strategies were a function of situation. The *results* showed that actors used avoidance the most frequently and aggression the least frequently, with the other strategies being used about equally. In terms of situation, excuses are likely to be used to counter mistakes, and justifications are used in response to faux pas. Humor was considered an appropriate response to an accident, as was remediation, while aggression was used exclusively in recipient situations. Escape and avoidance are general strategies used across situations. Observers used support more than any other strategy and provided little if any remediation. Empathy and humor were also frequently used. The strategies others used did not seem to be strongly related to situation. It is apparent that people use a variety of communication strategies to extricate themselves from embarrassing situations and to save face.

Source: Sandra Metts and William R. Cupach, "Situational Influence on the Use of Remedial Strategies in Embarrassing Predicaments," *Communication Monographs*, 56 (June 1989), 151–62.

McCall and Simmons believe that each factor's importance is determined by "some sort of *averaged past level* of that factor. ... The overall prominence of a given role-identity is, then, actually a weighted average of the average past levels of several factors."[51] The artist asks the following questions: How good am I as an artist (self support)? How well do others think I paint (social support)? How much do I enjoy being an artist (intrinsic gratification)? Aside from sheer enjoyment, how much do I get from being an artist (extrinsic gratification)? How deeply have I staked myself on being an artist (commitment)? Finally, How much time, energy, and resources have I put into my artistic career (investment)?[52] The answers to these questions are weighted and combined to determine the overall salience of the artist identity. If extrinsic gratification is the key factor, then economic rewards will be the determining factor. If commitment, however, overshadows the others, then our artist may retain his role identity even in the face of humiliation and starvation.

McCall and Simmons note that responses to these factors are highly subjective and often distorted. Once a role identity becomes prominent, actors will actively maintain it, often in the face of contradictory evidence. Through selective perception we may act in ways outside observers judge irrational.[53] To legitimize a role identity, we may overlook our incompetencies, interpret politeness as positive evaluation, or only place ourselves in situations likely to enhance existing identities. We may also rationalize our failure, blame others for them, reject or deprecate unsupportive audiences, or disavow those aspects of our work that threaten self identity. These mechanisms help us maintain a positive view of self within a given role, and they explain how we manage to hold on to identities that seem unwarranted to others.

Deciding whether a particular identity is warranted is not accomplished in isolation. McCall and Simmons agree with Goffman that we actively collaborate with others to maintain our sense of self. Two mechanisms determine are used: (1) *controlled presentation of self* and (2) *altercasting.*[54] While the first was explored in our discussion of Goffman, the second needs elaboration. Whenever we communicate, we not only indicate who we are, but we also express views of who the other, the alter, is. We cast our partners in roles that support our views of self. The infatuated individual, for example, casts herself as desireable and simultaneously casts the object of her affections in a complementary role. Whether or not such casting is warranted, she treats the person she loves as though that person were in love with her and interprets the other's protestations and denials as playing hard to get. The process of altercasting is performed by both parties and involves a negotiation process in which partners work out their respective roles and performances.

Criticism of the Role Identity Model. The McCall and Simmons model deepens our understanding of role identity formation. Their recognition that we choose from multiple identities and use several factors to decide among them is sound. Although their model of the factors involved in this choice is intuitively compelling, they fail to discuss how we go about weighting different factors. They do not explain why social support will be influential for some individuals, while others will weight extrinsic rewards more heavily. When McCall and Simmons speak of computing a factor's average past level and when they discuss weighted averages, they imply that their system is quantifiable, yet it is unclear how these factors can be measured. They suggest that a person can subjectively distort any of these factors, but they do not explain why some individuals are more objective than others. Despite these difficulties, their model of self and identity is clear and compelling.

The Narrative Approach to Social Identity

McCall and Simmons stress how central the task of achieving an identity is and how far we will go in protecting our sense of self. They remind us that we spend a great deal of time actively constructing who we are. One way we both create and display the constructed self is through the autobiographical stories we tell ourselves and others. Not only are we like performers acting out social scripts, we are also like authors, writing *narratives* in which we play a central part. We do, in fact, spend a good deal of our time making up stories: In our dreams and fantasies as well as in more mundane accounts and explanations, we explain our lives by placing ourselves in the midst of a series of unfolding events. Often our stories involve "good guys" and "bad guys," follow a recognizable plot, and illustrate a moral theme.

A story that several of my students tell concerns a childhood experience. The student takes candy or a toy from a store without paying. When the parent discovers this crime, he or she forces the child to return to the store, apologize to the store manager, and pay back the money. There is generally agreement about the moral of this tale: The child is transformed by the confrontation. He or she achieves moral awareness, becoming, from that moment on, an honest person. The story is always a personally involving one, and its telling is usually dramatic. It also has cultural resonance, either because it is the kind of thing that middle class families actually do, or because it is the kind of thing they imagine themselves doing. It can be found both in life and in art, and there is a general consensus about its meaning.

While we like to think our life stories are our own, they are not entirely so. Mary Gergen points out they always have a social component: "The individual is limited at the outset to a vocabulary of action that possesses currency within the culture. One cannot compose an autobiography of cultural nonsense. One is also constrained by the demands for narrative coherence. An autobiography typically tells a story in a particular form."[55]

They are also social because we seldom keep them to ourselves. We share our stories with others, often with others who appear as characters in them. To avoid rejection, we must make them understandable and acceptable to others. Indeed, in some cases our stories are coauthored, as in the case of family myths or folie à deux.

Like literary narratives, social narratives can be analyzed for character development, structure, style, theme, and so on. Jerome Bruner, for example, borrowing the terminology of the Russian formalists, argues that the three aspects of a story, *fabula* (theme), *sjuzet* (discourse), and *forma* (genre), can be used to analyze autobiographies.[56] We can take a self narrative and submit it to an essentially literary analysis. We can ask what its gist or moral is. Is it, for example, a story about jealousy or about obedience to authority or about moral transformation? We can also look at it in terms of the way it is told, analyzing its plot and language. Finally, we can ask questions about its genre. Is it, for example, told as a romance, farce, tragedy, coming of age, or some other common narrative form? Questions such as these can help us understand how the individual has constructed his or her sense of self. And they are by no means trivial questions. As Bruner remarks:

> Eventually the culturally shaped cognitive and linguistic processes that guide the self-telling of life narratives achieve the power to structure perceptual experience, to organize memory, to segment and purpose-build the very "events" of a life. In the end, we *become* the autobiographical narratives by which we "talk about" our lives. And given the cultural shaping to which I referred, we also become variants of the culture's canonical forms.[57]

Narrative is a form of communication that we use to make sense of our worlds at all levels. Not only do we spin tales to create and maintain individual identities, we do so in the group and public contexts as well. As we will see in chapter 9, when we look at symbolic convergence theory, narratives are often used to create group and organizational identity.[58] Narratives are also important aspects of legal proceedings, for the cases presented by defense and prosecution may be seen as competing narrative explanations.[59] Finally, there are national narratives as a number of researchers who study political myths have pointed out.[60] The study of narrative form and its use in creating personal and public identity is an important theoretical area. For a study of the way people from different cultural backgrounds create narratives, see Research Abstract 6.3.

Secord and Backman's Role Negotiation Model

As we have seen in our discussion of narrative, our attempts to construct our selves are seldom done in isolation. We often coauthor our accounts of self. Secord and Backman consider the importance of negotiation processes in the creation of role identities. They believe that "an actor and his role partners can be thought of as working out though negotiation, either direct or indirect, how each will behave in particular encounters and situations, as well as the more general features of their relationship that develop over time."[61] They carefully emphasize that the negotiation process may not necessarily be overt. Role negotiations are often subtle and may not be consciously recognized by the participants. Nevertheless, interactors work out agreements resulting in a mutually satisfying performance.

Secord and Backman identify six situations in which role negotiation is particularly important:

Role negotiation…is an especially important determinant of role behavior under the following circumstances: (1) where the limits of the roles are so broad as to leave unspecified the particular nature of role performances, (2) where the role expectations held by actor and role partner for their respective roles are not in agreement with each other, (3) where the actor's characteristics preclude performing the role in the usual way, (4) where situational demands interfere with role enactment, (5) where other roles intrude upon performance, and (6) where the disparity of social power between actor and role partner is not so great as to preclude negotiation.[62]

They offer seven additional factors that determine the nature of the role bargain that will be struck between participants.[63] The first is the *role-identities* of both parties. Since this idea has been well developed by Goffman and McCall and Simmons, it will not be elaborated here. Other factors, however, affect the outcome of negotiations. One of these is the *situational demands and opportunities* surrounding the interaction. In many cases, environmental demands are why couples assume the roles they do. For example, a husband and wife may have traditional roles: a relatively dominant one for him and a relatively dependent and nurturing role for her. However, if the husband loses his job and the wife must go to work to support the family, these scripts may need to be reassigned.

Another factor involves the *influence of third parties* who may intervene on behalf of one party or may act as advisor to both. While a husband and wife may be perfectly willing to work out traditional roles, other family members may intervene with advice and counsel. For example, the wife's sister may persuade her that traditional roles are limiting. This kind of influence is especially likely when extended families live together. Husband and wife have to meet not only each other's role demands but those of the in-laws as well.

The *intrusion of other roles* affects situated role negotiation. In a negotiation between couples, the wife, for example, not only enacts the wife role but simultaneously meets the demands of being daughter, young woman, employee, member of a religious or ethnic group, member of a certain social class, and so on. To the extent any of these gain salience, they affect the negotiation process. The wife who feels a need to change from her traditional role because of her membership in a political party is allowing roles other than that of wife to affect her negotiation.

Another factor affecting negotiation outcome is the *power* of each partner, determined by his or her respective dependencies, resources, and alter-

RESEARCH ABSTRACT 6.3 Culture and Narrative Style

The ways people interpret and retell stories is often determined by cultural norms. Each of us is brought up in an "interpretive community," which tells us how to understand stories and how to convey them to others. Tamar Liebes conducted a study in which she asked respondents to retell an episode of the American soap opera "Dallas." The *purpose* was to examine the relationship between cultural background and choice of narrative form.

Using interview *methods*, Liebes assembled 54 five to six person groups and asked them, "How would you retell the episode you just saw to somebody who has not seen it?" Groups were chosen from different subcultures in Israel (Arabs, Moroccan Jews, Russian immigrants, and second-generation Israelis living in a kibbutz) and from second-generation Americans in Los Angeles. Although Liebes expected to see differences in narrative form used by these groups, there were no specific hypotheses about these differences. The research strategy was to let the responses suggest the direction of the analysis.

The research team began by reading a sample of responses. This reading showed three basic types of retellings. The first of these narrative strategies was labeled "linear"; here, the retelling followed a sequential story line. The second, called "segmented, " focused on a description of the personality of characters in the episode. The final strategy was "thematic"; here, respondents ignored events and character in order to explain the moral of the story.

Liebes did an independent textual analysis of the story. The episode consisted of two interwoven parallel plots. Sue Ellen has left J.R. and taken her child, while Pam has attempted suicide. Both J.R. and Bobby resort to illegal acts to gain possession of a child, J.R. using kidnapping and Bobby deciding to buy a baby. Thus, the story was a complex combination of several story lines.

Having determined the episode's structure, the author's next step was to examine how each group decided to retell it. *Results* showed that although all the groups simplified the episodes and added subjective perceptions, there was an identifiable correlation between ethnicity and narrative choice. The Arab and Moroccan groups used linear retellings, telling the story in a closed form as though it were an inevitable progression. The American and kibbutz groups offered segmented retellings, focusing on the psychological problems and motivations of a single character, generally Pam. These retellings were open and future oriented. Finally, the Russian group used a thematic strategy, explaining the popularity of the series in terms of its politics. They saw the episode as an example of capitalist propaganda. Ignoring the story, they concentrated on the overall message of the piece. Thus, the Arab and Moroccan groups explained the story sociologically; the American and kibbutz groups, psychologically; and the Russians, ideologically.

This study illustrates the extent to which in understanding stories people bring their own cultural perspectives with them, perspectives reflected in the ways they edit the story and recast it when asked to recount it to others.

Source: Tamar Liebes, "Cultural Differences in the Retelling of Television Fiction," *Critical Studies in Mass Communication*, 5 (December 1988), 277–92.

natives. The partner who is economically and emotionally dependent on the spouse, who has no other alternatives, and who controls few resources, will be at a disadvantage in the bargaining process. *Interpersonal skills* are also important. The individual who is perceptive, who can accurately assess his or her bargaining position, who knows how to handle the other, is likely to control the negotiation process skillfully. Finally, *interpersonal dispositions*, learned ways of resolving problems of interdependence, will also determine outcomes. The person, for example, whose only way of handling relationships is through dominance, will use that disposition during negotiation.

Secord and Backman suggest that many factors other than that of social role enter into the relational definition process. They further believe that changes in the wider economic or social sphere will have an impact on power relationships in situated negotiations and that these will feed back on and modify cultural forms. For example, women's changing economic roles within social systems have resulted in more alternatives, fewer dependencies, and a better bargaining position. These, in turn, redefine the social roles of husband and wife. There is a reciprocal relationship among all of the factors affecting individual role negotiations and the social structure as a whole.

COMMUNICATIVE COMPETENCE: WHAT FACTORS DETERMINE COMPETENT SOCIAL COORDINATION?

Our discussion so far has been general in nature. It has suggested that communicators are under pressure to take on socially defined and negotiated roles and to coordinate these with others. A number of theorists have set as their task a description of the kinds of knowledge and ability it takes to achieve this kind of coordination. Given that it is through speech that we act out

dramaturgical processes and connect with others, what kinds of speech behaviors are most appropriate? In this section, we will look at three models: Weinstein's developmental theory of interpersonal competence, Hart and Burks' concept of rhetorical sensitivity, and Wiemann's model of communicative competence. All three directly follow the theoretical perspective established in previous sections, stressing that competent coordination involves enacting multiple social identities and the ability to assess others' goals and views of situation.

Weinstein's Interpersonal Competence Theory

Weinstein defines interpersonal competence as our ability to accomplish interpersonal tasks by controlling and shaping our responses from others.[64] Central is skill at establishing and maintaining desired identities for both self and other. Weinstein believes three abilities lie at the heart of interpersonal competence: (1) *empathy* or role-taking ability, (2) possession of a varied *repertoire of lines* of action, and (3) the *flexibility* to enact appropriate lines of action under appropriate circumstances.

First, competent communicators must be empathic. They must be able to assess accurately others' definitions of a situation. The empathic communicator must be able to infer the feelings and needs of others. Developmentally, empathic ability seems to occur in stages. Very early, children learn that others have feelings and needs that are like their own but separate from them. The ability to recognize cues to others' feelings and to *sympathize* with them shows mastery of this stage.

Next, *projective role-taking* occurs. Here, children learn that certain feelings are associated with certain situations. They are able to reason in effect, "I know how I would feel in this situation. Since my friend is in this situation, he or she must

RESEARCH ABSTRACT 6.4 The Development of Interpersonal Competence

Riccillo wanted to determine how very young children develop the ability to respond appropriately to communicative demands that vary in complexity. He proposed that, like grammatical ability, the ability to know when and how to use language occurs sequentially. His *purpose* was to test a developmental model of communicative competence.

His model was derived from an earlier one by Williams and Naremore. These authors viewed speech usage as ranging along a continuum from simple expressive utterances that are highly contextual to elaborative forms showing ability to adapt to the receivers' perspective. Using their work, Riccillo identified seven modes of communication: contactive (speaker simply makes verbal contact with another), conversative (speaker maintains conversational connection with another, the topic being irrelevant), descriptive (speaker tries to relate precise information to the receiver), directive (speaker tells the receiver how to do something), interpretive (speaker explains the meaning of an event, idea, or concept), narrative (an organized, developed story is related), and persuasive (speaker appeals to the receiver to change). Each mode of communication places a different demand on the individual speaker.

Riccillo wanted to see at what age each speech mode is mastered and whether communication forms including role-taking and audience adaptation occur at a later age. His *method* was to develop a set of questions that required each kind of language use. He used these probes to elicit language samples from 16 middle-class preschool children ranging in age from 2½ to 4½ years. Each child responded to a total of 14 probes, based on the seven com-

continued...

feel the way I would." *Positional role-taking* soon follows. Children learn that people in certain positions (mothers, fathers, teachers, friends) can be expected to act in particular ways.

Personality stereotyping is another stage in the development of empathy. Eventually, children learn to place others in personality categories. By the middle grades, children can class others as "grouchy," "conceited," "mean," and "nice," and they know the behavioral implications of these categories. Finally, *individuation* is mastered. Here children abandon stereotyped thinking and base role-taking on experiences with particular individuals.

Clearly, we all work back and forth between these stages, sometimes using stereotypes when other information is missing. Although generally developmental, the stages are by no means set in stone. Very young children can make surprisingly mature individual judgments, and we all know fully grown adults who at times exhibit the empathic skills of two year olds.

In addition to role-taking and empathic abilities, competent communicators must also develop a repertoire of interpersonal tactics. A child's first interpersonal tactic is that of crying. Although crying begins as a natural reaction to unpleasant stimuli, it soon becomes a voluntary act. With language development, a whole new series of tactics ensue, including direct requests, the delivery of positive sanctions in return for favors, and more complex forms of bargaining and exchange. By the time children reach adolescence, they have mastered an entire repertoire of methods for deal-

RESEARCH ABSTRACT 6.4 (*continued*)

munication modes. For example, the child's ability to respond descriptively was tested by asking him or her to describe what a favorite toy looked like.

Each response was scored on the basis of whether the child responded appropriately to the probe. Here are two examples. First, a child responds to a request to describe a toy by saying, "It's round and it's red and green." This is an appropriate response. Later, when asked to describe how it feels to go real fast on a tricycle (an interpretive probe), the child says, "I have a tricycle, it's red and my grandmother gave it to me. Sometimes I fall and have to go inside. My tricycle is red." Because the child does not explain the experience but instead describes it, this response is inappropriate.

Responses were analyzed by reporting the percentage of children at each age responding appropriately. Each speech mode was ordered in terms of the number of children at each level who were able to

respond to it. *Results* showed that all of the children communicated contactively and conversatively. Of the remaining probes, descriptive appeared to be mastered earliest, followed by explanative and directive. The narrative and persuasive modes were the most complex. None of the 2½ year olds could fulfill these communicative demands, and less than half of the 3 year olds. However, by 4 years of age, over 80 percent could narrate and over 77 percent could persuade.

Riccillo says, "The modes of speech categories do seem to describe increasingly complex functional abilities and serve to give an initial indication of the stages in the development of communicative competence."

Source: Samuel C. Riccillo, "Modes of Speech as a Developmental Hierarchy: A Descriptive Study," *Western Journal of Speech Communication*, 47 (Winter 1983), 1–15.

ing with others. Research Abstract 6.4 discusses how children develop interpersonal repertoires.

The individual with a limited repertoire of tactics, who fails to develop a range of persuasive tactics, is at a distinct disadvantage in communicating with others. Of course, having an arsenal of tactics does not ensure interpersonal competence. Knowing when and how to employ them, being interpersonally flexible, is also necessary. As Weinstein points out, "It is possible for some people to know how to get what they want and still, because of personality factors, be unable to do so."[65] Rigidity and rule-boundedness can interfere with interpersonal competence. In addition, individuals who are anomic or alienated, lack self-esteem, or have too little or too great a need for approval, will be unable to accomplish interpersonal tasks successfully.

Rhetorical Sensitivity

Hart and Burks and Hart, Carlson, and Eadie present another view of the factors involved in being a competent communicator.[66] The key construct in their model is that of *rhetorical sensitivity*. Like interpersonal competence, rhetorical sensitivity involves adaptation to the social identities of others and flexibility in communicating.

To understand their model we have to know what prompted it. In the late 1960s and early 1970s, a movement known as humanistic psychology was popular. Psychologists such as Carl Rogers and Fritz Perls argued that the most important aspect of healthy communication was presentation of an authentic and consistent self.[67] Communicating partners were urged to maintain their own unique identities while showing unconditional, positive regard for the unique identities of others. Through therapeutic interactions such as sensitivity training, T-groups, and the like, people were taught that self-acceptance, total honesty, and willingness to self-disclose lay at the heart of rewarding interaction. The original formulation of rhetorical sensitivity was, in part, a protest against an uncritical acceptance of this view.

Hart and Burks believed the humanistic view failed to come to terms with the importance of role-adaptation and the need of communicators to enact multiple selves. They argued that, in preaching total honesty and complete consistency, the humanists failed to account for the importance of adaptation. They identified three types of communicators. While they recognized that the person who has no sense of self and is willing to adapt totally to others (*the rhetorical reflector*) is not the ideal type, they also believed that the person who refuses to adapt in order to be "true to self" (*the noble self*) is also limited. They suggested a third type of individual (*the rhetorically sensitive*) who lies halfway between these extremes. This individual is truly socially competent because he or she combines a concern for self and others with a recognition of the importance of situational constraints.

According to Hart, Carlson, and Eadie, five factors lead to rhetorical sensitivity. First is *acceptance of personal complexity*. Rhetorically sensitive individuals recognize that a person is a "complex network of selves" and that different situations require the presentation of different aspects of this network. Second is *avoidance of communication rigidity*. The rhetorically sensitive individual must be flexible. A third factor is *interaction consciousness*. Individuals must balance their own ideals and goals with those of others. In addition, they must show *appreciation of the communicability of ideas*. Sometimes, communication and disclosure are inappropriate, and there are some ideas about which, in certain contexts, the individual should remain silent. *Tolerance for inventional searching* is the fifth factor

in rhetorical sensitivity. Communicators must recognize the different ways to impart an idea and must be able to adapt to audience and situation.

Wiemann's Communicative Competence Model

John Wiemann presents a final model of social competence.[68] He focuses on patterns of verbal and nonverbal behaviors that allow individuals to appear competent to others. Wiemann's definition of communicative competence is not radically different from those of interpersonal competence and rhetorical sensitivity. He sees communicative competence as "the ability of an interactant to choose among available communicative behaviors in order that he may successfully accomplish his own interpersonal goals during an encounter while maintaining the face and line of his fellow interactants within the constraints of the situation."[69]

Wiemann says the competent communicator balances two possibly conflicting goals. On the one hand, the individual wants to accomplish a personally defined goal, yet, on the other, he or she recognizes that this cannot be accomplished at the cost of the other, that relational maintenance is also crucial. "The competent communicator is the person who can have his way in the relationship while maintaining a mutually acceptable definition of that relationship."[70]

While his definition of communicative competence is very general, his model defines the specific behaviors used by communicators during situated activity. That is, Wiemann attempts to answer the question: What does the competent communicator actually say or do to present a self-image that others will accept? Wiemann develops five sets of easily recognizable cues that signal competence. The first set consists of *affiliation-support* cues that include eye behavior, use of status markers, head nods, duration of speaking time and speaking rate, pleasantness of facial expression, statements indicating "owning" one's perceptions about another, and physical proximity.

The second set consists of *social relaxation* cues, among which are general posture and movement, speaking rate, speech disturbances, and object manipulation. *Empathy* cues form the third set. Reciprocity of affect displays, verbal responses indicating feeling and understanding, and perceived active listening cues are in this set. The fourth set involves *behavioral flexibility* and includes verbal immediacy cues and use of status and affiliation markers. Finally, the fifth set is labeled *interaction management* and is based on two important skills, the "ability to establish and maintain a smooth and easy pattern of interaction" and the ability to plan and control the direction of an interaction without dominating. The first is established through allocation of turn-taking, suitable use of pauses and interruptions, and the amount of attention devoted to the encounter. The second is indicated through topic control.

The competent communicator is perceived as being supportive to his or her partner, empathic, relaxed during interaction, and flexible in reaction to others. He or she is also skillful at managing the flow of interaction and at regulating the direction of talk. The competent communicator knows how to use appropriate sets of verbal and nonverbal cues in all these areas.

Criticisms of Social Competence Models

The three models reviewed all stress the importance of empathy and behavioral flexibility. They do not go far enough, however, in specifying the actual competencies involved or explaining how these competencies are actualized in ongoing interaction. Weinstein's and Hart's models are general and say little about the molecular behaviors necessary for communicative performance. Wiemann goes further in this direction, but his model lacks research support and concentrates only on a small subset of nonverbal behaviors. The question of communicative competence is important for students of communication. The answer seems to be a prerequisite for understanding communication in all of its contexts. Luckily, in recent years, a number of scholars have considered this problem and developed research programs to supplement our understanding of the knowledge and skill necesssary for coordinated interaction.[71]

SUMMARY: SELF, COMMUNICATION, AND SOCIETY

Taken together, the theories just presented stress the notion that coordinated interaction is intimately tied to our ability to create and maintain definitions of self and others, that these definitions are created by society and supported by communication. Most theorists suggest that the relationship between self, communication, and society is a complex, circular one. Social structures originally tell us who to be and how to communicate, but these structures depend on communication for their maintenance. Through communication we can act on and change the very structures that create us. How is this possible?

Sheldon Stryker uses symbolic interactionist ideas to explain. As you will recall from our discussion in chapter 3, social interaction is guided by symbolic processes, in particular by the process of naming. Through interaction we learn to classify and name objects in the environment. In the process of naming, we learn how to act toward the objects we name because we create action plans. Through interaction, we "recognize one another as occupants of positions, name one another, and so invoke expectations for another's behavior."[72] These expectations help us organize our behaviors and serve as guides for subsequent actions.

Stryker tells us that social rules and expectations impose limits on our possibilities for interaction "by bringing only certain people together in certain places in certain times under certain conditions."[73] We are constrained by norms of interaction, by rules dictating how to talk, and by sanctions that reward or punish us for inappropriate communication.

At the same time, these social rules do not absolutely determine behavior. During situated activity, behavioral expectations and rules of interaction may be renegotiated, and novelty may be introduced. "Changes in the character of definitions, the names used in those definitions, and the possibilities for (further) interaction can occur," and such changes can feed back on social structures, causing their evolution and growth.[74] Meanings derived from immediate individual experiences and meanings derived from embeddedness in social roles together determine the nature of human communication. To communicate successfully, individuals must be aware of social expectations, must be able to empathize with others, must develop flexible repertoires of styles and tactics, and must manage the flow of interaction. The individual who masters these skills will have successfully mastered the problem of coordination and will be able to participate in all the important contexts of communication.

REFERENCES

1. Hugh Dalziel Duncan, "The Search for a Social Theory of Communication," in *Human Communication Theory: Original Essays*, ed. Frank E. X. Dance (New York: Holt, Rinehart & Winston, 1967), p. 253.

2. Theodore M. Newcomb, Ralph H. Turner, and Philip E. Converse, *Social Psychology: The Study of Human Interaction* (New York: Holt, Rinehart & Winston, 1965), p. 325.

3. *Ibid.*, p. 325.

4. Ralph Linton, *The Cultural Background of Personality* (New York: Appleton-Century-Crofts, 1945). See also Newcomb, Turner, and Converse, *Social Psychology*, p. 326, and Ralph Linton, *The Study of Man*, chap. 8 (New York: Appleton-Century-Crofts, 1936).

5. Newcomb, Turner, and Converse, *Social Psychology*, p. 325.

6. Erving Goffman, "Role Distance," in *Encounters: Two Studies in the Sociology of Interaction* (New York: Bobbs Merrill, 1961), p. 85.

7. Newcomb, Turner, and Converse, *Social Psychology*, p. 328.

8. Goffman, "Role Distance," p. 86.

9. Linton, *The Cultural Background of Personality*, p. 78.

10. Frank E. X. Dance and Carl E. Larson, *Speech Communication: Concepts and Behavior* (New York: Holt, Rinehart & Winston, 1972), p. 107.

11. Goffman, "Role Distance," p. 87.

12. George J. McCall and J. L. Simmons, *Identities and Interactions* (New York: The Free Press, 1966), p. 67.

13. This idea is presented by many writers. Erving Goffman is one of the chief proponents of this view, as are McCall and Simmons. In addition, see Paul F. Secord and Carl W. Backman, *Social Psychology*, 2nd ed. (New York: McGraw-Hill, 1974), and James T. Tedeschi, ed. *Impression Management Theory and Social Psychology* (New York: Academic, 1981).

14. McCall and Simmons, *Identities and Interactions*, p. 75.

15. Erving Goffman, *The Presentation of Self in Everyday Life* (Garden City, N. Y.: Doubleday, 1981).

16. Erving Goffman, "On Face-Work: An Analysis of Ritual Elements in Social Interaction," *Psychiatry*, 18 (August 1955), 213–31.

17. *Ibid.*, pp. 213–14.

18. *Ibid.*, p. 215.

19. *Ibid.*, p. 216.

20. *Ibid.*, p. 217.

21. *Ibid.*, p. 215.

22. *Ibid.*, p. 215.

23. *Ibid.*, p. 220.

24. *Ibid.*, p. 220.

25. *Ibid.*, p. 221.

26. *Ibid.*, p. 226.

27. *Ibid.*, p. 229.

28. *Ibid.*, p. 229.

29. *Ibid.*, p. 229.

30. Goffman, *Presentation of Self*, p. 252.
31. *Ibid.*, p. 252.
32. *Ibid.*, pp. 252–53.
33. *Ibid.*, p. 22.
34. *Ibid.*, p. 24.
35. *Ibid.*, p. 212.
36. *Ibid.*, p. 216.
37. *Ibid.*, p. 218.
38. *Ibid.*, p. 75.
39. Goffman, "Role Distance," p. 106.
40. *Ibid.*, p. 107.
41. *Ibid.*, p. 108.
42. *Ibid.*, p. 142.
43. *Ibid.*, p. 133.
44. *Ibid.*, p. 118.
45. *Ibid.*, p. 139.
46. *Ibid.*, p. 142.
47. McCall and Simmons, *Identities and Interactions*, p. 23.
48. *Ibid.*, p. 79.
49. *Ibid.*, p. 78.
50. *Ibid.*, p. 78.
51. *Ibid.*, p. 79.
52. *Ibid.*, pp. 264–65.
53. *Ibid.*, p. 96–97.
54. *Ibid.*, p. 139.
55. Mary M. Gergen and Kenneth J. Gergen, "The Social Construction of Narrative Accounts," in *Historical Social Psychology*, eds. Kenneth J. Gergen and Mary M. Gergen (Hillsdale, N. J.: Lawrence Erlbaum Associates, 1984), p. 185.
56. Jerome Bruner, "Life As Narrative," *Social Research*, 54 (Spring 1987), 11–32. For a general discussion of narrative including an explanation of the work of the Russian formalists, see articles by Hayden White, "The Value of Narrativity in the Representation of Reality," and Frank Kermode, "Secrets and Narrative Sequence," in *On Narrative*, ed. W. J. T. Mitchell, (Chicago: University of Chicago Press, 1984).
57. Jerome Bruner, "Life as Narrative," p. 15.
58. Ernest G. Bormann, "Symbolic Convergence Theory: A Communication Formulation," *Journal of Communication*, 35 (1985), 128–38.
59. W. L. Bennett, "Storytelling and Criminal Trials: A Model of Social Judgment," *Quarterly Journal of Speech*, 64 (1978), 1–22.
60. There is a large body of literature on narrative in political mythmaking. The following studies are a very small sample. Ernest G. Bormann, "A Fantasy Theme Analysis of the Television Coverage of the Hostage Release and the Reagan Inaugural," *Quarterly Journal of Speech*, 68 (1982), 133–45; Ernest G. Bormann, *The Force of Fantasy: Restoring the American Dream* (Carbondale: Southern Illinois University Press, 1985); William F. Lewis, "Telling America's Story: Narrative Form and the Reagan Presidency," *Quarterly Journal of Speech*, 73 (1987), 280–302; Umberto Eco, "Strategies of Lying," in *On Signs*, ed. Marshall Blonsky (Baltimore: Johns Hopkins University Press, 1985).
61. Secord and Backman, *Social Psychology*, p. 415.
62. *Ibid.*, p. 415.
63. Carl B. Backman, "Toward an Interdisciplinary Social Psychology," in *Advances in Experimental Social Psychology*, vol 16, ed. Leonard Berkowitz (New York: Academic, 1983).
64. Eugene A. Weinstein, "The Development of Interpersonal Competence," in *Handbook of Socialization Theory and Research*, ed. David A. Goslin (Chicago: Rand McNally, 1969), p. 755.
65. *Ibid.*, p. 769.
66. Roderick P. Hart and Don M. Burks, "Rhetorical Sensitivity and Social Interaction," *Speech Monographs*, 39 (1972), 75–91; Roderick P. Hart, Robert E. Carlson, and William F. Eadie, "Attitudes Toward Communication and the Assessment of Rhetorical Sensitivity," *Communication Monographs*, 46 (1980), 1–22.
67. See, for example, Carl Rogers, *On Becoming a Person* (Boston: Houghton Mifflin, 1961) and *Client-Centered Therapy* (Boston: Houghton Mifflin, 1951).
68. John M. Wiemann, "Explication and Test of a Model of Communicative Competence," *Human Communication Research*, 3 (Spring 1977), 195–213; John M. Wiemann, "Needed Research and

Training in Speaking and Listening Literacy," *Communication Education*, 27 (November 1978), 310–15; John M. Wiemann and C. W. Kelly, "Pragmatics of Interpersonal Competence," in *Rigor and Imagination*, eds. C. Wilder-Mott and John H. Weakland (New York: Praeger, 1981).

69. Wiemann, "Explication and Test," p. 198.

70. *Ibid.*, p. 198.

71. See, for example, Donald J. Cegala, "Interaction Involvement: A Cognitive Dimension of Communicative Competence," *Communication Education*, 30 (April 1981), 109–21; Donald J. Cegala and others, "An Elaboration of the Meaning of Interaction Involvement: Toward the Development of a Theoretical Concept," *Communication Monographs*, 49 (December 1982), 229–48; William A. Villaume and Donald J. Cegala, "Interaction Involvement and Discourse Strategies: The Patterned Use of Cohesive Devices in Conversation," *Communication Monographs*, 55 (March 1988), 22–40; Ruth Ann Clark and Jesse G. Delia, "*Topoi* and Rhetorical Competence," *The Quarterly Journal of Speech*, 65 (1979), 187–206; Brian H. Spitzberg and Michael L. Hecht, "A Component Model of Relational Competence," *Human Communication Research*, 10 (Summer 1984), 575–99; David R. Brandt, "On Linking Social Performance with Social Competence: Some Relations Between Communicative Style and Attributions of Interpersonal Attractiveness and Effectiveness," *Human Communication Research*, 5 (Spring 1979), 223–37.

72. Sheldon Stryker, "Social Psychology from the Standpoint of a Structural Symbolic Interactionism: Toward an Interdisciplinary Social Psychology," in *Advances in Experimental Social Psychology*, vol. 16, ed. Leonard Berkowitz (New York: Academic, 1983), p. 209.

73. *Ibid.*, p. 209.

74. *Ibid.*, p. 209.

chapter 7

THE DUAL PROBLEMS OF OUTCOME ACHIEVEMENT AND EVOLUTION

INTRODUCTION TO THE PROBLEM OF OUTCOME ACHIEVEMENT

Think for a moment about the place of communication in your life. What personal goals do you achieve through communication? How does it allow you to control and change your own behaviors and those of others? Think also what your life would be like if your communication remained stable, if you communicated today in the same ways you communicated 10 years ago. How does communication develop, both within individual interactions and across the life span? These questions deal with the complex relationship between communication and change. They are representative of the final two problems we will consider: the problem of outcome achievement and the problem of evolution.

In the first part of this chapter we will examine theories about the ways individuals control their social and personal worlds, theories directed to the problem of outcome achievement.

We have already defined communicative competence as the ability to accomplish goals through coordinated social interaction. This definition implies that communication is often undertaken for a purpose, that we use communication to achieve desired ends.

We will begin our discussion of this problem by considering some of the ways in which communication changes us and allows us to pursue goals. We will then focus on theories of motivation and influence. We will ask, What kinds of outcomes motivate human actors? What strategies are effective in influencing receivers? How are these strategies best communicated? These questions introduce the fourth major communication problem: achieving communicative outcomes.

FUNCTIONAL OUTCOMES: HOW DOES COMMUNICATION CHANGE US?

Dance and Larson's Functional Theory

Frank Dance and Carl Larson's functional theory stresses the far-reaching effects of communication on human cognition and behavior.[1] Dance and Larson begin by making a distinction between function and purpose. They define *purpose* as an intentional outcome desired by an actor and *function* as a natural and unintentional outcome. They then go on to outline three functions that always accompany communication: (1) the *linking* of the individual with the environment, (2) the development of *mentation*, and (3) the *regulation* of human behavior.[2]

Perhaps the easiest way to grasp what they mean by function is to consider mathematical functions. In the empirical sciences, two things bear a functional relationship if they are dependent, if changes in one result in changes in the other. For example, heat is functionally related to the dissipation of energy.[3] As energy is released, heat is produced. Although humans may purposefully use their knowledge of this functional relationship by turning on a stove to cook a meal, the relationship itself occurs whether or not humans wish it to. Dance and Larson argue that communication too has certain inevitable and natural outcomes.

The Linking Function. Dance and Larson's first proposition is that communication serves to link individuals to their environments. Through communication individuals act on and adapt to the world. In discussing this process, Dance and Larson draw on the work of the developmental psychologist Jean Piaget. Piaget believes that

organisms modify themselves by drawing upon their environments. If the transaction between organism and environment "is such that the organism, after the interchange, is better suited to maintain itself and better equipped to engage in further interchanges... , then we have an instance of *adaptation*."[4] Adaptation involves two related subprocesses: *assimilation* and *accommodation*. Through assimilation, the organism searches the environment for elements to incorporate into its structure. Through accommodation, it adjusts itself to surrounding objects.

Communicative adaptation involves both processes. On the basis of cognitive structures and prior experiences, individuals assimilate information. Once incorporated, this information changes us, creating new ways of perceiving and gathering information. Because communication is the process of acting on information and because we, as humans, are innately capable of processing information, linking is inevitable.

The Mentation Function. Communication also leads to mentation. By mentation, Dance and Larson mean the ability to engage in such higher mental processes as "memory, planning and foresight, intelligence, thinking, [and] judgment."[5] Dance and Larson believe that the ability to engage in abstract thought depends on the ability to manipulate symbolic codes, the defining characteristic of human communication.[6] To explain the relationship between thought and action, Dance and Larson turn to the research of the Russian psychologist Lev Vygotsky.[7]

Vygotsky argues that although infants possess rudimentary thought forms that are nonlinguistic (for example, perceiving and pointing to objects) and simple speech forms that are pre-intellectual (for example, babbling), at around the age of 2, these behaviors merge, "whereupon thought becomes verbal and speech rational."[8] At first, this verbal thought is external and highly egocentric. Soon, however, an "ingrowth" stage occurs in which "external operation turns inward and undergoes a profound change in the process. The child begins to count in his head, to use 'logical memory.'" This process is called *inner speech.*[9] Once speech turns inward, advanced levels of thought are possible. The ability to engage in higher mental processes is dependent on the internalization of speech communication. Thus, the abilities to manipulate symbols and to engage in mentation are functionally related.

The Regulatory Function. Human communication also allows us to regulate both our own and others' behavior. Although behavior regulation is often intentional, Dance and Larson argue that it is also functional because "the initial acquisition of speech communication automatically limits (and thus regulates) our range of linguistic and thus behavioral options."[10] Dance and Larson argue that there are three stages to regulation: regulation of self by others, regulation of self by self, and regulation of others by self.[11]

As infants we are regulated by the speech of others. We exist in a world of verbal instructions: "Smile for Mommy"; "No, Baby mustn't touch"; "Wave bye-bye." From the moment of birth, the infant "is immersed in a web of regulatory speech."[12] With age, children soon learn not only to follow orders but to address speech to themselves. By adulthood we are capable of silently regulating our own behavior, although when we find ourselves in tense situations we may actually talk out loud, telling ourselves to "Take it easy," or to "Calm down and think things through."

The third stage involves controlling others through talk. First with family, and later with outside contacts, we learn to use words to accomplish our purposes. In adulthood:

The use of oaths and vows, the use of verbal formulas such as "I pronounce you man and wife," or "I dub thee knight," testify to the traditional and deep-seated view of the spoken word as not only a powerful regulator of individual and social human behavior but also a formidable power to be used in changing social reality.[13]

Criticism of Functional Theory

Although certain questions are left unanswered (Are there other functions? How are functions related to purposes?), this model offers a valuable contribution to our knowledge of communication. The idea that communication inevitably results in the achievement of certain outcomes is intriguing, and the three functions are carefully developed. The Dance and Larson model reminds us of the fact that we are, by nature, communicators and that this ability affects all aspects of our nature.

THEORIES OF MOTIVATION: WHAT DO HUMANS WANT?

We have established the importance of communication in the attainment of functional outcomes. We have not yet considered, however, what outcomes people purposefully seek; nor have we discussed the ways these outcomes may be achieved. We now turn to a discussion of theories of motivation, learning, and social influence. Because the research in this area is large, we can only look at a small subset of the alternative theories explaining the forces that shape human behavior.

Katz's Functional Theory of Attitudes

A point of departure for discussing motivation can be found in Katz's functional theory of attitude change.[14] Katz's use of the term "functional" is different from that of Dance and Larson. For Katz, functions are the motivations behind the attitudes we hold. In brief, Katz believes that humans hold attitudes for a variety of purposes. Attitudes can help us attain rewards and avoid punishments, protect our egos from external threats, allow us to express valued identities, and simplify our mental words. The ways we think and feel about attitude objects are related to these basic functions.

Katz's theory is useful in several ways. First, it allows us to compare some of the basic ends desired by human actors. Second, his typology can help us organize our review of classical motivational and social influence theories. Finally, his model introduces the notion of attitudes as mediators of social behavior. Although the theories in this chapter differ in the extent to which they embrace the concept of attitude, all of them recognize that behavior is cognitively mediated in some way.

Attitudes as Internal Mediating Structures. Before discussing the functions of attitudes we should ask what an attitude is. The usual definition is a predisposition toward action, a set of cognitions and emotions that result in "general feelings of favorableness or unfavorableness toward the self or some external stimulus."[15] Attitudes affect the ways we respond to stimuli. They are mental guidelines for action. Philip Zimbardo and others point out three defining characteristics of attitudes: (1) They are learned rather than innate, (2) they are enduring rather than momentary, and (3) they are general rather than specific.[16] These characteristics all have important ramifications for the ways attitudes predispose us to act. Because attitudes are learned, the general principles that increase or decrease learning affect their formation. Because attitudes are enduring, they give rise to long lasting rather than short-lived changes in behavior. Finally, because they are generalized, a single attitude may manifest itself in a variety of specific actions.

An attitude is not directly observable. It is a hypothetical construct assumed to explain the existence of more directly observable behaviors. Some theorists reject all mental constructs because they are not directly quantifiable. Most theorists who take a cognitive approach, however, believe that the inclusion of a mental construct such as attitude increases the explanatory power of their models. While they recognize the difficulty of measuring internal states, they believe

that this problem is solvable and that mental concepts are useful in understanding behavior.

Most attitude theorists also note that, while attitudes predispose us to act in certain ways, the relationship between attitudes and behaviors is not totally predictable. Because attitudes vary in strength and salience, because a single attitude can be behaviorally manifested in many ways, and because humans hold conflicting attitudes simultaneously, we do not always act in accordance with our attitudes. In fact, the relationship between attitudes and behaviors is not unidirectional but reciprocal. While cognitive structures such as attitudes lead to actions, actions also lead to attitude formation. As Herbert Kelman tells us, "not only is attitude an integral part of action, but action is an integral part of the development, testing, and crystallization of attitudes."[17] The concept of attitude and its relationship to behavior is complex. The key point to remember is that actions are often produced by internal planning and thought processes. The reasons people prefer some lines of action to others is due to these internal processes.

Four Functional Outcomes. Katz believes that we hold the attitudes we do because they address certain functional needs. The four functions served by attitudes are (1) the adjustment function, (2) the ego defense function, (3) the value expression function, and (4) the knowledge function. The *adjustment function* (also called the instrumental or utilitarian function) originates in our desire to maximize external rewards and minimize external punishments. Katz believes that we hold positive attitudes toward those objects that satisfy current needs or that previously resulted in rewards. Holding such attitudes lets us adjust to our environments. If our needs change, or if we find that a new attitude leads to better rewards, then we usually change our attitudes. For example, a lifelong Democrat who strikes it rich may now find it more rewarding to vote Republican because of economic policies that allow tax advantages and investment incentives. He may also change political beliefs simply because he wants to fit in with a new set of friends. Whenever attitudes are held because they are rewarding, they serve an adjustment function.

Another function attitudes serve is the *ego defense* function. Individuals may hold attitudes to protect the self from threat. According to this view, the ego is a fragile construction requiring protection from information that would show it to be less than ideal. Many of our personal beliefs and perceptions may be ego defensive. The distortions that occur in dreams, and the presence of defense mechanisms such as projection or denial, are designed to protect the ego from recognizing unacceptable impulses. Social attitudes often result from an attempt to project our own insecurities and fears onto outside groups. The "Red Scare" that was so successfully manipulated by Joseph McCarthy and the House Unamerican Activities Committee in the 1950s, as well as many racial prejudices, can be interpreted as a process of turning our own insecurities outward to maintain ego organization.

Attitudes that fulfill a *value expressive function* allow us to express our personal values and role identities. They are rewarding because they allow us to establish and confirm valued social roles. In a sense, value expression is the flip side of ego defense. While the goal of ego defense is self-protection, in value expression the goal is a an overt expression of social identity. For example, if we consider ourselves to be enlightened intellectuals, then we will hold attitudes that show the world we deserve this label. Katz believes that voting behavior is often value expressive. Although we may vote for a particular candidate because we anticipate some external gratification (adjustment) or because we believe he or she will protect us from externalized threats to self (ego defense), we often vote simply because it is a symbolic expression of political identity (value expression).[18] People who vote a straight party ticket are affirming their identities and values. This function may well explain behavior at politi-

cal conventions where the speeches center on loyalty to the party and emphasize abstract values. Even the wearing of funny hats, the waving of banners, and the chanting of slogans are ways of expressing who we are.

The *knowledge function* is based on individuals' needs to structure their cognitive worlds. It is based on a search for meaning, on a need to organize beliefs in a clear, coherent, and consistent manner. Attitudes can help humans achieve an ordered and knowable world. Stereotypes often serve the knowledge function by enabling us to simplify our worlds, avoid contradictions, and make predictions. It is cognitively easier to believe that all members of a group are alike than to accept individual contradictions and differences. We hold some attitudes simply because they allow us more certainty than others.

Using the Katz Model to Achieve Desired Outcomes. Katz believes that attitude change techniques must be based on knowledge of the function a target attitude fulfills for those who hold it. In general we can change attitudes by showing receivers that the function their current attitude fulfills can be better served by a new attitude. Of course, this means that we must know the functions attitudes hold for the individuals we wish to change. An ego-defensive attitude cannot be changed in the same way as one based on adjustment, value expression, or knowledge.

If we want to change an adjustment attitude, we must enable the individual to see either that current attitudes are not rewarding or that the new attitude we advocate will result in greater need fulfillment. If ego defense is at issue, we must show either that existing beliefs lead to unexpected threats or that new beliefs result in greater psychological security. Changes in value expressive attitudes must focus on the utility of new attitudes for enhancing self-image and role identity. Finally, changes in knowledge-based attitudes must demonstrate that old attitudes contain inconsistencies and contradictions while new attitudes make better sense of the world.

Criticism of Katz's Theory. Perhaps the biggest criticism that can be made about this typology is that it is dated. Although it synthesizes theory that was current at the time, it fails to account for more recent concerns with cognitive organization and rule-following behavior. In addition, the model is eclectic, containing elements of learning theory, psychoanalytic theory, self-identity and ego-psychology theories, and consistency theory. Some critics wonder whether these theories can be reconciled with one another. Still, as an organization of classical outcome literature, the model is invaluable.

One of its strengths lies in its practicality. As Reardon points out:

Perhaps its simple logic does not sufficiently challenge our social scientific minds. Nevertheless, it is one theory which can be converted into action. Unlike several other theories which speculate about the nature of attitudes with little reference to techniques for changing them, Katz's approach provides both theory and technique. As such, it is worthy of more attention than it has received by those who wish to practice persuasion as well as study it.[19]

In his typology, Katz paves the way for a more detailed discussion of three important theories: learning, self-validation, and cognitive consistency. As we shall see, learning theories view rewards and punishments as the chief motivators of human action, thus emphasizing adjustment. Self-validation theories, on the other hand, give primary importance to value expression. Consistency theories say that reality testing and cognitive balance are the most important determinants of action: They stress the knowledge function. We shall now look at each of these theories of influence and motivation.

The theory most related to the ego defense function is psychoanalytic theory, which will not be discussed because it has not come to play a vary large part in models of social influence. Only a few attempts have been make to incorporate its insights into the social influence literature.[20] This general neglect may be due to a rejection of hidden impulses and unconscious drives as

mechanisms of human behavior, it may be based on the failure of psychoanalytic theory to ground itself in social as opposed to individual action, or it may simply result from a view of clinical theory as "unscientific." Whatever the reason, theories of ego defense processes have not been scientifically fashionable, and most students of communication have looked elsewhere for explanations of outcome control.

Learning Theories: Rewards and Costs as Determinants of Behavior

Its emphasis on the motivational force of rewards and punishments show the adjustment function is clearly related to *learning theory*. By this time you should be familiar with learning theory. It was discussed in chapter 3 as part of the psychological perspective, and in chapter 4 when we examined social exchange theory. Familiar concepts such as stimulus, response, and reinforcement are part of this approach to human behavior.

Of course, there are many different learning models. In this chapter we will look at some of the principles common to all learning models and then focus on Bandura's social learning theory. To explain the forces that shape human behavior, learning theories emphasize situational determinants of human action, focusing specifically on the consequences of behavior. According to most learning theories, the consequences of a behavior determine the extent to which it will reoccur. If the results of a certain behavior are positive, the behavior will be repeated. If they are negative, then it is unlikely that the behavior will reoccur.

Behaviorist Learning. Learning theories can be classed as behaviorist or cognitive, depending on whether they include internal representations of rewards and punishments. *Behaviorist learning theories* avoid internal mediation. In the extreme they propose that human behavior is directly controlled by its immediate consequences. A person acts, external consequences occur, and these consequences directly determine subsequent reactions. For example, a child touches a hot stove, experiences pain, and thereafter avoids the stove. As the child develops, he or she learns to avoid punishments and to seek rewards, building up a repertoire of behaviors that result in valued consequences.

Behaviorist formulations of learning theory view all human behavior as externally determined. They scrupulously avoid any consideration of internal cognitive functioning, arguing that cognitions "are inaccessible except through untrustworthy self-reports, that they are inferences from effects, that they are epiphenomenal, or that they are simply fictional."[21]

Social Learning Theory: A Cognitive Approach. *Cognitive learning theorists* avoid the extreme behaviorist stance, arguing that while some learning occurs through direct trial-and-error experience, other forms of learning, particularly observational learning, require cognitive mediation. Albert Bandura is one such theorist. His social learning theory adds a consideration of symbolic representations to a behaviorist base.

In the social learning view, people are neither driven by inner forces nor buffeted by environmental stimuli. Rather, psychological functioning is explained in terms of a continuous reciprocal interaction of personal and environmental determinants. Within this approach, symbolic, vicarious, and self-regulatory processes assume a prominent role.[22]

For Bandura, the rewarding and punishing consequences of behavior still form the basis of human action, but they need not be directly experienced. He argues that most learning is vicarious and results from the cognitive representation of rewards and punishments. People act as they do because they can anticipate and imagine, as well as directly experience, the consequences of behaviors. Bandura outlines two ways that rewarding and punishing outcomes determine our actions: (1) *antecedent determinants* may affect us before action by determining our expectancies, and (2) *consequent determinants* affect us after action by providing information about the results

of acting. In either case, cognitive structuring is involved.

CONSEQUENT DETERMINANTS. Before discussing antecedent determinants of action, let us examine consequent determinants. Like learning theorists before him, Bandura argues that the consequences of behavior are powerful determinants of human action. This is a central tenet of all learning theory and is not unique to Bandura. What is unique is his emphasis on how consequences affect future behaviors.

Bandura argues that *direct experience* is not the only way we experience outcomes that lead to learning. *Vicarious experience* or *modeling* also results in similar effects. "Observed outcomes can alter behavior in their own right in much the same way as directly experienced consequences. As a general rule, seeing behavior succeed for others increases the tendency to behave in similar ways, while seeing behavior punished decreases the tendency."[23] Vicarious reinforcements affect individuals in several ways. They let us know what behaviors will likely be rewarded, they motivate action, they arouse the observer's emotions and reduce inhibitions, they change the organization of an individual's value system, and they result in higher levels of responsiveness.[24]

In addition to direct and vicarious experience, *self-reinforcement* also determines action. Bandura demonstrates that individuals often set their own standards and reward themselves for meeting these standards. If a behavior meets internal standards, then individuals can evaluate themselves positively and even give themselves tangible rewards. Similarly, they can punish themselves for inadequate performance. Negative evaluations, since they lower self-regard, are severely punishing consequences to most people. Thus, Bandura stresses the significance of internally generated outcomes as action determinants.

ANTECEDENT DETERMINANTS. Because of our ability to represent outcomes symbolically, we do not have to wait until a behavior has occurred (either to self or other) to know its results. We are not at the mercy of consequent determinants. We use prior knowledge of reward-punishment contingencies to anticipate future outcomes. By coupling *outcome expectancies* (predictions that a particular behavior will result in particular rewards) with *efficacy expectancies* (predictions of how well we will be able to enact a behavior), we compute the probability of receiving rewards or punishments for a given action and, thus, plan our behaviors.[25]

To compute the probability of receiving a reward, individuals carefully scan the environment for signs that predict reinforcements. While this information can be partially gained by experiencing the results of actual behavior (using consequent information), it can be achieved in other ways. We can recall our experiences with related actions, and we can respond to verbal explanations and instructions that point out likely effects. Finally, we can observe consequences occurring to others.

Efficacy expectancies are built up in similar ways. The individual anticipates successful completion of a given behavior if it has been successful in the past, if the individual sees others succeed, if offered verbal encouragement by others, if the individual is in a proper mood, or if the conditions for the behavior are favorable.[26]

Bandura believes individuals act on the basis of anticipated rewards and punishments. Anticipation involves determining both outcome and efficacy expectancies. The knowledge for computing both comes from our own direct experience with similar actions, from verbal instruction, or from observational learning.

Using Social Learning to Change Others. According to learning theory we can influence others by controlling their rewards and punishments. If I need to influence you, I can do so directly, by punishing or rewarding you, or I can do so indirectly, by modeling the behavior I want you to enact. By letting you vicariously observe others being rewarded I can increase the likeli-

hood that you will respond as desired. Many advertisements employ modeling. An attractive model is rewarded for using a product. We therefore believe that if we use the product then we will achieve the same results. Education also employs vicarious learning and modeling by showing children how to perform successfully.

Direct instruction is yet another way we can influence others. We can explain to others the benefits of acting in a desired way. Through instruction we can offer symbolic representations of reward/punishment contingencies. Finally, we can use our knowledge of self-reinforcement to control others. By reminding people that certain actions will not meet their internal standards, we can cause them to reward or punish themselves. Social learning theory holds that we can attain desired ends by manipulating others' rewards and punishments, and we can do so through communication as well as direct control.

Criticism of Social Learning Theory. A problem of learning theory lies in its failure to define exactly what ends are rewarding and punishing for individuals. Learning theorists tend to believe that any action repeatedly undertaken is rewarding, but they offer no further definition of reward. Another problem is that many learning theories overlook cognitive mechanisms.

Social learning theory makes a significant contribution to the latter problem. It goes beyond behaviorist concepts by discussing symbolic representation and conceiving of humans as capable of foresight and planning. Thus, this model is actional at heart. In addition, the inclusion of standard-setting and self-regulation processes makes this model closer to current views of human behavior than previous models. Unlike behaviorist views, social learning theory incorporates a consideration of the self. Social learning theory is based on the psychological perspective. To the extent we accept the assumptions underlying that perspective, it can be a useful theory of learning and influence.

Self-Validation Theories:
Identity and Behavior

Katz's discussion of the value expressive function introduces us to a set of theories that focuses on self-validation and impression management as motivators of human action. We will begin our discussion with Milton Rokeach's work on value systems, a theory chosen not only because it is related to value expression but because it introduces the theme of self-concept and refines the idea of attitude. Since self-concept and attitude are two extremely important constructs in many communication theories, it deserves consideration.[27]

Rokeach's Value Theory. Rokeach's theory is an interesting combination of consistency principles and self-validation concepts. Basically, Rokeach believes that individuals are motivated by a desire to maintain a positive self-image. All of the elements in an individual's belief system exist to enhance the self. If there is inconsistency among them, then it will be impossible to have a stable self-concept. Rokeach expresses this view by stating, "the only postulated motive for the initiation of cognitive and behavioral change is the maintenance and enhancement of self-conceptions."[28]

Rokeach believes that action is a function of three kinds of internal construct: beliefs, attitudes, and values. Of the three, value is most closely related to self-conceptions. But before we look at how values are related to identity, we need to examine the relationship between beliefs, attitudes, and values.

Beliefs are propositions about "what is or is not true and beautiful and good about the physical and social world in which we live."[29] For Rokeach, "a belief is any simple proposition, conscious or unconscious, inferred from what a person says or does, capable of being preceded by the phrase 'I believe that... .'"[30] All of us hold "tens and possible hundreds of thousands" of beliefs that are systematically interrelated. While some beliefs are relatively unimportant and have little force in the total belief system, others are more central. "The more a given belief is functionally connected or in communication with other beliefs, the more implications and consequences it has for other beliefs," and the more central it will be in the individual's belief system.[31]

BELIEF TYPES. Rokeach describes five classes of beliefs. Each varies in centrality. At the core of the belief system are *Type A: Primitive Beliefs, 100 percent consensus.* These are basic, unquestioned beliefs that are universally supported by everyone and that come from direct experience. "I believe this is a table," "I believe this is my mother," "I believe my name is so-and-so" are some of Rokeach's examples.[32]

Type B: Primitive Beliefs, 0 percent consensus are the second type. These direct beliefs are also at the center of the belief system. They differ from Type A, however, because they are supported by the self rather than by others. "There are no reference persons or groups outside the self who could controvert such a belief."[33] Beliefs that can be prefaced by the statement, "No matter what others believe, I believe..." are Type B. Rokeach offers the following examples: "I believe my mother does not love me"; "I believe I am reasonably intelligent"; "Regardless of what others say, I believe in God."

Type C: Authority Beliefs are the next type. These beliefs and the following two types are not primitive. They do not have the taken-for-granted character of Type A and Type B. We develop them as we encounter differences of opinion. Authority beliefs are credibility beliefs about who can or cannot be trusted. "The police officer is your friend," "The Pope is infallible in matters of faith," and "Father knows best" are examples.

Type D: Derived Beliefs are the fourth type. They are beliefs about matters of fact that we receive indirectly. We believe them because we accept the authorities who tell us they are true. Beliefs about the population of Andorra, the circumference of the earth, the intentions of our national leaders, the issues at stake in local elections, or the morality of certain actions are Type D. Most of our beliefs are this type and are derived from the media or from what our friends and colleagues tell us.

The final class, *Type E: Inconsequential Beliefs*, concerns matters of personal taste and judgment. Although they may be intensely held, they are labeled inconsequential because "they have few or no connections with other beliefs."[34] "Rare steaks are tastier than well-done steaks" and "Seashore vacations are more desirable than mountain vacations" are examples cited by Rokeach.[35]

Rokeach suggests that the more central a belief the more difficult it is to change, because core beliefs involve reorganizing the entire belief system. "In the event of a conflict between two beliefs varying in centrality, the more central belief would win out."[36] While Type D and Type E beliefs are probably easy to change, authority and primitive beliefs appear more resistant to influence.

ATTITUDES AND VALUES. When several interrelated beliefs focus on a common object, they result in *attitudes*. While we hold hundreds of thousands of beliefs, we probably hold fewer attitudes, perhaps a thousand or so. Attitudes are specifically organized around particular objects. All our beliefs about a given object create an attitude toward that object, a set of predispositions guiding our thinking and evaluations.

In addition to beliefs organized into attitudes, another kind exists, more abstract and more closely connected to the self. This is a value. A *value* is "an enduring belief that a specific mode of conduct or end-state of existence is personally or socially preferable to an opposite or converse mode of conduct or end-state of existence. A *value system* is an enduring organization of beliefs concerning preferable modes of conduct or end-states of existence along a continuum of relative importance."[37] Values differ from atti-

tudes in several ways. Values are more general, more central to one's personality and self-conception and more immediately linked to motivations. While attitudes focus on particular objects, values transcend them. Finally, a person has fewer values than attitudes, perhaps only dozens.[38]

Rokeach believes that there are several basic values that all individuals hold regardless of culture. Values may be directed to desired end-states or toward ways of attaining those states. The first are *terminal values*, including such ends as a comfortable life, a world at peace, equality, self-respect, family security, and freedom. The second, *instrumental values*, includes characteristic ways of acting such as being ambitious, broad-minded, cheerful, forgiving, imaginative, logical, or loving.[39]

These values motivate us by "providing us with standards of competence and of morality, guiding or determining attitudes, behavior, judgments, comparisons of self and others, rationalizations and justifications, exhortative attempts to influence others, impression management, and self-presentations."[40] Rokeach tells us that a person's values exist

to help maintain and enhance one's total conception of oneself.... . Every person attempts at the very least to maintain and, insofar as possible, to enhance whatever self-conception he has managed to develop... . In other words, the ultimate purpose of one's total belief system, which includes one's values, is to maintain and enhance...the master of all sentiments, the sentiment of self-regard.[41]

Values and Behavior Control. Changes in beliefs can be achieved through what Rokeach calls *the method of self-evaluation*. If individuals can be made to feel dissatisfied with themselves, then they will change to reduce this "noxious affective state." This state is aroused when people become aware of holding values or attitudes or engaging in behaviors that "contradict their self-conceptions as competent or moral."[42] To reduce the resulting discomfort, people realign their belief systems according to socially defined and previously learned ideas of who they are.[43]

Self-evaluation is based on a human drive to reduce inconsistency. It therefore has much in common with the cognitive consistency theories we will examine. Rokeach's model is unique, however, because he believes the drive to reduce inconsistency occurs only between cognitions, "one of which is always about oneself and one of which is a value or attitude or behavior which...a person discovers to be inconsistent with the cognition about oneself."[44]

Other Self-Validation Theories. Rokeach is not the only theorist who emphasizes self-concept and identity maintenance as foundations of social action. Many of the theorists covered in chapter 6 argued that humans are motivated by the desire to maintain a socially defined self. This position is upheld by the impression management theorists. Social psychologists such as Barry Schlenker and James Tedeschi argue that humans actively work to control others' impressions of them.[45] These theorists are more other-directed than Rokeach but still focus on the value expressive function. Research on social comparison and group conformity, to be reviewed in chapter 9, carries a similar theme; thus, we will have occasion to reexamine matters of self-validation.

Criticism of Rokeach's Theory. Rokeach's theory is useful both theoretically and practically, particularly his view that beliefs are hierarchically organized systems. In categorizing belief types, he shows that beliefs are not isolated but interrelated, so that a change in one part of the system affects the entire system, particularly if the change involves a core belief.

The relationship between the need for self-enhancement and the origin and nature of values, however, is not well developed. Rokeach does not say how holding a particular value allows self-enhancement, nor does he tell us much about the original development of self. In addition, as Stephen Littlejohn points out, his operationalization of values seems questionable. Rokeach believes that, regardless of culture, all humans possess the

same values (although to different degrees). "His attempt to reduce all values to a standard list and to describe the value system in terms of a simple ranking is unrealistic at best and ludicrous at worst."[46] His dismissal of cultural variation also seems unrealistic. Finally, his evidence supporting the drive to reduce self-dissatisfaction is inconclusive. Many criticisms leveled against consistency theories also apply to Rokeach. Nevertheless, he presents a potentially useful theory. As Littlejohn summarizes, "The time may be right to modify Rokeach's approach so that it is consistent with recent action-oriented, rules-based notions of human behavior."[47]

Cognitive Consistency Theories: The Need for Stability

According to Katz's knowledge function, human actors try to simplify their cognitions of the world, actively seeking consistency and predictability. There is a large body of literature that focuses on individuals' need for internal consistency.[48] These theories view people as rational creatures who monitor the elements within their cognitive arenas, test new cognitions against old, and when inconsistencies or imbalances are found, realign the system in the most logical (or psycho-logical) manner possible. Individuals variously try to maintain consistency between cognitions and actions. Inconsistency is viewed as an uncomfortable state that people are driven to reduce. Although a number of such theories exist, the most influential is the cognitive dissonance theory.[49]

Festinger's Cognitive Dissonance Theory. According to Leon Festinger, the originator of dissonance theory, *cognitions* (individual beliefs or attitudes) may be related in three ways. They may be *consonant* if one follows from the other. They may be *dissonant* if they are contradictory (if the observe of one cognition follows from the other). Or they may be *irrelevant* to one another if they are psychologically unconnected.[50] For example, the cognitions "I am an intelligent person" and "I acted rationally in this instance" are consonant. The cognitions "I am an intelligent person" and "I just did something incredibly stupid" are clearly dissonant. Finally, the cognitions "I am intelligent" and "It is raining outside" are irrelevant to one another.

Whenever individuals become aware of holding dissonant cognitions, they are in a state of dissonance. This is a psychologically uncomfortable state. Individuals, therefore, actively avoid dissonance-producing situations, and, when this is impossible, they try to reduce as much dissonance as they can.

FACTORS AFFECTING DISSONANCE AROUSAL. The degree of dissonance an individual experiences depends on several factors. Clearly, some contradictory cognitions produce more dissonance than others. A cognitive set that includes "people who fall great distances will be seriously injured" and "I am jumping from this plane without a parachute" will produce more dissonance than one including the cognitions "I dislike chocolate ice cream" and "I just ordered a chocolate sundae." The two sets obviously vary in *importance*, and importance is a central variable affecting magnitude of dissonance.[51]

The *number of consonant and dissonant elements* within a given cognitive set also affects the amount of dissonance we feel. Let us try to determine how much dissonance you will feel when you decide to take a new job. If all your existing cognitions are consonant with the decision to accept the job, then there will be no dissonance. If, however, you fear that the job has few opportunities for advancement (a cognition dissonant with the decision to take the job), then you will feel some degree of cognitive discomfort. If you hold many dissonant cognitions—for example, you believe there will be little opportunity for advancement, you realize you will have to leave friends and family, and you find the wages are low—then deciding to take it should produce a large amount of dissonance. As the ratio of disso-

nant to consonant cognitions increases, the magnitude of dissonance aroused also increases.

Magnitude of dissonance is thus a function of both the importance and number of dissonant and consonant cognitions held in regard to any particular topic.[52] This relationship is represented by the following ratio:

$$\text{magnitude of dissonance} = \frac{\text{number of dissonant cognitions} \times \text{importance}}{\text{number of consonant cognitions} \times \text{importance}}$$

Accepting a new attitude or belief will result in a lot of dissonance when the number of dissonant elements outweighs the number of supporting consonant elements, especially when dissonant elements are highly important or when a combination of these factors exists. As we become more aware of contradictions between cognitions, we feel more discomfort and expend greater effort to reduce this discomfort. If we have many important reasons to believe that a certain action or belief shows bad judgment, then we will feel more uncomfortable than if only one or two reasons existed.

Of course, no one is completely consistent. You and I hold many contradictory beliefs and attitudes at this very moment. As long as we are unaware of them, however, or as long as we fail to perceive them as inconsistent, we will be quite able to live with them. It is only when they are brought to our attention that they arouse dissonance, and we are forced to act upon them.

There are several situations where dissonance helps determine our behavior; for instance, whenever we receive new information that is inconsistent with old information. In such a case we try to protect ourselves from the ensuing dissonance, either by avoiding situations where it is likely to occur or by rejecting dissonance-producing ideas. Through selective exposure and perceptions, we refuse to admit the new information.

There are times, however, when dissonance is unavoidable. Whenever we have to decide between two equally attractive alternatives (say, between two automobiles that we like or between two equally prestigious jobs), some dissonance occurs. Similarly, dissonance results whenever we are forced to take a stand that violates existing beliefs (arguing for something we do not believe or performing a task we consider tedious and boring). In the first case, most people avoid thinking about the alternative not chosen, or they try to increase the perceived attractiveness of the chosen alternative while decreasing that of the one not chosen. Studies show that individuals avoid information extolling the virtues of the unchosen alternatives and prefer information consonant with the alternative they chose. In the second case, people reduce dissonance by convincing themselves that their beliefs are actually closer to the position advocated than originally supposed or that they engaged in the behavior to achieve some external reward.

In both instances, more dissonance results if the decision involves *public commitment* and is perceived as voluntary or *volitional*. Jack Brehm and Arthur Cohen, two psychologists working in the dissonance tradition, are credited with emphasizing the importance of these conditions in arousing dissonance.[53] An additional example may help clarify their importance. Take the case of a student, we'll call her Barbara, deciding which college to attend. She recognizes the advantages of attending a large public institution but has always wanted to attend a small private college. Most of Barbara's cognitions are favorable to the small college and opposed to a large state university. Assume, however, that at the last minute, for whatever reason, Barbara accepts an offer from a large state university. She commits to a decision that has all of the hallmarks of producing dissonance. Because the decision is an important one, because she already holds a series of cognitions that fly in the face of her decision, the potential for dissonance is quite high. It becomes even higher if Barbara perceives her decision as volitional rather than as beyond control. If the decision is a matter of free choice, then she will experience a great deal of dissonance, for she has

made a choice in which she does not believe. If, on the other hand, the decision is not volitional— for example, if a reversal in family fortunes made the decision a financial necessity or if parental threats bullied her into the decision—then, although she will feel dissonance, it will be less than if the decision were a free choice. If the decision is nonvolitional, she can always say, "I don't really like this decision, but what can you do? Attending the university is better than not going to school at all." In the case of free choice, no justification is present. The extent to which a decision is perceived as voluntary will increase the amount of dissonance felt and, in turn, the pressure to reduce dissonance.

METHODS OF DISSONANCE REDUCTION. What can our hypothetical student do to reduce the dissonance? She has several options; the first and most obvious is to recant: to *change the decision*. She can avoid the cognitive discomfort she feels by changing her mind, by withdrawing her application, and by attending the private school after all. If already publicly committed to attending the university, however, this will be difficult. In fact, having told friends and family she is going to the university, she may feel greater dissonance by backing out than by proceeding with her plans.

Another tactic is to *deny volition* by saying she had little choice in the matter and convincing herself that attending the state university will please her parents or save money. Although she will still feel dissonance, it will have decreased in magnitude. In addition to these options, she can try to change previously existing beliefs and attitudes. Since these conflict with her decision, realigning them should decrease the resulting discomfort. This can be done in several ways. She can *reduce the importance of previous cognitions*, telling herself that choice of school is relatively unimportant and that what is really important is getting an education. She can also *increase the cognitive overlap* between the two choices, minimizing the difference between public and private schools. By convincing herself that in either case she can get an education, make new friends, and prepare for a career—that the similarities between the two schools really outweigh the differences—she increases their overlap and decreases dissonance.

She can also change the ratio of consonant to dissonant cognitions, either by *reducing the number of dissonant cognitions* or by *increasing the number of consonant cognitions.* First, she can deny the beliefs and attitudes she once held favoring private schools, viewing them as immature and ill-considered. Second, she can seek elements consonant with the choice of a state school, convincing herself there are advantages in attending state university: size, diversity of students, larger curriculum, better facilities, and so forth. The more she can list, the less dissonance she feels. Changing the importance and degree of overlap or the number of dissonant and consonant elements in her cognitive arena may even be better than revoking the decisions. If she can realign successfully preexisting cognitive elements, then she can operate comfortably on a day-to-day basis. She can build a new set of cognitions consistent with the decision, thus allowing herself to believe she was right all along.

ELEMENTS THAT MAKE AN ATTITUDE RESISTANT. We saw that the student had many ways to reduce dissonance. Now, we need to answer the question of whether there is any way to determine what methods will be used to reduce dissonance. Dissonance theorists argue that some cognitions are relatively resistant to change while others are less so. It follows that methods of dissonance reduction involving highly resistant elements will be chosen less frequently than methods involving low resistance.

Brehm and Cohen state:

Those cognitions with relatively low resistance tend to change first. The resistance to change of a cognitive element comes from the extent to which such change would produce new dissonance and from some joint function of the responsiveness of the cognitions to reality (what it represents) and the difficulty of changing the reality.[54]

Brehm and Cohen suggest that three factors are involved in determining resistance: (1) the difficulty of effecting a change in cognitions, (2) the cognition's relationship to an underlying reality, and (3) the degree to which a change produces more dissonance than it would reduce.

In a situation where an individual is aware of holding opposing cognitions, the difficulty involved in changing each cognition determines which will change. There are times when one of the cognitions cannot be changed. For example, an individual agrees to sell a valued object, a car, but later realizes he wants it back. If the person who bought the car refuses to break the deal, it becomes impossible to revoke the decision. Since the cognition "I sold the car" cannot be changed, the cognition "I want it back" must be modified. Or, suppose an individual constantly criticizes her children and feels uncomfortable about this behavior. To reduce dissonance, she must either stop criticizing or somehow allow herself to continue the behavior without dissonance. The easiest solution would seem to be changing the behavior. But, if her criticism is a long-standing interpersonal strategy, she may have no alternative. In that case, it will be easier for her to rationalize her behavior than change it.

The extent to which a particular cognition is supported by reality also affects how resistant it is to change. It is difficult to fly in the face of cold, hard facts. If you live in Arizona, it may be possible to hold the cognition "It never rains in Indianapolis in the summertime." It is impossible if you actually live in Indianapolis. Cognitions supported by social reality are also difficult to change. If all your friends and family say that you should believe X, it is difficult to believe Y. On the other hand, cognitions that are ambiguous and not well supported by either social or physical reality are fairly easy to change. Ambiguous emotional states, for example, are not highly resistant to change. If you are not sure what you are feeling, then a change of heart can occur.

The final factor determining dissonance reduction is the degree to which changing a cognitive element will lead to new dissonance. For example, assume you hear something discreditable about a friend, perhaps concerning involvement in a crime. This information is potentially very dissonant. To reduce this dissonance, you can either excuse the crime, change your views about your friend, or refuse to believe what you have heard. If you firmly support law and order, then excusing the crime might cause more dissonance than it would reduce. If your friend is very important to you, then denigrating the friend might also increase dissonance. The simplest solution might be to tell yourself it was all a mistake. This alternative would lead to the least possible dissonance. By convincing yourself that the police arrested the wrong person, you may temporarily reduce dissonance without adding any new contradictions.

Dissonance and Social Control. Dissonance theory is based on two hypotheses. First, dissonance is psychologically uncomfortable, and those who experience it will try to reduce it. Second, people will actively avoid situations and information that increase dissonance.[55] Thus, dissonance is an undesirable outcome that motivates individuals. Knowledge of the principles of dissonance reduction can therefore be used to influence others and control them.

To change someone, we must begin by arousing dissonance in them. How can we do this? One way is simply to confront individuals with their own inconsistencies. Most people unknowingly hold inconsistent views. If we bring these to their awareness, then they may change them. They may resist this perception, of course, but if we block their resistance, change may come about. A less obvious method also exists: getting people to engage publicly in the actions you want them to adopt. To change an individual's attitude, you could persuade the person to volunteer to adopt a contrary attitude just for the time being. If the person does so, you will have induced dissonance, for violating beliefs can produce strong dissonance. Zimbardo expresses this principle:

When the justifications for discrepant behavior are barely adequate to induce compliance, the person cannot readily point to sources outside himself or herself as the instigators of the behavior in question. The locus of the public compliance, then, is more likely to be internal. When this occurs, the need to be consistent changes private events to bring them in line with the public commitment. Then values, motives, beliefs, perceptions, and attitudes may all be modified—sometimes dramatically so—to make them consonant with the public behavior. Might gets compliance, but not attitude change.[56]

By putting the individual in a situation of voluntary public commitment you initiate a process during which the individual is compelled to persuade himself or herself that actions and beliefs are consistent. Research Abstract 7.1 shows an extension and an unusual application of this principle.

Criticisms of Dissonance Theory. Many social scientists find dissonance theory appealing partly because its predictions are counterintuitive. The prediction that "less is more," that people will experience less internal change the more their actions are externally justified, is counter to common sense, yet it holds up in most cognitive dissonance studies. Dissonance theory has probably generated more research than any other social psychological theory with, perhaps, the exception of attribution theory.

Its popularity does not mean it is free of problems. One is its inability to predict how dissonance will be reduced in a given case. Dissonance theorists argue that attitudes are easier to change than behaviors, but they do not say whether this is always true nor do they say why. In addition, most theorists overlook the possibility that people may simultaneously use several dissonance reduction tactics.

The motivational basis of dissonance reduction has also been questioned. Do we always seek predictability and consistency? Are there times when we look for the unexpected and the complex? People often enjoy being amazed or astounded (for example, by magic tricks, optical

RESEARCH ABSTRACT 7.1 On Eating Fried Grasshoppers

Zimbardo's major *purpose* was to test the idea that compliance with a disliked source leads to greater attitude change than compliance with a liked source. According to dissonance theory, receivers have little external justification for complying with a disliked communicator. In such a case, subjects will feel dissonance and try to reduce it through attitude change. In the case of a liked communicator, there is less reason for attitude change, since there is less dissonance.

Zimbardo's *method* involved attitudes toward a highly disliked food: fried grasshoppers. Army reservists were given a message indicating the need for a mobile army, the need to eat unusual survival foods, and the need to study reactions to these foods. In one condition the communicator was friendly; in the other he was unfriendly. Zimbardo wanted to determine whether subjects who agreed to eat grasshoppers would experience greater attitude change in the "unfriendly" condition than in the "friendly" condition.

The *procedures* were as follows. Subjects came to a large lecture hall and filled out a nine-point scale indicating attitudes to a range of foods including grasshoppers. After this, control subjects completed a post-attitudinal scale either immediately or after a suitable interval. The rest of the subjects received the experimental manipulation either in groups of 10 or singly. The communicator delivered his persuasive message and then played his friendly/unfriendly role. He did this by treating an assistant (who mistakenly brought in eels instead of grasshoppers) either in a pleasant or unpleasant manner. After this manipulation, a plate of grasshoppers was placed before each of the subjects, who were told to try at least one. In an incentive condition, they were offered 50 cents to do so. In a no-incentive condition, they were simply asked to eat. Afterward, a "civilian liaison" asked them to fill out a post-test on attitudes toward a number of foods, willingness to endorse eating grasshoppers, and evaluations of the communicator, his assistant, and the experimental conditions.

Results were as follows. Approximately 50 percent of the subjects in each experimental condition ate at least one grasshopper. This indicates that treatments did not affect public conformity. The treatments did, however, affect private acceptance. Whether attitude change was measured by the proportion of subjects who changed their attitudes in the desired direction or by mean ratings of attitude toward grasshoppers, more change occurred as a result of the negative than of the positive communicator. This difference was more apparent when no monetary incentive was offered. As Zimbardo concludes, "the results support a dissonance theory explanation of communicator characteristics as a source of justification in forced compliance situations."

Source: Philip Zimbardo and others, "Communicator Effectiveness in Producing Public Conformity and Private Attitude Change," *Journal of Personality*, 33 (1965), 233–55.

illusions, or paradoxical puzzles). Dissonance theory fails to recognize that humans have an exploratory drive, a desire to seek out novelty for its own sake. The result of dissonance reduction would be a completely stable, quiescent system.

Perhaps consistency is only part of the picture, and a larger theory is required to account for both consistency and complexity drives and to specify conditions under which both operate.

Finally, the research supporting dissonance theory has been questioned.[57] Most studies fail to measure directly whether dissonance has indeed been aroused. Theorists have recently reinterpreted the results of dissonance studies. Bem, for example, argues that dissonance effects are individuals' attempts to attribute meaning to their own behaviors. Others have interpreted them as attempts by subjects to manage the impressions the experimenter has of them.[58] Nevertheless, the dissonance formulation is intriguing and is included here because of its historical importance and as an interesting example of theory.

COGNITIVE INFLUENCE THEORIES: HOW ARE OUTCOMES CONTROLLED THROUGH COMMUNICATION?

Every so often, in the course of studying a problem, we witness the emergence of new perspectives that signals a subtle shift in the way the problem is viewed. We are currently experiencing such a shift in the study of attitude change and social influence. The labels applied to emerging social scientific theories clue us in to the nature of this concern. Information integration, cognitive schemata, social cognition, reasoned action, and cognitive response theories are just some of the models currently being proposed. The common term *cognition* signals a renewed interest in understanding what occurs in the human mind as we collect and process information. The behaviorist emphasis on external consequences and outcomes has been replaced by a major concern with internal information processing.

At the same time that internal psychological organization is gaining ground, we are becoming more interested in understanding the effects of social rules, roles, and norms on human behavior. People are not only regarded as information processors but also as social rule followers. An emerging interest in social coordination, shared social perception, and the logic of social interaction is founded on the realization that we exist within social structures and are governed by social rules. While these views seem to be contradictory—one focusing on psychological and the other on social processes—they are both concerned with structure and organization rather than with consequences and motivations. Rather than asking what factors (drives, motivations, consequences) cause human action, they want to know how human behavior is organized.

Cognitive Response Theories

Theories that investigate how thought affects actions are called *cognitive response theories*. Despite the similarity in name, they should not be confused with cognitive consistency theories. Cognitive consistency theories assume a drive to achieve consistency or consonance. Cognitive response theories, on the other hand, concentrate on the nature of cognitive structure (how individuals' cognitions are interrelated and organized), cognitive styles (how individuals differ in cognitions and the kind of information they seek), and information processing (how we go about "perceiving, abstracting, judging, elaborating, rehearsing, and recalling" information).[59]

Cognitive response theory addresses problems of persuasion and influence. It holds that the attitude change process can only be understood by examining the kind of thoughts that "pass through a person's mind while he or she anticipates a communication, listens to a communication, or reflects on a communication."[60] Anthony Greenwald, for example, suggests that the degree to which a new attitude is accepted or rejected is a function not only of information contained in the message (in the form of arguments and evidence) but of existing information.[61]

During and after a persuasive message (and sometimes when anticipating it) we relate old information to new and generate cognitions about the object of the message. These cognitions may either support or negate the position advocated. Sometimes, our self-generated cognitions may be so antagonistic that a boomerang effect occurs: We come away advocating an attitude opposite to

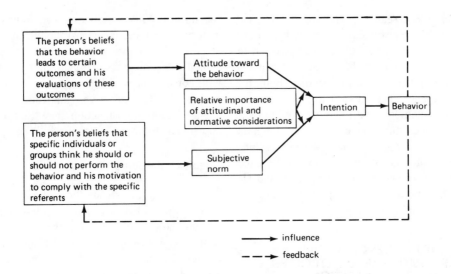

FIGURE 7.1: Relationship between beliefs, attitudes, intentions, and behavior. (From Martin Fishbein and Icek Ajzen, "Acceptance, Yielding and Impact: Cognitive Processes in Persuasion," in *Cognitive Responses in Persuasion* [Hillsdale, N.J.: Lawrence Erlbaum Associates, Publishers, 1981], p. 348).

the one presented in the message. According to cognitive response theory, a great deal of activity occurs during reception of a persuasive message. Communicators do not persuade individuals: "in effect, individuals persuade themselves to adopt (or reject) the position advocated by the communicator."[62] Research Abstract 7.2 shows an experiment on the effects of self-generated cognitions during persuasion.

Theory of Reasoned Action: Attitude Revisited

One of the problems that has plagued attitude theorists is the fact that the link between what we want to do (our attitudes) and what we actually do (our actions) is often weak. Martin Fishbein and Icek Ajzen try to solve this problem by describing the cognitive structures involved in deciding whether to act. In their theory of reasoned action, they describe the relationship between behavior change and beliefs, attitudes, norms, and intentions. (See Fig. 7.1.)

Behavioral Intentions. Fishbein and Ajzen believe that *behavioral intentions* are an important mediator between attitude and action.

The behavioral intention is viewed as a function of two factors: (1) the individual's *attitude* toward performing the behavior under consideration (A_B)—that is, his or her positive or negative feeling toward performing the behavior; and (2) the individual's subjective norm with respect to that behavior (SN)—that is, his or her belief that most important others think the individual should or should not perform the behavior.[63]

These two factors, attitude and subjective norm, vary in importance (w) in different situations. Fishbein and Ajzen present an equation to express the relationship between behavioral intention and attitudes and subjective norms:

$$B \sim I = f[w_1A_B + w_2SN]$$

The equation may be read as follows: One's behavioral intention to complete an action ($B \sim I$) is functionally related to (f) attitude toward that act weighted by its importance (w_1A_B) and belief about how others think one should act weighted by the importance of their views (w_2SN).

RESEARCH ABSTRACT 7.2   What Happens When Messages Are Repeated?

Studies of the effects of repeating a persuasive message show that over time attitude change first increases and then declines. When a message is repeated a moderate number of times, attitude change is favorable; but with more frequent exposure, however, this gain is lost. Moderate repetition allows the generation of cognitive responses that reinforce the message. With too frequent exposure, however, subjects either become bored or feel their freedom is threatened and react by generating negative thoughts. The *purpose* of this study was to test these ideas and to examine how persuasive effects are related to the cognitive responses receivers generate.

The *method* was experimental. One hundred ninety-three students were exposed to messages differing in position advocated (either pro or con existing attitudes) and in number of presentations (either one, three, or five). The design was a 2 × 3 factorial design. Six experimental conditions were prepared. One group heard a pro-attitudinal message once, a second heard it three times, and a third heard it five times. Three additional groups heard a counter-attitudinal message at each exposure level.

Researchers began by preparing two relevant and well-argued messages proposing a need for increasing university funding. Both messages argued that if more funds were available, then materials and services would improve. In the pro-attitudinal condition, subjects were told this could be done without tuition increase. In the counter-attitudinal condition, subjects heard that a tuition increase of $70.00 per quarter would be necessary.

The second step was exposing subjects to the messages. Subjects heard the message over headphones in language lab cubicles. After the appropriate number of exposures, they rated agreement with the message on a 15-point scale. To measure cognitive responses, the researchers asked them to list, in 3 minutes, all their thoughts while listening to the presentation. Researchers believed that "subjects are able to report accurately their recent and current thoughts and ideas." Subjects were also asked to recall and list as many message arguments as possible. Two independent judges then read the cognitive responses and classified them as either favorable, unfavorable, or neutral. Judges were able to agree on over 95 percent of the responses.

The *results* supported the importance of cognitive responses during attitude change. As expected, attitude change was related both to position and frequency of exposure. There was more agreement with the pro- than the counter-attitudinal advocacy, and more favorable attitude change was found in the moderate repetition condition. More important was analysis of the recall and cognitive response data. The authors found the correlation between number of arguments recalled and attitude change was near zero, indicating that change was not due to learning. Number of responses, however, was associated with attitude change. As repetitions increased, favorable cognitions first increased and then decreased, negative cognitions first decreased and then increased, and neutral thoughts continually increased. This indicated that moderate levels of repetition allow subjects to elaborate on message arguments, realizing their cogency and implications. At high levels, tedium or reactance seems to motivate subjects to attack the now offensive communication by generating negative or unrelated thoughts.

Source: John T. Cacioppo and Richard E. Petty, "Effects of Message Repetition and Position on Cognitive Response, Recall, and Persuasion," *Journal of Personality and Social Psychology*, 37 (1979), 97–109.

Assume that an individual is asked by the Red Cross to donate blood. B ~ I stands for the individual's intention to donate. The strength of this intention is determined both by attitude toward donating and social pressures. If the prospective donor's attitude is strongly favorable and if significant others urge him or her to donate—if A and SN are positive and have strong weights—behavioral intention will be high. The individual will be very likely to donate.

Both attitudes and subjective norms can be further analyzed. Attitudes are functionally related to the subjective probability that a given attitude object has certain attributes or characteristics (b_i) and to the extent the attribute in question is positively or negatively evaluated (e_i). Once again, this relationship can be expressed in an equation:

$$A_B = f [\Sigma_N b_i e_i]$$

This equation can be read as follows. An attitude toward a certain action (A_B) is a function (f) of the sum (Σ_N) of a person's beliefs regarding a particular action. These beliefs are based on whether an outcome is considered to be good or bad (e_i) and the subjective probability that it will actually be associated with the attitude object (b_i). For example, our blood donor's attitude is determined by combining all beliefs about donating blood. Our donor may believe that donating blood is painful, and also that donating blood will help save lives.[64] Each of these beliefs has two components. The first, subjective probability (or belief strength) refers to how strongly donating is connected with either pain or lifesaving. Evaluation refers to whether the latter terms are considered negative or positive. If our donor is afraid of pain, believes that donating will cause pain, and does not really believe that donating will save lives, his or her overall attitude will be negative. On the other hand, if our donor feels that the pain will be minimal, while strongly believing donating blood will save lives, then he or she will have a positive attitude about donating.

The second factor determining behavioral intention, subjective norm, can also be further analyzed. A subjective norm is based on several beliefs, each a function of the individual's personal estimation of what others think about an action and his or her motivation to comply with these others. A final equation expresses this relationship:

$$SN - f [\Sigma_N b_i m_i]$$

The equation tells us that the subjective norms related to a behavioral intention (SN) are a function (f) of the sum (Σ_N) of all salient beliefs about how others view the action in question. These beliefs are jointly determined by the subjective probability that significant others support the action (b_i) and by motivations to act in accordance with their desires (m_i). Intention will be related to whether or not our donor believes spouse or friends think donating is a good idea. If their support is strong, our donor will feel social pressure to comply. Together, attitudes and norms determine behavioral intentions. If the equations are troublesome, refer to the diagram in Fig. 7.1, which says in ordinary language what the three equations convey in more mathematical terms.

Using Knowledge of Behavioral Intentions to Control Others. This model clarifies the relationship between beliefs, attitudes, and behaviors by assuming an additional construct: behavioral intention. It also shows us how to change behaviors by changing attitudes and subjective norms. We can change an attitude in several ways. One way is to increase the way a given behavior is evaluated. In the example we have been using we could do this by showing the positive advantages of donating. We can also change the behavior's subjective probability: We can demonstrate that donating blood will actually save lives. Another option is to focus on social norms by stressing that credible others believe the behavior is positive or that social rewards will accrue from acting in the desired way. We could also try to weaken negative elements within the belief sets.

Fishbein and Ajzen sum up their model by suggesting that "only when the message brings about a shift in the summed products across the total set of underlying beliefs can it be expected to influence attitudes or subjective norms and, hence, intentions and behaviors."[65]

Criticism of Reasoned Action Theory. This theory has been positively received. The addition of intentions as an element linking attitudes and behaviors is seen as one of the model's strengths. By assuming that actions result from behavioral intentions that in turn consist of potentially conflicting beliefs, Fishbein and Ajzen help explain the difficulty other researchers have had in predicting action from single attitudes. By stressing subjective norms, they show that social relationships affect our belief sets.

The Fishbein and Ajzen model is only one theory in the cognitive response tradition. Many others focus not only on the underlying structure of belief systems but investigate additional areas. Models by Anthony Greenwald, Richard Petty and John Cacioppo, and Timothy Brock and others all examine the underlying cognitive responses that occur as individuals integrate new information and generate cognitions and arguments about objects of interest.[66]

Reardon's Approach to Persuasion: Rules and Change

The final model we will examine is being developed by Kathleen Reardon and others. Reardon believes behaviors are generated by internal rules "stored in the minds of individuals who use them to guide their behavioral choices."[67] Sets of regulative rules link antecedent conditions and desired consequences and prescribe actions by indicating behavioral options and specifying behavioral force.

In Reardon's own words, *antecedent conditions* are:

All those aspects of the present situation to which the individual attends and all of his or her memories of past successes and failures in such situations. *Behavioral options* are those particular behaviors from which the individual communicator may select. The level of *behavioral force* assigned to each behavior option indicates how necessary it is in the enactment of the episode, given the desired consequence… . Finally *desired consequences* are the goals of the communication.[68]

When confronted with situations in which they wish to achieve some end, individuals will search for an appropriate rule. Assume we want to borrow ten dollars from an acquaintance. We have a repertoire of regulative rules telling us how to act, each with a given amount of behavioral force. For example, some actions are prohibited: knocking the other to the ground or taking his or her wallet and removing the money. Others are sometimes permissible: bursting into tears, pleading, or threatening. Still others are preferred: making a polite request. Our regulative rules dictate how we enact goal-directed behaviors.

The need to persuade occurs when individual goals are blocked or threatened and when the threat is "sufficiently important to warrant the expenditure of effort involved in persuasion."[69] Persuasion may be accomplished by convincing a target to apply a preferred rule. The persuader must "render the application of that rule sensible" to the target. To do this, he or she must change the target's perception of antecedent conditions or show the target which rule is germane to the situation.

Reardon used a familiar example: beating a speeding ticket. In the example, a man is caught speeding while driving his pregnant wife to the hospital. By explaining his wife's pregnancy, he tries to persuade the police officer to "redefine the action of speeding as sensible in this emergency situation."[70] The driver is suggesting that under these antecedent conditions the desired consequence of punishing a lawbreaker should be supplanted by the desired consequence of helping in an emergency. If the officer accepts this behavioral logic, then he or she may redefine the context and apply a helping rule. If the officer gives the ticket anyway, then "we may assume that while a wife in labor may be sufficient reason for a husband to violate a speeding rule, it is insufficient grounds for policemen ... to apply another rule."[71]

Reardon believes persuasion requires sensitivity to the logic and cognitive processes of others. If the persuader understands the personal constructs and rules that others use to make sense of their worlds, he or she can demonstrate that an existing behavior is inconsistent, inappropriate, or ineffective according to these rules and can try to convince the other to abandon that behavior.[72] By using appropriate claims, the persuader can bring about four types of rule changes: *acquiescence*, in which target relinquishes a rule; *accomodation*, in which target revises rules; *compromise*, in which both target and persuader revise rules; and *coadjuvancy*, in which both generate a new rule or set of rules.

Criticism of Reardon's Model

Reardon's account of persuasion is heavily rules-based. It is in line with current concerns with cognitive processing, and it also takes into account the social nature of human actors. It defines persuasion as an act of coordinating rules. Like the cognitive response models, it sees persuasion not as something a persuader does to a target but as something a target does to himself or herself in cooperation with the persuader.

Whether or not this theory will be widely accepted will depend on the success of rules research. It is not completely obvious to some critics that the construct of rule is more useful than that of attitude or some other internal construct such as cognitive schema. Some consideration of how individuals process information is necessary, however, to understand how communicators control their social worlds, and this model seems to be a sound one. It remains to be seen whether rules-based models will supplant earlier formulations or not.

THE PROBLEM OF CHANGE AND GROWTH

Theories of outcome achievement point to a final problem, that of evolution and change. As we have seen, elements within the individual's cognitive arena constantly change and realign. Attitudes and beliefs may be reorganized, and outcomes may change their desirability. Behaviors affect attitudes, and rules are continually created, revised, and supplanted. Our social worlds are constantly changing.

Each communication act creates a new state of affairs that affects subsequent acts. A communicator who is incapable of change, accomodation, or assimilation will not be able to adapt to the world. The systems view of communication points this out better than any other view, for a general principle of systems theory is that a change in one element of the system affects every other element and the system as a whole.

Communicative interactions, whether interpersonal, group, or public, evolve and change. There are many theories that describe communicative stages. Some outline the changes that occur within a single interactional context; others describe changes that occur as individuals change over the course of their lives. We will save our discussion of interactional development for the next three chapters. There we will look at how interpersonal relationships blossom and fade, examine the phases through which problem-solving groups travel, and see how the relationship between speaker and audience changes over time. In the remainder of this chapter we will look at individual evolution and change, at some models of the changes we experience as we move from childhood to maturity.

The Life Span Approach

The selves we construct and the relationships we form through communication are not static throughout our lives. One of the most basic problems we face is adapting to life changes. Recently there has been a resurgence of interest in this problem and the development of a new approach to its study. Called the *life span approach*, this perspective holds that to understand human development we must understand the biological, psychological, social, and historical/political changes that affect humans across their lives.

David Featherman outlines some of the themes and premises of this new approach to human development.[73] Recognizing that development occurs over the entire course of an individual's life and not just during early childhood, life span theorists hold that there are multiple determinants affecting development. The changes we experience as we grow older are due to factors both outside the individual (for example social/psychological and historical trends) and within the individual (for example, individual attitudes and motivations). "Life histories are transactional products of the dialectics among the multiple determinants of development and the motivated, selectively responding person."[74] The fact that all life histories are in part unique means that it may be difficult to generalize across persons, especially in the last half of life. The fact that life histories are sensitive to social-historical conditions suggests that generalizations across generations are also problematic, as "each new birth cohort potentially ages through a different trajectory of life events, brought about by the impress of socio-historical change and by individual reactions to it."[75] Life span researchers ask us to remember that the individual is inherently adaptive and malleable, responsive to his or her environment, and capable of much more change than one might believe. Thus, static models of aging and universal models of child development are rejected.

Developmental psychologists have enthusiastically embraced the life span approach. So too have sociologists and historians. A life span orientation questions and modifies traditional beliefs in each of these fields, encouraging interdisciplinary dialogue.

Life span researchers include psychologists whose work seeks to describe individual changes across time as well as sociologists whose research emphasizes the effects of socializing structures on aggregates. It includes anthropologists with an interest in the cultural values associated with aging and social historians with an interest in changes in family dynamics over the centuries.

Early developmental theories often took the form of stage models, models that divide life into separate stages and then describe the behaviors typical for each stage. While recent life span models may also describe life stages, they are careful to take into account the fact that individuals are highly variable and that they develop in many ways at the same time. Life span theorists are also quick to point out that descriptions should not become prescriptions. Dale Goldhaber criticizes typical developmental models when he asks us how we should interpret the assertion that the average child can correctly copy a diamond at seventy-two months. "Should parents whose children copy a diamond at sixty months consider early admission to college? Should parents of children who don't copy the diamond until eighty months consider institutionalization?"[76] Obviously not. It is important to realize that children are highly variable. Goldhaber also points out that stage models contain implicit values. "What about Havighurst's statement that selecting a mate is one of the developmental tasks of young adulthood? What if someone doesn't want to select a mate? Can't single people be adults? ... The problem arises when what most people do (for example, marry) is equated with what people should do."[77]

Most developmental work in communication has centered on childhood development of language, on the acquisition of basic interpersonal skills such as comforting or persuasion, and on the communications skills necessary for success in educational settings.[78] There has been less work on communication through the entire life span. The two models we will review, while not specifically designed to describe communication, have implications for its study.

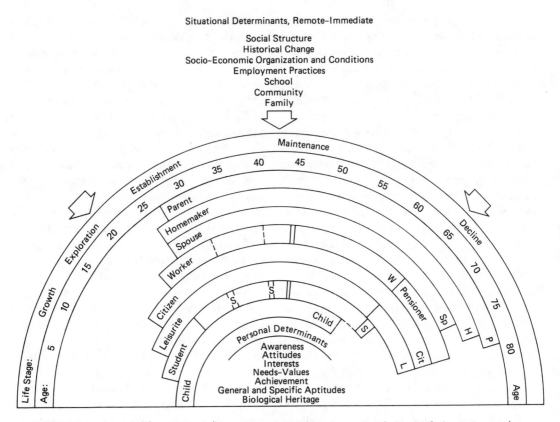

Situational Determinants, Remote-Immediate

Social Structure
Historical Change
Socio-Economic Organization and Conditions
Employment Practices
School
Community
Family

FIGURE 7.2: Super's life-career rainbow. (Source: Donald E. Super, "A Life-Span, Life-Space Approach to Career Development," *Journal of Vocational Behavior,* 16 [1980], 282–98.)

A General Life Span Model

Many of us have been exposed to discussions of "the mid-life crisis" or the "empty nest syndrome" and have seen graphs of individual "life lines" or have read about life cycle "passages" in the popular press.[79] These simple models attest to popular interest in life span processes. A more complex model of changing roles over our lifetimes is presented by Donald Super.[80] Super's model is fairly typical of the life span approach (see Fig. 7.2). Super takes as his central metaphor a rainbow, with the bands of color representing age-specific roles. Super argues that it is the transaction between situational determinants (such as changes in prevailing social structures)

and personal determinants (such as an individual's motivations, needs, and values) that determines the actual shape of an individual's life. Each individual's rainbow will be a variation on the general model, for each individual will decide how much time and how much emotional commitment to devote to each overlapping role.

Havighurst's Developmental Tasks

Robert Havighurst takes a slightly different approach to human development. Instead of outlining roles, he delineates the basic problems or tasks individuals must undertake throughout their lives. We should note that his model is sequential rather than age specific. That is, Havighurst does

FIGURE 7.3:   Havighurst's developmental tasks

Age	Developmental Tasks
Infancy and Early Childhood	Learning to walk Learning to take solid foods Learning to talk Learning bowel and bladder control Learning sex differences and sexual modesty Forming concepts and learning language to describe social and physical reality Getting ready to read
Middle Childhood	Learning physical skills necessary for ordinary games Building wholesome attitudes towards oneself as a growing organism Learning to get along with peers Learning an appropriate masculine or feminine role Developing basic skills in reading, writing and calculating Developing concepts necessary for everyday living Developing conscience, morality, and a scale of values Achieving personal independence Developing attitudes toward social groups and institutions
Adolescence	Achieving new and more mature relations with peers of both sexes Achieving a masculine or feminine role Accepting one's physique and using the body effectively Achieving emotional independence of parents and other adults Preparing for marriage and family life and for an economic career Developing an ideology (a set of values and an ethical system that guide behavior) Desiring and achieving socially responsible behavior
Early Adulthood	Selecting a mate and learning to live with a marriage partner Starting a family, rearing children, and managing a home Getting started in an occupation Taking on civic responsibility Finding a congenial social group
Middle Age	Assisting teenage children to become responsible and happy adults Achieving adult social and civic responsibility Reaching and maintaining satisfactory performance in one's occupational career Developing adult leisure time activities Relating to one's spouse as a person Accepting and adjusting to the physiological changes of middle age Adjusting to aging parents
Later Maturity	Adjusting to decreasing physical strength Adjusting to retirement and reduced income Adjusting to the death of one's spouse Establishing an explicit affiliation with one's age group Adopting and adapting social roles in a flexible way Establishing satisfactory physical living arrangements

not tie a particular stage of development to a particular age, although his model indicates that developmental tasks must be undertaken in order. According to Havighurst, a *developmental task* is "a task which arises at or about a certain period in the life of the individual, successful achievement of which leads to his happiness and to success with later tasks, while failure leads to unhappiness in the individual, disapproval by the society, and difficulty with later tasks."[81] Developmental tasks are the result of three factors: biological maturation, cultural pressure, and individual motivation. By using observation, surveys, and introspection, Havighurst developed six to nine tasks for each of six age groups. These are shown in Fig. 7.3.

While similar lists have been compiled by child language specialists or by communication competence scholars, their stage models have focused either on early language learning or on the competencies necessary to succeed during the school years. Havighurst's model is presented here because it spans the individual's entire life from infancy to old age. Although his model does not speak directly to communication, it should be clear that all of the tasks he outlines are accomplished through communication and many call upon the individual to learn new modes of interaction. The Havighurst model emphasizes that throughout one's life course it is necessary to adapt to social and biological changes and to find new ways of communicating.

Criticisms of the Havighurst Model

In her excellent review of life span research, Leonie Sugarman points out the advantages and disadvantages of this model.[82] First of all, it is very culturally specific and value laden, being not only a list of tasks the individual does but tasks he or she must do to be considered normal. Take, for example, its insistence that the individual achieve either a masculine or feminine role. The assumptions that (1) gender role differentiation is essential for successful development and (2) masculinity and femininity are the only two choices may well be questioned. Historical studies have shown that a list like this, which seems so self-evident, would have made only partial sense in, say, colonial America, where adolescence and middle age were not recognized as separate life stages.[82] Still, the general, content-free aspect of Havighurst's tasks makes it "a feasible candidate for trans-cultural and transhistorical transposition."[84] It also presents an excellent heuristic for applied research, inviting researchers to examine such problems as "mid-life career change; perception of aging by the self, the family and the community; personality change in the context of declin-ing health and vigor; and the attitudes towards death held by people of different ages."[85]

REFERENCES

1. Frank E. X. Dance and Carl E. Larson, *The Functions of Human Communication: A Theoretical Approach* (New York: Holt, Rinehart & Winston, 1976).

2. *Ibid.*, p. 48.

3. *Ibid.*, p. 42.

4. *Ibid.*, p. 63.

5. *Ibid.*, p. 92.

6. *Ibid.*, p. 100.

7. Lev Semenovich Vygotsky, *Thought and Language*, eds. Eugenia Hanfmann and Gertrude Vakar (Cambridge, Mass.: MIT Press, 1962).

8. *Ibid.*, p. 44.

9. *Ibid.*, p. 47.

10. Dance and Larson, *Functions*, p. 129.

11. *Ibid.*, p. 63.

12. *Ibid.*, p. 92.

13. *Ibid.*, p. 100.

14. Daniel Katz, "The Functional Approach to the Study of Attitudes," *Public Opinion Quarterly*, 24 (1960), 163–204.

15. Mary John Smith, *Persuasion and Human Action: A Review and Critique of Social Influence Theories* (Belmont, Calif.: Wadsworth, 1977), p. 38.

16. Philip G. Zimbardo, Ebbe B. Ebbesen, and Christina Maslach, *Influencing Attitudes and Changing Behaviors*, 2nd ed. (Reading, Mass.: Addison-Wesley, 1977), pp. 21–22.

17. Herbert C. Kelman, "Attitudes Are Alive and Well and Gainfully Employed in the Sphere of Action," *American Psychologist*, 29 (1974), 324.

18. Katz, "Functional Approach," p. 187.

19. Kathleen Kelley Reardon, *Persuasion: Theory and Context* (Beverly Hills: Sage, 1981), p. 68.

20. Irving Sarnoff, "Psychoanalytic Theory and Social Attitudes," *Public Opinion Quarterly*, 24 (1960), 251–79.

21. Albert Bandura, *Social Learning Theory* (Englewood Cliffs, N. J.: Prentice Hall, 1977), p. 10.

22. *Ibid.*, p. 12.

23. *Ibid.*, p. 117.

24. *Ibid.*, pp. 124–27.

25. *Ibid.*, p. 79.

26. *Ibid.*, pp. 80–83.

27. Milton Rokeach, "Value Theory and Communication Research: Review and Commentary," in *Communication Yearbook 3*, ed. Dan Nimmo (New Brunswick, N. J.: Transaction Books, 1979), pp. 7–28; Milton Rokeach, *The Nature of Human Values* (New York: The Free Press, 1973); Milton Rokeach, *Beliefs, Attitudes, and Values* (San Francisco: Jossey-Bass, 1972).

28. Rokeach, "Value Theory and Communication Research," p. 12.

29. Rokeach, *Beliefs, Attitudes, and Values*, p. 1.

30. *Ibid.*, p. 113.

31. *Ibid.*, p. 5.

32. *Ibid.*, p. 6.

33. *Ibid.*, p. 8.

34. *Ibid.*, p. 11.

35. *Ibid.*, p. 13.

36. *Ibid.*, p. 16.

37. Rokeach, *Nature of Values*, p. 5.

38. *Ibid.*, p. 18.

39. Rokeach, "Value Theory and Communication Research," p. 11.

40. *Ibid.*, p. 10.

41. Rokeach, *Nature of Values*, p. 216.

42. Rokeach, "Value Theory and Communication Research," p. 12.

43. *Ibid.*, p. 12.

44. *Ibid.*, p. 13.

45. See for example, Barry R. Schlenker, "Translating Actions Into Attitudes: An Identity-Analytic Approach to the Explanation of Social Conduct," in *Advances in Experimental Social Psychology*, vol. 15, ed. Leonard Berkowitz (New York: Academic, 1982), p. 195, and James T. Tedeschi, ed., *Impression Management Theory and Social Psychological Research* (New York: Academic, 1981).

46. Stephen W. Littlejohn, *Theories of Human Communication*, 2nd ed. (Belmont, Calif.: Wadsworth, 1983), p. 157.

47. *Ibid.*, p. 157.

48. Robert P. Abelson and others, eds., *Theories of Cognitive Consistency: A Sourcebook* (Chicago: Rand McNally, 1968).

49. For the original formulation of dissonance theory, see Leon Festinger, *A Theory of Cognitive Dissonance* (Stanford, Calif.: Stanford University Press, 1957); for a further development and research review see Jack W. Brehm and Arthur R. Cohen, *Explorations in Cognitive Dissonance* (New York: John Wiley & Sons, 1962).

50. Festinger, *Theory of Cognitive Dissonance*, pp. 9–11.

51. *Ibid.*, p. 16.

52. *Ibid.*, p. 17.

53. Brehm and Cohen, *Explorations.*

54. *Ibid.*, p. 4.

55. Festinger, *Theory of Cognitive Dissonance*, p. 3.

56. Zimbardo, Ebbesen, and Maslach, *Influencing Attitudes*, p. 72.

57. Fritz Heider, *The Psychology of Interpersonal Relations* (New York: John Wiley & Sons, 1958); Theodore M. Newcomb, *The Acquaintance Process* (New York: Holt, Rinehart & Winston, 1961).

58. Daryl J. Bem, "Self-Perception Theory," in *Advances in Experimental Social Psychology*, vol. 6, ed. Leonard Berkowitz (New York: Academic, 1972), pp. 1–62.

59. John T. Cacioppo, Stephen G. Harkins, and Richard E. Petty, "The Nature of Attitudes and Cognitive Responses and Their Relationship to Behavior," in *Cognitive Responses in Persuasion*, eds. Richard E. Petty, Thomas M. Ostrom, and Timothy C. Brock (Hillsdale, N. J.: Lawrence Erlbaum Associates, 1981), p. 36.

60. Richard E. Petty, Thomas M. Ostrom, and Timothy C. Brock, "Historical Foundations of the Cognitive Response Approach to Attitudes and

Persuasion," in Petty, Ostrom, and Brock, *Cognitive Responses in Persuasion*, p. 7.

61. Anthony G. Greenwald, "Cognitive Response Analysis: An Appraisal," in Petty, Ostrom, and Brock, *Cognitive Responses in Persuasion*.

62. Richard M. Perloff and Timothy C. Brock, "'...And Thinking Makes It So': Cognitive Responses to Persuasion," in *Persuasion: New Directions in Theory and Research*, eds. Michael E. Roloff and Gerald R. Miller (Beverly Hills: Sage, 1980), p. 67.

63. Martin Fishbein and Icek Ajzen, "Acceptance, Yielding and Impact: Cognitive Processes in Persuasion," in Petty, Ostrom, and Brock, *Cognitive Responses in Persuasion*, p. 341.

64. *Ibid.*, p. 342.

65. *Ibid.*, p. 344.

66. See Petty, Ostrom, and Brock, *Cognitive Responses in Persuasion*.

67. Reardon, *Persuasion*, p. 26.

68. *Ibid.*, p. 36.

69. *Ibid.*, p. 25.

70. *Ibid.*, p. 26.

71. *Ibid.*, p. 26.

72. *Ibid.*, p. 101.

73. David L. Featherman, "Life-Span Perspectives in Social Science Research," in *Life-Span Development and Behavior*, vol. 5, eds. Paul B. Baltes and Orville G. Brim, Jr. (New York: Academic, 1983).

74. *Ibid.*, p. 3.

75. *Ibid.*, p. 3.

76. Dale Goldhaber, *Life-Span Human Development* (New York: Harcourt Brace Jovanovich, 1986), p. 22.

77. *Ibid.*, p. 22.

78. For some studies on the development of communication competencies see Carl E. Larson, "Problems in Assessing Functional Communication," *Communication Education*, 27 (1978), 304–09; R. R. Allen and Barbara Sundene Wood, "Beyond Reading and Writing to Communication Competence," *Communication Education*, 27 (1978), 286–92; for the development of communication and language strategies see, Barbara S. Wood, *Children and Communication: Verbal and Non-Verbal Language Development*, 2nd ed. (Englewood Cliffs, N. J.: Prentice Hall, 1981); Jesse G. Delia, Susan L. Kline, and Brant R. Burleson, "The Development of Persuasive Communication Strategies in Kindergarteners Through Twelfth Graders," *Communication Monographs*, 46 (1979), 231–40; Wendy Samter and Brant R. Burleson, "Cognitive and Motivational Influences on Spontaneous Comforting Behavior," *Human Communication Research*, 11 (1984), 231–60.

79. Gail Sheehy, *Passages: Predictable Crises of Adult Life* (New York: E. P. Dutton, 1976).

80. Donald E. Super, "A Life-Span, Life-Space Approach to Career Development, " *Journal of Vocational Behavior*, 16 (1980), 282–98.

81. Robert J. Havighurst, *Developmental Tasks and Education*, 3rd ed. (New York: David McKay, 1972), p. 2.

82. Leonie Sugarman, *Life-Span Development: Concepts, Theories and Interventions* (New York: Methuen, 1986).

83. John Demos and Sarane Spence Boocock, *Turning Points: Historical and Sociological Essays on the Family*, Supplement to the *American Journal of Sociology*, vol. 84 (Chicago: University of Chicago Press, 1978); John Demos, *Past, Present, and Personal: The Family and the Life Course in American History* (New York: Oxford University Press, 1986).

84. Sugarman, *Life-Span*, p. 97.

85. *Ibid.*, p. 99.

chapter 8

INTERPERSONAL COMMUNICATION

INTRODUCTION

As we saw earlier, context affects communication. In any interaction the number of people present and their physical closeness affect how feedback is used, how messages are adapted and planned, and how people work out their roles. When two people are involved in direct, face-to-face interaction, they are in the interpersonal context. Feedback is generally immediate, messages are informal and spontaneous, and roles are generally reciprocal and equal. According to this line of reasoning, what is important in defining context is not the goals and behaviors of communicators but rather the situation in which they find themselves.

There is another view, however. Here, dyadic interactions are not defined just by situational factors. Instead, interactions become interpersonal as

certain changes occur within the interactors. This view suggests that interpersonal communication is the end product of a developmental process; it focuses attention on the emerging nature of dyadic encounters. We begin this chapter by examining this approach to interpersonal communication.

THE DEVELOPMENTAL VIEW: WHAT HAPPENS IN INTERPERSONAL COMMUNICATION?

Gerald Miller and Mark Steinberg present what is essentially an evolutionary theory.[1] They study the time dimensions of communication, describing the changes that occur as communicators learn more about one another through repeated interaction. They argue that as relationships follow a trajectory toward increased intimacy, three

159

changes occur: (1) changes in rules governing the relationship, (2) changes in the amount of data communicators have about one another, and (3) changes in participants' levels of knowing.[2]

Changes in Level of Rules

Like other theorists, Miller and Steinberg believe communicative interactions are constrained by layers of rules. Communicators are controlled by consensual agreements that outline the "procedural, structural and content factors which direct and shape a communicative relationship."[3] For example, agreements tell us how to use our common language, what nonverbal behaviors are culturally sanctioned, and how to participate in culturally accepted rituals. All members of a given culture are partially guided by generalized rules existing at this *cultural level*.

Individuals belong, however, not only to the culture at large, but to specific groups: professional groups, social groups, ethnic groups, and so on. Each defines its members' roles and establishes behavioral norms. These constraints modify general cultural rules. For example, while there are general cultural rules for greetings and leave-taking, specific groups have additional rules governing these processes. The military prescribes that soldiers salute one another when they meet. Similarly, social or ethnic groups establish their own style of greetings. Each organization to which we belong has unique agreements about appropriate communicative behaviors. These exist on what Miller and Steinberg call the *sociological level*.

Finally, individuals develop their own variations of larger cultural and sociological rules. As we become acquainted with one another, we develop unique interpersonal patterns of interaction. We become "the rule makers, rather than allowing the rules to be imposed from outside,"[4] For example, you and a friend may develop your own greeting rules, perhaps beginning your interactions with mild joking insults. These rules are not culturally or sociologically sanctioned but worked out on the *psychological level*.

Miller and Steinberg argue that interpersonal communication develops as we move from the cultural and sociological levels to the psychological level. For example, when new employees first enter an organization, they rely on cultural level rules to guide behavior. Their initial dyadic relationships are impersonal, not interpersonal. As they become better acquainted with the workings of the organization, they advance to the sociological level, using organizationally defined roles and rules to guide interaction. Finally, as they make friends, individual patterns of behavior develop. The rules constraining interaction are mutually negotiated. According to Miller and Steinberg, communication that remains entirely on the cultural and sociological levels may be characterized as *impersonal*, not interpersonal. Only when communication reaches the psychological level does it truly become *interpersonal*.

Changes in Level of Data

Miller and Steinberg agree with Charles Berger that communication involves a gradual process of uncertainty reduction.[5] Because we need to structure our social worlds, we seek data that afford us some predictive control over our environments. Miller tells us that "*at the outset of a relationship, communicators must rely on cultural and sociological information for making predictions since this is all the data they have available.*"[6] While knowledge of cultural and group affiliations reduces some of our uncertainty about others, psychological data are the most powerful information for predicting another's actions.

As relationships become more interpersonal, new information sources open. We attach unique meanings to others' actions. We know how our relational partners differ from other members of the culture, and we begin to recognize our partners' idiosyncrasies, becoming sensitive to cues not available to outsiders. Gaining access to these data is time-consuming and difficult. It is usually undertaken only when the relationship is important enough or long-lasting enough to warrant a great deal of attention. Not all relationships become interpersonal, although all can, given desire and commitment. As Miller points out, "serious attempts to acquire a large store of psychological information probably occur relatively infrequently."[7]

Changes in Level of Knowing

A change in level of data changes level of knowing. Miller and Steinberg discuss three ways we can "know" someone. First, we know a person by recognizing or identifying that person. This level of knowing is *descriptive*. Second, we know what a person will do in a particular situation. This level of knowing is called *predictive*. Finally, we know not only what a person will do in a given instance but *why*. Knowledge at this level is called *explanatory*.[8] As relationships become increasingly interpersonal, interactors move through these levels of knowledge, eventually developing a store of explanatory knowledge about each other.

For Miller and Steinberg, interpersonal communication is a special kind of dyadic communication, characterized by the development of personally negotiated rules, increased information exchange, and progressively deeper levels of knowledge. All dyadic encounters begin impersonally. Some stay at that level for months or years, while others develop, becoming increasingly more interpersonal over time. The study of interpersonal communication, therefore, involves the study of developing relationships.

Criticism of the Developmental View

The fact that dyadic encounters take different forms is undeniable. There is a vast difference between the hurried exchange of a supermarket clerk and a one-time customer and the interaction of longstanding friends (or enemies.) While the situational view classes both interactions as interpersonal, the developmental view proposes that different theoretical concepts are needed to understand them. The developmental approach

also recognizes that communicative transactions occur along a time dimension. It recognizes that relationships change and grow.

Its greatest difficulty is that it implies dyadic relationships inevitably lead to intimacy, that the only path relationships should take is toward increasing psychological involvement. While Miller and Steinberg do not mean to "sanctify" interpersonal relationships in this way, others who take the developmental view see intimacy as the only valuable end state of a relationship, and they pay little attention to dyadic communication that does not move in this direction. Jesse Delia has criticized this view of interpersonal communication. He argues that it is wrong to presume that the "natural or most important course of relationships is toward intimacy."[9] We all know people who work side-by-side for years without knowing one another on the psychological level. They stay within prescribed roles and polite norms, and they feel no pressure to deepen the relationship. Whether or not we label these interactions as "impersonal" or "interpersonal," they are proper subjects of theoretical study. To ignore or criticize them as incomplete is a serious error.

Our discussion of the developmental approach emphasizes the importance of evolution and change, a problem we will return to when we conclude this chapter by looking at stages in the creation and dissolution of long-term dyadic relationships. In the interim, we will look at how the other problems of communication are manifested in the interpersonal context: how interpersonal impressions are formed, how interpersonal influence is achieved, and how relational cultures are created and maintained.

INTERPERSONAL JUDGMENTS AND IMPRESSIONS: HOW DO WE CHOOSE RELATIONAL PARTNERS?

One area of great concern to theorists interested in interpersonal exchanges is person perception and impression formation. To decide on the communicative acceptability of potential relational partners, we gather information about them, organize this information to form an impression of their characteristics, and decide whether the dispositions we attribute to them attract us. In what follows we examine three theories that focus on how impression formation affects interpersonal communication.

Berger's Model of Uncertainty Reduction

Berger and his colleagues argue that one of the primary functions of communication is the reduction of uncertainty.[10] They believe that most people have a strong need to attain knowledge and understanding of others. Much of our communicative behavior is a drive to attain information to structure and control our environments. While acknowledging that under certain conditions "there is a competing drive for novelty, for exposure to a diverse range of stimuli," they believe that most people, most of the time, engage in uncertainty reduction, seeking out information about the characteristics of other human actors.[11]

The drive to acquire information about others is especially strong under certain conditions: (1) when others' behaviors are deviant, (2) when we anticipate repeated interactions with them, and (3) when there is a high probability of our receiving rewards or punishments from them.[12] Such conditions maximize our uncertainty and prompt us to seek additional information. We do not need to know much about others if we do not anticipate further interaction with them, but, if we must repeatedly communicate with important and powerful people whose actions we do not understand, then we will feel a strong need to find out more about them. Doing so has survival value for us.

Uncertainty Reduction Strategies. In cases where uncertainty is high, we employ strategies to gain more information. Berger and his colleagues identify six such strategies. The first two involve passive observation of the target. Berger and Calabrese argue that we choose to observe others in specific situations, situations that maxi-

mize the amount of information we can obtain. Most of us prefer to observe others actively engaged in social interaction rather than individuals who are alone. When we observe targets reacting to one another socially, we are engaged in *reactivity search*. Given a choice, we also prefer to observe others in informal contexts where they are relatively uninhibited by role constraints. When we seek this kind of information, we use a strategy called *disinhibition search*. In Miller and Steinberg's terms, we gain more information when we observe others interacting at the psychological level rather than the cultural or sociological levels. Research Abstract 8.1 provides empirical evidence for the use of both passive strategies.

Communication involves more than passive observation. We can also actively reduce uncertainty. The first active strategy that Berger and Calabrese discuss is that of *asking others about the target person*. The second involves *environmental structuring*. This latter strategy is used whenever we stage incidents to gain information about target persons' responses. By placing targets in situations where they must make choices, we learn more about how they will behave. Direct interactions with targets also serve as information sources. One such strategy is *interrogation*, asking targets direct questions. Finally, *self-disclosure* gives us information because when we disclose to others they often reciprocate by disclosing to us.

These strategies seem to be progressive. When we first decide we want to learn more about someone, we may observe how this person reacts to others (reactivity search) and pay special attention to his or her actions in unguarded moments (disinhibition search). We also approach mutual friends (asking others) and may even stage situations where the other will reveal his or her true nature (environmental structuring). On the basis of this information, we may interact directly, asking the target questions (interrogation) or trying to prompt disclosures by telling about ourselves (self-disclosure). Once this happens, we will be on a highly interpersonal level. Of course, we

RESEARCH ABSTRACT 8.1   Finding Out What Other People Are Like

Berger and Douglas's *purpose* was to see how people gather information about others. They theorized that we prefer to gather data in two situations: (1) when the target is with others rather than alone and (2) when the target is acting informally rather than formally.

To test these hypotheses, Berger and Douglas used the following *method.* Over a 2 month period, they took more than 200 slides of a woman engaging in a variety of natural behaviors in both private and public contexts. They randomly chose 15 of the best slides as stimulus pictures for the study. The slides showed the target with others or alone and in either a formal (having her blood pressure checked) or an informal (watching TV in a living room) context. Slides were presented two at a time in all possible combinations, and subjects were asked to indicate their preference for one of each pair. Subjects were 50 undergraduate students from Northwestern University.

Two experimental conditions were created. One-half of the subjects were told they would be interacting with the person in the picture. For the other half there was no anticipated interaction. Subjects were told to choose the slide from each pair that they believed gave them the most information. They also indicated how similar they felt to the target person and why they chose the slides they did.

The data were analyzed through a statistical procedure known as multidimensional scaling. This procedure allows the extrac-

tion of judgmental dimensions and shows how each subject's choices are influenced by each dimension. The *results* indicated the existence of two major dimensions. The first was amount of social interaction; the pictures were judged differently when the target was interacting with others than when she was alone. The second dimensions was formality. At one extreme, the target person was seen in a kitchen making coffee. At the other, she was in a highly public context (standing on a train platform or in a doctor's office). In the first case, few constraints were placed on her behavior, while in the second she was in a context requiring more normative behaviors.

While the majority of subjects preferred to judge the target in social situations, the results for the formal/informal dimensions were more variable. When the data for those anticipating future interaction with the target were examined separately, however, there was also a significant preference for informal situations. Berger and Douglas interpret their results as indicating that people prefer to observe targets in "contexts which will produce greater response variety from the target." By doing so, they afford themselves a maximum level of uncertainty reduction.

Source: Charles R. Berger and William Douglas, "Studies in Interpersonal Epistemology: III. Anticipated Interaction, Self-Monitoring, and Observational Context Selection," *Communication Monographs*, 48 (September 1981), 183–96.

may abandon our efforts anywhere along the line. Some initial passive strategies may give us enough information so we need go no further, or we may decide that the person is no longer of interest to us.

Criticism of the Berger Model. The strategies identified by Berger and his colleagues are reasonable descriptions of how we gather interpersonal information. We often intentionally use communication to reduce uncertainty about others. The Berger model focuses on this kind of rational, self-conscious, purposeful process of uncertainty reduction. It has little to say, however, about how we perceive others during normal, daily interactions where our primary focus is on the task at hand. The model also fails to explain when individuals will act to achieve certainty and when they will seek novelty. Berger and his colleagues admit that we are often attracted to people or situations because they increase our uncertainty. Without an explication of the conditions leading to novelty, a full theoretical explanation of uncertainty is incomplete. Still, the Berger model is an interesting description of information-gathering processes.

Individuals differ widely in the uses they make of the information they collect. Even when two people employ identical information-gathering strategies, the result, their interpretations of this information, will not be identical. Some of us are adept at forming accurate impressions of others. Others are often wrong about other people. What factors affect the impression formation process? Why are some individuals interpersonally sensitive and perceptive and others not? These questions can be answered in part by turning to a theoretical framework known as constructivism.

Constructivism

Constructivism is a label applied to the work of several researchers including Jesse Delia, Ruth Anne Clark, Daniel O'Keefe, and others.[13] Delia and other constructivists argue that experience is never directly apprehended; instead, it is cognitively interpreted or "constructed." Each individual creates his or her own social world. While a world of concrete objects and behaviors exists at some level, the impressions we form of them depend on our own mental makeup. You and I are different people in the eyes of every person who meets us, and we, in turn, perceive others in unique ways.

One way we differ from each other is in the complexity of our personal construct systems. As children, we only have a few basic constructs. All strangers seem the same to us. As we grow older, we develop more constructs and distinguish more characteristics of others. Throughout our lives our constructs become more differentiated, more abstract, and less egocentric. Even as adults we differ from each other in terms of the content and organization of our personal constructs. It is the nature of these constructs that affects the way we form impressions. Delia and his colleagues argue that when we observe others we transform surface cues into the categories contained in our personal construct systems. Individuals who are high in cognitive complexity, who have a large number of well-differentiated and well-integrated constructs at their disposal, form different impressions from those whose construct systems are less complex. To understand the constructivist approach to impression formation, we need to understand two concepts: personal constructs and cognitive complexity.

Personal Construct Theory. The idea of *personal constructs* was originally developed by George Kelly, who believed that an individual's activities are "psychologically channelized" by the ways he or she anticipates events.[14] To anticipate events, the individual constructs, or construes, those events by locating them in a cognitive framework that gives them shape and meaning.[15]

Each individual's construct system consists of an organized set of personal constructs. Some are of a higher order than others. For example, the construct "good/bad" might be a superordinate construct, including the constructs "intelligent/stupid," "attractive/unattractive," and "kind/cruel." "Intelligence," "attractiveness," and "kindness" are interrelated, belonging to the overall construct "good." Constructs, then, are not isolated but belong to an organized system. Furthermore, they change over time. As we experience our world, we modify our construct systems, replacing outmoded constructs with new ones or giving up those that no longer work.

For Kelly, a given construct may be broadly or narrowly applied. Some people use a single construct to apply to a large range of events. For example, an individual might interpret every action she encounters in terms of a "support/defiance" construct. For such a person, no action is innocent. If another inadvertently fails to return a greeting or is late for an appointment, she interprets their behavior as defiance. For others, the defiance construct only applies in cases of direct public confrontation. These people might prefer to use the "thoughtful/thoughtless" construct to interpret everyday slights, reserving "support/defiance" for a more limited range of events.

Constructs differ not only in range but in rigidity or permeability. Some individuals cannot expand their constructs to include new experiences and new situations. When confronted with the unexpected, they become confused. Other people are more capable of interpreting new events. Their construct systems are more resilient.

Personal Constructs and Cognitive Complexity. The constructivists take insights offered by Kelly's personal construct theory and apply them to communication. They investigate the notion of cognitive organization and detail how the complexity of an individual's construct system is related to the ability to form impressions, to assume the role of others, and to adapt to that role during interaction. The constructivists argue that, over time, individuals develop construct systems differing in content, number, degree of abstraction, and amount of organization. Following the lead of Walter Crockett, Delia and his colleagues believe that these systems develop along a simplicity/complexity dimension. A cognitive system is "considered relatively complex in structure when (1) it contains a relatively large number of elements and (2) the elements are integrated hierarchically by relatively extensive bonds of relationship."[16] Someone whose constructs are complex in this way is judged to be high in *cognitive complexity*.

This view of cognitive complexity focuses on two aspects of an individual's construct system: number of constructs and their organization. Cognitively complex subjects employ a larger number of constructs. If an individual's range of constructs is broad and varied, he or she can form differentiated and varied impressions. The total number of constructs, however, is not the only way construct systems differ. When judging others, we use different kinds of constructs. We class people at very concrete levels (according to their physical properties) or we use more abstract level constructs (employing dispositional and personality information). We also differ in our abilities to integrate variability in the behaviors we observe in others. For example, some of us may judge others as totally good or totally bad, but not as both. More cognitively complex individuals are better able to deal with "shades of gray," using higher level constructs to explain why others sometimes can be good and sometimes bad. This latter ability is highly important in impression formation.

As you will recall from our discussion of attribution theory in chapter 4, actors tend to view their own behavior as situationally bound but see others' behavior as the result of enduring dispositions. To the extent we can put ourselves in another's "cognitive shoes," we can recognize that situational constraints affect them as well as us. We will form more accurate impressions, be more empathic and understanding, and adapt our communications more readily. These abilities seems to be intimately related to cognitive complexity.

Programmatic research conducted by the constructivists shows that cognitively complex subjects form impressions that:

(a) are more extensive or differentiated, (b) better represent and integrate evaluative inconsistency and behavioral variability in others, (c) are more organized around motivational attributions, and (d) are characterized by greater evaluative stability. Complex subjects have also been shown to possess greater capacity for taking the perspective of others in social situations, and (e) performing beyond their normal level when given an experimental set to "understand" the other as a person.[17]

Research Abstract 8.2 gives one example of the kind of methodology used in this research program.

Criticism of Constructivism. The constructivists are responsible for a large body of research. They have systematically investigated the nature and development of construct systems and shown how construct systems are related to interpersonal

RESEARCH ABSTRACT 8.2 Cognitive Complexity and Conversational Content

Cognitive complexity is an important factor in our perceptual lives, for it affects the way we make sense of the world. It should, therefore, have an impact on the topics we find interesting and the way we interact with others. Delia and his colleagues' *purpose* was to examine how cognitive complexity affects the content of informal interpersonal interaction in an unstructured and ambiguous situation.

The *methods* they used were as follows. Fifty-eight students volunteered to take part. Prior to the actual study, each subject was asked to describe two known peers, one liked and one disliked. The total number of constructs used in these descriptions comprised the measure of cognitive complexity. Complexity scores were ordered and broken at the median. Those above the median were classed as complex, and those below the median were classed as noncomplex.

Subjects were taken to a room, two at a time, and told to wait for the person running the experiment. While they waited, their conversations were recorded by a hidden tape recorder. After 10 minutes they were told that the study was actually about first impressions, and they were taken to separate rooms to fill out a number of measures not actually relevant to the present study.

The content of their conversations was analyzed according to topic and type of utterance. Three topic categories were used: (1) externally oriented topics ("How many speeches does your class give?" "How many people in your fraternity are walking in the march on poverty?"), (2) topics oriented to the present situation ("What do you think the study is about?" "I'll bet there's a tape recorder somewhere." "This is a stupid study."), and (3) topics relevant to the immediate participants ("Where are you from?" "I'm an impatient kind of person."). In each category, utterances were divided into descriptions, evaluations, information giving, and information seeking comments. Noncontent utterances ("uh," "hm," "right") were also coded.

The *results* indicated that utterance type did not vary with cognitive complexity or topic. An interaction between topic and cognitive complexity was found, however. Complex subjects' talk included more participant-centered utterances than that of noncomplex subjects. Noncomplex subjects talked more about external matters than did complex subjects.

Delia and his colleagues interpret the results to indicate that highly complex subjects "appear spontaneously, and presumably quite tacitly, to structure their social worlds around the personalities and characteristics of the interactional participants themselves." The authors concluded that social cognitive processes seem to affect the ways individuals choose to organize communicative episodes and ways they choose to interact.

Source: Jesse G. Delia, Ruth Anne Clark, and David E. Switzer, "The Content of Informal Conversations as a Function of Interactants' Interpersonal Cognitive Complexity," *Communication Monographs*, 46 (November 1979), 274–81.

communication strategies. By combining the work of cognitive psychologists like Kelly with a symbolic interactionist perspective, they make a substantial contribution to our understanding of the relationship between internal cognitions and social interactions.

The major criticism of their research involves measurement procedures. In many studies, cognitive complexity is measured by asking subjects to describe two peers, one liked and one disliked. The total number of constructs produced in these descriptions is the measure of cognitive complexity. This procedure is somewhat problematic. Kelly, for example, was careful to point out that a construct is not the same as a symbol. We have many constructs that are not actualized into verbal descriptions. Measuring constructs by counting symbols, then, may lead to classifying highly articulate subjects as more cognitively complex than their more reticent counterparts. Delia and his colleagues face a methodological problem shared by all cognitive researchers: how to find an overt, observable measure for an internal cognitive state.

Measurement problems aside, cognitive complexity seems a promising explanation for differences in impression formation. The constructivists have conducted a very impressive series of research studies, each building on others, and their program addresses an important aspect of communicative behavior.

So far we have examined strategies for acquiring information about others, and we have looked at how cognitive complexity affects this process. We have not yet considered how we use this information to evaluate others. What kind of information leads us to accept others as communication partners? In the next section we will discuss the kind of cues that lead to interpersonal attraction.

Models of Interpersonal Attraction

The characteristics we value in others may vary in many ways. As the Cronkhite and Liska model discussed in chapter 4 indicates, individual goals and situations affect what we look for in a partner. Still, there appear to be general characteristics we value in others. In the interpersonal context, these tend to center around how likeable the other is; we are preoccupied with "judgments about whether we 'like' another person, whether we desire to associate or spend time with him, whether we 'feel good' in his presence, etc."[18] When a person meets these criteria, we feel *interpersonal attraction*.

Factors Affecting Attraction. A number of theories examine factors leading to feelings of attraction. One of these is offered by James McCroskey, Carl Larson and Mark Knapp. One of the first and most important foundations for attraction is *proximity*. McCroskey and his colleagues believe that proximity is an "almost sufficient" condition for attraction. Proximity refers to the physical closeness of individuals. People who live or work together are more likely to become attracted to one another than individuals separated by great distances. Although we sometimes hear about people who fall in love with unattainable strangers, in the normal course of affairs we choose our friends and lovers from among those who are in physical proximity to us. Of course, proximity does not always bear positive results. We may learn to dislike the people we live and work with. Still, it is a beginning, and a great deal of research ties familiarity and environmental closeness to the development of attraction.

According to McCroskey and his colleagues, the first true variable affecting our propensity to find others attractive is their *object characteristics*: factors such as physical attractiveness, appearance, and demeanor. In the early stages of dyadic exchange, these cues are all we have to go on. An indisputable finding in the attraction literature is that persons who meet cultural and personal norms of physical attractiveness are more highly evaluated and sought after than their less attractive counterparts.[19]

	Initial Phases	*Intermediate Phases*	*Subsequent Phases*
FOUNDATIONS FOR ATTRACTION	Properties of people Physical attractiveness	Social rewards Reinforcement	Interpersonal similarity Evaluative orientations
SOURCES OF THE FOUNDATIONS	Personal tastes and values	Orientation toward self	Orientation toward objects of discussion
IMPORTANT COMMUNICATION VARIABLES	Perception of object characteristics Judge's priorities	Nature of feedback Self-opinion and perception of evaluator	Perception of people characteristics Degrees of disclosure and importance of topics

FIGURE 8.1:   Changes for foundations in interpersonal attraction over time.   (From James C. Mc-Croskey, Carl E. Larson, and Mark L. Knapp, *An Introduction to Interpersonal Communication* [Englewood Cliffs, N.J.: Prentice Hall, 1971], p. 49.)

Another factor determining attraction, one that eventually overshadows object characteristics, is *personal rewards*. People who praise us, who positively evaluate us, who are instrumental in our attaining social rewards and avoiding social punishments will be highly valued. We like those who like and reinforce us.

A third factor affecting attraction is *interpersonal similarity*. Although the old saying "opposites attract" may hold in the short term, in the long term the true saying appears to be "birds of a feather flock together." We tend not to form lasting relationships with people of dissimilar attitudes or personalities. Although differences may be exciting at first, over the long haul people form bonds with those of similar family background, religious affiliation, ethnic group membership, intelligence, and so on.

The model in Fig. 8.1 shows how the bases of attraction change over time. While initially attracted to the most handsome or beautiful person, we gradually shift our concerns. The truly gorgeous stranger with an unpleasant personality will not interest us for long. The individual who differs in almost every way may fascinate us for a while, but eventually the differences may lead to conflict. Ultimately, we are happiest with those who see the world the way we do.

Criticism of the Attraction Model. Although the McCroskey, Larson, and Knapp model is not new, it holds up quite well. More recent discussions of the attraction process essentially agree with this early model. Steve Duck, for example, argues in his theory of acquaintanceship that the formation of interpersonal relationships is a filtering process by which "individuals assess the general population of those encountered against a distinct and sequentially ordered set of criteria, filtering them down to a few who become fast friends."[20] Duck argues that we progressively seek information that is more personal. In the beginning, proximity and physical characteristics are used to filter targets; later on, interactive and personal information predominate. For Duck, similarity is the key variable affecting filtering. At the outset we try to determine the similarities we share with others because similar others validate us.

Perhaps the strongest criticism that can be leveled against attraction models is that they view targets of perception as passive individuals who are either attractive or unattractive rather than as active individuals who manipulate others' impressions. While we are seeking information about others, they actively try to present us with positive impressions. Therefore, to understand how communicative relationships are formed, we must examine not only impression formation but impression management as well. This will be our next topic.

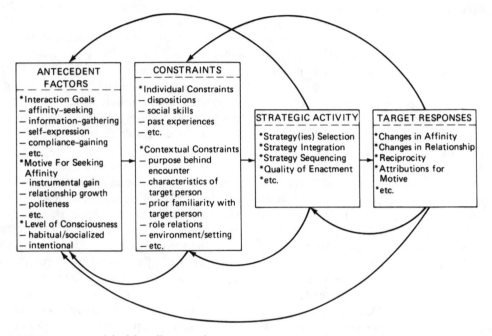

FIGURE 8.2: A model of the affinity-seeking process. (From Robert A. Bell and John A. Daly, "The Affinity-Seeking Function of Communication," *Communication Monographs*, 51 [June, 1984], 93.)

THEORIES OF SOCIAL CONTROL: HOW DOES INTERPERSONAL INFLUENCE WORK?

We spend a good deal of time and effort trying to get interpersonal partners to think highly of us. To forge friendships and romantic attachments, to receive positive evaluations from employers and to control subordinates, to maintain valued self-perceptions—in short, to achieve personal outcomes—communicators try to manipulate the impressions others have of them. From the first meeting, communicators are concerned with problems of control. They recognize their ability to achieve it depends on the impressions they give.

Bell and Daly's Affinity-Seeking Model

We begin our investigation of impression management by examining the affinity-seeking model offered by Robert Bell and John Daly. Like McCroskey, Larson, and Knapp, they are interested in attraction, but they approach the topic from a slightly different perspective. Their model describes the strategies people actively use to get others to like them. Bell and Daly define affinity-seeking as "the active social-communicative process by which individuals attempt to get others to like and to feel positive [sic] to them."[21] They view affinity-seeking as a strategic activity, presenting a general model showing the decision making processes people use when seeking affinity from others. Their model, illustrated in Fig. 8.2, focuses on four issues involved in affinity-seeking: antecedent factors, constraints, strategic activities, and target responses.

Factors Affecting Affinity. Antecedent factors are all those factors affecting the situation in which affinity-seeking will take place. The interactors' goals, their motives for affinity-seeking, and their level of consciousness all affect the outcome of the process. Sometimes, affinity-seeking itself may be the major goal of interaction: Actors seek affinity simply because they want to be liked. In other cases, affinity may be a means to another end. Affinity may be sought for professional gain, out of kindness, or to enhance relational growth. It may be produced intentionally or simply as a matter of habit. All these factors affect the ensuing process. In addition, *individual and contextual constraints* affect strategic selections. An individual's personal characteristics and past experiences affect his or her strategic repertoires. While some individuals have a great deal of behavioral flexibility, others habitually use the same strategies in every context. The parent who knows no other way to gain a child's love but to buy expensive presents is one example. The nature of the situation and of the target person are also important. Not only must individual repertoires be large, but they must be target and context sensitive as well.

Strategic activity is the enactment of actual strategies in context. During interaction, individuals must integrate and sequence chosen strategies with other behaviors and enact their strategies with the proper amount of skill. Sometimes, a simple smile is enough to induce liking; at other times, a carefully prepared and skillfully enacted set of behaviors must be used. Finally, the *target's response* must be considered, for the success or failure of a strategy determines whether it will be used again. The model is recursive. The results of each factor affect all others.

Besides presenting this model, Bell and Daly investigate some behavioral options that make up individuals' strategy repertoires. They list 25 general affinity-seeking strategies and show their interrelationships by dividing them into seven clusters, as shown in Fig. 8.3.

Criticism of the Affinity-Seeking Model. Bell and Daly recognize communication as an active process, and they view human actors as goal-oriented and self-determined. In addition, they ground their discussion in actual communicative

behaviors, allowing us to understand concrete ways in which liking may be induced. Rather than viewing attraction as the product of abstract variables such as object characteristics and similarity, they investigate the behaviors people use to make themselves attractive to others. By assuming the perspective of the affinity-seeker rather than of the individual making affinity judgments, they add another dimension to the study of attraction and liking.

Whether or not these strategies form a complete set, how strategies are related, and how a strategy is chosen are questions needing further investigation. An examination of Bell and Daly's methodology reveals that the strategy clusters were inductively generated. Undergraduate students were asked to list behaviors people could use to get others to like them. The lists were combined and 25 strategies extracted. These were then submitted to another group of subjects who were asked to group them according to similarity. Finally, a statistical analysis of the groupings resulted in the seven clusters.

Similar methods have been used by other researchers who assume that in generating and grouping strategies, subjects use some kind of internal organizing scheme mirrored in the results. Although this method is useful in the initial stages of theory building, by itself it appears to describe a data set rather than explain an underlying process. It is difficult to tell what criteria subjects are using when they perform such a task. Theories developed in this way are not highly explanatory. This criticism is not just directed at Bell and Daly. In point of fact, their research seems to be carefully and systematically done. Rather, it is a general criticism of the typologies currently being generated, and it can be applied to all the models in this section.

The Bell and Daly model focuses on only one kind of outcome, engendering liking. This is an important goal, but it is not the only impression human actors seek to achieve. We now turn to a broader approach to interpersonal impression management.

Cluster Description	*Strategies*
CONTROL AND VISIBILITY Strategies in which the actor presents self as a rewarding relational partner, able to control social rewards.	*Assume Control.* Present oneself as a person in control of whatever is going on. *Dynamism.* Present oneself as an active, enthusiastic person. *Personal Autonomy.* Present oneself as an independent, free–thinking person. *Physical Attractiveness.* Look and dress as attractively as possible in the presence of the target. *Present Interesting Self.* Present oneself to the target as someone interesting to know. *Reward Association.* Present oneself so that the target perceiving the affinity–seeker can reward the target for associating with him or her.
ESTABLISHMENT OF TRUST Strategies in which the actor presents self as both trustworthy and trusting.	*Openness.* Disclose personal information to the target. *Trustworthiness.* Present oneself as an honest, reliable person.
POLITENESS Strategies in which the actor presents self as cooperative and other–directed.	*Concede Control.* Allow the target to assume control over relational activities. *Conversational Rule–Keeping.* Adhere closely to cultural rules for polite, cooperative interaction with the target.
CONCERN AND CARING Strategies in which the actor presents self as nurturing and concerned with other.	*Altruism.* Strive to be of assistance to the target in whatever she or he is currently doing. *Elicit Other's Disclosures.* Encourage the target to talk by reinforcing the target's conversational contributions. *Listening.* Listen actively and attentively to the target. *Self–Concept Confirmation.* Demonstrate respect for the target and help the target to "feel good" about herself or himself. *Sensitivity.* Act in a warm, empathic manner toward the target. *Supportiveness.* Support the target in the latter's social encounters.
OTHER–INVOLVEMENT Strategies in which the actor presents self as an enthusiastic partner who includes others in activities.	*Facilitate Enjoyment.* Maximize the positiveness of relational encounters with the target. *Inclusion of Other.* Include the target in the affinity–seeker's social groups. *Nonverbal Immediacy.* Signal interest in the target through various nonverbal cues.
SELF–INVOLVEMENT Strategies in which the actor presents self as personally and intimately involved with other.	*Self–Inclusion.* Arrange environment to come into frequent contact with the target. *Influence Perceptions of Closeness.* Engage in behaviors that cause the target to perceive the relationship as closer than it has actually been.
COMMONALITIES Strategies in which the actor presents self as similar and equal to the other.	*Assume Equality.* Strike a posture of social equality with the target. *Comfortable Self.* Act comfortable and relaxed in settings shared with the target. *Similarity.* Convince the target that the two of them share many similar tastes and attitudes.
Strategy failing to cluster	*Optimism.* Present oneself to the target as a positive person.

FIGURE 8.3:   A typology of affinity-seeking strategies. (Adapted from Robert A. Bell and John A. Daly, "The Affinity-Seeking Function of Communication," *Communication Monographs,* 51 [June, 1984], 96–97, 110–111.)

Jones and Pittman's Self-Presentation Theory

Jones and Pittman define the phenomenal self as "a person's awareness, arising out of interaction with his environment, of his own beliefs, values, attitudes and the links between them, and their implications for his behavior."[22] These authors believe that an individual's notion of self is intimately related to choice of self-presentation strategy. On the one hand, the individual seeks consistency with the phenomenal self; on the other, he or she tries to achieve personal goals by presenting an advantageous self-image. "Pressures toward self-consistency (and long-range adaptation) may then compete with pressures toward shorter-range social gains in creating the conflicts and dilemmas of social life."[23]

The Nature of Self-Presentations. Strategic self-presentations are behaviors designed to "elicit or shape others' attributions of the actor's dispositions."[24] Although strategic self-presentation may sometimes involve creating an image that distorts the phenomenal self, it usually involves "selective disclosures and omissions, matters of emphasis and toning rather than of deceit and simulation."[25] Jones and Pittman point out that not all behavior is self-presentational. Self-presentation occurs only when the individual desires to "secure or augment his power to derive favorable outcomes" from another. It does not occur when individuals are so engrossed in a particular task that concerns with others' responses are momentarily set aside or when they are overwhelmed with emotion, engaging in ritualized social exchanges, or concerned with the integrity and authenticity of their actions.[26] Jones and Pittman's image of the human actor is not that of a manipulative and self-conscious individual but one of a person who cares about the impressions others have of him or her and puts his or her best foot forward. Jones and Pittman outline five methods of strategic self-presentation: ingratiation, intimidation, self-promotion, exemplification, and supplication.

Self-Presentational Strategies. *Ingratiation* involves presenting oneself as likeable. The ingratiator wants others to see him or her as characterized by "warmth, humor, reliability, charm, and physical attractiveness." Individuals try to achieve this image through conformity, flattery, doing favors, and describing the self in favorable ways.[27] Unfortunately, this often involves the individual in the *ingratiator's dilemma*; the more important it is for one to be liked, the more likely it is that others will distrust one's motives. For example, if an employee is highly dependent on a boss's approval, the boss may interpret compliments and favors as illegitimate or strategically motivated and doubt the employee's sincerity.

Intimidation is a second method of strategic self-presentation. The intimidators' goal is to appear dangerous.[28] The intimidator may appear ungovernably angry or emotional, leading targets to believe that he or she will act unpredictably, irrationally, or vindictively if crossed. The intimidator can also appear to be cold, unfeeling, lacking in compassion, and untouchable by normal appeals. While many intimidation methods seem to issue from strength, the intimidator may also manipulate weakness. By making others believe that he or she cannot stand stress or disappointment, the passive individual may control others just as effectively as the active individual. To avoid a scene, to stop hysterical weeping, or to protect the intimidator's health, the target of intimidation may repeatedly give in.

Self-promotion is a third strategic self-presentation technique. Individuals who seek the attribution of competence use self-promotion. By gaining respect from others they gain power over them. Just as there is an ingratiator's dilemma, so there is a *self-promoter's dilemma*. Truly competent people do not generally proclaim their own competence; therefore, too much self-advertisement may be mistrusted.

Exemplification involves the projection of integrity and moral worthiness. The exemplifier is the saint or martyr:

Examples such as Ghandi, Martin Luther King, the Ayatollah Khomeini come to mind. The power that may accrue from such dramatic exemplifications may be used for a variety of specific objectives: recruiting a following, raising funds, changing a law, fomenting a revolution.[29]

More commonplace examples of exemplifications also exist. Parents try to exemplify the virtues they want their children to adopt. The employee who arrives early, leaves late, and skips lunch to finish a report exemplifies the hard worker and has a decided moral edge over less dedicated colleagues.

Supplication is the final strategy used by those who lack the power or resources to engage in any of the preceding strategies. The "powerless" person can often exert power through helplessness or incompetence. Jones and Pittman cite the case of the traditionally sex-typed female paired with the traditionally sex-typed male:

She cannot change a tire, understand algebra, read a legal document, carry a suitcase, or order wine. Her classic male counterpart, of course, rushes in to fill the breach. His vanity is touched by the indispensability of his contributions to her survival in the world.[30]

To be fair, males indulge in supplication as well. The husband who cannot sew on a button, do the laundry, cook himself a meal, or handle the children by himself, can manage to manipulate his wife into giving up a trip or refusing to take a job because he would be lost without her. There is a heavy cost associated with the supplication strategy. One's self-esteem is bound to suffer if one's strategic choice is the advertisement of helplessness. The success of this strategy depends on the presence of a forebearing other who is willing to tolerate or even welcome incompetence in a partner.

Social norms limit our willingness to engage in strategic presentation. The norm of integrity often inhibits the use of manipulative interaction. It is important for most of us to retain a phenomenal self, worthy of respect. The nature of the phenomenal self mitigates the choice and frequency of self-presentation strategies.

Criticism of Jones and Pittman's Theory.
This model presents a useful sketch of some of the power bases that affect interpersonal relationships. But, like all typologies, it is not highly explanatory. It does, however, raise interesting questions. Under what conditions will each strategy be used? What determines whether a strategy will succeed or fail? How will repeated use of a strategy affect relational development, and how would such repetitions feed back on the phenomenal self? Jones and Pittman realize that a typology is only the beginning of a theory. Their eventual goal is not to classify people but to examine the communicative results of using one or a combination of these strategies in interaction.

Marwell and Schmitt's Compliance-Gain Model

Most of the time we use affinity-seeking or self-presentational processes to achieve specific ends. When we do so in the interpersonal context, the process is often labeled *compliance gain*. And just as there are many taxonomies of impression management strategies, so there are many taxonomies of compliance-gaining techniques.[31] The most popular, and one of the most comprehensive, is that offered by Marwell and Schmitt.[32]

Techniques for Gaining Compliance. Figure 8.4 lists 16 techniques for gaining compliance. As you can see, some seem to be identical with those we have already discussed. Promises, threats, liking, pre-giving, aversive stimulation, debt, and altruism all appear to fit one of the strategy styles discussed by Bell and Daly or by Jones and Pittman. The other techniques, however, add a new dimension, for they depend not on the source's ability to deliver positive or negative outcomes but on the target's own needs. Negative and positive expertise, for example, relate the target's needs to social circumstances in general, while moral appeal, altercasting, positive and negative self-feeling, and positive and negative esteem seem to depend on the target's own desire for social acceptance. Here, the mechanism resulting in compliance depends less on the impression the actor creates and more on the target's desires and needs. The target complies because of a belief that compliance will result in the attainment of individual goals.

To make their taxonomy more manageable, Marwell and Schmitt submitted it to the statistical

---

	Sixteen Compliance-Gaining Techniques with Examples from Family Situation
1. Promise	(If you comply, I will reward you) "You offer to increase Dick's allowance if he increases his studying."
2. Threat	(If you do not comply I will punish you) "You threaten to forbid Dick the use of the car if he does not increase his studying."
3. Expertise (Positive)	(If you comply you will be rewarded because of "the nature of things") "You point out to Dick that if he gets good grades he will be able to get into a good college and get a good job."
4. Expertise (Negative)	(If you do not comply you will be punished because of "the nature of things") "You point out to Dick that if he does not get good grades he will not be able to get into a good college or get a good job."
5. Liking	(Actor is friendly and helpful to get target in "good frame of mind" so that he will comply with request) "You try to be as friendly and pleasant as possible to get Dick in the 'right frame of mind' before asking him to study."
6. Pre-Giving	(Actor rewards target before requesting compliance) "You raise Dick's allowance and tell him you now expect him to study."
7. Aversive Stimulation	(Actor continuously punishes target making cessation contingent on compliance) "You forbid Dick the use of the car and tell him he will not be allowed to drive until he studies more."
8. Debt	(You owe me compliance because of past favors) "You point out that you have sacrificed and saved to pay for Dick's education and that he owes it to you to get good enough grades to get into a good college."
9. Moral Appeal	(You are immoral if you do not comply) "You tell Dick that it is morally wrong for anyone not to get as good grades as he can and that he should study more."
10. Self-Feeling (Positive)	(You will feel better about yourself if you comply) "You tell Dick he will feel proud if he gets himself to study more."
11. Self-Feeling (Negative)	(You will feel worse about youself if you do not comply) "You tell Dick he will feel ashamed of himself if he gets bad grades."
12. Altercasting (Positive)	(A person with "good" qualities would comply) "You tell Dick that since he is a mature and intelligent boy he naturally will want to study more and get good grades."
13. Altercasting (Negative)	(Only a person with "bad" qualities would not comply) "You tell Dick that only someone very childish does not study as he should."
14. Altruism	(I need your compliance very badly, so do it for me) "You tell Dick that you really want very badly for him to get into a good college and that you wish he would study more as a personal favor to you."
15. Esteem (Positive)	(People you value will think better of you if you comply) "You tell Dick that the whole family will be very proud of him if he gets good grades."
16. Esteem (Negative)	(People you value will think worse of you if you do not comply) "You tell Dick that the whole family will be disappointed (in him) if he gets poor grades."

FIGURE 8.4: Marwell and Schmitt's sixteen compliance-gaining techniques. (From Gerald Marwell and David R. Schmitt, "Dimensions of Compliance-Gaining Strategies: A Dimensional Analysis," *Sociometry*, 30 [1967], 350–64; 357–58.)

procedure known as factor analysis. They found five basic factors or dimensions: Rewarding activity (items 1, 5, 6), punishing activity (items 2, 7), expertise (item 4), activation of impersonal commitments (items 9 to 15 and 16), and activation of personal commitments (items 8, 13, and 16). Note that items 13 and 16 appear on both of the last two factors.

Criticism of the Marwell and Schmitt Model.

The same criticisms leveled at the Bell and Daly cluster analysis can be applied to the Marwell and Schmitt taxonomy. As Schenck-Hamlin and colleagues point out, the taxonomy-generating approach fails to describe relationship among strategies. What have we learned about communication from looking at a model like that of Marwell and Schmitt? Taxonomies often "appear more like a listing of elements in a department store catalogue, rather than elements growing out of an organic theory of compliance gaining."[33] This problem is compounded when different studies present different lists of strategies and when strategies are described in abstract and imprecise ways.

Taxonomies by themselves tell us very little. Only when investigators work out the relationships between strategies and answer questions about when, how, and, more important, why strategies are used, will they become useful approaches to understanding interpersonal influence. Luckily, a number of researchers are beginning to offer theoretical models of this process.[34] Research Abstract 8.3 cites one of these efforts.

The models we have just examined look at how senders influence receivers. They assume relatively autonomous communicators who independently seek to maximize self-defined out-

RESEARCH ABSTRACT 8.3 Interpersonal Influence Messages

Dillard and his colleagues believe that influence is a goal-driven activity. The primary goal in an influence situation is, of course, to get someone to undertake a desired action. But there are also secondary goals: Persuaders may also work to maintain a desired identity, try to follow norms of appropriateness, and strive to keep the costs of interaction down. The strength of the primary goal determines whether or not influence will be instigated, and the nature of secondary goals shapes the influence message. Dillard and his colleagues did three studies to see how goals affect influence.

Study 1. The purpose of this study was to find out people's goals and concerns during influence. The researchers used questionnaires that contained two hypothetical interpersonal influence situations. (There were five different versions of the questionnaire, so all together subjects responded to

10 interpersonal situations.) Following each situation there was a list of the 14 compliance-gaining strategies of Schenck-Hamlin. Respondents were asked to indicate whether or not they would use each strategy and then provide a written justification for their decision. Subjects were 100 undergraduate communication students. Open-ended responses were content analyzed. Analysis showed that subjects were most concerned with the primary goal, whether or not the influence attempt would work. They did show secondary goals, however, mentioning a need to maintain their identities ("It's not my style"), manage the interaction ("It's inappropriate for the situation"), maintain resources ("It would cost me my friendship"), and manage arousal level ("It would make me too nervous").

continued...

RESEARCH ABSTRACT 8.3 (*continued*)

Study 2. The purpose of this study was to learn more about the relationship between the primary influence goal and the secondary goals. A new questionnaire was given to 604 students. The first part of this instrument asked subjects to recall a recent influence attempt. Subjects then wrote their goals and recreated the dialogue that had occurred. The second part asked students to rate their agreement with researcher-generated statements based on the results of the first study. This instrument consisted of several statements for each previously identified goal. For example, the identity goal was reflected in the statement, "I was concerned about being true to myself and my values," and the relational resources goal was indicated by "I didn't really care if I made the other person mad or not." Factor analysis supported a six-factor model composed of the primary influence goal, as well as five secondary goals: identity, interaction, personal resources, relational resources, and arousal management. Statistical regression procedures were used to eliminate redundant items and shorten the scale.

Study 3. The purpose here was to test the hypothesis that the importance of the influence goal would determine how carefully the influence attempt would be planned,

how hard the person would work on it, and whether the message used would show directness (would it clearly explain the desired change?), positivity (would rewards and punishments be mentioned?), and logic (would logical arguments and evidence be included?). Planning and effort were measured by Likert items; directness, positivity, and logic were coded from subjects' dialogues. Results showed that the greater the subjects' primary goal, the more planning and effort they put into the message. In terms of message variables, when identity needs were of concern, directness tended to be low. When interaction goals were at stake and when relational costs were important, positivity was high. When subjects were concerned with managing arousal, directness, positivity, and logic were all low, indicating "the influence attempts of apprehensive persons resemble emotional outbursts more than considered attempts at producing behavioral change." There was no effect for personal resources. The authors concluded that a goals-directed approach to the study of influence would be a useful enterprise.

Source: James Price Dillard, Chris Segrin, and Janie M. Harden, "Primary and Secondary Goals in the Production of Interpersonal Influence Messages," *Communication Monographs*, 56 (March 1989), 19–38.

comes. To understand interpersonal communication fully, however, we must regard it as a coordinated social activity that is systemic in nature. This is particularly important in the interpersonal context, since one of the major functions of communication at this level is the creation and maintenance of relational culture. We will turn our attention to this problem next.

COORDINATING INTERPERSONAL RULES: HOW ARE RELATIONAL CULTURES CREATED AND MAINTAINED?

In this section we will consider how the problem of social coordination is manifested in the interpersonal context. Previously it was suggested that culture provides us with our identity and thus constrains our interactions. It was also proposed that we can free ourselves from social constraints and negotiate our own identities. Since much of this occurs in the interpersonal context, it is appropriate to discuss it in more detail here. We will begin by looking at how communicators develop a perception of self, and we will then discuss how the messages they exchange define and constrain relational trajectories.

Theories Concerning the Development of Self

Since our self-concept determines our perception of the world, the nature of our individual needs and goals, and our interactions with others, it is important to know how the phenomenal self develops. Almost every chapter in this book has acknowledged the importance of the individual self; however, little attention has been given to the development of self-conceptions. We are now ready to investigate how we know who we are and how our self-conceptions are affected by interactions. There are two ways we can learn about the self: (1) by observing our own behaviors and inferring what we are like and (2) by attending to relational cues from others and accepting these definitions of who we are. In both cases we learn who we are from communication.

Bem's Self-Perception Theory. Daryl Bem offers us a theory of the self based on our ability to perceive ourselves as objects. He summarizes his major point in the following way:

Individuals come to "know" their own attitudes, emotions, and other internal states partially by inferring them from observations of their own overt behavior and/or the circumstances in which this behavior occurs. Thus, to the extent that internal cues are weak, ambiguous, or uninterpretable, the individual is functionally in the same position as an outside observer, an observer who must necessarily rely upon those same external cues to infer the individual's inner states.[35]

Bem proposes that we know ourselves in the same way we know others. Just as we form impressions of others' attitudes and motivations by observing their overt behaviors, so we make attributions about ourselves from observing our own actions. At first, this may seem somewhat surprising. Are our emotions and motives not self-evident? Can we not rely on private internal cues to tell us how we feel and what we believe? Bem says no. He argues that our internal cues are not as clear, strong, or obvious as we might think. We must often look outside ourselves to discover our thoughts and feelings. This is especially true when our internal cues are ambiguous.

Take for example two states of emotional arousal, love and fear. Bem argues that to tell them apart we must look outside ourselves, for, internally, both these states are similar. In both we are physiologically aroused: our hearts beat faster than normal, our breathing speeds up, extra adrenalin may be released. On the basis of internal cues alone we may be hard pressed to tell the differences. We must therefore observe our situation and our own actions to tell which emotion we feel. If someone has put a gun to our head, we know what we feel is fear. If we are in a romantic setting, we interpret it as love. This may explain why strong emotions confuse us and why it is easy to switch from anger to love in a short time.

We often turn to external cues to tell us what we feel. We may find ourselves saying things like, "I must have been hungry; look how much I ate" or "I must really like him, we spend all our time together." Similarly, if we observe ourselves succeeding at a difficult task, we infer that we are bright, talented, or lucky; while, if we see ourselves fail, then we assume we are dull, incompetent, or unfortunate. External events give us information about who we are.

If Bem is correct, then we must revise our notions about the relationship between attitudes and behaviors. The traditional view says we use attitudes as a guide for action. Bem argues that often we behave first and then decide what we believe. Self-perception theory helps to explain how we learn what the phenomenal self is like.

We decide what we are like partly by making self-attributions on the basis of past and present behaviors.

Relational Exchange as a Source of Self-Definition.

While self-observation is one way of monitoring the self, we also determine who and what we are by observing others' actions and messages. While others may directly tell us how they expect us to behave and what they find acceptable, there are more subtle ways for them to define us. To examine this notion, we must turn to the work of a group of theorists known as the Palo Alto group, a group including such theorists as Gregory Bateson, Paul Watzlawick, Janet Bavelas, and Don D. Jackson.

The pragmatic theorists argue that communication has meaning on two levels: the content and relational levels. The *content level* is what the message is about; it is a proposition about the topic of discourse. The *relational level* presents information about the interaction in which content is being exchanged. Members of the Palo Alto group argue that every message presents both types of information. Assume you ask me what the weather outside is like, and I answer, "It's raining." On the content level, I offer a proposition about the weather. At the same time, I also deliver a relational message. If I smile and eagerly offer the information, then I tell you that I acknowledge your presence and am willing to interact with you. If I answer sharply, then I indicate that I resent your bothering me for such trivial information and wish you would leave me alone. In these two cases the content is similar but the relational information differs.

Sieburg's Model of Confirmation.

Assume that, on a particularly bad day, everyone you meet sends you a negative relational message. Although no one is overtly rude, you will pick up on their relational messages. You will probably feel depressed and unhappy, and you may doubt yourself. If this behavior is repeated over the course of weeks and months, then your self-concept will be undermined. Evelyn Sieburg has examined the effects of this kind of rejection. She argues that whenever we interact with others we present ourselves for their approval. Their responses serve as relational messages that either confirm or disconfirm the self we present.

Sieburg defines *confirming* and *disconfirming responses* in the following way:

> In interaction between persons A and B, confirming responses occur whenever person B responds to person A's communicative attempt in a way that causes A to value himself more. Disconfirming responses occur when B's responses to A's communicative attempts cause A to value himself less.[36]

Sieburg found 12 categories of confirming-disconfirming responses, as shown in Fig. 8.5. The disconfirming responses all present subtle relational messages that say, in effect, "You aren't worthy of consideration" or "You don't count." If heard once or twice, these responses may not be destructive, but over time they can lead to "feelings of alienation, interpersonal antagonism, and even mild forms of personal despair."[37] They can materially affect our notions of who we are and what we are worth. When disconfirmations become habitual, they define our relationships. Assume, for example, a child who needs approval. To gain this approval, the child tries to get his parent's attention. The parent, however, ignores the child. What does the child do? The child may amplify the message, making it louder and stronger. If the parent continues to ignore the child, he may use even more outrageous behavior, until his actions become so obnoxious or destructive that the parent stops ignoring and retaliates by punishing. Of course, amplifying the message is only one option the child can take. The child could also withdraw more each time disconfirmation occurs. In either case, a pattern is established that affects the relationship.

Theories About Relational Patterns

Patterns of interaction define relationships. Over time, an interpersonal culture is created that constrains interaction on an individual level in the

Disconfirming Responses

Response	Definition	Example
1. Impervious response	When B fails to acknowledge, even minimally, A's message.	A: Hi! What's happening? B: (Continue working, ignoring A completely)
2. Interrupting response	When B cuts A's message short while A is talking.	A: So then I. . . . B: Nice chatting with you, I've got to run.
3. Irrelevant response	When B's response is unrelated to what A has been saying.	A: So then we started yelling. B: I'm thinking of going to Bermuda over break.
4. Tangential response	When B acknowledges A's message but immediately takes the conversation in another direction.	A: I just don't know what to do. B: Gee, too bad. I'm thinking of buying a new car.
5. Impersonal response	When B conducts a monologue or uses nonimmediate, overintellectualized or cliche ridden language.	A: How can I improve my grade in your class, Professor Jones? B: Educationally speaking, adequate classroom performance is a function of cognitive and affective integration.
6. Incoherent response	When B's response is rambling, difficult to follow, and incoherent.	A: Tell me what's wrong. B: Well, uh, see it's a . . . . Gosh, see the thing is . . . I mean, uh, it's hard to say.
7. Incongruous response	When B's nonverbal and verbal behaviors are contradictory.	A: Are you angry with me? B: No, of course not. Why should I be? (said sarcastically)

Confirming Responses

Response	Definition	Example
8. Direct acknowledgment	B directly reacts to A's message.	A: Do you have time to talk? B: Not now, but what about later?
9. Agreement about content	B reinforces opinions offered by A.	A: I've definitely noticed a change in Joe lately. B: Right. I noticed it too.
10. Supportive response	B expresses understanding and reassurance to A.	A: I feel just awful about it. B: I understand your feeling, but I think you did the right thing.
11. Clarifying response	B tries to clarify A's message.	A: I'm not sure what to do. B: So you're confused and upset and a bit guilty, is that it?
12. Expression of positive feeling	B expresses positive feelings in relation to A's message.	A: No, what I meant is that we should discuss it with him. B: OK, now I know what you mean, and I agree.

FIGURE 8.5: Sieburg's taxonomy of confirming and disconfirming messages.   (Adapted from Frank E. X. Dance and Carl E. Larson, *Speech Communication: Concepts and Behavior* [New York, Holt, Rinehart & Winston, 1972], pp. 141–43.)

same way general cultural roles constrain more general behavior patterns. Because all enduring interactions become patterned, it is important to examine more closely the nature of relational patterning.

Rogers, Farace, and Millar: Interpersonal Control. Frank Millar and Edna Rogers offer an argument for examining relational patterns in the interpersonal context.[38] They believe emerging patterns are much more important in defining relationships than the participants' individual characteristics. Taking an essentially pragmatic approach, they note that patterned exchanges should be the unit of analysis for understanding interpersonal communication. Such a perspective "tries to look directly at the combinatorial rules characterizing the system's message-exchange process and not at the individual characteristics brought to the situation by the individual participants."[39]

They argue that there are three dimensions of relationship (control, trust, and intimacy), but they focus on relational control sequences. The control dimension "is concerned with who has the right to direct, delimit, and define the actions of the interpersonal system... ."[40] Three control patterns are described. The first is *complementarity*, "where the control directions are different and directionally opposite." If, for example, A seeks to take charge by saying, "I think we should begin by listing all our options," and B agrees to relinquish control by responding, "Fine, sounds good to me," then a pattern of complementarity is achieved.

A second pattern is *symmetry*, "where the control directions are the same." Here both parties seek to be dominant or submissive. Competitive symmetry occurs when both parties try to establish control. For example, A might say, "I think we should begin by defining the problem," and B might retort, "A better idea would be to brainstorm solutions." In submissive symmetry, both partners attempt to relinquish control. A says, "We'll do whatever you want to," and B says, "Maybe you should decide." Finally, a *transitional* pattern can occur, "where the parties' directions are different but not opposite," as when one interactor takes on or relinquishes control while the other seeks to "minimize the issue of control."

It is tempting to see complementarity as healthy and symmetry as unhealthy, but most authors warn against applying value judgments to these patterns. While complementarity might at first appear better because it satisfies both parties, it can also result in a very static relational system.

Similarly, while symmetry may lead to conflict in its competitive form, it can also generate new ideas and motivate both participants to do their best.

These patterns are useful in describing and understanding how message sequences define relationships. They help us see predominant patterns in relationships and aid us in examining the ebb and flow of these patterns across time. But how are they to be measured? Research abstract 8.4 presents one well-known coding system and illustrates how it can be used to analyze relationships.

Wilmot's Discussion of Relational Intricacies. The Rogers and Farace coding system allows us to discover patterns of relational messages in ongoing interactions. But complementarity and symmetry are just two of many patterns that can be identified. Wilmot reviews several additional patterns which either enhance or inhibit relational growth.[41] Included are spirals, paradoxes, and double binds.

In a *spiral*, A's definition of the relationship is intensified by B's reaction.[42] For example, A, wanting to discuss an issue with B but getting no response, becomes frustrated and makes sarcastic comments. B, frustrated by A's sarcasm, responds with coldness. When this occurs, A becomes more sarcastic and B even colder. Soon the two are locked in what Wilmot calls a regressive spiral. Eventually, the relationship becomes dysfunctional.

Spirals need not be regressive. Some are progressive. They move in a positive direction. Assume you have friend who is timid and uncertain about dating. You advise that friend and even go so far as to set the friend up with a blind date. No longer a "wall flower," your friend gains confidence. As others notice this confidence, they find your friend more attractive, and this in turn makes the friend more confident.

As Wilmot points out, all spirals have limits. The wall flower's confidence can conceivably increase so much that he or she begins to feel too good for others. At this point the spiral has peaked, and negative responses may occur that modify your friend's increasing sense of his or her own importance. As Wilmot says, "A progressive spiral will either whirl away unchecked and break a relationship, or short regressive phases will occasionally slow it down. In either event, it is clear that progressive spirals cannot continue unabated."[43] The same is true of regressive spirals. Participants must either move to less destructive behaviors or dissolve their relationship. Wilmot says dyadic relationships fluctuate between varying stages of progressive and regressive spirals. In cases where the outer limit is reached but the spiral is not reversed, the relationship will dissolve.[44]

Paradoxes are a particularly destructive kind of relational intricacy in which two equally valid but contradictory messages are simultaneously given. Imagine, for example, a young man saying to his love, "I adore you. But, then, of course, I always lie." The statement is contradictory. If everything he says is a lie, then he was lying when he said, "I adore you." But if he always lies, then the statement that he always lies is itself a lie, so perhaps he really does care. As a receiver you find yourself alternately believing and disbelieving. A classic example is the injunction, "Dominate me!" This is a command that cannot be obeyed, for, if you try to obey by being dominant, you are actually submitting to the command. If you try to disobey by being submissive, then you are actually being dominant. If you have trouble following these examples, then you are getting the point. Paradoxes are frustrating and confusing. They allow the receiver no resolution. The only way out of a paradox is to recognize it. Paradoxes, however, are generally so confusing

RESEARCH ABSTRACT 8.4   Coding Interpersonal Control Patterns

Rogers and Farace's *purpose* was to develop a method for examining control sequences during interaction. They wanted an objective method for coding utterances and uncovering patterns such as symmetry and complementarity. The first step was deciding that the basic unit to be coded would be the relationship of one utterance to what preceded it. For example, the statement, "No, it's not a good idea," would have a different meaning if it followed a proposal like "Let's go for pizza" than if it followed a statement like "Todd's idea doesn't seem to work." In the first case the statement would be dominant, and in the second it would be submissive.

It was decided that for every statement three things would be coded: who was talking, the kind of utterance made (assertion, question, talk-over, noncomplete statement, or other), and how the utterance related to what had gone on before. To code this last factor, the authors developed nine relational categories. An utterance is coded as *support* if it shows acceptance, approval, or agreement with a previous statement; it is coded as *nonsupport* if it expresses disagreement, rejection, or challenge; and it is an *extension* if it merely continues the flow of a previous message. An *answer* code is used for direct and substantive answers to questions, and *instruction* and *order* codes are used for direct suggestions and commands. *Disconfirmations* and *topic changes* each have their own code as does any utterance that *initiates or terminates* a discussion. Finally, an *other* category is also used.

continued...

RESEARCH ABSTRACT 8.4 (continued)

Rogers and Farace believed that different combinations of utterances show different amounts of control. They proposed three levels of control, a one-up (↑) bid to take control, a one-down (↓) attempt to yield control, and a one-across (→) movement to neutralize control. An *assertion* that *supports* a previous utterance, for example, is coded as one-down. An *assertion* that is an order, however, is a one-up. An *assertion* that acts as an *extension* is a one-across. They developed a chart to relate the three-digit code to control codes, as shown.

Source: L. Edna Rogers and Richard V. Farace, "Analysis of Relational Communication in Dyads: New Measurement Procedures," *Human Communication Research*, 1 (1975), 222–39.

Message Type and Control Direction
Third Digit

Second Digit	Support 1	Nonsupport 2	Extension 3	Answer 4	Instruction 5	Order 6	Disconfirmation 7	Topic Change 8	Initiates or terminates 9	Other 0
Assertion 1	↓	↑	→	↑	↑	↑	↑	↑	↑	→
Question 2	↓	↑	↓	↑	↑	↑	↑	↑	↑	↓
Talk–over 3	↓	↑	↑	↑	↑	↑	↑	↑	↑	↓
Noncomplete 4	↓	↑	→	↑	↑	↑	↑	↑	→	→
Other 5	↓	↑	→	↑	↑	↑	↑	↑	↑	→

		Message Code	Control Code	Transaction Code
Wife:	We don't do anything together anymore.	119	↑	↑↓
Husband:	What do you mean?	223	↓ ↑	↓↑ ↓→
Wife:	Well, as a family we don't do very much.	114		
Husband:	Oh, I don't know.	213	→ ↓	→↓ ↓↑
Wife:	Don't you feel I do the major portion of the disciplining of the children?	121		
Husband:	The time we're together you don't.	214	↑	↑↑
Wife:	Well, just for the record, I have to disagree.	112	↑	↑↑
Husband:	Well, just for the record, you're wrong.	212	↑	↑↑
Wife:	Well then, we completely disagree.	119	↑	

that we are unable to see them for what they are. As long as we stay within the conditions set up by the paradox, we are unable to escape it.

Double binds are special paradoxes in which the individual's relationship with the person creating the paradox is such that it is impossible to comment about or withdraw from the paradox. The necessary conditions for a double bind are described by Wilmot as follows:

1. Two persons, one of whom is the victim.
2. Repeated experience so that the double bind becomes an habitual expectation.
3. A primary negative injunction.
4. A secondary injunction conflicting with the first injunction, but at a more abstract level. Like the primary injunction, the second threatens punishment.
5. A tertiary negative injunction prohibiting the victim from escaping from the field.
6. A victim who begins to see the entire universe in double bind patterns.[45]

Take an example where a father says to his daughter, "I want you to be independent and make your own life," but whenever she tries to do so, the father gets sick and has to be taken care of. The daughter is the victim. She is told to be independent, but every time she tries to be she is punished for it. If she gives up her independence, then she is also punished, since she is disobeying her father. Because the relationship is important and long lasting, she cannot withdraw or escape. She may eventually see every choice as impossible.

Wilmot says that one way out of a double bind is to refuse to choose. If the daughter could say to her father, "Look, you have set up a choice that is impossible for me to make. If I leave, I feel guilty. If I don't I feel trapped. What can we do about this?" then perhaps they could extricate themselves from the situations. In a true double bind, however, it is difficult to do this, since the partners are trapped within the paradox.

RELATIONAL STAGES: HOW ARE INTERPERSONAL RELATIONSHIPS CREATED AND DISSOLVED?

Throughout this chapter we have stressed the fact that interpersonal relationships are characterized by progressive stages. We encountered this idea with Miller's developmental view, and it was also implied in our discussion of attraction stages and in our examination of spirals. We will conclude with yet another theory that explains the developing nature of interpersonal relationships: Julia Wood's 12-state model.

For Wood, relational culture is "a unique private world constructed and sustained by partners in a relationship."[46] The relationship between the individual and this culture is recursive. While individuals create their own relational cultures, the cultures work back on them, governing their understanding of others and the surrounding world. "Over time partners modify conceptions of themselves, the bond, and the appropriate standards for private and public behavior. As partners and external systems change, there is need for repeated definition and redefinition of the relational culture if it is to maintain its viability."[47] Through communication, the relationship is modified and changed.

Wood identifies 12 states that characterize the development and deterioration of a relational culture. We begin with the first state, *individuals*. At this point no relational culture exists, although because of prior relationships individuals have expectations about the characteristics of acceptable others and the qualities of an acceptable bond. Next comes *invitational communication (auditioning)*. Here communication is characterized by information acquisition and uncertainty reduction, and the mutual exchange of "initial identity declarations." Individuals are auditioning for the role of relational partners.

In *explorational communication*, communication serves to "reduce further uncertainties regarding areas of similarity and to define initial forms of exchange."[48] Communicators need to determine whether they are similar enough to build a common culture. The next state is *intensifying communication (euphoria)*, where interactors have decided to form a bond and create a common world, "to merge their previously distinct selves into a pair-identity."[49] Here, communication functions to (1) remove individuals from social roles into more privately agreed-upon relational roles, (2) allow agreement on relational definition, (3) give participants information about deeper levels of self, and (4) allow empathy and role-taking. Self-disclosure and confirmation characterize exchanges here.

Revising communication marks a transition between interactors' recognition of their bond and their decision to commit to a future together. The roles and rules developed earlier are revised and expanded. Problems ignored or repressed in the intensifying state are now acknowledged and negotiated. When *bonding communication* occurs, the communicators engage in some kind of public or private event marking a mutual commitment for an extended future. "This event radically transforms a relationship from one defined in the here-and-now to one implying a future in which each individual's life will be constrained by and connected with that of the other."[50]

Navigating communication is an extended process individuals use to maintain their relational culture at a satisfactory level. During this period, which may last for the remainder of the relationship, the couple must both confirm existing roles and rules and meet the changing demands of the external environment. Rituals are often enacted to confirm the existence of the culture (for example, anniversaries, birthdays, or holidays). At the same time, the partners negotiate role changes (moving, for example, from young couple to settled married couple to parents). As each change occurs, rules for conduct must be renegotiated.

Ideally, a couple could navigate smoothly for the rest of their lives, but relationships can fall apart. States 8–12 trace the disintegration of a relationship. *Differentiating communication* involves an attempt to reassert individuality. "Typi-

cally communications serve to challenge existing patterns in a relational culture, to highlight differences in partners, and to call attention to individuals' activities extrinsic to a bond, thus demonstrating independence of a relationship."[51]

In *disintegrating communication* attempts are made not only to exist in addition to and apart from the relational culture, but to disintegrate the bonds that tie one to the culture. The culture is denied, rules are purposefully violated, and breadth and depth of exchange are decreased. Communication centers on only a few topics and becomes progressively more distanced in style. By the time *stagnating communication* occurs, the relationship is at a standstill. The members are biding time before its final dissolution. What little talk there is, is highly superficial and formal, almost as though the two were strangers in a public place.

Terminating communication marks the end of the relationship. Here, communication is used to negotiate settlements and to define the form of future interactions, if any. In the last state, partners are *individuals* again, but, as Wood is careful to point out, they are not exactly where they started. Each has been changed by the relational culture, and each will bring this new self to future communicative exchanges in the interpersonal context.

REFERENCES

1. Gerald R. Miller and Mark Steinberg, *Between People: A New Analysis of Interpersonal Communication* (Palo Alto, Calif.: Science Research Associates, 1975); Cassandra L. Book and others, *Human Communication: Principles, Contexts, and Skills* (New York: St. Martin's, 1980); Gerald R. Miller, *Explorations in Interpersonal Communication* (Beverly Hills: Sage, 1976).

2. Book, *Human Communication*, pp. 113–20.

3. *Ibid.*, p. 23.

4. *Ibid.*, p. 113.

5. Charles R. Berger and Richard J. Calabrese, "Some Explorations in Initial Interaction and Beyond: Toward a Developmental Theory of Interpersonal Communication," *Human Communication Research*, 1 (1975), 99–112; Charles R. Berger and James J. Bradac, *Language and Social Knowledge* (London: Edward Arnold, 1982).

6. Book, *Human Communication*, p. 115.

7. *Ibid.*, p. 115.

8. Berger and Bradac, *Language and Social Knowledge*, pp. 8–9.

9. Jesse G. Delia, "Some Tentative Thoughts Concerning the Study of Interpersonal Relationships and Their Development," *Western Journal of Speech Communication*, 44 (Spring 1980), 99.

10. Berger and Bradac, *Language and Social Knowledge*, pp. 8–9.

11. *Ibid.*, p. 117.

12. *Ibid.*, pp. 15–18.

13. For a summary and references on many studies in the constructivist tradition, see Jesse G. Delia, Barbara J. O'Keefe, and Daniel J. O'Keefe, "The Constructivist Approach to Communication," in *Human Communication Theory: Comparative Essays*, ed. Frank E. X. Dance (New York: Harper & Row, 1982).

14. George A. Kelly, *The Psychology of Personal Constructs, Volume 1: A Theory of Personality* (New York: W. W. Norton, 1955), p. 46.

15. *Ibid.*, p. 53.

16. Walter H. Crockett, "Cognitive Complexity and Impression Formation," in *Progress in Experimental Personality Research, II*, ed. Brendan A. Maher (New York: Academic, 1965), p. 49.

17. Jesse G. Delia, Ruth Anne Clark, and David E. Switzer, "Cognitive Complexity and Impression Formation in Informal Social Interaction," *Speech Monographs*, 41 (1974), 299–308.

18. James C. McCroskey, Carl E. Larson, and Mark L. Knapp, *An Introduction to Interpersonal Communication* (Englewood Cliffs, N. J.: Prentice Hall, 1971), p. 38.

19. Ellen Bersheid and Elaine Walster, *Interpersonal Attraction* (Reading, Mass.: Addison-Wesley, 1969).

20. Steve Duck, "Interpersonal Communication in Developing Acquaintance," in Miller, *Explorations in Interpersonal Communication*. For a general discussion of attraction, see Ellen Bersheid, "Interpersonal Attraction," in *Handbook of Social Psychology*, 3rd ed., eds. Gardner Lindzey and Elliot Aronson (New York: Random House, 1985), pp. 413–84. See also, Steve Duck and Daniel Perlman, eds. *Understanding Personal Relationships: An Interdisciplinary Approach* (Beverly Hills: Sage, 1985).

21. Robert A. Bell and John A. Daly, "The Affinity-Seeking Function of Communication," *Communication Monographs*, 51 (June 1984), 91–114.

22. Edward E. Jones and Harold B. Gerard, *Foundations of Social Psychology* (New York: John Wiley & Sons, 1967), p. 716.

23. Edward E. Jones and T. S. Pittman, "Toward A General Theory of Strategic Self-Presentation," in *Psychological Perspectives on the Self*, ed. Jerry Suls (Hillsdale, N. J.: Lawrence Erlbaum Associates, 1980), p. 233.

24. *Ibid.*, p. 233.

25. *Ibid.*, p. 233.

26. *Ibid.*, p. 235.

27. *Ibid.*, p. 236.

28. *Ibid.*, p. 238.

29. *Ibid.*, p. 246.

30. *Ibid.*, p. 248.

31. William J. Schenck-Hamlin, Richard L. Wiseman, and G. N. Georgacarakos, "A Model of Properties of Compliance-Gaining Strategies," *Communication Quarterly*, 30 (1982), 92–100; Gerald R. Miller, Frank Boster, Michael E. Roloff, and David Seibold, "Compliance-Gaining Message Strategies: A Typology and Some Findings Concerning Effects of Situational Differences," *Communication Monographs*, 44 (1977), 37–51; Michael E. Roloff and Edwin F. Barnicott, "The Situational Use of Pro- and Anti-Social Compliance-Gaining Strategies by High and Low Machiavellians," in *Communication Yearbook 2*, ed. Brent D. Ruben (New Brunswick, N. J.: Transaction Books, 1978), pp. 193–205.

32. Gerald Marwell and David R. Schmitt, "Dimensions of Compliance-Gaining Behavior: An

Empirical Analysis," *Sociometry*, 30 (1967), 350–64.

33. Schenck-Hamlin and others, "Properties of Compliance-Gaining Strategies." See also Richard L. Wiseman and William J. Schenck-Hamlin, "A Multi-Dimensional Scaling Validation of an Inductively Derived Set of Compliance-Gaining Strategies," *Communication Monographs*, 48 (December 1981), 251–70.

34. Michael J. Cody and Margaret L. McLaughlin, "Perception of Compliance-Gaining Situations: A Dimensional Analysis," *Communication Monographs*, 47 (June 1980), 132–48; Miller and others, "Compliance-Gaining Message Strategies"; Roloff and Barnicott, "Situational Use."

35. Daryl J. Bem, "Self-Perception Theory," in *Advances in Experimental Social Psychology*, vol. 6, ed. Leonard Berkowitz (New York: Academic, 1973), p. 2.

36. Evelyn Sieburg, "Dysfunctional Communication and Interpersonal Responsiveness in Small Groups" (unpublished dissertation, University of Denver, 1969). For a discussion, see Frank E. X. Dance and Carl E. Larson, *Speech Communication: Concepts and Behavior* (New York: Holt, Rinehart & Winston, 1972), pp. 140–43.

37. Dance and Larson, *Speech Communication: Concepts and Behavior*, p. 143.

38. Frank E. Millar and L. Edna Rogers, "A Relational Approach to Interpersonal Communication," in Miller, *Explorations in Interpersonal Communication*.

39. *Ibid.*, p. 90.

40. *Ibid.*, p. 91.

41. William W. Wilmot, *Dyadic Communication*, 2nd ed. (Reading, Mass.: Addison-Wesley, 1979).

42. *Ibid.*, p. 121.

43. *Ibid.*, p. 125.

44. *Ibid.*, p. 125.

45. *Ibid.*, p. 133. See also, Gregory Bateson, *Steps to an Ecology of Mind* (New York: Ballantine, 1972).

46. Julia T. Wood, "Communication and Relational Culture: Bases for the Study of Human Relationships," *Communication Quarterly*, 30 (Spring 1982), 75. See also, Mark L. Knapp, *Interpersonal Communication in Human Relationships* (Boston: Allyn & Bacon, 1984); Steve Duck, ed., *Personal Relationships, 4: Dissolving Personal Relationships* (New York: Academic, 1982).

47. *Ibid.*, p. 77.

48. *Ibid.*, p. 79.

49. *Ibid.*, p. 79.

50. *Ibid.*, p. 80.

51. *Ibid.*, p. 80.

chapter 9

SMALL-GROUP COMMUNICATION

INTRODUCTION

In our discussion of the interpersonal context, we considered the notion of interpersonal trajectories: the idea that dyads change over time, usually in the direction of increasing intimacy. The same can be said about groups. Although we can define a group in purely situational terms, as any small aggregate of individuals in face-to-face interaction, most theorists believe a group is more than a mere collection of individuals. They argue that "groupness" develops over time as collections of individuals interact with one another, in the same way that "interpersonalness" happens in dyads; thus most theorists use what is essentially a developmental approach to defining groups.

To understand small-group communication, we need to understand what distinguishes a true group from a mere "heap" or aggregate of individuals. John Brilhart offers five distinguishing characteristics of a small group:

1. A sufficiently small number of people so that each will be aware of and have some reaction to each other (from 2 to rarely more than 20).
2. A mutually interdependent purpose in which the success of each person is contingent upon the success of the others in achieving this goal.
3. Each person has a sense of belonging or membership, identifying himself with the other members of the group.
4. Oral interaction (not all of the interaction will be oral, but a significant characteristic of a discussion group is reciprocal influence exercised by talking).
5. Behavior based on norms, values, and procedures accepted by all members.[1]

According to Brilhart's definition, not all collections of individuals are groups. For example, a robber and the police officers in pursuit are not a group.[2] Although they meet the size criteria and might exchange a few words during pursuit, they lack a common purpose, a sense of mutual identification, and accepted norms and procedures. Similarly, we would not call the five or six individuals waiting for a bus a group, although they could develop groupness. If they began talking, they might find enough in common to identify with each other, and, given enough time, they might also develop informal rules and norms of interaction, assigning each other status positions. They might even decide to take some collective action, perhaps working together to get the bus company to change policies. If this happened, then they would become a group, and all of the principles of group communication could be applied to their interactions.

Why distinguish groups from other collections of people? Because the behavior of groups is very different from the behavior of non-groups. Theoretical constructs and laws describing the first do not describe the second. This is why the definition of a group is so important. For our purposes, the small group will be defined as a collection of three or more interacting individuals who have a collective perception of their membership, who are interdependent so that any event affecting one member affects all members, and whose behaviors gradually become structured and patterned.

CHOOSING A GROUP: WHAT DETERMINES GROUP MEMBERSHIP?

We live in a society where being part of a group is essential. Although we can imagine getting away from it all, living alone in a mountain cabin or a tent in the wilderness, for most of us this is mere fantasy. In a sense, group membership is not a matter of choice at all. It is an inescapable fact of life.

Although it may be impossible to choose not to belong to *any* group, we still can choose *which* groups to join. Just as we choose our friends, preferring interpersonal bonds with some people and not with others, so we make judgments about group associations. We will begin this chapter by looking at two theories that explain how such

choices are made: Festinger's social comparison theory and Schutz's theory of interpersonal needs.

Festinger's Social Comparison Theory

Festinger argues that all humans have a basic need to evaluate their abilities and opinions. Because "the holding of incorrect opinions and/or inaccurate appraisals of one's abilities can be punishing or even fatal in many situations," satisfying this need is vitally important.[3] When objective, nonsocial sources of information exist, individuals will use them. When no objective criteria exist, however, individuals must seek others' opinions, engaging in *social comparisons*. Groups provide people with these comparisons. Festinger argues that individuals join groups primarily to gain information about themselves.

Groups as a Source of Information. Festinger hypothesizes that individuals seek others who are fairly similar to themselves. They are drawn to such associations because groups that diverge too greatly cannot provide useful or accurate comparisons. "Thus a college student, for example, does not compare himself to inmates of an institution for the feeble-minded to evaluate his own intelligence. Nor does a person who is just beginning to learn the game of chess compare himself to the recognized masters of the game."[4] Festinger believes that we feel more attracted to groups of people who are similar to us because we are better able to evaluate ourselves in such groups. We are unable to evaluate ourselves precisely if no comparison groups exist.

Pressures Toward Uniformity. Of course, even in the most homogeneous groups we will find discrepancies in opinions and abilities. When this occurs we feel a "pressure toward uniformity," a pressure to remove the discrepancy. Festinger says three mechanisms exist for correcting this state of affairs: We can (1) change our own opinions and abilities to bring them closer to those of the group, (2) change other members' opinions and abilities, or (3) narrow the comparability range by refusing to compare ourselves with deviant members. For example, assume someone joins a group thinking it consists of similar others, but then finds his or her performance considerably higher than other members. One way to deal with the pressures toward uniformity is to reduce performance over a period of time so as to be more like the others. The deviant might also "devote considerable time and effort to trying to improve the performance of the others in the group to a point where at least some of them are close to, but not equal to, [him or her]."[5] The third option is simply to stop comparing with the divergent others. The same processes occur if the discrepancy involves opinions rather than abilities. The deviant member can abandon divergent opinions, use social influences to change others' opinions, or narrow comparability range.

Festinger argues that pressures toward uniformity occur anytime the ability to make useful comparisons is threatened. He further argues that those close to the group norm will choose to influence others rather than changing themselves or ceasing to compare. We can expect the "normal" members of a group to exert pressures on deviants. We can also expect deviants either to respond to such pressures or to become isolated. The more important and attractive the group is and the more salient the ability or opinion in question, the more such pressures will be exerted. If the group is important to the deviant, then he or she may change to conform to group norms or may improve abilities to be closer to those of the group. This is especially likely if the deviant individual has no other comparison group to join.

People who share group membership will be similar to one another and dissimilar to members of other groups.[6] Festinger says, "It may very well be that the segmentation into groups is what allows a society to maintain a variety of opinions within it and to accommodate persons with a wide range of abilities. A society or town which was not large enough or flexible enough to permit such segmentation might not be able to accommodate the same variety [sic]."[7] Social comparison theory is not only a tool for understanding why individuals associate with similar others but an explanation of group conformity and social segmentation as well.

Criticism of Social Comparison Theory. For Festinger, the mechanism that drives the entire system is the need to reduce uncertainty about self. The theory assumes one central need: a cognitive need for certainty and balance. Festinger describes people as rational information processors, a theme developed more fully in his later work on cognitive dissonance. If we accept his definition of the human actor, then the arguments of social comparison theory fit. If, however, we view humans as sometimes less than rational, as driven by a variety of other needs, then the theory is less satisfying. Our acceptance of social comparison theory as an explanation of group membership rests on our acceptance of a universal drive to reduce uncertainty.

Schutz's Interpersonal Need Theory

Other theorists agree with Festinger that group membership is based on the perceived ability of a group to meet member needs, but they define these needs differently. William Schutz is one such theorist. In this section we examine his theory of the three basic interpersonal needs that explain group association: inclusion, control, and affection.[8]

Inclusion, Control, and Affection. *Inclusion* needs are based on the establishment and maintenance of a "satisfactory relationship with others in respect to interaction and association."[9] At heart, this need centers on establishing identity through association. Those with high inclusion needs join a group to strengthen their identity: The group makes them feel significant and worthwhile. As a result of group membership, they may say to themselves, "I must be a worthwhile person because I am a member of this group." These individuals may not like the other group members. They may not even receive very many external rewards from their membership. What they do get is a sense of group identity.

Control needs are based on the establishment and maintenance of a "satisfactory relationship with people with respect to control and power."[10] Important here are feelings of competence and responsibility. Individuals with strong needs to control others join groups to exercise power. They can say to themselves, "I must be a competent person because I exercise authority and leadership over others in my group." As long as these people can pull the strings, their need to feel competent is satisfied.

Finally, *affection* needs are based on the establishment and maintenance of a "satisfactory relation with others with respect to love and affection."[11] People with high affection needs join groups to satisfy their desire for intimacy and closeness. Such individuals say, "I must be a loveable person. Look at how many close friends I have." For such persons, group membership proves they are capable of close, intimate relationships.

Balancing Needs. So far, we have discussed an individual's needs in a general way. Actually, there are two aspects to each of those needs: the need to *express* inclusion, control, and affection to others and the need to *have others express* them to us. We must also avoid being what Schutz calls excessive or deficient in regard to a need. The person who is deficient in a particular need rejects the need and does not try to satisfy it. The person who is excessive constantly works toward its satisfaction. The ideal individual is one who has found a comfortable, satisfying relationship with others on that dimension.

Schutz's theory explains why people join or refuse to join groups. The individual with excessive inclusion needs, the *oversocial* individual, has a strong need to be a member. Schutz provides the example of a woman who attended a celebrity's funeral. When asked why, she explained, "Because our club all came together." "But," the interviewer asked, "why did you come here?" "I came here because the rest came here." "Were you fond of the dead man?" "Not especially," she answered, "but we always do things together."[12] The *undersocial* individual acts in an opposite manner. He or she may refuse to join groups or may withdraw, be late, or constantly leave early. This person prefers being alone to being rejected by the group. Schutz believes that both undersocial and oversocial individuals share the same anxiety. Even though they deal with it differently, both fear that they are not worthwhile.

Similar patterns are associated with control and affection. The individual with excessive control needs is called an *autocrat*. He or she may join groups to exercise dominance. The *abdicrat*, on the other hand, becomes a group member so that others will take responsibility for decisions. *Overpersonal* individuals are excessively concerned with affection and use groups to form extremely personal, intimate, confiding relationships. Those who are *underpersonal* may avoid group associations or act in a rejecting or antagonistic manner if the interaction becomes too personal.

If a group allows members to satisfy their needs, the group remains attractive. Compatibility between group members is largely a matter of intermeshing and satisfying interpersonal needs. For example, a group allowing those with high control needs to lead and those with low control needs to follow will be attractive to all parties. A group with members who all want to relinquish control, however, will be unsuccessful.

Criticism of Schutz's Theory. The interpersonal needs that Schutz identifies seem to be basic, and it seems logical to assume that need compatibility is one reason we join groups. Whether inclusion, control, and affection are the only important needs, however, is less certain, as is Schutz's explanation of their psychodynamics. His theory is based on a psychological perspective and will be attractive to those who share that view of communication. While the theory does not account for all group behavior, it is useful as a partial explanation of why we find some groups more attractive than others.

GROUP SOCIALIZATION: HOW DO GROUPS MAINTAIN THEMSELVES?

We have focused so far on how individual needs affect a prospective member's decision to join a group. To understand how groups stay together, we must look at the processes they use to maintain desired outcomes and control member behaviors. We now turn to this question.

Moreland and Levine's Model of Group Socialization

Richard Moreland and John Levine's primary goal is to describe "the passage of individuals through groups." Their model considers how individuals and groups become attracted to one another and how they maintain a satisfactory relationship through mutual influence and social control.[13] Moreland and Levine see group socialization as a transactional process. While individual members work to achieve their own needs, the group as a whole works to ensure that its members conform to group goals. Thus, group socialization is a dynamic, reciprocal process that must be studied from two perspectives: that of individual members and that of the group as a whole.

Their model explains two parts of group behavior: (1) the psychological processes that let groups and individuals interact successfully and (2) the temporal phases in individual/group relationships. Their goal is to understand how reciprocal processes of social control operate during the life of a group.

Psychological Processes in Group Interaction. Moreland and Levine believe that three important psychological processes repeatedly occur during group interaction: evaluation, commitment, and role transition. *Evaluation* occurs as

groups and individuals "assess and alter one another's rewardingness" by developing mutual expectations and monitoring differences between actual and ideal behaviors. *Commitment* occurs when a "motivational link" is forged between the group and the individual. When both parties perceive their relationship as more rewarding than alternative relationships, commitment increases. Conversely, as the amount of perceived reward diminishes, commitment weakens. During the life of a group, changes in commitment level continuously occur. Finally, as commitment changes, *role transitions* occur. During role transitions, new behavioral expectations are placed on group members, and new phases develop. The entire process is repetitive and recursive. Each role transition is followed by new evaluations, new levels of commitment, and new needs for role transition.[14] Thus, individuals pass in and out of different stages during the course of their association with a group.

EVALUATION. During the evaluation process, individuals and groups determine how much reward they will reap from their association. The group as a whole first determines the ideal behavior it desires from each member and then defines a range of tolerable behaviors. "Whenever the behavior of the individual falls within this range, the person will receive some degree of positive evaluation from the group."[15] If an individual's behavior falls outside of this range, then he or she will be negatively evaluated.

Normative expectations may change over time, and, as they do, so must the member's behavior if he or she wants to be evaluated positively. Moreland and Levine use the example of a group's norms for talkativeness. Initially, a moderate amount of talk may be expected. The person who talks too much or too little will receive mild negative evaluations. Over time, changes may occur in the group's expectations. The ideal amount of talk may change, and less individual variation may be tolerated. Rewards for acceptable levels of talk may grow stronger, and punishments for violations may become more severe.

Each individual is expected to keep step with these changes. Failing to do so results in corrective actions. "Such action can involve efforts to change the individual's behavior, alterations in the group's expectations, or rejection of the individual."[16] Of course, the relationship between group and individual is reciprocal. Just as groups have normative expectations for members, so do members have expectations for groups. If the group fails to meet a member's expectations, the member can take corrective action, which "might involve efforts to change the group's behaviors, alterations in the individual's expectations for the group, or rejection of the group."[17]

COMMITMENT. As a result of evaluation processes, groups and individuals develop a level of commitment toward one another. Commitment depends not only on the rewards to be gained from their mutual association but also on rewards to be gained from alternative associations. If the present relationship seems more rewarding than any alternative, then a high level of mutual commitment will occur.

For the individual member, commitment to the group results in "acceptance of the group's goals and values; positive affective ties to group members; willingness to exert effort on behalf of the group and to fulfill group expectations; and desire to gain or maintain membership in the group."[18] From the group's point of view, commitment to the individual results in similar outcomes. The group accepts the individual's values, becomes attracted to the individual, tries to meet his or her expectations, and tries to retain the individual as a member.[19]

ROLE TRANSITIONS. Commitment changes as rewards vary. Moreland and Levine argue that both parties formulate decision criteria about how much commitment is acceptable at any point in time. "When commitment rises or falls to a decision criteria, the individual is perceived as ready to undergo a role transition."[20] If a decision criterion is not reached, then no change in the mutu-

ally defined roles is necessary. Throughout the life of the group, role relationships will change as the group relabels the individual and as the individual relabels himself or herself. Role transitions may be smooth if both individual and group share the same decision criteria. However, they can be troublesome if one party wants to change roles while the other prefers the status quo.

Passage Through Group Phases. As role transitions occur, new relationships develop between the person and the group. Each transition marks a new phase in their relationship. Figure 9.1 shows the five major phases identified in the model: investigation, socialization, maintenance, resocialization, and remembrance. It also shows major role transitions: entry, acceptance, divergence, and exit.

The initial relationship between member and group involves a period of mutual *investigation.* The group as a whole engages in *recruitment.* It looks for potentially valuable new members and makes itself attractive to them. For prospective members, investigation involves a *reconnaissance* of potential groups. Individuals look for groups that can meet their needs and try to persuade these groups to accept them. As investigation proceeds, both group and individual may reject one another. In such a case, commitment fails to reach the first decision level and no association occurs. If the commitment level of both parties is high, however, then they form an association, and the prospective member assumes the role of new member.

Entry is the first major transition in the relationship between group and individual. Whenever a new member enters a group there is danger of group destabilization. The new member inevitably poses a threat to group integrity and stability. To minimize this threat, the group may use entry ceremonies to assimilate new members and generate additional commitment. Entry ceremonies may consist of special benefits (welcoming parties or gifts) or of unpleasant initiations (hazing and the like) designed to create commitment

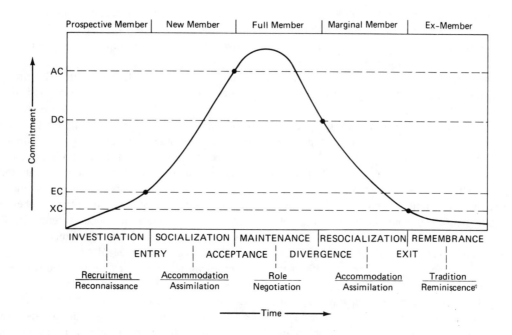

FIGURE 9.1: A model of group socialization. (Source: Richard L. Moreland and John M. Levine. "Socialization in Small Groups: Temporal Changes in Individual–Group Relations," in *Advances in Experimental Social Psychology*, vol. 15, ed. Leonard Berkowitz [New York: Academic, 1982], p. 153.)

through dissonance reduction. In either case, they manage some of the stress and threat that the group and the individual may feel.

After entry, a *socialization* phase occurs. During this time, the group seeks to *assimilate* members, teaching them the norms and rules it wants them to follow if they are to become full members. The group may use techniques such as indoctrination sessions, coaches who act as role models, training programs, or even debasement "in which the newcomer is forced to give up his or her prior self-image and seek a new one within the context of the group."[21] New members simultaneously try to induce the group to *accommodate* to their needs. Each member publicizes his or her needs and tries to motivate the group to meet them. This is difficult for a lone newcomer unless he or she is highly valuable. In groups admitting

several newcomers at the same time, however, the new members may band together to force accommodation and to resist assimilation pressures.

If the socialization process succeeds, then commitment from both parties rises. When it becomes high enough, the new member experiences the second major transition, *acceptance* as a full member. This transition is marked by special rites of passage. The group may allow the individual access to materials and resources previously reserved only for full members, share secret information, include the individual in informal cliques, or show special trust and respect. During this period the individual assumes the label of group member, begins to feel group solidarity, adopts the group's frame of reference, and exhibits willingness to assume additional group tasks.

Once acceptance occurs, a *maintenance* phase is entered, marked by high commitment, with both parties trying to maintain a satisfactory level of reward. *Role negotiation* occurs as member roles are worked out. The group finds a role for each member that maximizes group goals. Meanwhile, the member surveys possible roles and chooses the one that is most satisfying. Occasionally, a role is already occupied. The member then must consider the difficulty of evicting the incumbent. This is clearly a period of give and take. If both parties agree on role assignments, then commitment remains high. If agreement is not reached, however, commitment falls off and a new role transition may be in order.

Divergence is the third transitional state. While maintenance may occur for the life of the group, members and groups may also reach a stage where they consider separating. Some groups do not expect a member to remain indefinitely with the group. For example, the college community expects members to graduate after several years. In other groups, however, there are no natural limits to membership, and divergence is stressful and troublesome. If the group decides to terminate the relationship, then it must let the member know. The techniques used are often mirror images of those that marked acceptance. "Thus, the group may refuse to share valuable material resources with the individual, withhold special information, exclude the person from informal cliques, and so on."[22] If it is the individual who decides to separate from the group, then it is the individual who will begin to communicate divergence.

When divergence is expected because of natural time limits, both parties accept and prepare for the individual's eventual exit. In cases of unexpected divergence, however, efforts may be made to *resocialize* the member by providing the motivations and skills necessary for *reassimilation*. Especially when the individual is hard to replace, special *reaccommodation* efforts may be made by the group. During resocialization, commitment can rise or fall. If it rises, then a special role tran-

sition called *convergence* occurs as the individual once again becomes a full member. If it drops below exit criteria, however, then the association terminates.

Exit is the final role transition. The group decides how to terminate the member and may use covert rites of passage "including making secret arrangements for the individual to be recruited by another group, allowing the individual to resign quietly from the group, and giving the individual a 'grace period' before he or she must depart."[23] It may also use overt methods including social pressures to force the member to leave or even "status degradation ceremonies" designed to humiliate the marginal member publicly.[24] The member who decides to exit also faces the problem of communicating this decision. He or she may simply fail to participate or attend meetings, may notify the leader or a few members, or may publicly denounce the group. Exit may be stressful for both individual and group, especially if one does not desire termination.

Exit is followed by a period of *remembrance* in which the group "arrives at some consensus about how much the individual contributed to the group's goals when he or she was a member."[25] This allows the group to decide whether it will maintain a partial association with the former member or sever all ties. As time passes, the former member may pass into the group's *traditions*, becoming part of stories, legends, or jokes. For the individual, remembrance is a time for reflection and *reminiscence*. Depending on the outcome of this process, the ex-member may maintain some kind of association or abandon the group altogether. Over time the group passes into memory, which can often be distorted. "Probably the most important long-term effect of the group on the individual is the alteration of his or her expectations for other groups."[26]

Criticism of the Moreland and Levine Model

The Moreland and Levine model is comprehensive, integrating several theoretical concepts and principles. By using what is essentially a social exchange approach, it shows how need satisfaction leads to decisions to maintain or abandon group associations. It also accounts for structural variables (roles and norms) and shows how they change over time. This model touches on several communication problems: communicator acceptability, outcome achievement, evolution and change, and social coordination.

The most interesting aspect of this model is its emphasis on the reciprocal relationship between individual and group. While the authors acknowledge that viewing the group as a decision making entity with its own needs may be a form of reification, they argue that most individuals "unlike social psychologists, are quite comfortable thinking about groups as social entities."[27]

GROUP STRUCTURE: HOW DO RULES AND ROLES COORDINATE GROUP ACTION?

The Moreland and Levine model touches on the importance of roles and norms in guiding member action. We now examine these structural variables in more detail.

The Nature of Group Structures

Members of groups do not act identically or fulfill exactly the same functions. Some talk more than others, some exert more influence, some are more adept at particular tasks. Each participates according to his or her needs and skills. Group members become differentiated along the various dimensions that compose the group's activities. As Marvin Shaw tells us, "this pattern of relationships among the differentiated parts of a group is often referred to as *group structure*."[28] Because groups have different dimensions, there will be many structures, "in fact, as many structures as there are dimensions along which the group may be differentiated."[29]

Several constructs have been developed to describe structural differentiation. Within a

group, as within the society at large, positions, statuses, roles, and norms will emerge. A member's *position* within a group is defined as his or her characterization on each dimension of group activity. Thus, "a given group member may simultaneously be the person who talks the most, the person who is most active, the person who has least influence within the group, and so on."[30] Groups evaluate positions according to the importance of the member's position. This evaluation is the individual's *status*. Because some abilities and skills are more useful to the group than others, some positions will be of high status while others will be low.

The behavioral expectations the group places on the occupant of a particular position is his or her *role*. A college dean, for example, is expected to enact educational policy, supervise academic affairs, take care of disciplinary problems, and so on. A student, on the other hand, is expected to attend classes, complete assignments, and take tests. Deans are not expected to act like students nor are students expected to act like deans. Roles define for their incumbents what they are expected to do.

Finally, *norms* are rules of conduct group members are expected to follow. Norms refer to what *should* occur within the group. Each group develops its own norms over time, and norms can be quite stable, persisting even in the fact of changing membership. Departures from normative behavior tend to be punished, although there is latitude in the amount of conformity expected of individual members. Edwin Hollander, for example, argues that leaders build up what he calls *idiosyncrasy credits*, which may be exchanged for nonnormative behavior.[31] He argues that by initially conforming to group norms, the leader may eventually reach a position where he or she is allowed to institute innovative, nonnormative behaviors. Conversely, the leader who fails to conform at first will be sanctioned for innovative actions.

The concepts of position, status, role, and norm help us to describe the relationship between group members and to understand the group's structural properties. They show us what the group is like and how its members are linked to one another through communication.

Networks in Groups

Another way to describe group structure, one that is important from a communication viewpoint, is through *network analysis*. Networks are "patterns of channel linkages among individual members of a group. Such patterns consider a group in terms of which members transmit and receive messages to and from one another."[32] By examining networks, we examine the flow of messages within a group, the amount of each member's influence, and the relational patterns between individual members. Figure 9.2 illustrates a number of networks that might exist in a five-member group.

Two important concepts describe networks: centrality and distance.[33] The *distance* between two members is the shortest number of links through which a message may be transmitted and received. If two members are relatively isolated, then the distance between them will be great. The message will have to pass through many links. In the chain network, for example, E and A are very distant. A message must pass through four links before it is received. The distance between A and B, however, is minimal. They can address each other directly. Of all the networks, the all-channel most successfully minimizes distance, since direct links exist between all members.

Centrality is measured by summing the distances between a given position and all others in the network. In the wheel network, for example, C is highly central, since he or she can communicate with all members in four links. In the same network, it would take A seven links to get a message to everyone. Individual A is therefore less central than C. In Fig. 9.2, the number in parentheses next to each member shows that member's centrality. A network is considered centralized if

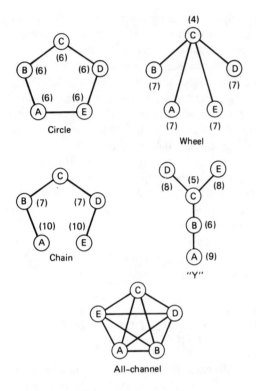

FIGURE 9.2: Some common networks in five-person groups. (Source: B. Aubrey Fisher, *Small-Group Decision Making*, 2nd ed. [New York: McGraw-Hill, 1980], p. 78.)

one member is in a more central position than others.

When we talk about networks, we are not necessarily talking about physical proximity but about who communicates with whom. A and B may sit next to one another, or have their offices on the same floor, but if they do not communicate, then they will not be connected in their network. As Shaw points out, "in a sense, we are dealing with topological space rather than Euclidian space."[34]

Research shows that centrality affects networks in several ways. The individual who occupies a central position has a good chance of emerging as leader (at least in experimental groups), and a single leader is less likely to emerge in decentralized networks.[35] Group morale is greater in decentralized (circle, all-channel) than in centralized (wheel or chain) networks. In addition, the individual most central in any network tends to be more satisfied than those who are peripheral.[36]

Problem-solving efficiency depends on type of task. Although, in experimental groups, centralized networks have been found to be faster and more efficient, this is subject to variation, with centralized networks being superior when "the task is relatively simple and requires only the collation of information" and decentralized superior when the task is more complex.[37]

Although experimental research favors the efficiency of centralized networks, Shaw warns us against accepting this result uncritically. Laboratory studies have used highly artificial methods to induce networks. While these studies may sometimes approximate conditions in complex organizations (where, for example, memos may be used to communicate), they have less bearing on face-to-face groups where networks are more direct. In addition, Shaw notes that the problems faced by natural real-life groups are more complex than those used in the laboratory. Aubrey Fisher also criticizes network studies, suggesting that the differences in efficiency between networks significantly diminish over time. He argues that "as soon as the group members accustom themselves to the network they are using, the particular pattern or network they employ should be of little consequence."[38]

This does not mean, however, that the structural properties of networks are unimportant in understanding group communication. While the networks emerging in "real life" small groups are not as clear cut as those in Fig. 9.2, group members do form differential links with one another, and certain members are more central and influential. Coalition formation is a particularly important aspect of group linkage, one that can materially affect group interaction. Examining patterns of communication preference within

groups shows how messages flow within the group and can indicate the relative importance of group members.

Leadership Theories

One role of great concern to theorists studying small groups is that of leader. Leadership is an interesting theoretical area because it illustrates how underlying philosophical assumptions affect approaches to theory. It also reveals the natural tendency of social scientists studying practical problems to formulate prescriptive rather than descriptive models. In the remainder of this section, we will examine three approaches to leadership: the trait, the styles, and the situational approaches.

The Trait Approach to Leadership. A natural way to approach the question of leadership is to ask: What characteristics separate people with leadership ability from those without it? If you phrase your question in this way, then a method at once suggests itself. Find groups of successful and unsuccessful leaders and test them to determine differences in their abilities, skills, and personality characteristics. This approach, the *trait approach*, seems so natural you may be unaware of its hidden assumptions. It assumes that leadership is a trait or skill. Shaw traces this assumption to a general philosophy of individualism prevalent at the beginning of the twentieth century.[39] He explains, "it was believed that a man could become whatever he wished to become, so long as he had the ability and persevered. Thus, leaders become leaders because of their own personal efforts and attributes."[40] The trait approach assumes that leadership springs from personality, that those who rise to leadership status possess natural traits largely lacking in nonleaders.

In 1974, Ralph Stogdill presented a comprehensive review of more than 150 studies of leader characteristics. Figure 9.3 lists some of the traits associated with leadership. Stogdill summarized his findings as follows:

Leadership Traits

Physical Characteristics	Social Background
Activity, energy	Education
Age	Social status
Appearance, grooming	Mobility
Height	
Weight	*Personality*
	Adaptability
Intelligence and Ability	Adjustment, normality
Intelligence	Aggressiveness, assertiveness
Judgment, decisiveness	Alertness
Knowledge	Ascendance, dominance
Fluency of speech	Emotional balance, control
	Enthusiasm
Social Characteristics	Extroversion
Ability to enlist cooperation	Independence, nonconformity
Administrative ability	Objectivity, tough-mindedness
Attractiveness	Originality, creativity
Cooperativeness	Personal integrity, ethical conduct
Nurturance	Resourcefulness
Popularity, prestige	Self-confidence
Sociability, interpersonal skills	Strength of conviction
	Tolerance of stress
Social participation	
Tact, diplomacy	

Task–Related Characteristics
Achievement drive, desire to excel
Drive for responsibility
Enterprise, initiative
Persistence against obstacles
Responsibility in pursuit of objectives
Task orientation

FIGURE 9.3: Some commonly studied leadership traits. (Adapted with permission of The Free Press, a Division of Macmillan, Inc. from Ralph M. Stogdill, *Handbook of Leadership: A Survey of Theory and Research* [New York: The Free Press, 1974], pp. 74–75. © 1974 by The Free Press.)

The leader is characterized by a strong drive for responsibility and task completion, vigor and persistence in pursuit of goals, venturesomeness and originality in problem solving, drive to exercise initiative in social situations, self-confidence and sense of personal identity, willingness to accept consequences of decisions and actions, readiness to absorb interpersonal stress, willingness to tolerate frustration and delay, ability to influence other persons' behavior, and capacity to structure social interaction systems to the purpose at hand.[41]

He concludes that, when combined, these traits "generate personality dynamics advantageous to the person seeking the responsibilities of leadership," although singly, they hold little predictive significance.[42]

While possessing these virtues would no doubt be advantageous to anyone seeking leadership (or to anyone, for that matter), knowing this does not tell us very much about the leadership process or about leader behaviors. To study leadership in this way implies that what the leader does is less important than who he or she is. There is now consensus that studying leader attributes is a weak way to approach leadership.

The Styles Approach to Leadership. Those who use a *styles approach* prefer to investigate how a leader's behavioral style affects his or her success. They argue that a leader's behavior is more important than his or her attributes, and they

RESEARCH ABSTRACT 9.1 Leadership Styles

This essay describes an early study of leadership behavior. Four groups of 10-year old boys were subjects. Each group consisted of five members who met after school to engage in hobbies and social activities. Four adult leaders were trained to exhibit three types of leadership: autocratic, democratic, and laissez faire. The leaders were shifted from group to group every 6 weeks. Each time they moved to a new group, they changed their leadership behavior. Each group, therefore, experienced each style in a different order and with a different leader.

In the autocratic climate, the leader determined all policy, gave instructions one step at a time, told the boys exactly what to do and who to work with, and was personal in praise and criticism. In the democratic climate, all policies were determined by the group with the leader's assistance, tasks were outlined in advance, members could work with whomever they chose to, and praise and criticism were objective. Finally, in the laissez faire climate, the group had complete freedom with a minimum of leader participation. The leader supplied information only when asked, did not dictate task or work partners, and made no attempt to appraise performance. Individual differences in acting out the roles seemed to be minor.

The boys' behaviors under these conditions were observed and analyzed. The results were as follows. *Laissez faire was not the same as democracy.* In the laissez faire climate, there was less and poorer work and more play, and the boys expressed preference for the democratic leaders. *Democracy was efficient.* Although the quantity of work under autocracy was greater, originality and work motivation were stronger with democracy. *Autocracy can create discontent that does not appear on the surface.* There were more dropouts and discontent in autocracy, and "release" behaviors upon transition to a freer atmosphere suggested previous frustration. *There was more dependence and less individuality in autocracy.* The boys were submissive and dependent in this climate, with less variation in conversation and individual behaviors. *There was more group mindedness and more friendliness in democracy.* Spontaneous subgroups were larger. Group-minded remarks were more marked as was mutual praise, friendliness, and willingness to share.

The results show that leadership style does affect the climate sustained and the kinds of worker behaviors that result.

Source: Ralph K. White and Ronald Lippitt, "Leader Behavior and Member Reaction in Three 'Social Climates'," in *Autocracy and Democracy*, eds. Ralph K. White and Ronald Lippitt (New York: Harper & Row, 1960).

seek to determine the best leadership style. The classic study under this approach was conducted in 1939 by Ralph White and Ronald Lippett. Although this study has been criticized, it clearly illustrates a second approach to studying leadership. Research Abstract 9.1 reviews this study.

While the study of leadership styles is closer to our interests as students of communication than the traits approach, it too makes some questionable assumptions. First, styles research uses fairly broad and abstract definitions of style, generally distinguishing between only two styles of leadership: person oriented and task oriented. Second, it assumes that a single style works in all situations and for all leaders. A third approach modifies styles research by examining the interaction between styles and situations. It is appropriately called the *situational approach.*

The Situational Approach to Leadership.

FIEDLER'S CONTINGENCY MODEL. One of the most influential situational theories is that of Fred Fiedler, who investigated the conditions under which strongly task oriented and strongly person oriented leaders would be effective.[43] Fiedler measured leader orientation by asking leaders to rate the coworker they least prefer (LPC.) The leader with a low LPC score perceives his or her least preferred coworker in unfavorable terms. Fiedler argues that this type of leader tends to be concerned primarily with task performance. The low-LPC leader wants to get the job done and is concerned with relationship only in so far as it leads to task completion. The high-LPC leader, on the other hand, describes the least preferred coworker in relatively favorable terms and is primarily concerned with successful interpersonal relationships. The high-LPC leader may sometimes focus on task but does so primarily to maintain successful relationships.[44]

Fiedler argues that leaders will be successful under different conditions. The three major factors that he believes affect leader effectiveness are (1) the amount of influence and power the leader has within the group, (2) the structure of the task, and (3) the personal relationship between the leader and the group. The leader's position may be considered as highly favorable, moderately favorable, or highly unfavorable. A leader's position is highly favorable if he or she has great influence, if the task is clearly structured, the decision easily verified, and if the group loyally accepts the leader.

According to Fiedler, the low-LPC leader is effective when his or her position is either highly favorable or highly unfavorable. The high-LPC leader is effective when his or her position is moderately favorable. Shaw sums up this view:

That is, when the situation is very favorable, the leader can be managing and controlling without arousing negative responses by group members; because things are

going well, there is no reason to reject the directive behaviors of the leader. On the other hand, when the situation is highly unfavorable, things are going badly, and the group is in danger of falling apart, then directive leadership is required, and again the low-LPC leader is more effective. But if the situation is only moderately favorable, the group expects to be treated with consideration, and the permissive, high-LPC leader is more effective.[45]

HERSEY AND BLANCHARD'S SITUATIONAL MODEL. Fiedler's model is not the only situational theory. Hersey and Blanchard present a model that adds a time dimension to the analysis.[46] Like Fiedler and others, Hersey and Blanchard divide leadership into two dimensions: task and relationship. They assume that leaders can combine these behaviors. They can be high in both, high in one and low in the other, or low in both. The effectiveness of these combinations depends on the group's maturity. Maturity level is determined by whether a group can set its own goals and take responsibility for its actions and whether its members are experienced at working together. The leader's style should match the maturity level of the group on a particular task. Figure 9.4 illustrates this relationship.

There are four leadership styles based on the leader's orientation to task and leadership. A *telling* style is strongly directive. Here, the leader tells the group what to do. The *selling* style is also directive, but it couples this with a concern for group acceptance. In selling, the leader persuades the group to internalize task goals. The *participating* style is primarily concerned with relationships. Group members share in decision making. Finally, in the *delegating* style, the leader steps back and allows the group a high degree of autonomy. Hersey and Blanchard recommend that telling be used with relatively immature groups, selling with groups who are slightly more mature, and participating and delegating styles with mature groups.

Consider teaching style as a form of leadership. Hersey and Blanchard would suggest that at the beginning of a course of study, with inexperienced students, a highly directive telling style is

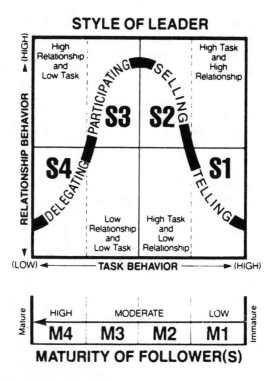

FIGURE 9.4: Hersey and Blanchard's situational theory. (From Paul Hersey and Kenneth Blanchard, *Management of Organizational Behavior: Utilizing Human Resources*, 3rd ed. [Englewood Cliffs, N.J.: Prentice Hall, 1977]. Reprinted by permission.)

best. The teacher who says to freshmen on the first day of class, "You decide what and how you want to learn," will fail because students are not yet ready to take full responsibility for their own education. As the course progresses, however, and as the students feel more comfortable with the material and one another, the teacher might use selling and participating styles, and, perhaps at the end, a delegating approach could be used. According to this theory, the teacher, as leader, should be aware of students' maturity levels and be willing to exert and relinquish control when appropriate. As groups mature, their preferences for interaction style will change, whether they be students in a classroom or employees in an office. The leader must be flexible.

Criticism of Leadership Theories. Each theory is based on different assumptions. The trait approach clearly locates leadership within the personality and psychology of the individual. The styles approach is more concerned with behavior patterns but assumes that research should uncover and describe the one "correct" style. The situational approach uses a more transactional view, simultanously considering characteristics of leader, situation, and group. However, this approach too has its problems. Both Fiedler's and Hersey and Blanchard's models are based on a rather global dichotomy between task and relationship. They have little to say about subtle variations in style and orientation, and they do not focus on actual behavior during group interaction. Like most leadership theories, they prescribe "good" leadership behavior rather than describing the leadership process itself. More explanatory theories are necessary before we can understand this important aspect of group behavior.

MESSAGE PATTERNS: HOW DO VERBAL PATTERNS AFFECT GROUPS?

The failure of the styles and situational approaches to focus on the verbal and nonverbal acts resulting in effective group interaction is unfortunate from a communication standpoint. Luckily, other theorists examine group message variables. Two methods in particular have been used to study verbal patterns in groups. The first, by Bormann, is concerned with the function of symbolic themes in the life of the group. The second takes a more microscopic view, analyzing patterns of verbal utterances through the process of interaction analysis. Both address problems of message exchange in the small-group context.

Bormann's Symbolic Convergence Theory

In analyzing the way message exchange affects group structure and outcomes, Ernest Bormann and his colleagues focus on stories and anecdotes during group interaction.[47] Bormann argues that the stories that groups create about themselves and about outside groups allow members to build a shared identity and inform each other of important rules and norms. The process of analyzing these kinds of communications he calls *fantasy theme analysis*. The theory explaining how group fantasies are created is called *symbolic convergence theory*.

Fantasy and Identity. Symbolic convergence theory assumes that through jokes, stories, reminiscences, anecdotes, and rituals the members of a culture build up a common consciousness, a shared symbolic understanding of the culture and of what it means to be a member. Narratives, especially, create a dramatic world where the central characters' actions mirror important themes in

the life of the culture's members. By identifying with events and characters of the narrative, individuals jointly experience emotions and learn to interpret common experiences in similar ways.

For Bormann, the phenomenon "of several or more people participating in a narrative contained in a dramatizing message" is called sharing a group fantasy.[48] He describes this process in the following way:

Typically a group in a task-oriented meeting will be discussing matters in a matter-of-fact and businesslike way when a member will use dramatic imagery, wordplay, or, more often, tell a story in which characters enact a dramatic scenario in some other place or time than the here-and-now of the unfolding group experience. One or more of the others will be caught up in the narrative and begin to participate in the dramatic action. They may laugh, several may speak at once; they may become emotional and forget their self-consciousness. The mood of the meeting becomes charged and the participants become committed and involved in the conversation.[49]

During the sharing of a group fantasy, members become involved with the narrative's heroes, identifying with the character's efforts to overcome obstacles. Fantasy themes are often narratives about people within or known to the group or about some future outcome involving the group. While fantasy themes can be imaginary, they are often reenactments or reinterpretations of actual events. In either case, they are the group's way of creating and sharing a story that embodies important themes and lessons and defines group.

Shared Narrative Forms. Bormann believes the basic unit of analysis is the *fantasy theme*.[50] As an example, he refers to a story widely circulated within IBM. It concerned a young woman whose job was checking the identity of individuals entering security areas. When the chairman of the board unexpectedly approached her checkpoint, she would not let him enter because he lacked proper identification. Although others in his entourage were shocked at her behavior, the chairman calmly stopped and asked one of his party to get the appropriate badge. The function of this story becomes apparent when compared to another story circulating at IBM about the same time. This story involves the same situation but another corporation. According to the second story, when stopped by the security guard, the chairman turned to her and said, "When you pick up your final paycheck next week, check the signature and you'll see who I am and who you *used* to work for."

Both stories have a similar theme (a low-level employee caught in a *faux pas* with top management), but, because their resolution is so different, they give IBM employees a clear description of their organization. In the IBM version, the leader is forebearing, approves of the guard's actions, and plays by the rules. In the second version, the leader is portrayed in much less sympathetic terms. The theme of an employee unknowingly coming into contact with top management is of understandable significance to individuals working in powerful organizations.

Bormann suggests that a group may circulate several stories similar in theme and action. The narrative frame will be the same, but the characters and situations will differ. Similar stories may be classed together into a single fantasy type. A *fantasy type* is a general narrative framework addressed to a particular question or problem, such as "What is our leader like?"[51] Other narrative types in a complex organization might center on how the organization deals with employees during labor negotiations, how employees can rise in rank, or what the personal characteristics of the ideal employee are.

When individuals in a group share several fantasies and fantasy types, they develop what Bormann calls a *rhetorical vision*, a broader view of who and what they are in relation to each other and the outside world.[52] Often the rhetorical vision can be summed up by a master analogy or slogan, for example, "We are one big, happy family." This analogy integrates members' experiences and clarifies the meanings of individual fantasy themes and types. Those who buy into the

rhetorical vision become a *rhetorical community*, with a shared sense of their own identity.[53] They accept the actions of their fantasy heroes and disdain those of the villains. They know how to relate to one another. Those who do not accept the rhetorical vision become outsiders.

Although these examples are drawn from complex organizations, all groups use fantasies to build cohesion. Families will often share anecdotes that embody fantasy themes ("Remember when Dad got so angry when we...") and subscribe to family-based rhetorical visions ("We Kennedys are achievers" or "We Medicis never get mad, we get even"). Bormann argues that part of becoming a group is indulging in a shared symbolic experience. Through symbolic convergence, stories are created that build cohesion, set the group off from others, and instruct members in appropriate behavior.

Criticism of Symbolic Convergence Theory. Fantasy theme analysis is especially noteworthy for communication study because it focuses directly on the way spoken symbols affect group structure and cohesion. It tells us that seemingly trivial and innocent processes (the swapping of stories, the telling of anecdotes, the use of jokes) can reveal hidden meaning behind a group's actions. Currently, narrative analysis is becoming an important tool for understanding communication not only at the group but at the public level as well. (See Research Abstract 10.3 in the next chapter for an example of public narrative.) There are still questions that need to be answered about Bormann's formulation and about the other narrative models that are being used. Nevertheless, the idea that we make sense of our world by constructing stories is an important insight that deserves to be examined in more detail.

Interaction Analysis

While Bormann's system focuses on global, thematic patterns in groups, other methods of analyzing verbal exchanges focus more closely on individual utterances. These methods describe and identify redundant patterns of interaction. They may try to determine the effects of these patterns on overall group functioning or show their relationship to phases in the life of the group. The most common method involves interaction analysis, the use of category systems for coding utterances that occur during group interaction.

Many coding systems have been proposed.[54] Rather than reviewing all of them, we will look at two, one concentrating on the task dimensions and the other focusing on the social or relational dimension. Because Fisher and his colleagues have used coding systems in many influential studies and because they provide a theoretical rationale for their use, we will concentrate on their work.[55]

Fisher and Hawes' ISM Model. One of the clearest descriptions of how interact sequences lead to small-group theory is provided by Aubrey Fisher and Leonard Hawes in their Interaction System Model (ISM).[56] They present a three-level model showing the relationship between interaction categories, phases, and cycles. Fisher and Hawes begin by making a strong case for *grounded theory*, a type of theory construction we have not yet discussed.

They point out that the most widely used method of building theory is to start with *a priori* assumptions, make deductions based on these assumptions, generate testable hypotheses from these deductions, and then collect data to see whether the hypotheses are upheld or falsified. This method is called the *logico-deductive approach*, and it forms the basis of discussion in Appendix A.

Fisher and Hawes propose that an alternative method should be used to study small-group interaction. Instead of using data to verify preexisting hypotheses, data can be used inductively to create theory. By examining, replicating, reanalyzing, and reevaluating observations of actual communication, patterns can be identified and

models can be created. This is the essence of grounded theory.[57]

Besides advocating the use of grounded theory, Fisher and Hawes argue that small groups are open systems capable of structuring and regulating themselves. Believing that "the system is its own best explanation," they argue that the best way to study the small group is to describe what occurs within the system, focusing on what is said and done during message exchange. While the notion of the group as a system is not new, previous approaches viewed individual members as the key elements in the system and focused on member characteristics in order to understand the system. Fisher and Hawes call this the *Human System Model (HSM)*. They propose, instead, that a group should be regarded as an interrelated system of behaviors rather than as an interrelated system of individuals. This is the *Interaction System Model (ISM)*. It is concerned not with characteristics of group members but with codable verbal and nonverbal units of behavior.[58]

The smallest unit of behavior in the ISM is the *act*, which is one unit of behavior emitted by one individual. A set of two contiguous acts (an act by one member and a response by another) is called an *interact*. For Fisher and Hawes, as for Karl Weick, the interact is the crucial unit of behavior.[59] An act by itself can hardly be considered a unit of communication. When an interact occurs, however, we have the beginnings of a patterned relationship and, therefore, a meaningful unit of communication.

The first level in ISM research involves categorizing interacts. By using one of the interact category systems, researchers can describe verbal and nonverbal behaviors and look for recurring sequences that define the way the group operates. The second level of ISM research identifies recognizable phases of task progression, redundant patterns from level 1 analysis. As groups engage in a series of tasks, certain phases may reoccur cyclically. The third level of ISM research involves identifying cycles in the life of the group. "The three levels of the ISM are aimed specific-

Interaction Analysis—Decision Functions

UNIT: Each member's uninterrupted comment. If it represents two categories, it is considered two units.

CODING: Each interaction unit is assigned a code on the basis of the 'function' it performs regarding the decision proposal being considered by the group.

CATEGORIES:

1. *Interpretation*: a unit of interaction reflecting a simple value judgment regarding a decision proposal. No evidence, reasons, or explanations are given. Each interpretation may be considered to be:
   f-favorable toward the decision proposal
   u-unfavorable toward the decision proposal
   ab-ambiguous (unit combines both favorable and unfavorable evaluation)
   an-ambiguous (unit is neutral)
2. *Substantiation*: a unit of interaction including supporting evidence or reasons enhancing the believability of the decision proposal. As in code 1 above, each unit may be; f, u, ab, or an.
3. *Clarification*: a unit clarifying or rendering a decision proposal more understandable. Contains no evaluation.
4. *Modification*: a unit amending or modifying the decision proposal.
5. *Agreement*: a unit expressing support of the immediately preceding act.
6. *Disagreement*: a unit expressing nonsupport for the immediately preceding act.

FIGURE 9.5: From B. Aubrey Fisher, *Small-Group Decision Making,* 2nd ed. [New York: McGraw-Hill, 1980], pp. 323–24.

ally at discovering the movement through time of the group system's organizing function—communication (or interaction)."[60]

In the ISM model, the key element is the process of interaction the group uses to organize itself as a system. Individual variables (member personalities, statuses or positions, degree of commitment to the task and group, or amount of power wielded) are of interest only to the extent they correlate with interact patterns, phases, or cycles. In other words, the elements from the HSM will only be studied in terms of their relation to the ISM. Concern centers on directly observable patterns of organization within the interact system.

Although the ISM model is not a theory of small-group behavior per se, it tells us what to examine to understand groups. It serves as a guide for conducting grounded research on groups. The first step in ISM research is to identify interact patterns, a task accomplished by using a standardized coding system. Next we examine two coding systems developed to analyze interaction.

Interaction Analysis on the Task Dimension. The first coding system focuses on the task dimension.[61] It is designed to analyze the way members respond to decision proposals. Fisher suggests that, in attempting to arrive at consensus, members offer proposals they believe will lead to a decision. Each member's contribution is either the introduction of a decision proposal or a comment on one previously introduced. Fisher's coding system uses various categories to indicate how a particular verbal act functions on a given proposal. Figure 9.5 shows this system, and Fig. 9.7 uses the system to code a sample transcript of group interaction.

The unit of analysis is each uninterrupted comment of a group member, which is classed according to its "function": whether it is an interpretation, substantiation, clarification, modification, agreement, or disagreement regarding a decision

Interaction Analysis—Relational Messages (Rel/Com)

UNIT: Any uninterrupted verbal utterance, independent of length.

CODING: Each unit is coded in relation to the previous utterance. Thus, an act agreeing with the directly preceding utterance is coded as *deferring;* one which denies or shows disagreement with a preceding act is coded as *structuring.*

CATEGORIES:

1. *Domineering* (↑ +): An attempt to restrict severely the behavioral options of the other. Included are: orders, abrupt topic changes, acts that disconfirm the previous comment by ignoring it, challenges, justifications following a challenge, personal attacks or nonsupports.
2. *Structuring* (↑ −): An attempt to restrict the other's behavioral options while leaving the other some options. An attempt to control the flow of interaction. Included are: assertions extending previous ideas, assertions about procedures to be followed, agreements with extensions, and disagreements.
3. *Equivalence* (→): An attempt at mutual identification that does not control the flow of interaction. Included are: simple extensions such as repetitions, restatements and clarifications, conditional agreements, agreements extended with personal experience; agreements that restate the preceding comment, and incomplete or uncodable utterances.
4. *Deferring* (↓): An act showing a willingness to relinquish some behavioral options while retaining others. A behavior allowing the other to control the flow of interaction. Included are simple agreements and requests for information.
5. *Submitting* (↓ +): An act showing a willingness to relinquish behavioral options while retaining little choice. Included are statements of personal support and nonextended ideas.

FIGURE 9.6:   Adapted from B. Aubrey Fisher, "RELCOM: A System for Analyzing Relational Control" (mimeo, Department of Communication, University of Utah), and B. Aubrey Fisher, *Small-Group Decision Making,* ([New York: McGraw-Hill, 1980], Appendix 2: Analysis of Small-Group Interaction, p. 327).

proposal. By using this system, the researcher can discover patterns, compute the frequency of particular acts, and identify general sequences or chains of interacts. Ultimately, phase progressions can be discovered.

Interaction Analysis on the Relationship Dimension. In chapter 8 we examined the Rogers and Farace scheme for coding dyadic control sequences. Don Ellis, B. Aubrey Fisher, and their colleagues offer another coding system for identifying control patterns. Figure 9.6 presents this system, labeled Rel/Com, and Fig. 9.7 illustrates its use on a sample transcript. Like the Rogers and Farace system, Rel/Com assumes that interactions may function to seek, relinquish, assume, or minimize control as a dimension of interaction. It also assumes that each utterance gains meaning through its relationship to a previous utterance.[63]

Rel/Com, unlike the Rogers and Farace system, uses five categories to explore the nature of control: domineering, structuring, equivalence, deferring, and submitting. Their definitions are shown in Fig. 9.6.

Criticism of Interaction Analysis

Fisher and his colleagues are not the only researchers offering interactional analysis sytems. Others have their own systems, and Fisher himself uses several additional systems.[64] The goal of this section has not been to review all available approaches but to introduce the concept of analyzing interaction patterns by coding utterances. Fisher says:

These systems of interaction analysis...are by no means ideal or standardized tools for analyzing interactions. But they do provide some explanation of the difficulties involved in observing the ongoing process of

Sample Transcript Coded According to Task and Relational Dimensions

Decision	Rel/Com	Transcript
lan0₁*	not coded	A: Would we want to spend $2,000 this first quarter to find out what the cost of our plant expansion is going to be?
3 (asks for)	→	D: The cost of what?
3	→	A: Our fixed expenses. Would we like to know how much they are going to be?
lu	↑ −	B: No. I'm not really worried about that.
lu	→	D: No. I'm not concerned about that.
2f	↑ +	A: But if we are concerned about production and profit, that's a factor. That is a fixed operating cost we will have to live with. We should know in advance what it is going to cost us.
6	↑ −	B: No.
2u	↑ −	C: But knowing it won't influence our decision to expand or not.
2u	↑ +	D: Why pay $2,000 to get it if we are going to have to pay it anyway?
2f	↑ +	A: Until we do it the first time, we've got no idea if this is going to be another $6,000 or whether it's going to be as high as $30,000. That might influence us considerably on our long–range goals.
2u	↑ +	B: We are going to have to expand in spite of that, though.
2u	↑ −	D: I don't think we are ever going to refuse to expand. So the first time that we do expand, we are going to find out the fixed operating cost.
5	↓ −	G: Yes.

FIGURE 9.7: Transcript taken from B. Aubrey Fisher, *Small-Group Decision Making*, 2nd ed. [New York: Mc-Graw Hill, 1980], Appendix 2: Analysis of Small-Group Interaction, pp. 325–26, 28. Coding is also Fisher's. *The decision proposal being considered is that the corporation should discover what its fixed costs will be after the proposed plant expansion has been completed. This decision proposal is ambiguously introduced by A at the beginning of the transcript. The O₁I refers to the fact that this is the introduction of decision proposal 1.

group communication. They should also demonstrate that, despite these difficulties, group communication can be observed reliably with just a little practice and familiarity with the categories. The important point is not to determine which is the "best" method of interaction analysis, but to realize that interaction analysis does provide one method, however, imperfect, for observing and understanding group communication as a process during group decision-making.[65]

Fisher acknowledges that current systems are not perfect. Indeed, all coding systems have problems. O'Donnell-Trujillo discusses some of them.[66] The major problem lies in the coding systems' inabilities to yield consistent results when used by different researchers. Coders trained by different researchers often code transcripts differently, making it difficult to compare research results. "Differential training is evidence of disparate operationalizations and suggests that

slightly different theoretical domains guide our research in…communication."[67]

There are also questions about the validity of the coding schemes. For example, are the utterances coded as one-down actually instances of submission? Is an act identified within a coding system as a one-up indeed a bid for control? How do people actually experience these acts? While attempts have been made to validate different systems, more work remains to be done. As O'Donnell-Trujillo points out, "clearly the issue of coding validity must be resolved before we can fully assess the findings derived from relational communication coding schemes."[68]

Coding systems assume that message exchanges determine group success or failure. Although we have reviewed several coding systems, we have not examined their actual use in research. Several researchers, for example, have tried to correlate group performance with the fre-

RESEARCH ABSTRACT 9.2 An Examination of Group Problem-Solving Effectiveness

---

Hirokawa's *purpose* was to determine whether successful and unsuccessful problem-solving groups interact differently over time. The subjects were 80 introductory speech communication students from a large university. They were screened to be sure they had no prior instruction in group discussion and that they were unfamiliar with the tasks used in the study.

Subjects were randomly divided into 20 four-member groups. *Methods* involved asking each group to solve a problem about how to control speeding in a large metropolitan area. Each group was videotaped during a 30-minute discussion of the problem. Two National Highway Safety Administration officials evaluated whether group solutions would remedy the problem, were economically feasible, and were free of sociopolitical problems.

Evaluations were made by rating each solution on a scale from 1 to 7 for each criterion. A successful group was one receiving at least a 6 on all three criteria, while an unsuccessful group had to receive no greater than a 2 on all three criteria. Five groups were identified as successful and four as unsuccessful.

Each utterance of each group member was coded in terms of the function it performed for the group. Each utterance was coded as an analysis of the problem, an establishment of evaluation criteria, a generation of alternative solutions, an evaluation of alternative solutions, an establishment of operating procedure, a positive

socioemotional comment, or a negative socioemotional comment.

To *analyze* the data, Hirokawa divided each session into eight equal time segments. The total percentage of units in each category was then computed. This allowed him to look for overall differences in terms of how often and when groups used a particular kind of comment. He could thus determine whether a certain kind of comment was used more frequently in certain phases than in others.

The *results* were as follows. Successful groups analyzed the problem before seeking a solution, while unsuccesfull groups began to work on a solution immediately. In addition, successful groups tended to produce fewer negative socioemotional utterances than unsuccessful groups. While these general findings were clear, Hirokawa did not find evidence for similarities in phase sequences either within each type of group or between them. Each group appeared to follow its own individual path toward task accomplishment. These results indicate either that groups do not pass through similar task phases or that the functions used in his coding system are not adequate for differentiating phases in group interaction.

Source: Randy Y. Hirokawa, "Group Communication and Problem-Solving Effectiveness: An Investigation of Group Phases," *Human Communication Research*, 9 (Summer 1983), 291–367.

---

quency of certain communicative behaviors to determine the differences in verbal interaction between successful and unsuccessful groups. Research Abstract 9.2 presents one such study that uses a different coding scheme from the ones we have so far considered.

Another use for interaction analysis was outlined in Fisher and Hawes' ISM model: identifying group phases. We will now examine in more detail a phase model developed from one of Fisher's studies and offer a general critique of phase models.

GROUP PHASES: HOW DO GROUPS EVOLVE?

A question that intrigues researchers in the small-group field is whether or not there is a natural process through which groups progress as they make decisions. Several researchers have focused on this problem and have identified group phases.[69] Although we could discuss any one of these, we will turn our attention to Fisher's four-phase model of decision emergence.

Fisher's Model of Decision Emergence

Research Abstract 9.3 outlines the methods used to develop this phase model. According to Fisher, groups experience the following phases: orientation, conflict, emergence, and reinforcement. Although every group may not experience these phases the same way, phases exist in many groups and follow a logical progression.

Orientation. The *orientation phase* is marked by a high degree of primary tension. During this phase, members are uncertain about their relationship to one another and about the direction for subsequent interaction. Because they do not know how others will respond to their decision proposals, their contributions are ambiguously phrased and tentatively offered. Interaction is characterized by politeness, uncertainty, unwillingness to take a strong stand, and frequent silences and pauses. Initial meetings of new groups are generally characterized by this kind of behavior, and groups may start subsequent meetings with a brief orientation phase.

Conflict. Once primary tension is overcome, members move into a more active, less tentative phase. Here, decision proposals are more directly introduced, members argue about opposing proposals, coalitions emerge, and struggles for dominance and leadership become evident. The ambiguity and uncertainty of the beginning phase is gone. Interaction during the conflict phase is characterized by direct argument, statements favoring or opposing different porposals, and polarization around different leadership contenders. During this phase, conflict is not a sign of a dysfunctional group but is instead a natural process allowing generation of opposing ideas.

Emergence. During the emergence phase, conflict and dissent dissipate. Opposing ideas are no longer reinforced as the group settles on its ultimate decision. Members who were previously in disagreement with this decision back down. Ambiguity reoccurs, this time allowing dissenting members to express tentative approval of the group's opinions. Coalitions gradually break up. During this phase, the eventual outcome of the group's decision-making process begins to emerge.

Reinforcement. Final consensus occurs during the reinforcement phase. Now conflict has almost totally dissipated. The group agrees on both decisions and roles. The major goal now is to support and reinforce these agreements. Ambiguity vanishes once again, and interaction is marked by positive, favorable expressions. Interactors often continue to support these expressions with evidence and reasons, but these substantiations no longer serve the argumentative purpose they did during the conflict stage. The function is now to reinforce a decision already made. Interaction here is often loud, boisterous, and self-congratulatory as the group commits itself to the position.

Both task and socioemotional elements are connected as the group decision emerges. Groups tack back and forth between these two dimensions until they reach the reinforcement phase when both task and relational problems have been resolved. Fisher sums up his discussion:

Decisions are not so much *made* by a group as they *emerge* from group interaction. This emergence of decisions is illustrated in the four-phase model of orientation, conflict, emergence, and reinforcement, each phase characterized by a distinctively different interaction pattern."[70]

RESEARCH ABSTRACT 9.3 Discovering Small-Group Phases

Fisher's *purpose* was to investigate the interaction patterns characterizing groups as, over time, they move toward decisions. The general *method* he employed involved interaction analysis of all of the verbal contributions of group members during their entire interaction history. Ten groups were chosen according to seven basic criteria: (1) each group's goal was to achieve consensus, (2) their interaction was primarily verbal, (3) they operated in an emerging context, (4) their entire history was available, (5) a written record of task performance was available, (6) they successfully completed the task, and (7) they formed outside of a classroom context. The groups varied in size (from four to 12 members), sex composition, age (teens to 60s), and time spent together (25 minutes to over 30 hours). Over 3,000 units of interaction were analyzed.

Fisher's interaction analysis category system coded each unit of talk according to its function and whether it was favorable, unfavorable, or ambiguous toward each decision proposal. Group interaction was divided into 5-minute segments. For each segment, a "static analysis" was used to determine how many utterances fell into each coding category and a "contingency analysis" looked at the frequency of different combinations of units. Fisher was particularly interested in identifying interact

patterns. For example, comments favorable to a given proposal that were immediately followed by comments unfavorable to that same proposal indicated a conflict pattern. On the other hand, favorable units followed by additional favorable units indicated group members were reinforcing each other's proposals. Ambiguous responses following an argument suggested tentativeness or ambiguity on the part of group members. By plotting these combinations of acts, Fisher saw emerging patterns in the data.

As Fisher reviewed these patterns, he identified four different phases. He used statistical tests of association to *analyze* the accuracy of this perception. The *results* indicated the presence of four phases that he named orientation, conflict, emergence, and reinforcement. Each phase showed a different pattern of ambiguous, conflicting, and reinforcing interacts.

Fisher argues that these results indicate a consistent progression. While he admits that the amount of time devoted to each phase may vary in different groups and that external controls might modify these patterns, he believes similar task behavior patterns can be expected to emerge in a variety of groups.

Source: B. Aubrey Fisher, "Decision Emergence: Phases in Group Decision-Making," *Speech Monographs*, 37 (March 1970), 53–66.

Criticism of Fisher's Model. The four-phase model has been widely accepted. Perhaps the greatest problem is that it is too general. Although successful groups seem to go through a similar process, there may be individual variations. The time spent in a particular stage may vary among groups; and a single phase, say, conflict, may be repeated. We do not know what conditions trigger movement to a new phase, nor how the process of resolving task and relational problems at each stage is accomplished.

Marshall Scott Poole offers one of the most complete criticisms of phase models. He contends that viewing group decision making as a series of discrete, consecutive phases is an oversimplification that has created a "blind spot" in current group research.[71] Poole argues that theories built on an inductive, or grounded, approach can "lead to the assimilation of observations to expectations, to the sharpening of some occurrences and the neglect of others in the service of a coherent story. They can quite easily become self-fulfilling and blind the researchers to the 'marvelous particularity' of the object of study."[72] Once the reseacher discovers a particular pattern in an initial study, he or she may confirm it in subsequent research even if this results in oversimplification. Researchers trying to confirm phase models, he tells us, often "divided discussions into the same number of segments as the expected phases" and have "combined data across groups," thereby failing to see differences.[73] Poole also believes that the coding systems focus on only a small number of functions, ignoring others that could qualify results.

Poole's Model of Decision Development

Poole believes detailed examination of particular groups reveals a much more complex picture than simple phase models currently yield. He himself offers a model that views group activity not as a series of simple sequential "blocks" but as a set of parallel strands that "evolve simultaneously and interlock in different patterns over time."[74] When the different tracks converge in a simple pattern, classic phases emerge. In other cases, however, the development of each track may be uneven. They may not interlock coherently. Poole believes at least three activity tracks exist:

1) Task process activities: those activities the group enacts to manage its task; 2) Relational activities: those activities that reflect or manage relationships among group members as they relate to the group's work, and 3) Topic focus: the substantive issues and arguments of concern to the group at a given point in the discussion.[75]

Other possible tracks include control strategies and various conflict-management activities. As the group progresses, it moves along each track simultaneously, but unevenly. Although changes in one track (a movement from problem orientation to solution design on the task track) may be accompanied by changes on other tracks (a move-

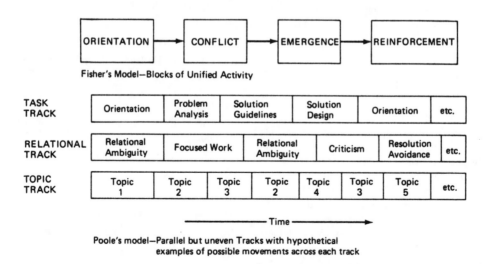

Fisher's Model—Blocks of Unified Activity

| ORIENTATION | → | CONFLICT | → | EMERGENCE | → | REINFORCEMENT |

TASK TRACK	Orientation	Problem Analysis	Solution Guidelines	Solution Design	Orientation	etc.
RELATIONAL TRACK	Relational Ambiguity	Focused Work	Relational Ambiguity	Criticism	Resolution Avoidance	etc.
TOPIC TRACK	Topic 1	Topic 2	Topic 3	Topic 2	Topic 4	Topic 3	Topic 5	etc.

◀——————— Time ———————▶

Poole's model—Parallel but uneven Tracks with hypothetical examples of possible movements across each track

FIGURE 9.8: Comparison of Fisher's phase model and Poole's model of decision development. (Adapted from discussions in Marshall Scott Poole, "Decision Development in Small Groups, III: A Multiple Sequence Model of Group Decision Development," *Communication Monographs*, 50 [December 1983], 321–41.)

212 Chapter 9 Small-Group Communication

ment from noncritical interaction to opposition on the relational level), the coordination between them is not always complete. The development of these tracks will be uneven and broken at various points by transitions. "Sometimes these break points interrupt only one thread, sometimes two or all three. The end effect is halting development with the strands pushing forward at different rates depending on the number of breakpoints and with differing degrees of association and coordination between tracks as the discussion unfolds."[76] Figure 9.8 compares Poole's approach to Fisher's. There are advantages to both models. The Fisher model is simple. The Poole model is more detailed. Poole's approach is in the process of being worked out, but it suggests that refinement of the classic phase models may be desireable.

REFERENCES

1. John K. Brilhart, *Effective Group Discussion*, 3rd ed. (Dubuque, Iowa: William C. Brown, 1978), pp. 20–21.
2. *Ibid.*, p. 21.
3. Leon Festinger, "A Theory of Social Comparison Processes," *Human Relations*, 2 (May 1954), 117–140, p. 117.
4. *Ibid.*, p. 120.
5. *Ibid.*, p. 127.
6. *Ibid.*, p. 136.
7. *Ibid.*, p. 136.
8. William Schutz, *Firo: A Three-Dimensional Theory of Interpersonal Behavior* (New York: Holt, Rinehart & Winston, 1958), and *The Interpersonal Underworld* (Palo Alto, Calif.: Science and Behavior Books, 1966). For a short summary see "The Postulate of Interpersonal Needs," in *Messages: A Reader in Human Communication*, 2nd ed., ed. Jean M. Civikly (New York: Random House, 1977), pp. 174–84.
9. Schutz, "Postulate of Interpersonal Needs," p. 174.
10. *Ibid.*, p. 174.
11. *Ibid.*, p. 175.
12. *Ibid.*, p. 181.
13. Richard L. Moreland and John M. Levine, "Socialization in Small Groups: Temporal Changes in Individual-Group Relations," in *Advances in Experimental Social Psychology*, vol. 15, ed. Leonard Berkowitz (New York: Academic, 1982), pp. 137–93.
14. *Ibid.*, p. 182.
15. *Ibid.*, p. 141.
16. *Ibid.*, p. 143.
17. *Ibid.*, p. 144.
18. *Ibid.*, p. 148.
19. *Ibid.*, p. 149.
20. *Ibid.*, p. 149.
21. *Ibid.*, p. 164.
22. *Ibid.*, p. 172.
23. *Ibid.*, p. 176.
24. *Ibid.*, p. 176.
25. *Ibid.*, p. 179.
26. *Ibid.*, p. 181.
27. *Ibid.*, p. 140.
28. Marvin E. Shaw, *Group Dynamics: The Psychology of Small-Group Behavior*, 3rd ed. (New York: McGraw-Hill, 1981), p. 263.
29. *Ibid.*, p. 213.
30. *Ibid.*, p. 263.
31. Edwin P. Hollander, "Conformity, Status, and Idiosyncrasy Credit," *Psychological Review*, 65 (1958), 117–27.
32. B. Aubrey Fisher, *Small-Group Decision-Making*, 2nd ed. (New York: McGraw-Hill, 1980), p. 76.
33. *Ibid.*, pp. 76–81.
34. Shaw, *Group Dynamics*, p. 151.
35. *Ibid.*, p. 153.
36. *Ibid.*, p. 154.
37. *Ibid.*, pp. 155–56.
38. Fisher, *Small-Group Decision-Making*, p. 79.
39. Shaw, *Group Dynamics*, p. 316.
40. *Ibid.*, p. 324.
41. Ralph M. Stogdill, *Handbook of Leadership: A Survey of Theory and Research* (New York: The Free Press, 1974), p. 81.

42. *Ibid.*, p. 82.

43. Fred E. Fiedler, "A Contingency Model of Leadership Effectiveness," in *Advances in Experimental Social Psychology*, vol. 1, ed. Leonard Berkowitz (New York: Academic, 1964); see also *A Theory of Leadership Effectiveness* (New York: McGraw-Hill, 1967).

44. Fiedler, *Theory of Leadership Effectiveness*, pp. 45–46.

45. Shaw, *Group Dynamics*, p. 341.

46. Paul Hersey and Kenneth Blanchard, *Management of Organizational Behavior: Utilizing Human Resources*, 3rd ed. (Englewood Cliffs, N. J.: Prentice Hall, 1977).

47. Ernest G. Bormann, "Symbolic Convergence: Organizational Communication and Culture," in *Communication and Organizations: An Interpretive Approach*, eds. Linda L. Putnam and Michael E. Pacanowsky (Beverly Hills: Sage, 1983), pp. 99–122. See also Bormann, *Discussion and Group Methods: Theory and Practice*, 2nd ed. (New York: Harper & Row, 1975); Ernest G. Bormann, Jerie Pratt, and Linda Putnam, "Power, Authority and Sex: Male Response to Female Leadership," *Communication Monographs*, 45 (June 1978), 119–155.

48. Bormann, "Symbolic Convergence," p. 103.

49. *Ibid.*, p. 103.

50. *Ibid.*, p. 107.

51. *Ibid.*, p. 110.

52. *Ibid.*, p. 114.

53. *Ibid.*, p. 115.

54. Robert F. Bales, *Interaction Process Analysis: A Method for the Study of Small Groups* (Reading, Mass.: Addison-Wesley, 1950) offers the classic group interaction coding system; see also Randy Hirokawa, "Group Communication and Problem-Solving Effectiveness: An Investigation of Group Phases," *Human Communication Research*, 9 (Summer 1983), 291–305; Randy Hirokawa, "Group Communication and Problem Solving Effectiveness, I: A Critical Review of Inconsistent Findings," *Communication Quarterly*, 30 (1982), 134–41; Henry Mintzberg, Daru Raisinghani, and Andre Theoret, "The Structure of 'Unstructured' Decision Processes," *Administrative Science Quarterly*, 21 (1976), 246–75; Marshall Scott Poole, "Decision Development in Small Groups, II: A Study of Multiple Sequences in Group Development," *Communication Monographs*, 50 (September 1983), 206–32; Marshall Scott Poole, "Decision Development in Small Groups, III: A Multiple Sequence Model of Group Decision Development," *Communication Monographs*, 50 (December 1983), 321–41.

55. Fisher, *Small-Group Decision Making*, Appendix 2. See also Donald G. Ellis and others, *Rel/Com* (unpublished coding manual, University of Utah); B. Aubrey Fisher and Leonard C. Hawes, "An Interact System Model: Generating a Grounded Theory of Small Groups," *Quarterly Journal of Speech*, 57 (December 1971), 444–53.

56. Fisher and Hawes, "An Interact System Model."

57. Barney G. Glaser and Anselm L. Strauss, *The Discovery of Grounded Theory: Strategies for Qualitative Research* (Chicago: Aldine, 1967), p. 6.

58. Fisher and Hawes, "An Interact System Model."

59. See, for example, Karl E. Weick, *The Social Psychology of Organizing* (Reading, Mass.: Addison-Wesley, 1969).

60. Fisher and Hawes, "An Interact System Model," p. 451.

61. Fisher, *Small-Group Decision Making*, Appendix 2.

62. *Ibid.*; Ellis and others, *Rel/Com*.

63. Nick O'Donnell-Trujillo, "Relational Communication: A Comparison of Coding Systems," *Communication Monographs*, 48 (June 1981), 91–105.

64. B. Aubrey Fisher, Gay Lloyd Dreksel, and Wayne S. Werbel, *Social Information Processing Analysis* (unpublished coding manual, University of Utah).

65. Fisher, *Small-Group Decision-Making*, p. 329.

66. O'Donnell-Trujillo, "Coding Systems."

67. *Ibid.*, pp. 104–05.

68. *Ibid.*, p. 105.

69. Robert F. Bales and Fred L. Strodtbeck, "Phases in Group Problem-Solving," *Journal of Abnormal and Social Psychology*, 46 (1951), 485–95; Warren G. Bennis and Herbert A. Shepard, "A Theory of Group Development," *Human Relations*, 9 (1956), 415–37; Bruce Tuckman, "Developmental Sequences in Small Groups," *Psychological Bul-*

letin, 63 (1965), 384–99. See also, Donald G. Ellis and B. Aubrey Fisher, "Phases of Conflict in Small Group Development: A Markov Analysis," *Human Communication Research*, 1 (Spring, 1975), 195–212.

70. Fisher, *Small-Group Decision Making*, p. 163.

71. Poole, "Decision Development III," p. 321.

72. *Ibid.*, p. 323.

73. *Ibid.*, p. 323.

74. *Ibid.*, p. 326.

75. *Ibid.*, p. 326.

76. *Ibid.*, p. 328.

chapter 10

PUBLIC COMMUNICATION

INTRODUCTION

Our final context will be face-to-face public communication. Here, a single speaker delivers a message to many receivers at the same time. Public communication differs from interpersonal and small-group in many ways. In most cases, the speaker addresses a specially convened group of strangers. There is no opportunity for speaker and audience to get to know each other gradually; rather, an immediate impression must be made, one not usually open to revision.

In addition, audience size and heterogeneity are important. In many public speaking situations, the speaker may address hundreds, or even thousands, of people. This makes it impossible to tailor the message to individual audience members. For the transaction to proceed in an orderly fashion, the role relationship between speaker and listeners must be formal. The person delivering the message plays the active role of speaker, and audience members play the more passive role of listener.

Because of these factors, the message must be preplanned. Although a skilled speaker can adapt a presentation in minor ways during the speaking event, communication is far from spontaneous. The speaker must anticipate audience responses and carefully compose the message ahead of time.

Although public communication is different in all these ways from other contexts, the basic problems of communication still apply here. Audience members must evaluate each speaker's acceptability. And speakers must concern themselves with problems of signification and message exchange, carefully crafting the language and organizations of their messages. Although roles are more formalized in public situations, the speaker is still concerned with social coordination; that is, he or she must meet audience expectations. The problem of outcome achievement is of primary importance as speakers actively try to transform the beliefs, attitudes, and values of their listeners. Even problems of evolution and change play their part, for audience members take the message away with them, and, as they reflect on it and encounter similar messages, their reactions change. Public communication, although different in many ways from interpersonal or group communication is still communication, and involves the same basic processes affecting all communicative exchanges.

THE PUBLIC CONTEXT: WHAT CONSTITUTES THE PUBLIC EXPERIENCE?

There are many approaches to understanding the nature of public communication. In chapter 1, we examined one: the canons of rhetoric proposed by the early Greek and Roman rhetoricians. This model examined how a speaker develops persuasive messages. By breaking this process down into invention, style, arrangement, memory, and delivery, the model offers prescriptive guidelines for effective message exchange. This approach has proven itself so useful that, even today, public speaking texts are organized around the ancient canons of rhetoric.

We can also benefit from modern descriptions of the factors that constitute public communication. We will look at two recent models: one using a rhetorical, philosophic approach and one based on psychological, social-scientific principles.

Burke's Dramatistic Model

One way to view public communication, or any act of human communication, is to use a dramatic metaphor. When we observe a real-life performance we are like an audience watching a play. Just as spectators decipher the meaning of a play by carefully observing its setting, costumes, props, blocking, and dialogue, so individuals use these same cues to characterize everyday interactions.

Kenneth Burke used a dramatic analogy to analyze how people attempt to make sense of their social worlds.[1] He isolated five factors people use to assign meanings to social acts. All *acts*

are embedded in *scenes* and realized by *agents* who employ some *agency* to accomplish their *purposes*. These five dramatic factors are known as the *pentad*. By analyzing each one, we can more fully understand human action.

Burke developed the pentad to describe the factors people use to attribute motives to others. He addressed the question, "What is involved when we say what people are doing and why they are doing it?"[2] He believed that each of us concentrates on a different aspect of the pentad, which in turn affects what we think and say about the events we observe. As Charles Larson tells us, if you were to describe a particular action, then "your words would reflect your preference. If you thought that men control their own destiny, you would focus on the agent. If you felt that circumstances compelled action, you would focus on the scene. If you felt that high principles and ideals carried even weak men through trying times, you focus on the purpose."[3]

In focusing on a particular aspect of the pentad, individuals are guided by their philosophies about human motivation. Burke argues that each of the major Western philosophies reflects a part of the pentad. *Materialists*, for example, believe that *scene* or situation is the primary cause of human action, that environmental conditions help determine why a person acts as he or she does. *Idealists* concentrate on the *agent*, believing that the explanation for human action lies in the nature of the person acting, that personal goals and motivations determine behavior. *Pragmatists* focus on *agency*, the means or instruments the actor uses to achieve an end. *Mystics*, on the other hand, emphasize *purpose*. They believe people are governed by powers and purposes beyond their control, that human action results from a divine purpose. Finally, *realists* concentrate primarily on the form or pattern of the *act*, believing that what is most important and most "real" are observable human actions and patterns of behavior. By identifying which aspects of the pentad a speaker refers to, we can identify his or her philosophy about human motivation.

Individual speakers can use the pentad in composing speeches. A speaker, for example, can sway an audience by concentrating on scene, agent, agency, purpose, or act. A trial lawyer can argue that a defendant's act was caused by poverty (scene) or by conflicting religious or moral values (purpose). The lawyer's opponent, on the other hand, can focus on the personal character and reputation of the defendant (agent), on how the crime was committed (agency), or on the nature of the crime itself (the act). Thus, both lawyers can assign blame or excuse an action by emphasizing a different aspect of the pentad.

Because a speaker's arguments emphasize different dramatic factors, the rhetorical critic can use the pentad to analyze the nature of communicative acts. He or she can analyze the force of a persuasive argument by determining how successfully it uses different aspects of the pentad. The critic can uncover "the underlying beliefs or key elements of an advocate and also...discover and...label a persuader's characteristic symbols and rituals."[4] Research Abstract 10.1 takes a famous speech and employs a dramatistic perspective to analyze its effectiveness.

We can also use the pentad to understand the dramatic nature of public speaking itself. Public speaking is, after all, an act and always involves a scene, an agent, and a purpose. Each element contributes to the overall communicative effect. If the message style does not fit with the setting, with the speaker's personal characteristics, or with the speaker's purpose, then communication fails. The relationship, or what Burke calls the *ratio*, between each element of the pentad determines the nature and interpretation of a particular act of communication.[5] The skillful communicator knows, for example, how to set the stage so the message will have the greatest impact on the audience. He or she knows the styles and methods that best fit the purpose and realizes the importance of consistency among all the dramatic elements of the speaking situation. The factors of scene, act, agent, agency, and purpose always

come into play in any communicative act and are especially important in public communication.

The dramatistic model focuses our attention on the importance of the scene or situation. While the canons analyze how the public speaker creates a message, the pentad explains how audience members interpret the speech. The pentad reminds us that audience members work hard to make sense of messages and that receivers' interpretations are just as important as speakers' intentions in determining the success or failure of public communication. A second model also examines the part the receiver plays in communication, this time by looking at psychological processes inside the receiver. We now turn our attention to this model.

The Yale Attitude Model

In the 1950s, several social psychologists at Yale University embarked on a research program designed to investigate what makes a persuasive communication effective.[6] The Yale researchers used social learning principles to explain public communication. For them, messages were stimuli capable of causing psychological responses in audience members. They argued that if these stimuli provide enough incentives, then the listener's response will be favorable. The model developed by the Yale Attitude group outlines the kinds of stimuli that are most effective in achieving a desired response, and it describes the psychological processes that operate in receivers as they listen to a speech. Figure 10.1 outlines this model.

The Yale group recognized that the stimulus/response link between speaker and listener is cognitively mediated. As listeners process symbolic stimuli, they actively filter these stimuli, interpreting them according to internal cognitive predispositions. The model suggests that a persuasive stimulus can generate several responses. After hearing a public speech, listeners may experience changes in perceptions, emotions, or

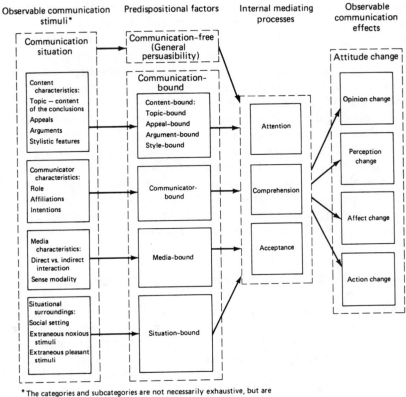

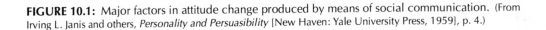

*The categories and subcategories are not necessarily exhaustive, but are intended to highlight the main types of stimulus variables that play a role in producing changes in verbalizable attitudes.

FIGURE 10.1: Major factors in attitude change produced by means of social communication. (From Irving L. Janis and others, *Personality and Persuasibility* [New Haven: Yale University Press, 1959], p. 4.)

behaviors. They may also change their opinions and attitudes. While all these responses are important, the Yale model emphasizes opinion and attitude change.

Opinion Change. According to Carl Hovland, Irving Janis, and Harold Kelley, opinions are *"verbal 'answers' that an individual gives in response to stimulus situations in which some 'question' is raised."*[7] For example, if you ask yourself, "Will current economic policies lead to prosperity?" your answer will reflect beliefs about government policies. Every time you make a mental judgment about a subject, you express

an opinion, and these opinions predispose you toward that subject. Such predispositions are known as attitudes. If, for example, it is your opinion that current economic policies are ill-conceived because they lead to inflation and unemployment, then you will be negatively predisposed toward government policies. If, on the other hand, you hold favorable opinions of this subject, then your attitude is likely to be positive. Hovland and his colleagues explain: "Our assumption is that there are many attitudes which are mediated by verbal beliefs, expectations, and judgments and that one of the main ways in which communications give rise to changes in

RESEARCH ABSTRACT 10.1   A Rhetorical Examination of Motives

On the evening of July 18, 1969, Senator Edward Kennedy was involved in a traffic accident in which a passenger, Mary Jo Kopechne, died. On July 25, he described the accident to the people of Massachusetts and to a national audience.

Ling's *purpose* was "to examine some of the rhetorical choices Kennedy made … in his address and to suggest the possible impact of these choices on both short- and long-term audience responses." The *method* was a rhetorical analysis using Burke's pentad. For Ling, the speech consists of two parts. The first explains the accident, and the second discusses Kennedy's future. The function of the first is to absolve Kennedy of full responsibility for the death of Miss Kopechne; that of the second is to place responsibility for his political future in the hands of the people of Massachusetts.

Although Kennedy states he does not place blame "either on the accident or on anyone else," Ling argues that the speech is designed to portray Kennedy as a helpless victim of the scene. Ling identifies the following elements in the first part of the speech: "The scene (the events surrounding the death of Miss Kopechne), the agent (Kennedy), the act (Kennedy's failure to report the accident immediately), the agency (whatever methods were available to make such a report), and the purpose (to fulfill his legal and moral responsibilities)."

In describing the accident, Kennedy establishes the scene as the controlling element. He emphasizes that the road was unlit and unsafe, and that he nearly died: "Then water entered my lungs and I actually felt the sensation of drowning. But somehow I struggled to the surface alive." He later expresses concern that "some awful curse did actually hang over the Kennedys," thus implicating fate in the accident and portraying himself as the victim of an uncontrollable situation.

In the second part of the speech, Kennedy seeks to make the people of Massachusetts co-agents in his decision to stay in office. The pentad once again operates: "The scene (current reaction to the events of July 18), the agent (the people of Massachusetts), the act (Kennedy's decision not to resign), the agency (statement of resignation), and the purpose (to remove Kennedy from office)."

Kennedy emphasizes that "whispers" and "innuendo" constitute the scene. He says that should the people of Massachusetts lack confidence in a senator's character, "with or without justification," then that senator must resign, suggesting that the kind of people who would force his resignation are the kind of people who believe unfounded rumors. The favorable response of the people of Massachusetts showed they chose not to accept this characterization.

Ling concludes by examining the long-term effects of Kennedy's rhetorical strategies. Polls showed that close to 90 percent felt his chances of becoming president had been hurt. Ling gives three reasons. First, Kennedy presented himself as a person unable to act in extraordinary conditions, the kind of agent who is not what a president should be. Second, it was common knowledge that advisors helped write the speech, suggesting that Kennedy's role as agent might have been manipulated. Finally, Kennedy did not explain why he and Miss Kopechne were where they were, leaving the audience wondering whether he was, in fact, responsible for the incident.

Source: David A. Ling, "A Pentadic Analysis of Senator Edward Kennedy's Address to the People of Massachusetts, July 25, 1969," *The Central States Speech Journal*, 21 (Summer 1970), 81–86.

attitudes is by changing such verbal responses."[8] By presenting arguments, a public speaker changes an audience's opinions and therefore its attitudes and ultimately its actions.

Persuasive Responses. In order for a persuasive stimulus to result in opinion and attitude change, the receiver must experience three internal responses: *attention, comprehension,* and *acceptance.* Although all are important, acceptance is most crucial in achieving change. The Yale model proposes two major sets of variables affecting acceptance: stimulus variables and receiver variables. Stimulus variables include characteristics of the message, the speaker, the media of transmission, and the speaking environment. Receiver variables have to do with the ways receivers filter the message through their own cognitive structure.

Receivers are not blank slates upon which the speaker writes a message. They have predispositions that affect message perception. Audience predispositions may be general or may be bound to certain aspects of the stimulus. For example, individuals differ in how open they are to arguments on a particular topic, how acceptable a given message is, how much they like a speaker's style, and so on. They also favor some speakers over others and respond differently to different media and different speaking situations. If speakers are to achieve the attention, comprehension, and acceptance they desire, then they must take into account not only the form and content of message stimuli but also the ways audience members are likely to filter and interpret these stimuli. The speaker must recognize the importance of receiver variables.

The Yale researchers embarked on a series of empirical studies that tested relationships between speaker, message, and receiver. They believed that the proper method for testing theory was through experimental research. Several Yale experiments focused on how speaker credibility affects message reception. Others investigated the kinds of appeals and arguments likely to lead to message acceptance. These studies asked, for example, What are the effects of fear appeals? In what order should arguments be presented? Is a one-sided or two-sided presentation most acceptable? How specifically should conclusions be stated? They also investigated how audience predispositions and characteristics affect the speaker's ability to present a message, posing additional questions such as, How does general level of persuasibility affect message reception? Do different personalities accept different types of appeals? How much does audience intelligence affect responses? These questions will be answered as we proceed through the rest of this chapter.

Criticisms of the Yale Model and the Pentad. Although the underlying perspectives of Burke's dramatistic analysis and the Yale attitude approach differ, they share some similarities. Both say that the way an audience characterizes an agent is important. Both emphasize the role that scenic factors play in determining communicative success or failure. In addition, both see the receiver as an active participant who processes and interprets information. The Yale model goes beyond the pentad, however, by describing the receiver's psychological responses as he or she assigns meaning to acts of communication.

Both models also give us implicit directions for studying public communication. The pentad suggests that, as students of communication, we can understand persuasive messages by analyzing how a speaker uses the pentad. The Yale model favors a more scientific approach, saying that by conducting experimental studies we can discover scientific laws explaining the psychology of audiences.

In what follows, we will examine the major factors identified by both systems. Since both emphasize the characteristics of the agent or speaker, we will address this topic first.

CREDIBILITY AND ETHOS: HOW DO SPEAKER CHARACTERISTICS AFFECT AUDIENCE RESPONSE?

Speaker characteristics have long been recognized as important to success in the public context. We have already seen that the attributions we make about our communicative partners affect our willingness to communicate. If audience members judge a speaker to be incompetent, untrustworthy, or unworthy of respect, then they are unlikely to attend to, comprehend, or accept a message.

Aristotle and the Nature of Ethos

Aristotle first drew our attention to the importance of speaker characteristics more than 25 centuries ago. In the *Rhetoric*, he analyzed and described the nature of speaker characteristics. He believed that a public speaker could persuade an audience in three ways: (1) by demonstrating his personal character, (2) by manipulating the audience mood, and (3) by providing, within the speech itself, logical proof for the positions being advocated. The first of these, the character of the speaker, Aristotle called *ethos*. He said:

Persuasion is achieved by the speaker's personal character when the speech is so spoken as to make us think him credible. We believe good men more fully and more readily than others: this is true generally whatever the question is, and absolutely true where exact certainty is impossible and opinions are divided.[9]

For Aristotle, the speaker's character was the most important persuasive tool he could possess.

Aristotle divided the concept of ethos into three parts: good sense, good moral character, and good will. He believed that errors and false statements can always be attributed to a lack of one of these. Speakers will be mistrusted if the audience believes they are inherently unable to form true opinions, that they are liars, or that they lack concern for the best interest of the audience. If an audience perceives these faults, then it will reject the speaker's message. Aristotle, therefore,

advised speakers to build their ethos in each of these areas.[10]

The first way a speaker can increase persuasive impact is to show that he or she possesses *good sense* or competence. Aristotle did not specify whether good sense meant native intelligence or common sense, but he did imply that good sense involved the ability to discover the correct or best solution to a particular problem.[11] The speaker with good sense is trusted to hold true opinions and to make wise decisions.

The second way the speaker can increase ethos is by demonstrating *good will*, which reflects concern for the welfare of the audience. By demonstrating candor, humility, and respect for others, a speaker may capture the confidence of an audience and, therefore, be effective in a persuasive situation.[12] Finally, the speaker should exhibit *good character*. If listeners believe a speaker is ambitious, vain, selfish, or otherwise morally reprehensible, they will not accept his or her message. The speaker must appear to be above reproach.

Source Credibility

Aristotle's analysis, written so many centuries ago, is relevant today. Although the methods of modern credibility theorists differ from Aristotle's, their interests are similar. They agree that a speaker's perceived ethos determines effectiveness, and they generally accept the importance of good sense and good will as dimensions of speaker acceptability.

The Yale Approach to Credibility. The Yale group was also concerned with speaker characteristics. They believed speakers could achieve attention, comprehension, and acceptance by offering incentives. Some of these incentives were related to the audience's desire to form a symbolic bond with the speaker; that is, a highly admired speaker offers the reward of social approval. By accepting his conclusions, audience members see themselves as someone the speaker would approve of, and they can associate themselves with groups to which the speaker belongs.[13]

A speaker can also control audience members through negative incentives. Speakers who are perceived as powerful, as controlling valued resources, can inspire fear in an audience. To disassociate themselves from threatened punishments, audience members may accept messages. Of course, more rational incentives may also be presented. In the speech, the speaker may use logical arguments to point out the rewards and punishments associated with particular opinions. To accept these arguments, the audience must believe the speaker is knowledgeable and well disposed toward them.

The ability to control rational incentives is known as *credibility*. Achieving audience response by presenting logical arguments is the method of gaining acceptance that most interested the Yale researchers. They therefore tried to define the factors contributing to a speaker's credibility. For Hovland and associates, credibility consists of two major dimensions: "(1) the extent to which a communicator is perceived to be a source of valid assertions (his 'expertness'), and (2) the degree of confidence in the communicator's intent to communicate the assertion he considers most valid (his 'trustworthiness')."[14]

Several cues are associated with each aspect of credibility. Expertness, for example, may be indicated by the speaker's age, leadership position, social background, or professional standing. Trustworthiness may be shown by the speaker's sincerity and candor. High credibility speakers, those judged as expert and competent, will more successfully change attitudes than low credibility speakers. Hovland and his colleagues believed that it was not attention or comprehension that was most affected by the speaker's credibility but rather acceptance. They argued that people may pay as much attention to and learn as many facts from a low credibility source, but they fail to accept the opinions of this source. Sources low in credibility are simply unable to motivate audience members, while sources high in credibility are better able to provide their listeners with the rewards necessary to effect a positive response.[15]

The Yale group conducted studies designed to test the relationship between credibility and persuasive ability. They approached credibility as an independent variable. In a typical study, identical messages were attributed to two sources differing in credibility. For example, a message might be prepared on a medical topic. Under one experimental condition, the message would be attributed to a prestigious medical journal (the high credibility source), and in the other the message would be attributed to a mass circulation pictorial magazine (the low credibility source).[16] The researcher would then measure the amount of attitude change that each source achieved. Any difference between audience responses under these two conditions was assumed to be due to credibility, since all other stimuli were held constant.

A Scale for Evaluating Message Sources. Later researchers refined the original credibility construct. They believed the concept of source credibility was ambiguous, and they wanted to examine its underlying dimensions. Their goal was to extend the work of the Yale researchers by "investigating the criteria actually used by receivers in evaluating message sources."[17] Instead of using credibility as an independent variable, they proposed to measure it directly as a dependent variable. By measuring audience perceptions of a speaker directly, they could compare the credibility of different speakers and examine different dimensions of the credibility construct.

David Berlo, James Lemert, and Robert Mertz were the first in a long line of researchers interested in developing scales for measuring source acceptability. Research Abstract 10.2 outlines the procedures they used to develop their measurement instrument. Through the use of factor analytic techniques, they identified three aspects of credibility: *safety*, *qualification*, and *dynamism*. The first two seemed conceptually similar to the

RESEARCH ABSTRACT 10.2   An Examination of the Nature of Source Credibility

Berlo, Lemert, and Mertz wanted to determine whether credibility is a two-dimensional construct consisting of trustworthiness and competence as Hovland and his associates had supposed, or whether it involves additional dimensions. Their *purpose* was to find out how many dimensions account for a source's credibility, to test whether these dimensions are independent, and to describe the responses that characterize each dimension. They also wanted to develop a measurement instrument to evaluate sources.

Their first task was to develop the instrument. As items, they used pairs of bi-polar adjectives separated by a seven-point rating scale. (For example, "Good 1 2 3 4 5 6 7 Bad"). Respondents were to circle where on this continuum they rated a source. The instrument consisted of several similar scales. To select these scales, the researchers interviewed residents of Lansing, Michigan. Respondents were asked to name acceptable and unacceptable sources and then to provide detailed descriptions of their qualities. For these interviews and from a review of other studies, 128 scales were derived. Then only the most easily understood were chosen, reducing the number to 83.

They tested the scales on several kinds of sources, sources that were recognizable and would elicit both positive and negative responses. They tested general public sources (*The New York Times*, Dwight Eisenhower), public sources in relevant contexts (Khruschev on foreign policy), public sources in irrelevant contexts (Perry Como on organized crime), and interpersonal sources (people only the subjects knew). They tested this instrument in two studies.

Study 1. They asked 91 MSU students and spouses to rate each source on each of the 83 scale items. The responses were then factor analyzed, allowing the grouping of similar scale items. Four dimensions were identified in the instrument. The first was labeled *safety*. It included characteristics such as kindness, honesty, and sincerity. The second was *qualification*. It included experience, authoritativeness, and expertness. The third was *dynamism*. Here, items rated were energy, boldness, and aggressiveness. The fourth factor was unstable and consisted of two scales: sociable-unsociable and cheerful-gloomy. This factor was tentatively labeled *sociability*.

Study 2. In a second study the number of scales and sources was reduced and a more representative sample selected. Eight scale items were chosen to represent each of the first three factors from study 1. The two original sociability items were also retained, and nine others were added. One hundred seventeen subjects chosen from the Lansing telephone directory were asked to evaluate 12 sources on 35 scales. Factor analysis was again used. The *results* showed three major factors. The following items were identified as most representative of each factor. Safety: safe-unsafe, just-unjust, kind-cruel, friendly-unfriendly, honest-dishonest. Qualification: trained-untrained, experienced-unexperienced, skilled-unskilled, qualified-unqualified, informed-uninformed. Dynamism: aggressive-meek, emphatic-hesitant, bold-timid, active-passive, energetic-tired. No sociabilty factor emerged. Berlo and his colleagues conclude that an audience evaluates a source in three ways: according to perceived safety, qualification, and dynamism.

Source: Berlo and others, "Dimensions for Evaluating the Acceptability of Message Sources," *Public Opinion Quarterly*, 15 (1951), 635–50.

dimensions of trustworthiness and expertness identified by Hovland and his colleagues as well as to Aristotle's constructs of good sense and good will.

The dynamism dimension had not been identified by earlier researchers. It measures how active and potent a communicator is. As Berlo and his associates state, "the dynamism factor appears to tap an evaluative dimension that could be referred to as 'disposable energy'; i.e., the energy available to the source which can be used to emphasize, augment, and implement his suggestions."[18] They suggest that dynamism is less an independent dimension than an intensifier of the other two. "In other words, given an evaluation of a source as safe or unsafe, qualified or unqualified, the polarity or intensity of these evaluations of the source is intensified through perceptions of high dynamism. Under this assumption, low energy sources would seldom if ever be perceived as either extremely safe or unsafe, extremely qualified or unqualified."[19]

Other Dimensions of Credibility. Since the work of Berlo, Lemert, and Mertz, many scholars have defined credibility dimensions. James McCroskey and Lawrence Wheeles, for example, describe three additional dimensions: sociability, composure, and extroversion.[20] Roderick Hart, Gus Friedrich, and William Brooks add five more to the basic competence/trustworthiness dyad: power, good will, idealism, similarity, and dynamism.[21] Although these authors agree that the audience's perception of source characteristics is an important determinant of message acceptability, they vary greatly in their definitions of these characteristics.

Criticisms of Credibility Research. Critics have recognized flaws in the credibility research. Some attack its methodology, while others criticize it on general, theoretical grounds. Gary Cronkhite and Jo Liska do an excellent job of uncovering methodological problems in this research.[22] They believe credibility researchers place too much emphasis on factor analysis of semantic differential scales (the kind of scale used in the original Berlo, Lemert, and Mertz study). They note that the standard method is for researchers to either make up their own scales or borrow them from other studies, instead of turning, as Berlo and his colleagues did, to respondents themselves and asking them to identify the characteristics they use to judge speakers. Clearly, if the scales are chosen haphazardly, the results will be questionable. By choosing scale items themselves, researchers place themselves in a position of discovering what they already know. Simply borrowing previous items only compounds this problem. Cronkhite and Liska sum up this criticism as follows: "Two questions emerge from this analysis: First, how many other dimensions may be lurking in the semantic underbrush? Second, how much of the strength of the dimensions which have been observed is due to the inclusion of similar scales and the exclusion of scales which might represent other dimensions?"[23]

Cronkhite and Liska also see problems in the way factors are named. They point out that credibility researchers often find different clusters of scales in different studies but give them similar names, making the research look more cohesive than it is. A single scale item (good/bad) may wind up on different factors in different studies. Cronkhite and Liska reviewed a number of studies and found that the "good/bad" scale was identified as part of all the following factors: safety, authoritativeness, character, general evaluation, character-sociability, competence, and trustworthiness.[24]

Other problems may be cited. Little attention is paid either to the speaker's physical characteristics or to the speaker's behavior during the speech (language use, arguments, organizational strategies). Topic and situation are factors affecting source believability, but the use of general scales masks their effects. It may be that very different underlying dimensions will arise in different situations.

Gerald Miller and Michael Burgoon criticize the credibility construct as part of their general commentary on persuasion research.[25] They argue that the concerns of credibility researchers have been too limited. They feel the concept of credibility should be expanded. For example, our understanding might be improved by integrating some of the attraction literature. The same argument can be made for attribution and social judgment theories. Credibility researchers focus on one context and let traditional ways of studying it blind them to other potentially useful approaches.

The biggest criticism leveled against credibility research is that it has little theoretical grounding; that is, it says little about how a speaker achieves a desired response. No one disagrees that a speaker's credibility is an important factor in his or her ultimate success. As a coherent theoretical construct, however, credibility leaves much to be desired. We know surprisingly little about it and how it operates.

All credibility critics point out that researchers have paid little attention to how a speaker's actual wording and organization of a speech affect credibility. Yet, these are clearly part of the stimulus presented to the audience. We will now turn our attention to a general consideration of message variables in the public context.

LANGUAGE IN THE PUBLIC CONTEXT: WHAT MESSAGE VARIABLES LEAD TO PERSUASION?

Language use in the public context contrasts with language use in private conversations. Public messages are longer and more carefully composed and organized. In most cases, the public speaker's purpose is to advocate a particular position. In terms of style, public messages use linguistic forms designed to capture and maintain audience attention.

In this section we examine language variables that lead to success or failure in the public context, particularly speaker style, appeal type, and message organization. There is a huge body of literature on public communication in the areas of rhetoric and public address. Unfortunately, most of this literature is beyond the scope of this book. If you find yourself interested in learning more about this context, you should consider consulting this literature or taking a course in public address or rhetoric. In the interim, this chapter can give you a small sampling of the kind of theories that have been developed by using the social science approach and, to a lesser extent, the rhetorical approach.

Style Variables in the Public Context

A public speech is generally formal and may even, in the words of a great speaker, be a work of art. Extraordinary modes of expression are commonly used in this context. Skilled speakers know they must capture audience attention and present claims and arguments in unique and expressive ways. They often use figures of speech infrequently used in daily conversations, including alliteration, personification, repetition, extended metaphor, rhetorical questions, antitheses, and "literary" figures. John Wilson and Carroll Arnold say that such figures often "argue" as sharply as the arguments illustrated in logic and debate books.[26]

Weaver's Analysis of Grammatical Forms. Richard Weaver suggests that the grammatical forms a speaker uses can be effective in subtle ways.[27] He contends that simple sentences, for example, concentrate our attention on subject and predicate classes, presenting them as stable and substantial. Complex sentences, on the other hand, qualify the world, telling us that some ideas or objects are of more value than others. Complex sentences present ideas in relationship to one another, one detail dynamically emerging from another. Compound sentences show balance, and they suggest a symmetrical, settled view of the world as two ideas bid for equal attention.

Weaver also says individual parts of speech have complex and subtle effects. Nouns, he tells us, are substantial, expressing things "whose being is completed, not whose being is in process, or whose being depends upon some other being."[28] Adjectives, on the other hand, are less forceful and are secondary to the noun they describe. Adverbs are judgmental words, indicating the speaker's evaluations. Verbs are forceful and vigorous and can modify the acts they assert. For example, a speaker describing someone who is moving quickly can modify our view of that act by choosing from among words such as: hasten, rush, scramble, scurry, bolt, or flee. The choice of words and sentence types affects how a message is received. There is rhetorical force in grammatical categories. Just as a poet or novelist's choice of form affects message content, so the speaker's use of language provides subtle arguments for his or her points.

Spoken vs. Written Language. While language in the public context is often as carefully chosen as literary language, the two are not identical. Aristotle remarked, "It should be observed that each kind of rhetoric has its own appropriate style. The style of written prose is not that of spoken oratory, nor are those of political and forensic speaking the same."[29] Later on he suggests, "Compared with those of others, the speeches of professional writers sound thin in actual contexts. Those of orators, on the other hand, are good to hear spoken, but look amateurish enough when they pass into the hands of a reader."[30]

Wilson and Arnold suggest that good spoken style has the following characteristics: more personal pronouns, variety in sentence type and length, more simple sentences and sentence fragments, and more monosyllabic words. It often employs contractions, interjections, and familiar words. It also tends to use rhetorical questions, repetitions, indigenous language, connotative words, euphony, figurative language, and direct quotation.[31]

Intensity, Immediacy, and Diversity. Language style is important for several reasons: It captures audience attention, drives home points, and allows us to make inferences about the speaker and the speaker's intentions. James Bradac, John Waite Bowers, and John Courtwright tell us that "language expresses more than ideas. Effortlessly, automatically, receivers infer from speakers' language styles their attitudes, moods, and affiliations. Some evidence indicates that language in the form of connected discourse is an especially potent determinant of receivers' inferences about sources."[32]

If every speaker used the same style, then little information could be gleaned from language variables. Many features of language, however, vary among individuals and groups. An individual's background and group memberships, cognitive states, and other situationally determined factors vary the way he or she frames messages. These variations are of predictive use to observers. "As social animals, we generally can (and do) ignore safely that which is perfectly certain or predictable. But mutation, surprise, anomaly compels us to attend and explain. To make judgments, we must perceive differences."[33] Three language variables that give us this kind of information are language intensity, verbal immediacy, and lexical diversity.

Language intensity is defined as "the quality of language which indicates the degree to which the speaker's attitude toward a concept deviates from neutrality."[34] It indicates the emotion the speaker exhibits. For example, a speaker who describes the "total devastation" felt at someone's "despicable action" uses more intense language than one who says he or she is "somewhat taken aback" by another's "inappropriate behavior." There are several kinds of language intensity: language using highly charged connotative meanings, strong adjectives, obscenities, and opinionated statements.

Many experiments have studied the effects of a speaker's use of intense language on variables such as ratings of source credibility and amount of audience change. In addition, sex of speaker, audience and speaker's level of arousal, type of intensity (obscenity), and direction of message (pro or con audience beliefs) have also been found to modify the general effects of using intense language.[35]

Overall, the effects of intense language suggest a connection between intensity and stress. When speakers and listeners are under stress, they prefer low intensity language, presumably because intense expressions lead to additional arousal. If an audience is already aroused by a topic, then highly intense language is not recommended. Intense language, especially obscenity, can damage a speaker's competence ratings. Speakers with high credibility who agree with audience opinions may achieve attitude change through intensity, but they risk damaging their credibility by doing so. Generally, the person who can most successfully use intense language will be a credible male addressing an unaroused audience and advocating a position with which they agree. The least successful will be a low credibility female delivering a speech to an aroused, hostile audience.

Verbal immediacy is the degree to which speakers directly associate themselves with the message or the receivers. Immediacy measures psychological closeness. The more specific speakers are and the more they use spatial or temporal indicators of proximity (here versus there, now versus then), then the more immediate their language will be. Verbal immediacy can be increased by speakers' use of pronouns indicating inclusion (we versus you and I). Finally, speakers who choose a course of action as opposed to being forced into it (I want versus I may) are using immediate forms.[36] The person who says, "I'd like it if we could get together today to discuss the matter" is more immediate than one who says, "Perhaps you and I should talk about things sometime." The first signals involvement and liking, a psychological closeness between addresser and addressee. The second implies more distance.

Studies on the effects of verbal immediacy show that it generally leads to positive effects. Speakers who are immediate are seen as high in competence, character, and similarity. They are judged to be relaxed and positively disposed both to the audience and to message content. They are also judged to be similar to audience members, especially when the content of the message is congruent with audience attitudes.[37]

Lexical diversity indicates the range of a speaker's vocabulary. One way to measure lexical diversity is to compute the ratio of the number of different words to the total number of words employed. In a sense, lexical diversity is the opposite of redundancy; that is, the speaker who frequently repeats the same words has low lexical diversity. Studies on the effects of diversity show it to be positively associated with positive judgments of source's social class and competence. It is positively correlated with similarity to receivers and with message effectiveness and negatively correlated with stress. It also appears that the effects of diversity are strengthened when the source has high status.[38]

Overall, a speaker who shows diversity, exhibits immediacy, and refrains from high intensity under most conditions will be more successful than one who shows opposite characteristics.

Of course, many other language variables affect message acceptance. Charles Berger and James Bradac review several, including _familiarity and goodness_.[39] Certain words are familiar and acceptable, while others are unacceptable (sexually explicit words, or words related to death and decay). All else being equal, we value speakers who refrain from using taboo words and instead uses "charmed" words. _Grammatical choices_ also affect audience response, as does the use of _power words and phrases_. There is evidence that a powerful style leads to positive evaluations of communicator credibility and effectiveness. _Dialects_, _idiolects_, and _phonetic variations_ indicate class and ethnic membership and can affect audience evaluations of a speaker. Even _volume_ and _rate_ may reduce audience uncertainty.

Narrative Style in Public Discourse. Our discussion so far has emphasized single words rather than overall stylistic strategies. Narrative theory allows a more macroscopic view. As we saw earlier, people tell stories to make sense of events and of others. Speakers also make use of this universal form of perception by spinning narratives to convince their listeners. Rhetorical theorists and critics have begun to explore how speakers use narrative forms in public speech. They have also raised questions about the criteria for judging "narrative rationality," and there is a heated debate about whether narrative is a broad paradigm encompassing all symbolic action (as in Walter Fisher's narrative paradigm)[40] or whether it is best thought of in more limited ways as a particular form of discourse.[41] Research Abstract 10.3 illustrates the use of a narrative criticism of public address.

Public Communication and Message Appeals

A public speaker's purpose is often to convince the audience. To do so, he or she uses message appeals. Theorists divide message appeals as either emotional or logical, although admittedly, it is sometimes difficult to differentiate them. In the next section we will look at one of the most commonly studied of emotional appeals: the fear appeal.

Emotional Appeals: Inducing Fear. Research on fear appeals shows that factors affecting message acceptance are very complex. Single hypotheses that account for one variable at a time may oversimplify the issue. Originally, researchers thought that strong fear appeals should be avoided, because the resulting arousal would lead an audience into defensive avoidance. This proposition was based on research evidence showing the relationship between message acceptance and the intensity of fear appeals to be an inverted U. Low fear appeals were relatively ineffective, moderate fear appeals highly effective, and very

strong fear appeals ineffective. This conclusion was qualified by later research.

It is important at the outset to realize that fear appeals are part of a larger argumentative sequence. In using fear appeals, a speaker argues that a particular action will have adverse consequences if audience members refuse to adopt the speaker's recommendations. In this way, the speaker induces fear. He or she then provides assurances that the fear can be averted. The reassurances cause the attitude change, not fear induction itself. The speaker must, therefore, provide "information verifying the effectiveness of the remedy as well as specific instructions regarding the taking of recommended preventative measures."[42]

While, in general, moderate levels of fear are the most successful, this depends on the importance and relevance of the topic, the receivers' personalities, and the source's credibility. Extremely anxious people respond best to low levels of fear. When a topic is highly salient and is accompanied by simple instructions for avoiding the induced threat, strong appeals are most effective. High credibility sources may use higher levels of fear than low credibility sources. In general, we can say that it is not the short-term arousal that makes fear appeals so effective but rather the kind of long-term cognitive processing that accompanies them.[43] Research Abstract 10.4 presents a typical fear appeal study.

Rational Appeals: The Toulmin Model. While emotional arousal is one way to affect an audience, what is important is cognitive processing, and one way to ensure cognitive acceptance of a message is to present logical appeals. The Toulmin model helps us understand the structure of rational argument.[44] Stephen Toulmin was interested in the kind of working logic individuals use when they make arguments. The question he wanted to answer was, "What, then, is involved in establishing conclusions by the production of arguments?"[45] His model outlines the parts of an

RESEARCH ABSTRACT 10.3 Reagan as Hero and Storyteller

Whether or not people agreed with the policies of former President Ronald Reagan, there was general consensus that he was one of the West's most gifted communicators. Reagan could make mistakes and could appear inconsistent, yet his supporters remained loyal. What can account for his remarkable popularity? Lewis believes the answer lies in the predominance of narrative form in Reagan's speeches. Lewis' *purpose* was to examine how Reagan used stories to shape his message.

Reagan used two kinds of stories. He was adept at short anecdotes, jokes, and incidents that illustrated simple precepts; because the stories seemed true or true to life, audience members accepted their morals. Reagan also used a larger and more important type of story, the myth. Reagan's myth was a story about America, its origin and its destiny. Lewis believes that the Reagan myth showed America as a "chosen nation, grounded in its families and neighborhood, and driven inevitably forward by its heroic working people toward a world of freedom and economic progress unless blocked by moral or military weakness."

The narrative form is especially powerful because it encourages identification. In Reagan's narrative, ordinary audience members could see themselves either as the active participant who makes America strong or as the irresponsible onlooker who, through lack of faith, courage, hard work, and compassion, contributes to its decline. What is Reagan's place in the story? Reagan is at once the mythic hero, the active force who rights wrongs and protects the country, and the narrator, who realistically and simply tells us the truth of the story. According to Lewis, Reagan's popularity can be explained by his "exclusive and explicit reliance" on this single story.

What was important to the audience was the spell of the story. Reagan's inaccuracies were simply dismissed as unimportant details that did not affect the overall truth of the narrative. His failures in policy were also seen as unimportant when contrasted with the rightness of his aims. By using a mythic narrative, he deemphasized means in favor of noble ends. Finally, his narrative was grounded in simple, common-sense actions. He was the hero who realized that the solutions to problems were simple, although not easy. Thus his supporters could "recognize Reagan as 'no rocket scientist' and still respect his intelligence."

Lewis believes that Americans accepted Reagan's story. They wanted to see him both as the compassionate and courageous hero and as the realistic narrator. They also judged his errors from within the frame of the story, where they were relatively unimportant. Because his story reflected popular morals and common sense, it had enormous appeal.

Source: William F. Lewis, "Telling America's Story: Narrative Form and the Reagan Presidency," *Quarterly Journal of Speech*, 73 (1987), 280–302.

argument: claim, data, warrant, reservation, rebuttal, and backing.

When a speaker addresses an audience, he or she presents that audience with a *claim*. The speaker may assert, for example, that a given law is unfair, that a given proposal should be enacted, or that a given defendant is innocent or guilty. Although the speaker's claim may be accepted without question, he or she must be prepared to defend it by answering the question, "What have

RESEARCH ABSTRACT 10.4 The Use of Fear Appeals

Hewgill and Miller recognized that high fear appeals may be less effective than mild fear appeals if they cause subjects to employ defense mechanisms and thereby tune out the message. They reasoned, however, that under some circumstances, high fear appeals are more effective than mild. They thought this effect would occur when the speaker's credibility is high and when the threat is made not to the receiver but to the receiver's family, so they designed a message directing fear toward family members. They hypothesized that, with such a message, high fear appeals would be more effective if the speaker's initial credibility were high and that low fear appeals would be more effective if the speaker's initial credibility were low.

They used the following *methods*. The message was a taped question-and-answer interview in which a speaker advocated community fallout shelters rather than family shelters. All messages contained the same basic content, but, in the high fear conditions, 13 statements concerned physical injury or death to spouse and children. Credibility was manipulated by introducing the speaker either as (1) a professor of nuclear research or (2) a high school sophomore whose information came from a term paper. The four versions of the message (high fear/high credibility, high fear/low credibility, low fear/high credibility, and low fear/low credibility) were presented to 90 members of a PTA group in Flint, Michigan.

Each group was told the reseachers were considering using the interview to educate the public on fallout protection and that they needed personal reactions. Subjects filled out scales on concern for family during the message, attitudes to community and family fallout shelters, and perceptions of the speaker's competence, trustworthiness, and dynamism. To test treatment validity, the researchers examined levels of anxiety aroused by the message. Overall, the high fear conditon led to more anxiety than the low fear condition, but this difference was significant only for the high credibility speaker.

The *results* showed that, for the high credibility speaker, high fear appeals were more effective in producing attitude change than low fear appeals, as hypothesized. No attitude difference between types of appeals was found for the low credibility speaker, but this may have been due to a failure of the experimental induction in this condition. Regardless of this fact, the study was deemed a success in that "it is one of the few reported experimental results in which a highly threatening message was more effective than one posing a limited threat." It appears that source credibility is an important factor in the success of emotional appeals.

Source: Murray A. Hewgill and Gerald R. Miller, "Source Credibility and Response to Fear-Arousing Communications," *Speech Monographs*, 32 (1965), 95–101.

you got to go on?"[46] The answer to that question, the ground that supports the claim, is known as *data*. For example a lawyer's claim that a defendant is guilty of speeding must be supported with data: police testimony that the defendant was driving at 70 mph. A claim without data has no grounding and can be dismissed by an audience.

An argument can consist of a simple claim accompanied by data, or it can consist of more complex lines of reasoning. The listener needs to

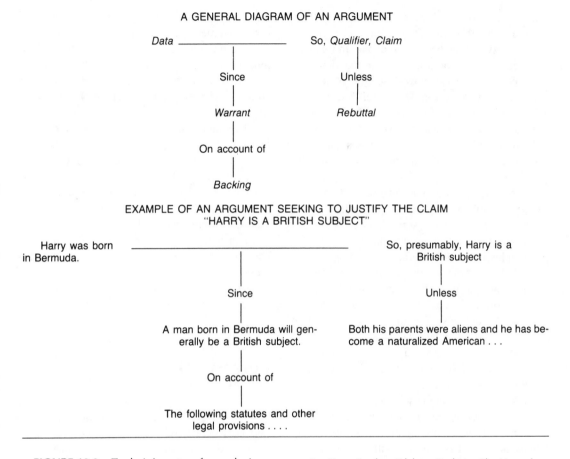

FIGURE 10.2: Toulmin's system for analyzing arguments. (From Stephen Edelston Toulmin, *The Uses of Argument* [Cambridge: Cambridge University Press, 1958] p. 99.)

know not only what data the speaker uses to back up a claim but also how data and claim are connected. This connection is called a *warrant*. The warrant for the claim that someone driving at 70 miles per hour in a zone where the posted limit is 55 can be found in the traffic laws. While we expect most jurors to know that it is illegal to disobey traffic signs in the United States, there are more complicated cases where jurors do not know the laws upon which a claim rests. In that case, the lawyer has to make the warrant explicit.

Toulmin suggests that data, warrant, and claim provide a skeletal outline of an argument. Figure 10.2 diagrams these basic parts of an argument by using an example provided by Toulmin. The data (Harry was born in Bermuda) leads to the claim (Harry is a British subject) because of the warrant (A man born in Bermuda will be a British subject).

Warrants differ in force. Some automatically lead to a claim, while others do not. Sometimes there are exceptions that may qualify a claim. Toulmin therefore introduced two more parts of an argument: *qualifiers* and *rebuttals*. To use Toulmin's example, the claim that someone holds a particular citizenship can usually be decided by knowing his or her place of birth; however, this is not true all the time. People may change their nationality or may be born to aliens. In that case, the claim will not follow from the data. The speaker must always know the degree of certainty associated with a claim. In Toulmin's example in Fig. 10.2, the qualifier "presumably" is added because there are exceptions under which the claim might be set aside (if Harry has applied for a new citizenship or if his parents were not British).

One final question that may occur to an audience is why the warrant is justified. Standing behind each warrant is some kind of *backing*. A warrant that "a whale is a mammal" is backed by principles of zoological classification. A warrant that "a Saudi Arabian will generally be a Muslim" can be backed by statistics about the distribution of religious beliefs in Saudi Arabia. If the warrant is that "Bermudans are British subjects," then the backing is based on legal statutes.

While the only necessary parts of an argument are data and claim, speakers may need to complete the rest of their arguments. The explicitness of a speaker's reasoning will depend on the audience. For some audiences, a speaker may need to provide the entire argument, including reservations and rebuttal. Others will accept a claim based only on a small amount of data. In any case, speakers who have a clear argument and a carefully identified warrant, backing, and rebuttal are better equipped to argue logically, regardless of how explicitly they present their argument in the speech.

Message Placement and Organization

In addition to language style and use of appeals, a final aspect of public messages involves placement and organization. Messages must be structured and appeals presented appropriately. Introductory texts on public speaking contain standard patterns of speech organization. For example, a speaker can organize a speech in time, space, or topic order or use a problem solution or motivated

sequence pattern.[46] Simply put, a structured and organized message is more effective than a disorganized one. In organizing a speech, the speaker must decide how to place arguments so that they have maximum impact. Figure 10.3 summarizes common wisdom on the effects of placement and organization.

The goal of this chapter has not been to report all of the findings on the effects of message variables. Rather it has been to illustrate the nature of research in the field. Unfortunately, much of this work has consisted of testing single propositions about the effects of one or two variables rather than developing more global theories. Still, we can consider these isolated findings as potential components of an overall prescriptive model of message effects in the public context. Certainly, message choices affect audience willingness to accept or reject a speaker's message.

OUTCOME ACHIEVEMENT: HOW CAN WE PREDICT ATTITUDE CHANGE?

A large part of public communication theory is persuasive. Because chapter 7 reviewed general theories of motivation and social influence, we will not repeat them here. In this section we will examine two new theories that predict the amount and direction of change after exposure to persuasion. Both suggest that the initial attitudes of audience members are powerful determinants of the amount of attitude change a speaker can achieve.

Social Judgment-Involvement Theory

Muzafer Sherif and his colleagues in the Yale Attitude group developed a theory of attitude change based on the nature of social judgments.[47] They argue that when audience members receive a message, they need to evaluate it. To do so, they compare the message to preexisting opinions and attitudes that serve as *anchor points*. A receiver's

Guidelines for Presenting Arguments

One–sided vs. Two–sided Arguments:
Present one side of the argument when the audience is generally friendly, when your position is the only one that will be presented, or when you want immediate, though temporary, opinion change.
Present both sides of the argument when the audience disagrees with you, or when it is probable the audience will hear the other side of the argument from another source.

Speaking Order:
When opposite views are presented one after another, the one presented last will probably be more effective. (The greater impact of what comes first is called a primacy effect; the greater effectiveness of the last message is a recency effect.) Primacy effects predominate when the second side immediately follows the first; recency effects predominate when the opinion measures come immediately after the second side.

Drawing Conclusions:
You will probably cause more opinion change if you explicitly state your conclusions rather than let the audience draw their own, except when they are intelligent. Then, implicit conclusion drawing is better.

Placement of Arguments:
It is inconclusive whether the opening or closing parts of a speech should contain the more important material.

Distractions and Forewarnings:
Cues that forewarn the audience of the speaker's manipulative intent increase resistance to it, while distractors simultaneously presented with the message decrease resistance.

FIGURE 10.3: Evidence on the effects of some common variables. (Taken from Philip G. Zimbardo, Ebbe B. Ebbeson, and Christina Maslach, *Influencing Attitudes and Changing Behavior*, 2nd ed. [Reading, Mass.: Addison-Wesley, 1977] pp. 98–99.)

anchors determine how much he or she will change after a persuasive message.

Anchors, or reference points, are necessary to make any kind of judgment. For example, if you were asked to guess how heavy a set of weights is, with no objective means to produce an answer you would rate them by comparing them. If you were told that one weighed five pounds, then you would use that as an anchor, estimating the heaviness of the other in comparison. All judgments are, in essence, comparative. In the middle of winter, 50 degrees feels quite warm. In the middle of summer, it would feel cold. Judgments, then, are always relative.

Research on the judgments of the weight of physical objects showed Sherif that subjects often distort their judgments in relation to their anchor points. Objects similar to an anchor are judged closer than they actually are. This is called an *assimilation effect*. Objects divergent from an anchor are judged as farther away than they actu-

ally are. This is called a *contrast effect*. Comparisons to anchors, then, lead subjects to overestimate or underestimate the properties of objects.

Sherif believed that the same effects occur with social judgments. Audience members use anchors to judge messages, and these anchors force assimilation or contrast effects. If you are an advocate of women's rights, for example, then you may perceive a speaker who favors equal rights legislation as being just as committed as you, even though this may not be the case. You may view another speaker, one who is generally favorable but who raises some objections to the legislation, as extremely negative. Your response to these speakers depends on how far their positions are from your reference point.

How can a speaker predict whether assimilation or contrast will occur? Sherif and colleagues suggest that audience attitudes on any given topic be placed along a continuum from highly favorable to highly unfavorable. Somewhere along that

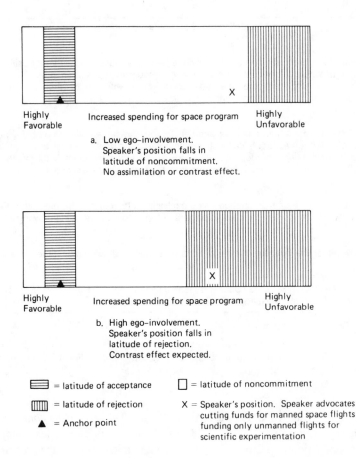

a. Low ego–involvement.
   Speaker's position falls in
   latitude of noncommitment.
   No assimilation or contrast effect.

b. High ego–involvement.
   Speaker's position falls in
   latitude of rejection.
   Contrast effect expected.

≡ = latitude of acceptance   ☐ = latitude of noncommitment

▥ = latitude of rejection   X = Speaker's position. Speaker advocates
cutting funds for manned space flights
▲ = Anchor point   funding only unmanned flights for
scientific experimentation

FIGURE 10.4: Latitudes of acceptance, noncommitment, and rejection

continuum lies the audience member's anchor point: the position closest to his or her stand on that topic. Surrounding the anchor is the *latitude of acceptance*, all other positions that are also acceptable to the audience member. The continuum also contains the *latitude of rejection*, made up of all positions that are totally unacceptable. Between the two is the *latitude of noncommitment*, the positions about which the receiver is undecided or ambiguous.[48]

Assume that the topic of a speech is the amount of money to be budgeted for the space program. At one end of the continuum is the position advocating large expenditures for manned space flight. At the other is the position that space program funding should be cut. Between the two are more moderate positions. The position closest to an audience member's thinking is his or her anchor. Assume that a segment of the audience favor increased spending but think space exploration should not be a top governmental priority. This is their anchor. The positions that they also find acceptable constitute their latitude of acceptance, and those they find unacceptable are their latitude of rejection. Figure 10.4 indicates this situation.

If a speaker advocates a position within our audience members' latitudes of acceptance, then assimilation occurs. The message will be favorably perceived, although attitude change will not be great since speaker and listeners already agree. If the speaker advocates a position within the audience members' latitudes of rejection, contrast occurs: The message will appear more divergent than it actually is, resulting in a boomerang effect. A speaker advocating a position within members' latitudes of noncommitment has the greatest potential for change, simply because there is more room for movement.

Individuals differ in the relative size of their latitudes of acceptance and rejection. One person may be very accepting, and another may reject all positions that deviate from his or her own attitudes. *Ego involvement* is one factor determining the shape of our latitudes of acceptance and rejection. A person who is personally affected by a policy (in our example, a person who works for NASA or who is an aeronautical engineer) will be more ego involved in the topic of space exploration than the average person. Research shows that those who are ego involved not only have wider latitudes of rejection but have stronger anchor points, use fewer categories to process information, and show greater assimilation/contrast effects. Those highly ego involved are more resistant to persuasion than those less ego involved. A public speaker can understand an audience better by considering both their current positions and the strength of their ego involvement. With a highly involved audience, the speaker should advocate moderate rather than extreme views.

Congruity Theory

Attitude change theories are theories of evolution since they emphasize how speakers can modify audience beliefs over time. Congruity theory makes this explicit, saying that attitude change is not only a function of the speaker's position but also a function of his or her credibility.[49] Using these factors, it tries to predict the direction and the amount of change that will occur as a result of persuasive messages.

At heart, congruity theory is a balance theory, for it holds that individuals need to maintain a stable and balanced world view. It assumes that an individual will feel uncomfortable when valued sources advocate positions that are not valued. Generally, people are attracted to similar others. If someone we admire and respect differs from us on a pertinent topic, then we lose our cognitive balance and must do something to restore it.

For example, assume a friend suddenly takes a moral position you find reprehensible (say the friend advocates cheating on taxes). This is likely to make you feel uncomfortable. You may be torn between thinking that your friend is wrong and thinking that cheating is justified. Balance theories suggest that you will reevaluate either your friend or the issue on which you disagree. Balance predictions also apply to the public context. The same kind of conflict you felt when you found your friend cheating will occur when you discover that an admired source advocates a position you dislike. Some sort of attitude change will have to occur. Congruity theory predicts the kind and amount of change.

According to congruity theory, two relationships may exist between a source and an attitude object. The source may advocate the attitude object, in which case an *associative bond* exists, or the source may oppose the object, resulting in a *dissociative bond*. Let us begin with associative bonds. Assume, for example, that political candidate Jones advocates raising taxes. If your attitude toward both Jones and the tax proposal is the same, then a congruity exists, and you feel no pressure to change. If, on a scale from −3 to +3 you rate Jones as a +3 and rate raising taxes as a +3, then your cognitive system will be perfectly balanced. If, however, you evaluate Jones as a +3 but your feelings about tax increases is only a mild +1, some imbalance will be felt. Any deviations between your ratings of source and attitude object, no matter how slight, will result in a state of imbalance.

Since you feel pressured to change, you have two options. You can lower your estimation of

Jones or you can increase your estimation of Jones's tax proposal. What congruity theory suggests, and what makes it unique from other balance theories, is that you will change your ratings of *both* source and issue. Your positive attitude about Jones will increase slightly your attitude toward the tax proposal. At the same time, your uncertainty about Jones's proposal will decrease Jones's popularity. Think of source and attitude evaluations as weights placed on an old-fashioned scale. If the weights are uneven, the scale will be out of balance. The only way to restore balance is to add more weight to the light side, and subtract some weight from the heavy side so that both are equal.

But where is the point at which balance will be reestablished? According to congruity theory, the balance point between a source valued as a +3 and an attitude object valued as a +1 turns out to be +2.5. You may ask why the balance point is not a +2, as this is halfway between the +3 and +1. Congruity theory says that the more extreme evaluation will exert greater influence than the less extreme evaluation. Because, in our example, the source was originally more highly valued, it will move less; and because the attitude object was less extreme, it will move more. Congruity theory provides a mathematical formula to predict the balance point in any situation:

$$R_o = \frac{|A_o|}{|A_o| + |A_s|} A_o + (d) \frac{|A_s|}{|A_o| + |A_s|} A_s$$

where R_o = the balance point or resolution for the attitude object

A_o = the original attitude toward the object

A_s = the original attitude toward the source

d = whether the bond between source and object is associative (+1) or dissociative (−1)

Figure 10.5 shows the computations for the example we have been using.

So far we have only examined associative bonds. What about dissociative ones, bonds in which a source *opposes* an attitude object? The balance point for dissociative bonds occurs when

attitude toward source is the mirror image of attitude toward the issue. If, for example, a highly admired source argues against a position that you also dislike, then a perfect state of equilibrium exists. For example, say you rate candidate Jones as +3 and a proposal for increased military spending as a −3, and Jones comes out against military spending. Any deviation from this situation, however, is imbalanced and produces pressures to realign attitudes. Assume that a +3 source, candidate Jones, gives a speech that strongly opposes equal pay for equal work, an issue that you agree with and rate a +2. This is a highly imbalanced state for you, and once again you will have to resolve it. Figure 10.5 shows what will happen. You will realign your attitudes so that Jones ends up as a +1 and the proposal as a −1. Jones drops two points in your estimation, while the idea of equal pay for equal work drops three points. Because there is a dissociative bond you end up devaluing both source and attitude object.

Research findings generally agree about the direction of change although the actual numbers deviate from the predictions of the congruity formulas. This has led Charles Osgood and Percy Tannenbaum to add two correction factors. The correction for incredulity accounts for the tendency to disbelieve that sources we value disagree with us. The assertion constant accounts for a tendency to adjust our attitudes toward issues more than our attitudes toward sources.[50]

Determining the exact balance point is less important than realizing that attitudes toward both sources and the positions they advocate will change as a result of persuasive messages. The implications are many. Congruity theory can explain the ebb and flow of a speaker's credibility as he or she advocates various positions. A politician, for example, forms many bonds during a campaign. His or her popularity will decrease as he or she advocates unpopular ideas and opposes popular issues. The politician can increase it by favoring admired attitude objects (motherhood and apple pie) and by denouncing unpopular issues (crime and drugs). He or she can also

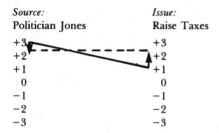

Source:
Politician Jones

Issue:
Raise Taxes

Example of an associative bond: Jones advocates raising taxes. Jones' original rating is +3; original rating of tax raise is +1.

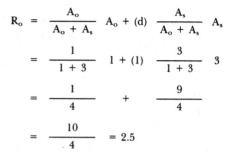

$$R_o = \frac{A_o}{A_o + A_s} \; A_o + (d) \; \frac{A_s}{A_o + A_s} \; A_s$$

$$= \frac{1}{1 + 3} \; 1 + (1) \; \frac{3}{1 + 3} \; 3$$

$$= \frac{1}{4} \quad + \quad \frac{9}{4}$$

$$= \frac{10}{4} \; = 2.5$$

Resolution Point = 2.5. After the message, both Jones and the policy of raising taxes are rated +2.5.

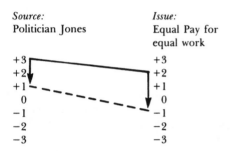

Source:
Politician Jones

Issue:
Equal Pay for
equal work

Example of a dissociative Bond: Jones comes out against equal pay for equal work. Jones' original rating is +3; original rating of issue is +2.

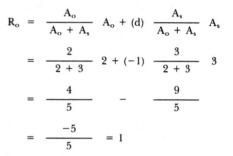

$$R_o = \frac{A_o}{A_o + A_s} \; A_o + (d) \; \frac{A_s}{A_o + A_s} \; A_s$$

$$= \frac{2}{2 + 3} \; 2 + (-1) \; \frac{3}{2 + 3} \; 3$$

$$= \frac{4}{5} \quad - \quad \frac{9}{5}$$

$$= \frac{-5}{5} \; = 1$$

Resolution Point = −1. After the message, Jones is rated +1, while equal pay for equal work is rated −1.

FIGURE 10.5: Computation of resolution points, congruity theory (without correction for incredulity). (See Kenneth K. Sereno and Edward M. Bodaken, *Trans-Per: Understanding Human Communication* [Boston: Houghton Mifflin, 1975], for similar graphic illustrations and for additional examples.)

increase in popularity by associating with celebrities or popular political figures. Of course, popular figures must be careful not to endorse too many unpopular candidates, since they could lose their own credibility.

Conversely, congruity theory can predict what will happen if an unpopular or neutral attitude object is repeatedly associated with popular sources. We can expect it to increase gradually in popularity as the prestige of the various sources rubs off. There is a dynamic balance between source and issue that constantly changes over time as receivers work toward equilibrium.

REFERENCES

1. Kenneth Burke, *A Grammar of Motives* (Berkeley and Los Angeles: University of California Press, 1969).

2. *Ibid.*, p. xv.

3. Charles U. Larson, *Persuasion: Reception and Responsibility*, 2nd ed. (Belmont, Calif.: Wadsworth, 1979), p. 46.

4. *Ibid.*, p. 27.

5. Burke, *Grammar of Motives*, pp. 3–20.

6. See for example, Carl I. Hovland, Irving L. Janis, and Harold H. Kelley, *Communication and Per-*

suasion (New Haven: Yale University Press, 1953); Carl I. Hovland and others, *The Order of Presentation in Persuasion* (New Haven: Yale University Press, 1957); Irving L. Janis and others, *Personality and Persuasibility* (New Haven: Yale University Press, 1959).

7. Hovland, Janis, and Kelley, *Communication and Persuasion*, p. 6.

8. *Ibid.*, pp. 7–8.

9. Aristotle, *Rhetoric*, trans. W. Rhys Roberts and *Poetics*, trans. Ingram Bywater (New York: The Modern Library, 1954), pp. 24–25.

10. *Ibid.*

11. Edward Rogge and James C. Ching, *Advanced Public Speaking* (New York: Holt, Rinehart & Winston, 1966), p. 210.

12. *Ibid.*, pp. 212–14.

13. Hovland, Janis and Kelley, *Communication and Persuasion*, p. 20.

14. *Ibid.*, p. 21.

15. *Ibid.*, p. 37.

16. Carl I. Hovland and W. A. Weiss, "The Influence of Source Credibility on Communicative Effectiveness," *Public Opinion Quarterly*, 15 (1951), 635–50.

17. David K. Berlo, James B. Lemert, and Robert J. Mertz, "Dimensions for Evaluating the Acceptability of Message Sources," *Public Opinion Quarterly*, 15 (1951), 565–76.

18. *Ibid.*, p. 575.

19. *Ibid.*, p. 576.

20. James C. McCroskey and Lawrence R. Wheeles, *Introduction to Human Communication* (Boston: Allyn & Bacon, 1976), pp. 103–05.

21. Roderick P. Hart, Gustav W. Friedrich, and William D. Brooks, "Source Credibility," in *Contexts of Communication*, ed. Jean Civikly (New York: Holt, Rinehart & Winston, 1981).

22. Gary Cronkhite and Jo Liska, "A Critique of Factor Analytic Approaches to the Study of Credibility," *Communication Monographs*, 43 (June 1976), 91–107.

23. *Ibid.*, p. 94.

24. *Ibid.*, p. 96.

25. Gerald R. Miller and Michael Burgoon, "Persuasion Research; Review and Commentary," *Communication Yearbook II*, ed. Brent D. Ruben (New Brunswick, N. J.: Transaction Books, 1979).

26. John F. Wilson and Carroll C. Arnold, *Public Speaking as a Liberal Art*, 3rd ed. (Boston: Allyn & Bacon, 1974), p. 239.

27. Richard M. Weaver, "Some Rhetorical Aspects of Grammatical Categories," in *Methods of Rhetorical Criticism: A Twentieth Century Perspective*, 2nd ed., eds. Bernard L. Brock and Robert L. Scott (Detroit: Wayne State University Press, 1972).

28. *Ibid*, p. 287.

29. Aristotle, *Rhetoric*, p. 96.

30. *Ibid.*, p. 197.

31. Wilson and Arnold, *Public Speaking*, pp. 225–26.

32. James J. Bradac, John Waite Bowers, and John A. Courtright, "Lexical Variations in Intensity, Immediacy, and Diversity: An Axiomatic Theory and Causal Model," in *The Social and Psychological Contexts of Language*, eds. Robert N. St. Clair and Howard Giles (Hillsdale, N. J.: Lawrence Erlbaum Associates, 1980), p. 193.

33. *Ibid.*, p. 195.

34. John Waite Bowers, "Language Intensity, Social Introversion, and Attitude Change," *Speech Monographs*, 30 (1963), 345.

35. Bradac, Bowers, and Courtright, "Lexical Variations," pp. 197–202.

36. Albert Mehrabian, "Attitudes Inferred from Nonimmediacy of Verbal Communications," *Journal of Verbal Learning and Verbal Behavior*, 6 (1967), 294–95. See also Charles R. Berger and James J. Bradac, *Language and Social Knowledge: Uncertainty in Interpersonal Relations* (London: Edward Arnold, 1982), p. 57.

37. Bradac, Bowers, and Courtright, "Lexical Variations," pp. 203–04.

38. *Ibid.*, p. 205–07.

39. Berger and Bradac, *Language and Social Knowledge*, pp. 57–66.

40. Walter R. Fisher, "Clarifying the Narrative Paradigm," *Communication Monographs*, 56 (March 1989), 55–58; Walter R. Fisher, "The Narrative Paradigm and the Interpretation and Assessment

of Historical Texts," *Argumentation and Advocacy*, 25 (1988), 49–53; Walter R. Fisher, "Narration as a Human Communication Paradigm: The Case of Public Moral Argument," *Communication Monographs*, 51 (1987), 1–22.

41. Robert C. Rowland, "Narrative: Mode of Discourse or Paradigm?", *Communication Monographs*, 54 (September 1987), 264–75; Robert C. Rowland, "On Limiting the Narrative Paradigm: Three Case Studies," *Communication Monographs*, 56 (March 1989), 39–54.

42. Mary John Smith, *Persuasion and Human Action: A Review and Critique of Social Influence Theory* (Belmont, Calif.: Wadsworth, 1982), p. 232.

43. *Ibid.*, p. 232.

44. Stephen Edelston Toulmin, *The Uses of Argument* (Cambridge: Cambridge University Press, 1958).

45. *Ibid.*, p. 97.

46. See for example, Alan H. Monroe and Douglas Ehninger, *Principles and Types of Speech Communication* (Glenview, Ill.: Scott, Foresman, 1974).

47. Carolyn W. Sherif, Muzafer Sherif, and Robert E. Nebergall, *Attitude and Attitude Change: The Social Judgment-Involvement Approach* (Philadelphia: W. B. Saunders, 1965); Muzafer Sherif and Carl I. Hovland, *Social Judgment: Assimilation and Contrast Effects in Communication and Attitude Change* (New Haven: Yale University Press, 1961); Muzafer Sherif and Carolyn W. Sherif, "Attitude as the Individual's Own Categories: The Social Judgment-Involvement Approach to Attitude and Attitude Change," in *Attitude, Ego-Involvement and Change*, eds. Carolyn W. Sherif and Muzafer Sherif (New York: John Wiley & Sons, 1967).

48. Sherif and Sherif, "Attitude as the Individual's Own Categories," p. 115.

49. For a discussion of congruity theory see Percy H. Tannenbaum, "The Congruity Principle Revisited: Studies in the Reduction, Induction, and Generalization of Persuasion," in *Advances in Experimental Social Psychology*, vol. 3, ed. Leonard Berkowitz (New York: Academic, 1967). See also the discussion on congruity and balance in Kenneth K. Sereno and Edward M. Bodaken, *Trans-Per: Understanding Human Communication* (Boston: Houghton Mifflin, 1975).

50. Charles E. Osgood and Percy H. Tannenbaum, "The Principles of Congruity in the Prediction of Attitude Change," *Psychological Review*, 62 (1955), 42–55.

appendix A

EVALUATING MODELS

COMMON SENSE MODEL BUILDING

The process of creating models (or sets of interrelated guesses about how the world and the people in it operate) is not mysterious. We constantly try to explain, predict, and control the world around us. Indeed, we cannot make decisions about our actions without using common sense models, many of which are prompted by practical problems. You probably already have rules of thumb, stock solutions, or stereotyped judgments you use to guide your actions in everyday situations. These rules may not be very sophisticated or very just, but they are rudimentary theories about human actions. For example, you may have developed the rule, "people who come from a common background have a better chance for building a successful relationship than people who are different," or "people who return direct eye contact are indicating interest." These rules help you decide about other people. Because these propositions are guesses about others' motivations or qualities, they are implicit models of social action.

Not all models are prompted by practical problems. Sometimes we ask questions simply because we want to know facts. Thus, we may ask ourselves, "Do women use language differently from men?" or "What are the effects of using different methods of presenting evidence in an informative speech?" These are what Julienne Ford calls factual questions. Finally, some questions simply arise from the desire to understand why. When we ask questions like, "Why do some relationships grow while others deteriorate?" or "Why do people join groups?" or "Why are some people chosen as leaders?" we are motivated by theoretical problems.[1] Any attempt to understand and control the world is a form of theorizing or model building. Whether we are trying to solve practical problems, factual problems, or theoretical problems, we spend much of our time in constructing common sense models of reality.

SCIENTIFIC MODEL BUILDING

There are two major differences between common sense solutions and those proposed by scientists. First, scientists use a more systematic, objective set of criteria to develop and criticize their models; and second, true scientific model building seeks to answer the theoretical "why" questions. Irwin Deutscher argues that science must do more than predict, it must explain:

One may accurately predict without ever understanding why the prediction works. Malaria, for example, could be related to the presence of stagnant water in warm climates and effectively brought under control with no knowledge of the particular breed of mosquito that carried it, much less any knowledge of what that mosquito carried. This is effective and valuable social action in the public health arena; it has nothing to do with science. Nehemia Jordan, in a personal communication, puts it this way:

Imagine the green man from Mars coming in his space ship and giving us the gift we have all been looking for—the perfect computer. The computer is an unopenable black box with two slots, one for inputting the questions and the other for outputting empirical predictions to observable events. Perfect prediction is observed. Does this toll the death knoll for science? Not at all. The scientists of the existing disciplines will be compelled to try to figure out why the predictions are correct. And a new science will undoubtedly develop to try to answer the most burning question of them all. The name of this science will be a Graeco-Latin neologism which will mean: "How the hell does this damn black box work?"[2]

While common sense model building may consist of reaching into one's storehouse of knowledge for an explanation that fits the situation and that satisfies one's curiosity, the scientific process must be more objective and more rigorous. The scientific model's goal is to generate explanatory hypotheses that may be tested through careful observation.

STEPS IN BUILDING MODELS

The basic logic of model building is simple. Charles Lave and James March break the process down into four simple steps:

Step 1
Observe some facts.

Step 2
Look at the facts as though they were the end result of some unknown process (model). *Then speculate about the processes that might have produced such a result.*

Step 3
Then *deduce other results* (implications/consequences/predictions) *from the model.*

Step 4
Then ask yourself *whether these other implications are true and produce new models if necessary.*[3]

Let us take an example of a model and follow it through the four steps.[4]

Step 1: Observing

The first step in model building involves observing a fact or series of related facts. These facts should be of a special kind; they should be what Robert Dubin calls *phenomena.*[5] Dubin distinguishes between facts that are *historical events* because they occur only once and those that are *phenomena* because they are likely to be repeated and related to other facts. The scientist is more interested in reoccurring facts than in one-of-a-kind occurrences. For example, an argument between you and your brother is a single event and is not the stuff of which important theories are made. However, if the fight is an example of a wider class of occurrences—sibling rivalry—then you have a phenomenon about which a theory may be built.

Consider two observations of phenomena, one made by Tertullian in the third century A.D., the second made early in the twentieth century by several social scientists:

Observation one: If the Tiber overflows into the city, if the Nile does not flow into the countryside, if the heavens remain unmoved, if the earth quakes, if there is famine and pestilence, at once the cry goes up: "To the lions with the Christians."

Observation two: If the per-acre value of cotton in the southeastern section of the United States is low, the number of lynchings of Negroes in the area is high.[6]

A few moments' consideration should show that these two observations bear a striking resemblance to one another and describe an important social phenomenon. Both imply that "catastrophe leads to persecution" and both have important social consequences. They are excellent observations for theory building.

Step 2: Explaining

The scientist must next develop a general explanation from which the observed facts, and others, may be logically deduced. Let us consider two possible explanations for the observed facts. The first is as follows: "Catastrophe is a sign of the gods' displeasure. Their wrath may be placated by sacrificing those who angered them. The observed tortures and lynchings were ways members of both societies defer divine judgment." Let us call this the divine placation hypothesis. While this model explains the facts, it would probably not be accepted by very many today. Fortunately, a more general and more satisfactory model has been developed to account for the observations. This model, originally developed by Dollard and others in 1939, is known as the frustration-aggression hypothesis.[7] It states, "When frustrated, individuals direct aggression toward the agent seen as the source of frustration; however, when direct aggressive acts are inhibited, aggression will be displaced onto other members of a society." The observed aggression is explained by economic conditions that lead to frustration. Direct attacks against society, however, were inhibited, and thus the aggressive impulses were directed against marginal low power groups (in our examples, Christians and Blacks).

Alternate models are always available, some better than others. As Julienne Ford points out, models are like fairy tales: They are stories designed to explain observable facts and "there is

nothing whatever to prevent you from inventing a totally different story to explain the same facts."[8] Models are products of the scientists who create them. They must be continually tested, criticized, and revised.

Step 3: Predicting

Lave and March's third step is to find other cases that fit the model and make predictions about them. The frustration-aggression hypothesis can be used to make predictions about sibling aggression in response to parental punishment or the conditions leading to child abuse. It also predicts that an "attack on the actual cause of frustration may be a more successful means of preventing persecution than steps aimed directly at the persecution itself."[9]

March and Lave say:

In ordinary thinking when we have a result to explain, we are usually content to think of some simple explanation and then stop. This is incomplete thinking; it stops before the process is fully carried out. The real fun is to continue thinking and see what other ideas the explanation can generate, to ask ourselves: *If this explanation is correct, what else would it imply?*[10]

Step 4: Testing

The final step is determining whether step three predictions hold true in the world of observable events. The scientist does this by conducting research to determine whether the model should be rejected or refined. Appendix B discusses some of the ways this kind of research may be accomplished.

WHAT MAKES A GOOD MODEL?

Following the steps in model building does not guarantee correct outcomes. Models are constantly being revised, abandoned, or replaced by newer ones. As a consumer of theories, you must be able to critique the models you encounter. In this section we look at some of the ways theories and models may be evaluated. Perhaps the best way to go about this is to ask the question: What makes a good model?

A Good Model Is Risky

The most important criterion for a model is that it be testable: Its predictions must match observable facts. Models which are not open to empirical test may be right or wrong, but they are not scientific. An instance of this kind of nonscientific thinking appears in an example given by Lave and March:

When the Rain Dance ceremony is properly performed, *and all the participants have pure hearts*, it will bring rain.[11]

There is something scientifically wrong with this model. The problem is not that it cannot be *proved* through observation but rather that it cannot be *disproved*. If the ceremony is performed and it rains, then the model is verified; but, if the ceremony is performed and it does not rain, then the model is also verified. The rainmaker simply says that the lack of rain proves some participants were not pure of heart. In the absence of any way of determining purity of intentions, the model cannot be disproved. This model does not open itself to risk. Thus, it exists in the realm of magic not in the realm of science.

Many others examples exist. Self-styled psychics use a similar argument. When their predictions fail, they often say that someone in the room (usually a scientist) produced "bad vibrations" that spoiled the prediction. Or, take the proposition, "people always act in their own self-interest." Whenever you try to give a counter example (for example, when you say, "What about Mother Teresa's work with the poor?"), your opponent is likely to say, "She wouldn't do it if it weren't in her own interests to do so."

There are two points to remember. First, a model based on circular reasoning is a bad one. Second, no model can ever be proved. Attempts to prove theory by pointing to corroborating instances are never adequate tests, for a clever person can always come up with another model that would equally well explain the corroborating observations. Then, how can scientific models be proved through observation? The answer is that scientists do not try to prove their theories. They try to disprove or falsify them. Scientists try to make observations which, from the model's standpoint, are absolutely forbidden to appear. If these observations do appear, the scientist must be willing to discard or modify the theory and again attempt to disprove it. This idea is known as *falsification* and was developed by the philosopher Karl Popper.[12] Popper believes that the only statement that can be made about the truth of a model is whether it has or has not been falsified. As Ford points out, however, "this does not mean that there is no point in testing theories, for the more tests a theory has withstood, the better basis it affords for making predictions about the events in the real world."[13]

A Good Model Is Simple

A second important criterion of a good model is its simplicity. A simple, or *parsimonious*, model is preferable to a complicated one. To understand this more fully, consider the case in Fig. A.1. Lave and March propose two models to explain the behavior in the figure.[14] The first says that "individuals have innate preferences for walking in a clockwise or counterclockwise direction. Among a group of neighbors these preferences will be shared. Group A prefers to go clockwise to shop and counterclockwise to pray. Group C prefers the opposite. Group B prefers always to go counterclockwise. Group D prefers the opposite."[15] With some ingenuity, this model could be tested (one way might be to move the locations of church and store and observe the results). Its problem is not that it is not testable but that it is overly complicated. A simpler model based on fewer assumptions is preferable; for example:

THE CASE OF THE LAZY VILLAGERS

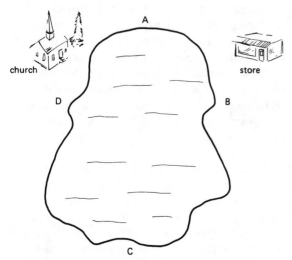

"All of the people in the village live along the shore of the lake, and a visiting anthropologist has noticed that they can be divided into four groups:

Group A
Lives on the north end of the lake. A-type people generally travel clockwise to the store and counterclockwise to the church.

Group B
Lives on the east shore of the lake. B-type people generally travel in a counterclockwise direction regardless of where they are going.

Group C
Lives on the south shore of the lake. C-type people generally travel clockwise to the church and counterclockwise to the store.

Group D
Lives on the west shore of the lake. D-type people generally travel in a clockwise direction regardless to where they are going."

FIGURE A.1: Map of hypothetical village describing behaviors of the groups living in the village. (From Charles A. Lave and James G. March, *An Introduction to Models in the Social Sciences* [New York: Harper & Row, 1975], p. 62.)

"Humans try to accomplish their goals with the least possible effort."[16] Be suspicious of overly complicated models that make unnecessary assumptions. Try to simplify them by finding more direct and efficient ways to explain phenomena.

A Good Model Is Novel and Productive

A good model should be simple but not simpleminded: It should yield non-obvious predictions. A scientific model should be capable of surprising us with its implications: The more trite it is, the less acceptable it is. One model that fits the novelty criterion is dissonance theory. Its beauty is that it allows us to make counterintuitive predictions. Dissonance theory may not pass all of the tests of a good model, but it clearly exhibits novelty.

A good model is also productive, capable of generating a whole series of interesting predictions. It is applicable to many different events. The frustration-aggression hypothesis is productive because it allows us to understand a series of events, from why Fred kicks the cat when he is mad to instances of racial prejudice. The frustration-agression hypothesis applies to any case in which goal-directed behaviors are blocked. It is general and, therefore, productive. When you examine a model, ask whether it tells you anything new—whether it results in genuinely interesting predictions. If it does not, then it is probably not a good model, and you should look for one which is more novel and more productive.

A Good Model Exhibits Adequacy

So far, the rules for judging models apply to both the natural and social sciences. The social scientist, however, observes different events than does the natural scientist. One of his or her goals is to examine how people explain their own and others' behavior. Alfred Schutz points out that while atoms and electrons do not create meanings, people do. The social scientist often creates models to explain how these meanings are created.[17]

Goals, for example, are abstract concepts created by human beings to explain actions. Models of goals are one step farther removed. When social scientists create models involving second-order concepts such as "goals," "frustration," or "trust," they must make sure that these second-order explanations are adequately related to the first-order explanations. Alfred Schutz explains: "each term in…a scientific model of human action must be constructed…[so] that a human act performed within the real world by an individual actor as indicated by the typical construct [in the theory] would be understandable to the actor himself as well as to his fellow-men in terms of common-sense interpretations of everyday life."[18] The idea that scientific concepts of social action must be founded on common sense concepts is known as the postulate of adequacy.

There is controversy about whether adequacy should be a criterion of a good theory. If we take it to mean that theoretical constructs should all be recognizable as stated by social actors, then it probably should not, for it is clear that social actors cannot always be relied upon to understand the nature of their own motivations and actions. However, if adequacy means that social scientific constructs should realistically reflect the actions on which they are based, then it seems reasonable to include this as a criterion of a good theory. It is especially important if you take a phenomenological or critical approach to theory. When encountering a model that purports to explain how people make sense of their social worlds, you should ask whether its explanations adequately represent the way people really think. If not, then the model is inadequate.

A Good Model Is Based on Tenable Assumptions

Although it would be comforting to think that models can be divorced from real-world concerns, existing in some realm of pure thought, this is not the case. Models always hold implications for the ways we implement social action. Although these assumptions are hidden and often unquestioned, they have powerful effects on our behavior.

For example, many social scientists have noted differences in language use between the middle and working classes. The debate over the meaning of these differences is known as the difference-deficiency controversy.[19] One side views language of the working class as grammatically *deficient*, implying there is something wrong with their culture, that they are incapable of using language systematically. The other side argues that lower class patterns are as systematic and rule-governed as middle class patterns and that the two groups simply follow *different* sets of rules. Basil Bernstein, for example, argues that language has different functions for each class and that these functions make sense, given differences in their living conditions.[20]

The point is that each view is based on different assumptions, each makes different statements about the individuals whose behavior is being modeled, and each would call for different intervention strategies. If we cannot accept the statements a model makes, then we should not accept the model.

A CHECKLIST FOR EVALUATING MODELS

Below are a series of questions based on our discussion of what makes a good model. Considering them should help you determine whether or not to accept a particular model. As an exercise, you might submit one of the theories from the text to this series of questions. You should also try to come up with your own criteria for evaluating models.

Risk:
   Is the model testable?
   Does it open itself to risk?
   Can I falsify the model through empirical test?

Simplicity:
   Is the model overly complicated?
   Does it make too many unnecessary assumptions?
   Is there a simpler way of explaining behavior than the explanation offered by this model?

Novelty:

Can the model make interesting predictions?

Does it help me see social phenomena in a new light?

Is my reaction to the model, "I see things now that I never thought of before," or is my reaction, "Ho-hum?"

Productivity:

Is the model applicable to a wide range of phenomena?

Can I explain many different puzzling things with this model?

If the model is too limited, can I think of ways to make it more general and productive?

Adequacy:

Is the model a realistic explanation of people's behavior?

Do the constructs and concepts used in the model fit the way people think about their worlds?

Do people act according to the principles the model offers?

Nature of Assumptions:

Which perspective comes closest to being the basis of this model?

Am I willing to accept the model's assumptions?

What image of human beings is implied by the model?

What are the model's practical implications?

If the model is accepted, how will it be used by people to solve actual communication problems?

REFERENCES

1. Julienne Ford, *Paradigms and Fairy Tales: An Introduction to the Science of Meanings*, vol. 1 (Boston: Routledge and Kegan Paul, 1975), p. 34.

2. Irwin Deutscher, "Looking Backward: Case Studies on the Progress of Methodology in Sociological Research," *The American Sociologist*, 4 (1969), 35–40.

3. Charles A. Lave and James G. March, *An Introduction to Models in the Social Sciences* (New York: Harper & Row, 1975), p. 19.

4. Claire Selltiz, Marie Jahoda, Morton Deutsch and Stuart W. Cook, *Research Methods in Social Relations*, rev. ed. (New York: Holt, Rinehart & Winston, 1959), pp. 481–86.

5. Robert Dubin, *Theory Building* (New York: The Free Press, 1969).

6. Selltiz, *Research Methods*, p. 481.

7. John Dollard and others, *Frustrations and Aggression* (New Haven: Yale University Press, 1939).

8. Ford, *Paradigms*, p. 97.

9. Selltiz, *Research Methods*, p. 486.

10. Lave and March, *Models*, p. 20.

11. *Ibid.*, p. 57.

12. Karl R. Popper, *The Logic of Scientific Discovery*, 2nd ed. (New York: Harper Torchbooks, 1958).

13. Ford, *Paradigms*, p. 101.

14. Lave and March, *Models*, p. 63.

15. *Ibid.*, p. 63.

16. *Ibid.*, p. 63.

17. Alfred Schutz, "Concepts and Theory Formation in the Social Sciences," *Journal of Philosophy*, 51 (1954), 266.

18. *Ibid.*, p. 271.

19. Dennis Lawton, *Social Class, Language and Education* (New York: Schocken, 1968).

20. Basil Bernstein, "Social Class, Linguistic Codes and Grammatical Elements," *Language and Speech*, 5 (1962), 221–40.

appendix B
RESEARCH METHODS

DOING RESEARCH

Although it may seem esoteric and far removed from normal concerns, research is something we engage in daily. Whenever we search for information to test the truth of our ideas, we are doing research. "To research is to search again, to take another, more careful look, to find out more… . What the research attitude presumes is that the first look—and every later look—may be prone to error, so that one must look again and again, differently and thoroughly each time."[1] Scientists know the difficulties of this enterprise and consciously check and challenge their own work. Good scientists, like good detectives and good investigative reporters, are suspicious. "Scientists are professional troublemakers: they must challenge old beliefs, create new ones, and then turn the challenge upon those new ones."[2]

Research methods are the procedures that guide scientific inquiries. We will discuss five such methods used in speech communication. This is not an exhaustive review. It depends heav-

ily on the traditional deterministic approach and has less to say about interpretive and critical approaches. Still, these are some of the most popular research methods currently used to test theory. Although we will examine these methods separately, they are not mutually exclusive; it is possible to use them in combination. As Eugene Webb and others point out, "When a hypothesis can survive the confrontation of a series of complementary methods of testing, it contains a degree of validity unattainable by one tested within the more constricted framework of a single method."[3] The use of multiple methods is known as triangulation, a topic we will return to at the end of the appendix.

THE RESEARCH CONTINUUM

Research methods can be arranged on a continuum. At one end are those labeled as *qualitative* or naturalistic; at the other end are *quantitative* methods. Qualitative methods take an interpretive approach and are based on direct observation and comprehension of naturally occurring events. Researchers immerse themselves in everyday experience, examining it from their subjects' perspectives. Such research is neither controlled, objective, nor carefully preplanned. Researchers try to interfere as little as possible with "natural" events. An anthropologist going in to an unknown culture to record its language and customs uses a qualitative model.

At the other end of the continuum are highly controlled laboratory methods. Researchers carefully preplan their observations and intentionally intervene in the behavior of those being studied. The researcher's role is that of an objective outsider who sets events in motion and observes the results of these manipulations. A quantitative social psychologist interested in the effects of authority on conformity might ask subjects in a laboratory setting to conform to an experimenter's demands and then record their reactions.

At one end of the continuum, then, we study events as they naturally occur, avoid numerical measurement, and present results in the form of essays that explain events from the subjects' point of view. Our goal is to understand the rules of human action. At the other end of the continuum, we control the occurrence of events and use preplanned, public, highly objective categories to analyze data. Reliable and valid numerical measurement is a key part of this method, with the results often including statistical tables. Our goal here is to specify the laws that explain human behavior.

FIVE METHODS OF SPEECH COMMUNICATION RESEARCH

In the following pages we begin with the qualitative end of the research continuum and work toward the quantitative end. We start with a consideration of participant observation and then move to the life history method. We next look at ways to analyze message systems, including conversational, relational, and content analyses.

Finally, we move on to survey research, and we end with the experimental method.

Participant Observation

Overview. Participant observation is the most naturalistic research method. The researcher may actually "move in" with the subjects of study, participating in their daily activities. The goal is to get a feel for the subjects' symbolic worlds. The research design is deliberately unstructured. The researcher may start with a rough working hypothesis but will be eager to modify that hypothesis in response to emergent meanings. The researcher observes, as unobtrusively as possible, subjects' communications, deciphering their social meanings. He or she participates in their daily activities, recording observations in detailed field notes. Respondent interviewing and the recording of ongoing verbal and nonverbal behaviors may also be used.

Steps in Participant Observation. Participant observation is one of the least structured research methods, making it difficult to systematize its steps. Next we will look at some of the activities of the participant observer, remembering that the key principle of this method is the avoidance of rigid systems of observation.

STEP 1: ENTERING THE FIELD AND ASSUMING A ROLE. Participant observation occurs in the field, not in the research lab, but on the subjects' turf. The researcher must gain access to the research setting, deciding on an appropriate role to assume during the study. He may choose a *covert role* in which he "is wholly concealed, his scientific intents are not made known, and he attempts to become a full-fledged member of the group under investigation."[4] Researchers fulfilling covert roles confront contradictory role demands. "In effect, the complete participant finds himself simultaneously responding to demands of his hidden self, his pretended self, and his self as observer."[5] While this role conflict may be a burden, it can also be advantageous. By considering their

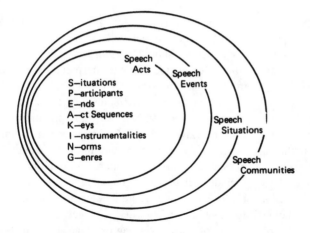

FIGURE B.1: Components of an ethnography of communication. (Developed from Dell Hymes' discussion of ethnographies of communication in *Foundations in Sociolinguistics* [Philadelphia: University of Pennsylvania Press, 1974], pp. 47-66.)

responses as they move between roles, researchers may gain insights about the phenomena being studied. Researchers may also choose *overt roles*, making their presence known to the subjects. Overt observers can ask direct questions about behaviors which are puzzling. Although overt observers face less role conflict, they must gain the subjects' trust so that subjects feel comfortable enough to act naturally and answer questions honestly.

These two roles illustrate the balance the researcher must maintain between objectivity and involvement. As Howard Schwartz and Jerry Jacobs point out, they mirror his two goals:

First, he wants to learn the actor's "definition of the situation"—to see what the actor sees, know what he knows, and think as he thinks. Second, having accomplished this reconstruction of the other's reality, the researcher hopes to transcend this view, to see what the actor does *not* see—the formal features, processes, patterns, or common denominators that characterize the actor's view and situation.[6]

STEP 2: MAKING OBSERVATIONS. There are some general elements of communicative behaviors that most observers will want to record. In his "ethnography of communication," Dell Hymes describes the major elements that should be observed in order to describe a culture's beliefs and communication practices.[7] Figure B.1 represents some of the factors discussed by Hymes.

Hymes believes all ethnographic investigations begin with identification of a *speech community*. The participant observer usually investigates communication practices within a particular community that shares "knowledge of rules for the conduct and interpretation of speech."[8] An ethnic urban neighborhood is a good example of such a community. Philipsen's study of Teamsterville, reported in Research Abstract 5.3, employs many of the features of Hymes' approach.

Within each speech community are clearly marked *speech situations*. Culturally defined and differentiated, they call for different kinds of speech. Examples are ceremonies, fights, meals, lovemaking, and so on. The observer who wishes to understand the culture must begin by determining its important speaking situations.

Each situation usually contains several speech events, activities directly governed by norms for the use of speech: conversations, sermons, lectures, comedy routines, and so on. *Speech acts* are the minimal units of interaction embedded within speech events. They are the specific actions performed by individual utterances: requests, commands, assertions, compliments, and so forth. Consider, for example, behavior at a wedding. A number of events involving speech occur, including conversations among the guests, responses during the ceremony, and ritual compliments in the receiving line. Each event is in turn made up of speech acts: During a conversation, a guest may wish to assert status, flatter the host, apologize for a gaffe, or perform some other act. The participant observer wishes to uncover the many rules for speaking that exist within this situation and which govern its events and acts.

Hymes suggests that participant observers should record eight factors designated by the mnemonic SPEAKING: Situation, Participants, Ends, Act sequences, Key, Instrumentalities, Norms, and Genres. *Situation* refers to the setting (time, place, physical circumstances) as well as the scene (the psychological or cultural definition of the occasion) in which the behaviors being studied occur. *Participants* is a description of who is involved in the interaction and may include not only the speaker and hearer but other people as well. Sometimes, for example, a message may be relayed from person to person before it gets to the receiver or a speaker may speak to one person to be overheard by another. Often, more people than one would think are involved in interaction. As Hymes points out, "the common dyadic model of speaker-hearer specifies sometimes too many, sometimes too few, and sometimes the wrong participants."[9]

Ends are outcomes and goals. Some goals may be encouraged and others prohibited within a speech community. In either case, the form of speaking participants use depends on what they are trying to accomplish. *Act sequences* refers to message content and form. Often, observers record the content of a topic but fail to specify how the content was phrased. Careful attention of the sort found in literary criticism should be paid to message form. *Key* is the tone, manner, or spirit of a particular speaking act. Is an argument to be taken seriously, or is it a mock attack? Is a compliment perfunctory or sincere? One of the basic elements of communicative competence is the ability to signal and recognize key. It is one of the hardest for an outside observer to recognize.

Instrumentalities are channels for speech forms. Channel is the medium of transmission (whether the message is spoken, written, or visually signaled, and, if spoken, whether it is whis-

pered, sung, chanted, etc.). Within a speech community, some channels will be favored over others, a fact that should be recorded by the observer. *Norms* for interaction and interpretation are also important for an observer to understand. Norms of interaction tell participants how to act in relation to one another. Norms of interpretation indicate the value and belief systems of the community. Finally, *genres* are the important categories of speech marked within a community. They include such things as "poem, myth, tale, proverb, riddle, curse, prayer, oration, lecture, commercial, form letter, etc." Because each genre has a different set of rules governing its usage and formation, the participant observer must clearly identify the important genres within the community.

STEP 3: RECORDING OBSERVATIONS. The researcher records and analyzes observations through the creation of field notes. During the observation period, the researcher makes brief notes about important events and, as soon as possible, converts these notes into detailed descriptions, usually in the form of a running log. The log includes concrete descriptions of subjects' behaviors, as well as the observer's self-observations, feelings, and interpretations of the meanings of events. Successful observation depends on the sensitivity of the observations and the quality of insights reflected in field notes. As the observation period may last for many months, and the observer's interpretations may change as more data are obtained, detailed field notes covering the entire study period are essential.

STEP 4: ANALYZING AND INTERPRETING DATA. The participant observer's goal is to understand the social meaning of observed communication events and to articulate the rules governing speech within a particular community. The final step is the presentation of results to the scientific community, using formalized conclusions and detailed descriptions as evidence for these conclusions. Other scientists can compare these results with their own and formulate new questions for study.

Life History or Case Method

Overview. A research method closely related to participant observation is the life history or case method, which also seeks to understand the subjective experiences of the individual subject through use of qualitative data. It differs in two ways, however: It concentrates on a single case, and it depends heavily on the use of documents and records rather than on direct observation. The method chooses a single case (perhaps an organization or group but often a single individual) and reconstructs its history by pulling together personal and public records illuminating the case's perceptions, feelings, experiences, and motivations. Understanding the case results in general insights applicable to other groups or individuals.

This method is often used in sociological and psychological research. A sociologist, for example, may seek insights into delinquency or deviance by studying the life history of a single delinquent. The researcher will record the subject's experience and, in doing so, will examine letters, diaries, newspaper accounts, court records, reports by social workers, accounts from the individual's family, and even transcripts of unstructured interviews with the individual.

Steps in the Life History Method.

STEP 1: SELECTING THE SUBJECT. The goal of the social scientist doing a life history is to understand a broader population from which the case is drawn. We study *this* delinquent because we want to understand *other* delinquents as well. The researcher begins with a topic of study, delinquency or gang membership or the experiences of women in the work force, and selects a specific delinquent, gang leader, or female executive to study.

Claire Selltiz and others, in discussing the use of insight-stimulating examples in exploratory research, argue that "cases that provide sharp contrasts and have striking features are most useful."[10] They suggest using strangers or newcomers, marginal people (emigrants, displaced persons), people in transition (adolescents, retirees), deviants, and "pure" cases (an extremely authoritarian personality or an excessively shy person). They also suggest that much can be learned by comparing those who fit into the social system with those who do not (teacher's pet versus classroom troublemaker) or individuals from different positions in the social structure (workers as well as managers in an organization). Finally, they believe that the investigator's own experiences, derived through self-analysis, may also lead to insights.[11]

STEP 2: GATHERING LIFE HISTORY DATA. Several data sources are available to the researcher including public archive records such as actuarial records, political and judicial records, government or state records, and mass media data.[12] Private documents may also be used including diaries, letters, results of projective tests, interviews, and verbatim reports.[13] A common and important personal document is the life history autobiography. The researcher may ask the subject to write an autobiography in response to specific research questions. As the subject writes the autobiography, the researcher works with him or her, probing for additional details to highlight emerging hypotheses or to fill in areas where coverage seems inadequate. The researcher may focus the subject's concerns, trying "to make the story jibe with matters of official record and with materials furnished by others familiar with the person, event, or place being described."[14] Norman Denzin notes that the final product will not be a conventional autobiography but will "have rather the character of confessions, intimate personal documents intended to record not so much external events as to reveal sentiments and attitudes."[15]

STEP 3: CRITICAL EXAMINATION OF DATA. Because the data are subjective, they may contain inaccuracies. The researcher must corroborate details with independent evidence that may come from witnesses or public materials. In either case, the researcher triangulates by source and perspective to get an accurate account. Once the data are corroborated, the researcher may present a draft of the life history to the subject for reaction and possible revision.

STEP 4: INTERPRETING THE DATA. As Denzin suggests, the final step is to "rework the report in its natural sequence in light of the above reactions. Present the hypothesis and propositions that have been supported. Conclude with its relevance for theory and subsequent research."[16] The life history method has not been widely used in speech communication, except in the study of organizational cases. It would seem, however, to have applications in the interpersonal area, for example, to gain insight into the growth and dissolution of dyadic relationships or in the communicative experiences of individuals undergoing transitions. Studies of physician-patient communication problems could also be handled this way. Given the growing interest in our field in qualitative approaches, the life history method may once again become popular. Its potential in communication studies has not been tapped.

The Analysis of Message Systems

Overview: Conversational, Relational, and Content Analysis. Traditionally, the study of the message holds a privileged place in the field of speech communication. Although the methods for analyzing messages differ widely, they all involve collecting samples of actual messages and message sequences. Although sometimes classed as observational, in actual practice these methods use a set of procedures distinct enough from the participant observation method to warrant a separate discussion.

This kind of inquiry is generally unobtrusive, with little contact between investigator and subjects. The focus of interest is not individuals but patterned exchanges resulting from their interaction. Because the investigators know their presence might be reactive, they remain as removed from the subjects as possible. In message analy-

sis, the researcher records a message and then analyzes its content or form. In the case of content, the researcher is looking for themes, ideas, metaphors, words, or topic sequences within a conversation. If the case of form, then he or she examines how message sequences are ordered and how message exchanges are patterned.

Steps in Message System Analyses. There are several ways to examine messages. In this section, three will be discussed: conversational or discourse analysis, interactional or relational analysis, and content analysis. We will begin by examining the general steps that apply to all of these variations.

STEP 1: COLLECTING A SAMPLE. The first step is to collect a sample (or corpus) of messages. Written messages pose little problem, but spoken messages must be recorded, either through the use of shorthand or audio or video tape recordings. Before recording, however, the researcher must decide what messages to collect. If the researcher assumes a stable rule system for generating messages, then any message belonging to this system is relevant, and it is unnecessary to collect a representative sample. Any message, providing it is naturally occurring, will do. Other researchers want to compare message classes and insist on gathering samples that are representative of their type.

After the message selection criteria have been determined, the messages are recorded. Message originators can either be filmed or recorded in natural settings without their knowledge, wired for sound and allowed to go about their business, or placed in rooms with recording equipment and asked to interact. Sometimes they are interviewed so that the investigators can elicit very specific language samples.

STEP 2: SCRUTINIZING THE SAMPLE. Once the recording has been made, the researcher reviews it, searching for patterns. If the orientation is qualitative, the investigator will describe the nature of the underlying code or rules by which the message was constructed. The researcher will often generate a rule that fits a particular message and test it by generating other messages and comparing them with the rule.

If the orientation is quantitative, then the researcher will test laws that link message variables, using a deductive, hypothesis-testing strategy. The investigator formulates a hypothesis about the message characteristics and then checks the data to see if the hypothesis is falsified. The researcher may use counts of message characteristics as research evidence, collected by a process of categorizing and coding.

STEP 3: ANALYZING AND INTERPRETING RESULTS. The final step is to interpret and explain the results of the analysis, either by describing patterns in the form of an interpretive essay or as a fully explained set of rules or by presenting counts of the frequencies of relevant variables. Regardless of the form the results take, the researcher must explore the meaning of the new information in relation to other research and theory.

Varieties of Message System Analyses.

CONVERSATIONAL OR DISCOURSE ANALYSIS. The method closest to the qualitative end of the continuum is conversational analysis. Michael Stubbs defines it this way:

Roughly speaking, it refers to attempts to study the organization of language above the sentence or above the clause, and therefore to study larger linguistic units, such as conversational exchanges or written texts. It follows that discourse analysis is also concerned with language in use in social contexts, and in particular with interaction or dialogue between speakers.[17]

The project of the conversational analyst is to uncover the rules regulating conversation and allowing the accomplishment of goals through talk, discovering how people go about complaining, excusing, boasting, joking, teasing, and so on. While this concern with ordinary conversa-

tion may seem trivial to some, to the conversational analyst it is an important social activity:

Talk seems to be almost a compulsion among humans. Of all the social activities they engage in, this one seems to be their favorite.... Its occurrence within daily life strikes us as remarkably unmomentous. Yet these millions of small verbal episodes may be the main vehicle for shaping what each of us become, know, and experience throughout our social life. Like the incessant sculpting of rocks by the sea, natural conversations may have more to do with shaping the nature of individuals and societies than wars, child-rearing practices, and political elections.[18]

Schwartz and Jacobs catalogue many topics of concern to conversational analyst, including the turn-taking system that regulates conversational exchanges, the recursive organization by which current utterances are given meaning through reference to previous utterances, the overall structural organization of conversational sequences, the structural organization of single utterances, and the rules allowing interconversational patterns.[19]

To investigate these topics, the researcher begins with a sample of conversation, which may consist of a single conversational exchange[20] or of a larger collection of utterances.[21] When analyzing a single conversation, the researcher only needs to locate an interesting conversation and examine it. So long as it is considered appropriate by speakers of the culture and is naturally occurring, it will serve the research purpose. The researcher who wants to collect a sample of utterances containing important variants of a single structure may either ask subjects to supply sample utterances or record them as they occur. Labov's important study of ritual insults, reported in Research Abstract 5.2, was a combination of these two methods.

The researcher's goal is to describe the structure of messages, generally in the form of a rule. Once the rule is formulated, it can be tested to see if it can generate further utterances that can be presented to informants for their approval or subjected to the researcher's own linguistic intuitions.

INTERACTION OR RELATIONAL ANALYSIS. Interaction analysis moves closer to the quantitative end of our continuum. In this method, the researcher is no longer interested in determining the structure of codes. The researcher is now interested in examining how messages are exchanged. The researcher draws samples of dyads or groups, records their interaction, and then codes the function of each utterance by employing one of the standard interaction coding schemes or devising a new one.[22] What most coding schemes have in common is a concern with relational categories. They concentrate on determining *how* an utterance functions rather than on *what* is said. The studies by Hirokawa (Research Abstract 9.2) and Fisher (Research Abstract 9.3) use this kind of analysis.

Codes are designed to be objective and public. They represent a way of reducing highly novel utterances to a series of well-defined and publicly agreed upon categories. In the process, some information is lost, but if the researcher's goal is hypothesis testing, then the use of codes is helpful.

CONTENT ANALYSIS. A third way to analyze message systems is content analysis, which differs from the other methods we have just reviewed because it emphasizes the content of a message. Content analysis assigns message units to categories and counts the frequency of units in each category. Content analysis can be used to describe the content of a specific set of messages or to compare different messages.

Because content analysis looks at message subsets, it involves sampling. A researcher wishing to compare liberal versus conservative newspaper coverage of the Vietnam War could never hope to code all of the news accounts during that time period. Rather, the researcher would have to limit the sample to several newspapers or to certain dates or to only a portion of the coverage (say, lead articles or editorials).

In content analysis, the sample consists not of people but of messages, and the researcher devises a category system designed to fit the content. This system may be inductively generated from the data, or it may be deductively generated from theory and previous research. The categories must be exhaustive (every message unit must be codable) and mutually exclusive (categories must not overlap). To assure the objectivity of the coding process, the researcher computes coding *reliability* figures. The coding is considered reliable if, on a satisfactory amount of messages, independent coders are in substantial agreement on category assignment.

A number of our research abstracts use content analysis in one form or another. The Metts and Cupach study on embarrassment (Research Abstract 6.2), the Riccillo study on children's competence (Research Abstract 6.4), and the Delia, Clark, and Switzer study on interpersonal conversations (Research Abstract 8.2) are a few of the studies that content analyze language samples.

Survey Research

Overview. Survey research is the first of the clearly quantitative methods. What makes it so is not only the way data are gathered but also the procedures used to select subjects and to process data after collection. In survey research, data must make a statement not only about the subjects in the study but about a larger group as well. A pollster, for example, cares little about the voting intentions of the 300 people interviewed. Instead the pollster wants to know how the voting population as a whole will cast their ballots. The interviewees are of interest only because their ideas approximate those of the population at large. A major methodological concern is with accurate measurement of population characteristics. It is this statistical orientation, more than the process of asking questions, that makes surveys quantitative.

Of course, in surveys, researchers do ask people questions. Thus, the method is based on a belief in the adequacy of self-reports. We have seen that inquiry into human communication can be made by observing people, by studying documents reporting their actions, and by examining traces of their behaviors. Survey research adds another method: asking people about themselves. As a method, it succeeds only in those cases where subjects are aware of, and capable of talking about, their experiences. From a humanistic point of view, it is the most optimistic and most trusting of methods.

Steps in Survey Research

STEP 1: SELECTING THE SAMPLE. The cornerstone of survey methodology is sampling. The researcher begins by identifying a population of interest. The term *population* refers to all members or *elements* of the particular group being studied. For example, if we want to study voting behavior of U.S. citizens, then all citizens of the United States at the time of our study constitute the population. We then locate a small collection or *sample*, representing some but not all members of a population. The success of the research depends on choosing a sample typical of the population at large.

The way a researcher chooses a sample is the *sampling plan*, of which there are two types: *probability* and *nonprobability*.[23] In probability sampling, it is possible to know the exact probability of a particular population element's being part of the sample. In nonprobability sampling it is not. Suppose that from a population of 5,000 students we decide to sample 100. If we stop the first 100 students who enter the cafeteria on a certain day, then we have no way of knowing the probability that a particular student will be included in the sample, for an individual student may decide to go for pizza or skip the meal or come to dinner late and thus avoid being in the sample. This is an example of a nonprobability plan. But, if we choose our sample by programming the school's computer to generate 100 names randomly from among all the college's students, then each student has an equal chance of being chosen, and we know this chance is pre-

cisely 1 in 50. By using the computer method we have increased our knowledge about the sample and reduced its bias. We can also employ statistical laws to judge the adequacy of our sample, to determine its size, and to test its properties. Probability samples are thus to be preferred in most cases.

One of the best known probability sampling plans is *simple random sampling* (SRS). In this method, each element of a population has an equal chance of being chosen in much the same way that each ticket in a fair lottery has a chance of being the winner. In picking an SRS, the researcher numbers each element of the population, generates random numbers, and then puts into the sample those elements in the population whose numbers match the random ones. In using this procedure, the researcher ensures a representative sample.

Probability samples are statistically advantageous but are costly and time consuming because each element of the population must be enumerated. So, the researcher may choose a nonprobability sample because it is easier and faster than probability methods, although more likely to contain biases. A basic type of nonprobability sampling is *accidental sampling*, called such because "one simply reaches out and takes the cases that are at hand, continuing the process until the sample reaches a designated size."[24] Interviewing students in cafeteria lines is an example of an accidental sample, as is using students enrolled in a class. Whether or not it is justified, much of the social science research is based on accidental sampling.

STEP 2: SURVEY CONSTRUCTION. Designing a good survey is a difficult job because getting people to answer questions truthfully is not as easy or natural as it at first seems. People often do not know what they think or have trouble expressing themselves. Often they are reluctant to open up to others or are anxious to create a good impression. All this makes the process of interview and questionnaire construction difficult for the researcher.

There are two kinds of surveys. A *questionnaire* is a written survey that respondents themselves fill out. In an *interview* the researcher personally asks respondents questions. There are advantages and disadvantages to both. In an interview, if respondents have trouble answering questions, then the interviewer can intervene, thus enhancing the quality of the data. An unskilled interviewer, however, can cue the respondent to the expected or preferred answers, unconsciously biasing the results. It is also expensive to train interviewers and to send them into the field. Questionnaires are usually cheaper and more efficient. They can be mailed to respondents and answered by them at their leisure. Their wording and order are uniform and not subject to the interviewer's whims. On the other hand, there is less control over the conditions under which the questions are answered. It is also easy to toss aside the questionnaire before it is done or to forget to mail it.

Regardless of whether the survey is conducted by interview or questionnaire, the researcher must formulate questions. *Open questions* are those in which responses are not limited to a particular set of alternatives. "Describe an incident in which one of your students did something you felt was inappropriate for the classroom," is open-ended because the respondent is not limited to choosing options provided by the researcher.

Closed questions are just the opposite. The researcher presents alternatives and asks the respondent to choose from among them. "Is this your first year of teaching?" is closed-ended because it asks for a yes or no. The following questions are also closed: "What percentage of your students would you class as having poor communication skills?" "On a scale from 1 to 10, how inappropriate are each of the following behaviors?" "How often do you encounter students who talk back to you? Very seldom, seldom, occasionally, often, or very often." When the response options are provided, the interview must be sure they are mutually exclusive and exhaustive. If the topic being investigated is new, then the researcher may have difficulties providing realistic response options, and the open question is best. Open questions, however, are quite difficult to quantify, making statistical analysis difficult.

A researcher must also decide the sequence of questions. Starting with open questions and working toward specific, closed questions is called a *funnel sequence*. The opposite order is an *inverted funnel*. When a researcher wants to avoid leading the respondent, the first strategy is usually employed. When the researcher fears that a general question may be too difficult and wants to focus the respondent's attention on more specific matters, an inverted funnel is often used.

Survey construction is difficult. Questions must be worded so that they are unambiguous, unthreatening, clearly understandable, and neutral in emotional tone and response acceptability. Questionnaires must be readable and must avoid needless complexity. The order and form of the survey design can substantially affect the study's results. The best way to avert problems is to pretest the survey with a pilot group and rework problematic questions. After hundreds of questionnaires have been mailed out is a poor time for the researcher to realize that the questions are ambiguous.

STEP 3: CODING AND ANALYSIS. The survey researcher uses statistical methods of analysis. These may be as simple as counting the number of "yes" answers to a particular question or as complicated as computing the degree of statistical association between two variables. Either way, data must be translated into numerical form: This process is called *coding*. The purpose of coding is to create response alternatives if none were originally provided and assign numbers to each alternative. With open questions, both parts of the process must occur; with closed responses, only numerical assignment is necessary. The number assigned may indicate membership in a category (the number of people who answered yes and no respectively on a particular question), the order of preference among responses (one's first, second, and third choice among alternatives), or scale values of alternatives (the average rating on a seven-point scale for each item). Each numerical assignment allows for a different kind of statistical analysis. More will be said about statistical analysis in the discussion of experimental design.

STEP 4: INTERPRETING THE DATA. Once the data have been coded and analyzed, the researcher must determine their meaning and how they fit theoretical models; thus, the last step in survey research is the same as for all methods: interpreting the data in terms of theory. Several of our abstracts employ survey methodology. The Sillars article used a questionnaire (Research Abstract 4.1) and the Riccillo study used an interview to obtain language samples (Research Abstract 6.4).

Experimental Research

Overview. Although the term *experiment* is often used to refer to all forms of social science research, technically it has a more limited meaning. True experiments are based on three processes: *manipulation*, *control*, and *comparison*. The experimenter systematically manipulates or varies part of the environment while controlling all other aspects. He or she then compares what happens in the presence of the manipulation with what happens when the manipulation is absent. That part of the environment manipulated by the researcher, the hypothetical cause, is called the *independent* or treatment *variable*. The reaction of the subject, the measured effect, is called the *dependent variable*.

The experimenter wants to determine whether the independent variable causes a change in the dependent variable and does this by making comparisons. The simplest comparison is observing values of the dependent variable in the presence of the independent variable and again in its absence. If the dependent variable stays the same in both cases, then no effect is attributable to the independent variable. If the dependent variable

changes in these two situations, and other explanations are ruled out, then we assume a causal connection. This type of comparison is generally made by observing reactions of separate groups of subjects. Each group is exposed to a different level of the independent variable. Any difference between groups on the dependent measure is then attributable to the independent variable.

It is important to realize that in experimental research, situations can be investigated in different ways under different conditions. In most research studies, there are many possible stimuli that can represent the independent variable, many possible responses that can measure the dependent variable, and numerous subjects who can respond to those variables. Philip Zimbardo argues that in every study the experimenter must select a particular set of stimuli, measurement procedures, and subjects from among the many that might test the hypothesis.[25] If these are selected reliably and validly, then they should represent the general process that the researcher wants to study, and what happens in the lab will reflect the general relationship the researcher wants to test.

Steps in Experimental Research

STEP 1: SELECTING A SAMPLE OF SUBJECTS. Care must be taken that selected subjects are typical of the target population. The guidelines for sampling given in the previous section on survey research apply here. The generalizability of the study depends on the adequacy of the sampling procedures used to select subjects.

STEP 2: DESIGNING THE STUDY. The difference between the experimenter and other researchers is that he or she does not wait for a communication behavior to occur naturally "but creates the conditions which he or she believes will elicit its occurrence. In this sense, the experimenter creates an artificial environment... ."[26] In designing this artificial environment, the experimenter decides three things: the number of treatment groups to use, how subjects are assigned to these

---

Design One: One-Group Pretest-Post-test Design
a. Prior to any treatment, a pretest is given to a single group of subjects to measure their responses to the dependent variable.
b. These subjects are then exposed to a single level of the independent variable. This is the treatment.
c. Finally, a post-test is given to see if any change has occurred in the dependent variable.

Design Two: Pretest-Post-test Control Group Design
a. Subjects are randomly assigned to one of two comparison groups.
b. Subjects in both groups are given a pretest on the dependent variable.
c. Subjects in one group are given a single level of the independent variable; subjects in the other group either receive no treatment (act as controls) or receive a second level of the independent variable.
d. Finally, a post-test is given to both groups to see if they differ on the dependent variable.

Design Three: Post-test-Only Control Group Design
a. Subjects are randomly assigned to one of two comparison groups.
b. Subjects in each group are given their respective treatments (or treatment and control.)
c. After the treatment, a post-test is given to both groups to see if they differ on the dependent variable.

FIGURE B.2: Some sample designs for the experiment. (For further discussion see Donald T. Campbell and Julian C. Stanley, *Experimental and Quasi-Experimental Designs for Research* [Chicago: Rand McNally, 1966], p. 8.)

groups, and when to make observations. We will now discuss three designs that illustrate the importance of these decisions: a one-group pretest/post-test design, a pretest/post-test control group design, and a post-test only control group design.[27]

Pretest means that at the start of the experiment, before the treatment for independent variables has been presented, an initial reading of the dependent measure is taken. A repeat of the original observation, taken after the subjects have received a dose of the independent variable, is known as a *post-test.*

In a *one-group, pretest/post-test design,* the researcher takes a single group, administers a pretest, exposes the subjects to the independent variable, administers a post-test, and then compares pretest and post-test scores to see if there is a difference. As an experimental design, this lacks one of the three factors necessary for a true experiment, comparison between treatment groups. Because of this, no valid conclusions can be drawn, even if there is a change from pretest to post-test. Stop for a minute and see if you can figure out why.

The answer is that the researcher has no way to tell whether any observed change is due to the treatment or to other factors that could change the subjects' reactions such as outside events, changes in the testing instrument, or changes in the subjects themselves through maturation or fatigue. Without an equivalent comparison group, it is impossible to rule out these explanations. Thus, no valid inferences can be drawn. As soon as we add an equivalent comparison group (as in the next two designs), we are home free, since all the alternative factors can be expected to affect the second group the same way they do the first group. Therefore, if we compare the post-test scores of the two groups and still see a difference, then it can only be due to the experimental treatment, the only factor differing between the two groups.

The logic of experimental inference depends on comparison of two or more initially equivalent groups. The researcher can ensure that these groups are equivalent by *random assignment of subjects to treatment groups.* Under random assignment, any initial bias between groups is removed and individual differences between subjects are equally distributed between the experimental groups. Thus, the groups begin as equivalent. Both the *pretest/post-test control group* and the *post-test only control group designs* use comparison groups to which subjects are assigned at random. What happens to each group is identical except for the treatment received. Both designs are true experimental designs from which valid inferences can be drawn. The only difference is that the second uses a pretest while the third does not. Figure B.2 summarizes these designs.

STEP 3: SELECTING TREATMENT STIMULI AND MEASUREMENTS.   After designing the study, the researcher determines which stimuli will represent the independent variable and which responses will be measured as the dependent variable. The researcher begins with general *conceptual definitions* of the variables that must then be *operationally defined* or translated into a set of specific, observable operations. The researcher specifies procedures to be followed to manipulate and measure these concepts.

The researcher who wants to measure a communication construct must be sure that the procedures used are *reliable* (that they consistently yield the same results) and *valid* (that they actually measure the concept of interest). First, the researcher must be able to rely on his or her measure to give consistent results. For example, a simple bathroom scale is expected to give the same weight reading every time the same person mounts it (as long as that person has not actually changed weight). A scale that fluctuates five pounds in five minutes is not reliable. Similarly, an attitude scale designed to measure an enduring trait like prejudice is unreliable if it classes a person as prejudiced on one occasion and unprejudiced on a second (always assuming that in the interim the person has not actually undergone a change of attitude). A scale that is unreliable is clearly useless to the researcher. But just because a scale gives a reliable reading time after time does not mean it is valid. I could set my bathroom scale to read a consistent five pounds less than I

actually weigh. The scale would be reliable, but it would be invalid, because it would not give a true reading. Similarly, I could devise a reliable attitude scale that would be invalid because it classed prejudiced people as unprejudiced.

Reliability refers to a measure's consistency. But consistency can mean different things: stability, equivalence, or homogeneity. *Stability* means that the measurement remains stable over time. If the results fluctuate too widely over time, then it is unreliable and must be improved before being used in an experiment. *Equivalence* of testing procedures means a particular person's scores on a specific measurement instrument should be the same no matter who administers or scores the test. If one judge or coder fails to notice certain behaviors or scores them differently from other judges, then the measure lacks equivalence.

Homogeneity means that all the items on a particular measure are consistent with one another. If you have a 20-item test measuring a certain attitude, all items must measure the same thing. Many statistical procedures can be used to measure the degree of association between test items, or *internal consistency*. An instrument that fails this test has "bad items" and must be corrected.

Just as there are different kinds of reliability, so there are different ways a test can be valid. It can have content, construct, concurrent, or predictive validity.[28] *Content validity* refers to the measurement of all applicable aspects of the concept being studied. If, for example, a professor tests students on 50 pages of reading, but asks questions only on the first three pages, then the test lacks content validity. To guarantee content validity, all relevant items that could measure the construct should be defined in advance and represented in the test.

Construct validity is the extent to which a test acts as one would expect it to. To ensure this kind of validity, the researcher formulates hypotheses about the nature of the construct being measured and tests to see if these hypotheses are confirmed. For example, an instrument designed to measure prejudice should be correlated with related constructs (authoritarianism, ethnocentrism) and should allow us to distinguish certain kinds of people from others (groups known to be prejudiced should not score the same as those who are liberal). Each of these relationships can be tested to determine construct validity.

Concurrent validity means that measurement procedures yield the same results as other tests of the same construct. For example, the results of a paper-and-pencil test of anxiety should be similar to results of other measures of anxiety such as physiological or projective measures. *Predictive validity* means that predictions made on the basis of the test actually occur. For example, a test designed to measure how well an individual will succeed at a job can be validated by giving it to people before they take a job and then waiting to see what their actual job achievement is. If high scorers do well and low scorers do not, then we have predictive validity. Whenever a researcher develops measurement procedures, he or she must submit them to detailed pretesting and analysis. They should always be valid and reliable.

STEP 4: ANALYZING AND INTERPRETING THE DATA. Once the experimenter runs the study and collects the data, he or she must decide whether the results falsify or support initial predictions. The researcher compares scores of experimental groups to see whether or not they differ. In most cases there will be some differences. The problem is to determine how large the difference must be to be meaningful. To do this, the researcher uses inferential statistics.

Assume the experimental treatments in a study have no effect on the dependent measure. Even in such a case, chance variations will give one group a slightly higher score than the other, although this difference will be due to chance rather than to significant effects caused by the independent variable. Chance fluctuations are called *error variance*, a kind of random noise in the system that should not be confused with meaningful differences or *explained variance*.

Statistical tests help researchers distinguish error variance from explained variance. If most of the difference between groups is due to error, then the researcher cannot conclude an effect due to the treatment variable. If most of the variance is explained, then the researcher can conclude a cause-effect relationship between the treatment and subjects' responses. Most of the commonly used inferential statistics are estimates of the ratio between explained and error variance. The researcher computes this ratio and then consults statistical tables that give the probability of obtaining that ratio by chance alone. The researcher never really knows if the differences he or she uncovers indicate a true effect. All that is known is the probability associated with the ratio that has been computed. Generally, if the ratio is large (if there is more explained than error variance), then there is low probability that the effect is due to chance, and the researcher can be fairly confident that a true relationship exists between variables. The results of experiments usually include not only the ratio between explained and error variances but also an estimate of the probability that the reported differences are not due to a causal relationship between variables but to chance alone. The researcher is always involved in a gamble, and it is up to him or her to decide how large a gamble is worthwhile.

STRENGTHS AND WEAKNESSES OF THE METHODS

The advantages of one research method are often the disadvantages of another; in choosing a particular method, we are engaged in a kind of trade-off. The strength of qualitative naturalistic studies lies in their flexibility and lack of artificiality. Since communication research seeks to understand how people communicate in the real world, it makes sense to observe them in natural settings. Because qualitative methods avoid prejudgments about the data and because they are not bound by rigid data-gathering conventions, they provide a fluidity and flexibility not found in quantitative methods.

There are, however, two serious weaknesses in qualitative studies. First, the impressionistic, unstructured nature of these methods does little to ensure the validity of the researcher's conclusions. These methods depend on the researcher's ability to achieve accurate insights and interpretations. There are few safeguards against the researcher's unwarranted conjectures. Qualitative observations seldom involve precise, public, operational rules, so that concepts often appear vague and ill-defined. It is difficult to know whether another independent observer would arrive at the same conclusions.

Second, there is a problem of generalizability. There is little way to know whether the patterns uncovered in a particular case are representative of other cases or are idiosyncratic. Because of the need to develop explanations for phenomena rather than to report one-time events, this problem is a potentially damaging one. Quantitative or laboratory studies, on the other hand, allow a degree of control not found in the qualitative realm. As the researcher focuses on specific variables and holds others constant, he or she can test causal hypotheses more accurately than the qualitative researcher.

Quantitative studies are generally geared to the aggregate rather than to the individual. Use of sampling theory principles means results can be generalized. If the goal of communication science is to understand how large groups of people behave, then there are obvious advantages to quantitative studies. The chief problem of quantitative studies is their dependence on the testing of preexisting hypotheses and their artificiality. Quantitative methods are generally deductive. Researchers begin with a preconceived idea or hypothesis, deduce the results if the hypothesis is true, and set up a situation in which the hypothesis can be falsified. The researcher must formulate the hypothesis before rather than during the research. Data are primarily used to test the valid-

ity of hypothesis rather than to discover new ideas. Naturalistic research, on the other hand, is inductive, beginning with data and using them to generate an explanation that best fits. In a very simplified sense, induction allows the creation of hypotheses. Deduction allows us to test them.

While there is disagreement about the advantages of deduction and induction, there is little argument about the artificiality of quantitative methods. First, the laboratory environment is artificial. Subjects who sign up for an experiment sign up for a situation unlike everyday situations. Subjects also generally see the experiment as a testing situation, and they take special effort to do whatever is expected of them. Experimental settings encourage subjects to perform according to the experimenter's expectations. The cues subjects use to guide their behaviors regarding the environment are called demand characteristics.[29] Experimental *demand characteristics* can cause subjects to act in ways that are "abnormal."

Artificiality may also be a problem in the area of measurement. While some human behaviors are easily quantifiable (frequency and duration of particular acts, for example), others are more problematic: How, for example, do we measure attitudes? Critics of this methodology question the need to reduce human action to numbers.

MULTIPLE METHODS AND TRIANGULATION

One way out of the dilemma posed by the qualitative/quantitative trade-off is to encourage multiple methods. Approaching a research problem from multiple perspectives is known as *triangulation*. Earl Babbie believes qualitative methods are excellent vehicles for initial, exploratory work, but that their resulting insights should be replicated by the use of more rigorous and controlled designs.[30] Although many writers argue that qualitative methods may be more useful in the initial hypothesis-generating stages and quantitative in later theory-testing stages, this is probably an oversimplification. A more adequate view recognizes that each method may be used at anytime during the process and that the researcher should work back and forth between methods depending on current findings and the questions they raise. Denzin states it well when he says:

No investigation should be used in a static fashion. Researchers must be ready to alter lines of action, change methods, reconceptualize problems, and even start over if necessary. They must continually evaluate their methods, assess the quality of the incoming data, and note the relevance of the data to theory…methodological triangulation involves a complex process of playing each method off against the other… . [Assessment] is an emergent process, contingent on the investigator, his research setting, and his theoretical perspective.[31]

REFERENCES

1. Claire Selltiz, Lawrence S. Wrightsman, and Stuart W. Cook, *Research Methods in Social Relations*, 3rd ed. (New York: Holt, Rinehart & Winston, 1976), p. 2.

2. *Ibid.*, p. 5.

3. Eugene J. Webb and others, *Unobtrusive Measures: Non-reactive Research in the Social Sciences* (Chicago: Rand McNally, 1966), p. 174.

4. Norman K. Denzin, *The Research Act: A Theoretical Introduction to Sociological Methods* (Chicago: Aldine, 1970), p. 189.

5. *Ibid.*, p. 190.

6. Howard Schwartz and Jerry Jacobs, *Qualitative Sociology: A Method to the Madness* (New York: The Free Press, 1979), p. 48.

7. Dell Hymes, *Foundations in Sociolinguistics: An Ethnographic Approach* (Philadelphia: University of Pennsylvania Press, 1974), p. 51.

8. *Ibid.*, pp. 47–62.

9. *Ibid.*, p. 54.

10. Selltiz, *Research Methods*, pp. 99–101.

11. *Ibid.*, p. 101.

12. Denzin, *Research Act*, p. 224.

13. *Ibid.*, p. 225.

14. Howard S. Becker, "Introduction," in Clifford Shaw, *The Jack-Roller* (Chicago: University of Chicago Press, 1966), p. vi.

15. Robert E. Park, *Human Communities: The City and Human Ecology*, eds. Everett C. Hughes and others (New York: The Free Press, 1952), p. 204. Quoted in Denzin, *Research Act*, p. 227.

16. Denzin, *Research Act*, p. 254.

17. Michael Stubbs, *Discourse Analysis: The Sociolinguistic Analysis of Natural Language* (Chicago: University of Chicago Press, 1983), p. 1.

18. Schwartz and Jacobs, *Qualitative Sociology*, pp. 340–41.

19. *Ibid.*, p. 342.

20. See, for example, the B-K conversation in Robert T. Craig and Karen Tracy, eds., *Conversational Coherence: Form, Structure, and Strategy* (Beverly Hills: Sage, 1983), pp. 299–320.

21. William Labov, "Rules for Ritual Insults," in *Studies in Social Interaction*, ed. David Sudnow (New York: The Free Press, 1972), pp. 120–69.

22. For a review of coding systems see L. Edna Rogers and Richard V. Farace, "Analysis of Relational Communication in Dyads: New Measurement Procedures," *Human Communication Research*, 1 (1975), 222–39.

23. Isidor Chien, "Appendix A: An Introduction to Sampling," in Selltiz, *Research Methods*, pp. 511–40.

24. *Ibid.*, p. 517.

25. Philip G. Zimbardo, Ebbe B. Ebbesen, and Christina Maslach, *Influencing Attitudes and Changing Behaviors*, 2nd ed. (Reading, Mass.: Addison-Wesley, 1977), pp. 199–200.

26. *Ibid.*, p. 198.

27. Donald T. Campbell and Julian C. Stanley, *Experimental and Quasi-Experimental Designs for Research* (Chicago: Rand McNally, 1966).

28. Selltiz, *Research Methods*.

29. See Robert Rosenthal and Ralph L. Rosnow, eds., *Artifact in Behavioral Research* (New York: Academic, 1969).

30. Earl R. Babbie, *The Practice of Social Research* (Belmont, Calif.: Wadsworth, 1975), p. 220.

31. Denzin, *Research Act*, p. 310.

BIBLIOGRAPHY

Abelson, Robert P. and others, eds., *Theories of Cognitive Consistency: A Sourcebook*. Chicago: Rand McNally, 1968.

Allen, R. R. and Barbara Sundene Wood, "Beyond Reading and Writing to Communication Competence," *Communication Education*, 27 (1978), 286–92.

Althusser, Louis, *For Marx*, trans. Ben Brewster. New York: Penguin, 1969.

_____, "Ideology and Ideological State Apparatuses," in *Lenin and Philosophy and Other Essays*, trans. Ben Brewster. London: New Left Books, 1971.

Aristotle, *Rhetoric*, trans. W. Rhys Roberts, and *Poetics*, trans. Ingram Bywater. New York: Modern Library, 1954.

Asch, Solomon E., "Forming Impressions of Personality," *Journal of Abnormal and Social Psychology*, 41 (1946), 258–90.

Babbie, Earl R., *The Practice of Social Research*. Belmont, Calif: Wadsworth, 1975.

Backman, Carl B., "Toward an Interdisciplinary Social Psychology," in *Advances in Experimental Social Psychology*, vol. 16, ed. Leonard Berkowitz. New York: Academic, 1983.

Bales, Robert F., *Interaction Process Analysis: A Method for the Study of Small Groups*. Reading, Mass.: Addison-Wesley, 1950.

_____ **and Fred L. Strodtbeck**, "Phases in Group Problem Solving," *Journal of Abnormal and Social Psychology*, 46 (1951), 485–95.

Bandura, Albert, *Social Learning Theory*. Englewood Cliffs, N. J.: Prentice Hall, 1977.

Barnlund, Dean C., "A Transactional Model of Communication," in *Foundations of Communication Theory*, eds. Kenneth K. Sereno and C. David Mortensen. New York: Harper & Row, 1970.

Barthes, Roland, *Mythologies*, trans. Annette Lavers. London: Cape, 1972.

Bateson, Gregory, *Naven*, 2nd ed. Stanford, Calif.: Stanford University Press, 1958.

_____, *Steps to an Ecology of Mind*. New York: Ballantine, 1972.

Becker, Howard S., "Introduction," in *The Jack-Roller*, ed. Clifford Shaw. Chicago: University of Chicago Press, 1966.

Bell, Robert A. and John A. Daly, "The Affinity-Seeking Function of Communication," *Communication Monographs*, 51 (1984), 91–114.

Belsey, Catharine, *Critical Practice*. New York: Methuen, 1980.

Bem, Daryl J., "Self Perception Theory," in *Advances in Experimental Social Psychology*, vol. 6, ed. Leonard Berkowitz. New York: Academic, 1972.

Bennett, W. L., "Storytelling and Criminal Trials: A Model of Social Judgment," *Quarterly Journal of Speech*, 64 (1978), 1–22.

Bennis, Warren G. and Herbert A. Shepard, "A Theory of Group Development," *Human Relations*, 9 (1956), 415–37.

Berger, Charles R. and James J. Bradac, *Language and Social Knowledge: Uncertainty in Interpersonal Relations*. London: Edward Arnold, 1982.

_____ **and Richard J. Calabrese**, "Some Explorations in Initial Interaction and Beyond: Toward a Developmental Theory of Interpersonal Communication," *Human Communication Research*, 1 (1975), 99–112.

_____ **and William Douglas**, "Studies in Interpersonal Epistemology: III. Anticipated Interaction, Self-Monitoring, and Observational Context Selection," *Communication Monographs*, 48 (1981), 183–96.

Berger, Peter L., "Sociology of Knowledge," in *Interdisciplinary Approaches to Human Communication*, eds. Richard W. Budd and Brent D. Ruben. Rochelle Park, N. J.: Hayden, 1979.

Berlo, David K., "The Context for Communication," in *Communication and Behavior*, eds. Gerhard J. Hanneman and William J. McEwen. Reading, Mass: Addison-Wesley, 1970.

_____, **James B. Lemert, and Robert J. Mertz**, "Dimensions for Evaluating the Acceptability of Message Sources," *Public Opinion Quarterly*, 33 (1969), 563–76.

Berne, Eric, *What Do You Say After You Say "Hello?"*. New York: Bantam, 1972.

Bernstein, Basil, "Social Class, Linguistic Codes and Grammatical Elements," *Language and Speech*, 5 (1962), 221–40.

Bersheid, Ellen, "Interpersonal Attraction," in *Handbook of Social Psychology*, 3rd ed., eds. Gardner Lindzey and Elliot Aronson. New York: Random House, 1985.

_____, **and Elaine Walster**, *Interpersonal Attraction*. Reading, Mass.: Addison-Wesley, 1969.

Birdwhistell, Ray L., *Introduction to Kinesics*. Louisville: University of Kentucky Press, 1952.

_____, *Kinesics and Context*. Philadelphia: University of Pennsylvania Press, 1970.

Blonsky, Marshall, ed., *On Signs*. Baltimore: The Johns Hopkins University Press, 1985.

Blumer, Herbert, "Symbolic Interaction," in *Interdisciplinary Approaches to Human Communication*, eds. Richard W. Budd and Brent D. Ruben. Rochelle Park, N. J.: Hayden, 1979.

_____, *Symbolic Interactionism: Perspective and Method*. Englewood Cliffs, N. J.: Prentice Hall, 1969.

Book, Cassandra L. and others, *Human Communication: Principles, Contexts, and Skills*. New York: St. Martin's Press, 1980.

Bormann, Ernest G., *Communication Theory*. New York: Holt, Rinehart & Winston, 1980.

_____, *Discussion and Group Methods: Theory and Practice*, 2nd ed. New York: Harper & Row, 1975.

_____, "A Fantasy Theme Analysis of the Television Coverage of the Hostage Release and the Reagan Inaugural," *Quarterly Journal of Speech*, 68 (1982), 133–45.

_____, *The Force of Fantasy: Restoring the American Dream*. Carbondale: Southern Illinois University Press, 1985.

_____, "Symbolic Convergence: Organizational Communication and Culture," in *Communication and Organizations: An Interpretive Approach*, eds. Linda L. Putnam and Michael E. Pacanowsky. Beverly Hills: Sage, 1983.

_____, "Symbolic Convergence Theory: A Communication Formulation," *Journal of Communication*, 35 (1985), 128–38.

_____, **Jere Pratt, and Linda Putnam**, "Power, Authority, and Sex: Male Response to Female Leadership, *Communication Monographs*, 45 (June 1978), 119–55.

Bowers, John Waite, "Language Intensity, Social Introversion, and Attitude Change," *Speech Monographs*, 30 (1963), 345–52.

Bradac, James J., John Waite Bowers, and John A. Courtright, "Lexical Diversity: An Axiomatic Theory and Causal Model," in *The Social and Psychological Contexts of Language*, eds. Robert N. St. Clair and Howard Giles. Hillsdale, N. J.: Lawrence Erlbaum Associates, 1980.

Brandt, David R., "On Linking Social Performance with Social Competence: Some Relations Between Communicative Style and Attributions of Interpersonal Attractiveness and Effectiveness," *Human Communication Research*, 5 (1979), 223–37.

Brehm, Jack W. and Arthur R. Cohen, *Explorations in Cognitive Dissonance*. New York: John Wiley & Sons, 1962.

Brilhart, John K., *Effective Group Discussion*, 3rd ed. Dubuque, Iowa: William C. Brown, 1978.

Brown, Penelope and Stephen Levenson, "Universals in Language Usage: Politeness Phenomena," in *Questions and Politeness: Strategies in Social Interaction*, ed. E. Goody. Cambridge: Cambridge University Press, 1978.

Bruner, Jerome, "Life As Narrative," *Social Research*, 54 (1987), 11–32.

Bullock, Theodore, "Neurons as Biological Transducers and Communication Channels," in *Concepts of Communication: Interpersonal, Intrapersonal, and Mathematical*, eds. Edwin F. Beckenbach and Charles B. Tompkins. New York: John Wiley & Sons, 1971.

Burgoon, Judee K. and Jerold L. Hale, "Nonverbal Expectancy Violations: Model Elaboration and Application to Immediacy Behaviors," *Communication Monographs*, 55 (March 1988), 58–79.

_____, **and Thomas Saine**, *The Unspoken Dialogue: An Introduction to Nonverbal Communication*. Boston: Houghton Mifflin, 1978.

Burke, Kenneth, *A Grammar of Motives*. Berkeley and Los Angeles: University of California Press, 1969.

Cacioppo, John T., Stephen G. Harkins, and Richard E. Petty, "The Nature of Attitudes and Cognitive Responses and Their Relationships to Behavior," in *Cognitive Responses in Persuasion*, eds. Richard E. Petty, Thomas M. Ostrom, and Timothy C. Brock. Hillsdale, N. J.: Lawrence Erlbaum Associates, 1981.

_____ **and Richard E. Petty**, "Effects of Message Repetition and Position on Cognitive Response, Recall, and Persuasion," *Journal of Personality and Social Psychology*, 37 (1979), 97–109.

Campbell, Donald T. and Julian C. Stanley, *Experimental and Quasi-Experimental Designs for Research*. Chicago: Rand McNally, 1966.

Cantor, Nancy and Walter Mischel, "Prototypes in Person Perception," in *Advances in Experimental Social Psychology*, vol. 12, ed. Leonard Berkowitz. New York: Academic, 1979.

Carterette, Edward C. and Donald A. Norman, "On the Uses of Sensory Information by Animals and Men," in *Concepts of Communication: Interpersonal, Intrapersonal, and Mathematical*, eds. Edwin F. Beckenbach and Charles B. Tompkins. New York: John Wiley & Sons, 1971.

Cegala, Donald J., "Interaction Involvement: A Cognitive Dimension of Communicative Competence," *Communication Education*, 30 (1981), 109–21.

_____ **and others**, "An Elaboration of the Meaning of Interaction Involvement: Toward the Development of a Theoretical Concept," *Communication Monographs*, 49 (1982), 229–48.

Charlesworth, W. R. and M. A. Kreutzer, "Facial Expressions of Infants and Children," in *Darwin and Facial Expressions: A Century of Research in Review*, ed. Paul Ekman. New York: Academic, 1973.

Chein, Isidor, "Appendix A: An Introduction to Sampling," in *Research Methods in Social Relations*, 3rd ed., Claire Selltiz, Lawrence S. Wrightsman, and Stuart W. Cook. New York: Holt, Rinehart & Winston, 1976.

Chomsky, Noam, *Language and Mind*. New York: Harcourt Brace Jovanovich, 1968.

_____, *Rules and Representations*. New York: Columbia University Press, 1980.

Clark, Ruth Ann and Jesse G. Delia, "*Topoi* and Rhetorical Competence," *Quarterly Journal of Speech*, 65 (1979), 187–206.

Cody, Michael J. and Margaret L. McLaughlin, "Perceptions of Compliance-Gaining Situations: A Dimensional Analysis," *Communication Monographs*, 47 (1980), 132–48.

Cooley, Charles Horton, *Human Nature and the Social Order*. New York: Charles Scribner's Sons, 1902.

Craig, Robert T. and Karen Tracy, eds., *Conversational Coherence: Form, Structure, and Strategy*. Beverly Hills: Sage, 1983.

Crockett, Walter H., "Cognitive Complexity and Impression Formation," in *Progress in Experimental Personality Research II*, ed. Brendan A. Maher. New York: Academic, 1965.

Cronen, Vernon E. and W. Barnett Pearce, "Logical Force in Interpersonal Communication: A New Concept of the 'Necessity' in Social Behaviors," *Communication*, 6 (1981), 5–67.

_____, **W. Barnett Pearce, and Lonna M. Snavely**, "A Theory of Rule-Structure and Types of Episodes and a Study of Perceived Enmeshment in Undesired Repetitive Patterns ('URPS')," in *Communication Yearbook 3*, ed. Dan Nimmo. New Brunswick, N. J.: Transaction Books, 1979.

Cronkhite, Gary and Jo Liska, "A Critique of Factor Analytic Approaches to the Study of Credibility," *Communication Monographs*, 43 (1976), 91–107.

Cushman, Donald P. and W. Barnett Pearce, "Generality and Necessity in Three Types of Theory and Human Communication with Special Attention to Rules Theory," *Human Communication Research*, 3 (1977), 344–53.

Dance, Frank E. X., "The 'Concept' of Communication," *Journal of Communication*, 20 (1970), 201–10.

_____, *Human Communication Theory: Comparative Essays*. New York: Harper & Row, 1982.

_____, "Swift, Slow, Sweet, Sour, Adazzle, Dim: What Makes Human Communication Human," *Western Journal of Speech Communication*, 44 (1980), 60–63.

_____ **and Carl E. Larson**, *The Functions of Human Communication: A Theoretical Approach*. New York: Holt, Rinehart & Winston, 1976.

_____ **and Carl E. Larson**, *Speech Communication: Concepts and Behavior*. New York: Holt, Rinehart & Winston, 1972.

Delia, Jesse G., Change of Meaning Processes in Impression Formation," *Communication Monographs*, 43 (1976), 142–57.

_____, "Some Tentative Thoughts Concerning the Study of Interpersonal Relationships and Their Development," *Western Journal of Speech Communication*, 44 (1980), 97–107.

_____, **Ruth Ann Clark, and David E. Switzer**, "Cognitive Complexity and Impression Formation in Informal Social Interaction," *Speech Monographs*, 41 (1974), 299–308.

_____, **Ruth Ann Clark, and David E. Switzer**, "The Content of Informal Conversations as a Function of Interactants' Interpersonal Cognitive Compexity," *Communication Monographs*, 46 (1979), 274–81.

_____, **Barbara J. O'Keefe, and Daniel J. O'Keefe**, "The Constructivist Approach to Communication," in *Human Communication Theory: Comparative Essays*, ed. Frank E. X. Dance. New York: Harper & Row, 1982.

_____ and Lawrence Grossberg, "Interpretation and Evidence," *Western Journal of Speech Communication*, 41 (1977), 32–42.

_____ and others, "The Development of Persuasive Communication Strategies in Kindergarteners Through Twelfth Graders," *Communication Monographs*, 46 (1979), 231–40.

Demos, John, *Past, Present, and Personal: The Family and the Life Course in American History*. New York: Oxford University Press, 1986.

_____ and Sarane Spence Boocock, *Turning Points: Historical and Sociological Essays on the Family*, Supplement to the *American Journal of Sociology*, vol. 84. Chicago: University of Chicago Press, 1978.

Denzin, Norman K., *The Research Act: A Theoretical Introduction to Sociological Methods*. Chicago: Aldine, 1970.

Deutsch, Karl W., "Some Notes on Research: On the Role of Models in Natural and Social Science," *Synthese*, 7 (1948–1949), 506–33.

Deutscher, Irwin, "Looking Backward: Case Studies on the Progress of Methodology in Sociological Research," *The American Sociologist*, 4 (1969), 35–40.

van Dijk, T. A., *Studies in the Pragmatics of Discourse*. The Hague: Mouton, 1981.

_____, *Macrostructures: An Interdisciplinary Study of Global Structures in Discourse, Interaction, and Cognition*. Hillsdale, N. J.: Lawrence Erlbaum Associates, 1980.

Dillard, James Price, Chris Segren, and Janie M. Harden, "Primary and Secondary Goals in the Production of Interpersonal Influence Messages," *Communication Monographs*, 56 (March 1989), 19–38.

Dizard, Jan E. and Howard Gadlin, "Family Life and the Marketplace: Diversity and Change in the American Family," in *Historical Social Psychology*, eds. Kenneth J. Gergen and Mary M. Gergen. Hillsdale, N. J.: Lawrence Erlbaum Associates, 1984.

Dollard, John and others, *Frustration and Aggression*. New Haven: Yale University Press, 1939.

Dubin, Robert, *Theory Building*. New York: The Free Press, 1969.

Duck, Steve, "Interpersonal Communication in Developing Acquaintance," in *Explorations in Interpersonal Communication*, ed. Gerald R. Miller. Beverly Hills: Sage, 1976.

_____, ed., *Personal Relationships, 4: Dissolving Personal Relationships*. New York: Academic, 1982.

_____ and Daniel Perlman, eds., *Understanding Personal Relationships: An Interdisciplinary Approach*. Beverly Hills: Sage, 1985.

Duncan, Hugh Dalziel, "The Search for a Social Theory of Communication," in *Human Communication Theory: Original Essays*, ed. Frank E. X. Dance. New York: Holt, Rinehart & Winston, 1967.

Duncan, S., Jr. and D. W. Fiske, *Face to Face Interaction: Research, Methods, and Theory*. New York: John Wiley & Sons, 1977.

Eco, Umberto, "Strategies of Lying," in *On Signs*, ed. Marshall Blonsky. Baltimore: The Johns Hopkins University Press, 1985.

_____, *A Theory of Semiotics*. Bloomington: Indiana University Press, 1976.

Ehninger, Douglas, "Dominant Trends in English Rhetorical Thought, 1750–1800," *Southern Speech Journal*, 18 (1952), 3–11.

Ekman, Paul and W. V. Friesen, "The Repertoire of Nonverbal Behavior: Categories, Origins, Usage, and Coding," *Semiotica*, 1 (1969), 49–98.

Ellis, Donald G. and B. Aubrey Fisher, "Phases of Conflict in Small-Group Development: A Markov Analysis," *Human Communication Research*, 1 (1975), 195–212.

Fay, Brian, *Social Theory and Political Practice*. New York: Holmes and Meier, 1975.

Featherman, David L., "Life-Span Perspectives in Social Science Research," in *Life-Span Development and Behavior*, vol. 5, eds. Paul B. Baltes and Orville G. Brim, Jr. New York: Academic, 1983.

Festinger, Leon, *A Theory of Cognitive Dissonance*. Stanford, Calif.: Stanford University Press, 1957.

_____, "A Theory of Social Comparison Processes," *Human Relations*, 2 (1954), 117–40.

Fiedler, Fred E., "A Contingency Model of Leadership Effectiveness," in *Advances in Experimental Social Psychology*, vol. 1, ed. Leonard Berkowitz. New York: Academic, 1964.

_____, *A Theory of Leadership Effectiveness*. New York: McGraw-Hill, 1967.

Fishbein, Martin and Icek Ajzen, "Acceptance, Yielding, and Impact: Cognitive Processes in Persuasion," in *Cognitive Responses in Persuasion*, eds. Richard E. Petty, Thomas M. Ostrom, and Timothy C. Brock. Hillsdale, N. J.: Lawrence Erlbaum Associates, 1981.

_____ and Icek Ajzen, *Belief, Attitude, Intention, and Behavior*. Reading, Mass.: Addison-Wesley, 1975.

Fisher, B. Aubrey, "Decision Emergence: Phases in Group Decision Making," *Speech Monographs*, 37 (1970), 53–66.

_____, *Perspectives on Human Communication*. New York: Macmillan, 1978.

_____, *Small-Group Decision Making: Communication and the Group Process*, 2nd ed. New York: McGraw-Hill, 1980.

_____, "A View from System Theory," in *Human Communication Theory: Comparative Essays*, ed. Frank E. X. Dance. New York: Harper & Row, 1982.

_____, Gay Lloyd Dreksel, and Wayne S. Werbel, "Social Information Processing Analysis." Unpublished coding manual, University of Utah.

_____ and Leonard C. Hawes, "An Interact System Model: Generating a Grounded Theory of Small Groups," *Quarterly Journal of Speech*, 57 (1971), 444–53.

Fisher, Walter R., "Clarifying the Narrative Paradigm," *Communication Monographs*, 56 (March 1989), 55–58.

_____, "Narration as a Human Communication Paradigm: The Case of Public Moral Argument," *Communication Monographs*, 51 (1987), 1–22.

_____, "The Narrative Paradigm and the Interpretation and Assessment of Historical Texts," *Argumentation and Advocacy*, 25 (1988).

Freud, Sigmund, *The Interpretation of Dreams*, trans. James Strachey. New York: Avon, 1965.

Frings, Hubert, "Zoology," in *Interdisciplinary Approaches to Human Communication*, eds. Richard W. Budd and Brent D. Ruben. Rochelle Park, N. J.: Hayden, 1979.

Ford, Julienne, *Paradigms and Fairy Tales: An Introduction to the Science of Meanings*, vol. 1. Boston: Routledge and Kegan Paul, 1975.

Gadlin, Howard, "Private Lives and Public Order: A Critical View of the History of Intimate Relations in the United States," in *Close Relationships: Perspectives on the Meaning of Intimacy*, eds. George Levinger and Harold L. Raush. Amherst, Mass.: University of Massachusetts Press, 1977.

Galvin, Kathleen M. and Bernard J. Brommel, *Family Communication: Cohesion and Change*. Glenview, Ill.: Scott, Foresman, 1982.

Gergen, Kenneth J., "Social Constructionist Inquiry: Context and Implications," in *The Social Construction of the Person*, eds. Kenneth J. Gergen and Keith E. Davis. New York: Springer-Verlag, 1985.

_____ **and Keith E. Davis**, eds., *The Social Construction of the Person*. New York: Springer-Verlag, 1985.

Gergen, Mary and Kenneth J. Gergen, "The Social Construction of Narrative Accounts," in *Historical Social Psychology*, eds. Kenneth J. Gergen and Mary M. Gergen. Hillsdale, N. J.: Lawrence Erlbaum Associates, 1984.

Gibb, Jack R., "Defensive Communication," in *Messages*, 3rd ed., ed. Sanford B. Weinberg. New York: Random House, 1980.

Glaser, Barney G. and Anselm L. Strauss, *The Discovery of Grounded Theory: Strategies for Qualitative Research*. Chicago: Aldine, 1967.

Goffman, Erving. "On Face-Work: An Analysis of Ritual Elements in Social Interaction," *Psychiatry*, 18 (1955), 213–31.

_____, *The Presentation of Self in Everyday Life*. Garden City, N. Y.: Doubleday, 1959.

_____, "Role Distance," in *Encounters: Two Studies in the Sociology of Interaction*. New York: Bobbs-Merrill, 1961.

Goldhaber, Dale, *Life-Span Human Development*. New York: Harcourt Brace Jovanovich, 1986.

Gould, Stephen Jay, "Triumph of a Naturalist," *New York Review of Books*, vol. 31, no. 5 (March 29, 1984).

Greenwald, Anthony G., "Cognitive Response Analysis: An Appraisal," in *Cognitive Responses in Persuasion*, eds. Richard E. Petty, Thomas M. Ostrom, and Timothy C. Brock. Hillsdale, N. J.: Lawrence Erlbaum Associates, 1981.

Grice, H. P., "Logic and Conversation," in *Syntax and Semantics*, vol. 3, eds. Peter Cole and Jerry L. Morgan. New York: Academic, 1975.

Gumperz, John J., "Introduction," in *Directions in Sociolinguistics*, eds. John J. Gumperz and Dell Hymes. New York: Holt, Rinehart & Winston, 1972.

Hall, A. D. and R. E. Fagen, "Definition of System," *General Systems Yearbook*, 1 (1956), 18–28.

Halliday, M. A. K., *Language as Social Semiotic: The Social Interpretation of Language and Meaning*. London: Edward Arnold, 1978.

_____ **and R. Hasan**, *Cohesion in English*. London: Longman, 1976.

Hanson, Norwood R., *Patterns of Discovery*. Cambridge: Cambridge University Press, 1958.

Harper, Nancy, *Human Communication Theory: The History of a Paradigm*. Rochelle Park, N. J.: Hayden, 1979.

Harre, Rom, ed., *Life Sentences: Aspects of the Social Role of Language*. New York: John Wiley & Sons, 1976.

_____, *Personal Being: A Theory for Individual Psychology*. Cambridge, Mass.: Harvard University Press, 1984.

_____, *Social Being*. Oxford: Basil Blackwell, 1979.

_____, *The Social Construction of Emotions*. New York: Blackwell, 1986.

_____, "Some Remarks on 'Rule' as a Scientific Concept," in *Understanding Other Persons*, ed. Theodore Mischel. Oxford: Blackwell, 1974.

_____, **David Clarke, and Nicola de Carlo**, *Motives and Mechanisms: An Introduction to the Psychology of Action*. New York: Methuen, 1985.

Hart, Roderick P. and Don M. Burks, "Rhetorical Sensitivity and Social Interaction," *Speech Monographs*, 39 (1972), 75–91.

_____, **Robert E. Carlson, and William F. Eadie**, "Attitudes Toward Communication and the Assessment of Rhetorical Sensitivity," *Communication Monographs*, 46 (1980), 1–22.

_____, **Gustav W. Friedrich, and William D. Brooks**, "Source Credibility," in *Contexts of Communication*, ed. Jean M. Civikly. New York: Holt, Rinehart & Winston, 1981.

Havighurst, Robert J., *Developmental Tasks and Education*, 3rd ed. New York: David McKay, 1972.

Hawkes, Terence, *Structuralism and Semiotics*. Berkeley and Los Angeles: University of California Press, 1977.

Heider, Fritz, *The Psychology of Interpersonal Relations*. New York: John Wiley & Sons, 1958.

_____, "Social Perception and Phenomenal Causality," *Psychological Review*, 51 (1944), 358–74.

Hersey, Paul and Kenneth Blanchard, *Management of Organizational Behavior: Utilizing Human Resources*, 3rd ed. Englewood Cliffs, N. J.: Prentice Hall, 1977.

Hewgill, Murray A. and Gerald R. Miller, "Source Credibility and Response to Fear-Arousing Communications," *Speech Monographs*, 32 (1965), 95–101.

Hewitt, John P., *Self and Society: A Symbolic Interactionist Social Psychology*. Boston: Allyn & Bacon, 1976.

_____ **and Randall Stokes**, "Disclaimers," *American Sociological Review*, 40 (1975), 1–11.

Hirokawa, Randy, "Group Communication and Problem Solving Effectiveness, I: A Critical Review of Inconsistent Findings," *Communication Quarterly*, 30 (1982), 134–41.

_____, "Group Communication and Problem-Solving Effectiveness: An Investigation of Group Phases," *Human Communication Research*, 9 (1983), 291–305.

Hollander, Edwin P., "Conformity, Status, and Idiosyncrasy Credit," *Psychological Review*, 65 (1958), 117–27.

Homans, George Caspar, *Social Behavior: Its Elementary Forms*. New York: Harcourt Brace Jovanovich, 1959.

Hovland, Carl I., Irving L. Janis, and Harold H. Kelley, *Communication and Persuasion*. New Haven: Yale University Press, 1953.

_____ **and W. A. Weiss**, "The Influence of Source Credibility on Communicative Effectiveness," *Public Opinion Quarterly*, 15 (1951), 635–50.

_____ **and others**, *The Order of Presentation in Persuasion*. New Haven: Yale University Press, 1957.

Hymes, Dell, *Foundations in Sociolinguistics: An Ethnographic Approach*. Philadelphia: University of Pennsylvania Press, 1974.

Jackson, Don D., "The Study of the Family," in *The Interactional View*, eds. Paul Watzlawick and John H. Weakland. New York: W. W. Norton, 1977.

Jakobson, Roman, "Closing Statement: Linguistics and Poetics," in *Style in Language*, ed. Thomas A. Sebeok. Berkeley and Los Angeles: University of California Press, 1977.

Janis, Irving and others, *Personality and Persuasibility*. New Haven: Yale University Press, 1959.

Johnson, David W., *Reaching Out*. Englewood Cliffs, N. J.: Prentice Hall, 1972.

Jones, Edward E. and Keith E. Davis, "From Acts to Dispositions: The Attribution Process in Person Perception," in *Advances in Experimental Social Psychology*, vol. 2, ed. Leonard Berkowitz. New York: Academic, 1965.

_____ **and Harold B. Gerard**, *Foundations of Social Psychology*. New York: John Wiley & Sons, 1967.

_____ **and Richard E. Nisbett**, "The Actor and the Observer: Divergent Perceptions of the Causes of Behavior," in *Attribution: Perceiving the Causes of Behavior*, 2nd ed., eds. Edward E. Jones and others. Morristown, N. J.: General Learning Press, 1972.

_____ **and Thane S. Pittman**, "Toward a General Theory of Strategic Self-Presentation," in *Pychological Perspectives on the Self*, ed. Harry Suls. Hillsdale, N. J.: Lawrence Erlbaum Associates, 1980.

Katz, Daniel, "The Functional Approach to the Study of Attitudes," *Public Opinion Quarterly*, 24 (1960), 163–204.

_____ **and Robert L. Kahn**, *The Social Psychology of Organizations*. New York: John Wiley & Sons, 1966.

Kelley, Harold H., "Attribution Theory in Social Psychology," *Nebraska Symposium on Motivation*. Lincoln: University of Nebraska Press, 1967.

Kelly, George A., *The Psychology of Personal Constructs, Volume 1: A Theory of Personality*. New York: W. W. Norton, 1955.

Kelman, Herbert C., "Attitudes are Alive and Well and Gainfully Employed in the Sphere of Action," *American Psychologist*, 29 (1974), 310–24.

Kermode, Frank, "Secrets and Narrative Sequence," in *On Narrative*, ed. W. J. T. Mitchell. Chicago: University of Chicago Press, 1984.

Kessler, Suzanne J. and Wendy McKenna, *Gender: An Ethnomethodological Approach*. New York: John Wiley & Sons, 1978.

Knapp, Mark L., *Essentials of Nonverbal Communication*. New York: Holt, Rinehart & Winston, 1980.

_____, *Interpersonal Communication in Human Relationships*. Boston: Allyn & Bacon, 1984.

_____ **and others**, "The Rhetoric of Goodbye: Verbal and Nonverbal Correlates of Human Leave-taking," *Speech Monographs*, 40 (1973), 182–98.

Kramarae, Cheris, *Women and Men Speaking: Frameworks for Analysis*. Rowley, Mass.: Newbury House, 1981, p. 3.

Krippendorf, Klaus, "Values, Modes and Domains of Inquiry into Communication," *The Journal of Communication*, 19 (1969), 105–33.

Krivonos, Paul and Mark L. Knapp, "Initiating Communication: What Do You Say When You Say Hello?" *Central States Speech Journal*, 26 (1975), 115–25.

Labov, William, "Rules for Ritual Insults," in *Studies in Social Interaction*, ed. David Sudnow. New York: The Free Press, 1972.

Lakoff, Robin, *Language and Woman's Place*. New York: Harper & Row, 1975.

Larson, Carl E., "Problems in Assessing Functional Communication," *Communication Education*, 27 (1978), 304–09.

Larson, Charles U., *Persuasion: Reception and Responsibility*, 2nd ed. Belmont, Calif.: Wadsworth, 1979.

Lave, Charles A. and James G. March, *An Introduction to Models in the Social Sciences*. New York: Harper & Row, 1975.

Lawton, Dennis, *Social Class, Language and Education*. New York: Schocken, 1968.

Leavett, Harold J., "Some Effects of Certain Communication Patterns on Group Performance," *Journal of Abnormal and Social Psychology*, 46 (1951), 38–50.

Levi-Strauss, Claude, *From Honey to Ashes: Introduction to a Science of Mythology, 2*. New York: Harper & Row, 1973.

Lewis, William F., "Telling America's Story: Narrative Form and the Reagan Presidency," *Quarterly Journal of Speech*, 73 (1987), 280–302.

Liebes, Tamar, "Cultural Differences in the Retelling of Television Fiction," *Critical Studies in Mass Communication*, 5 (December 1988), 277–92.

Ling, David A., "A Pentadic Analysis of Senator Edward Kennedy's Address to the People of Massachusetts, July 25, 1969," *The Central States Speech Journal*, 21 (1970), 81–86.

Linton, Ralph, *The Cultural Background of Personality*. New York: Appleton-Century-Crofts, 1945.

Littlejohn, Stephen W., *Theories of Human Communication*, 3rd ed. Belmont, Calif.: Wadsworth, 1989.

Lyman, Peter, "The Fraternal Bond as a Joking Relationship: A Case Study of Sexist Jokes in Male Group Bonding," in *Changing Men: New Directions in Research on Men and Masculinity*. Beverly Hills: Sage, 1987, pp. 148–63.

Marcel, Gabriel, *The Mystery of Being*, vol. 1. Chicago: Henry Regnery, 1960.

Marwell, Gerald and David R. Schmitt, "Dimensions of Compliance-Gaining Behavior: An Empirical Analysis," *Sociometry*, 30 (1967), 350–64.

McCall, George J. and J. L. Simmons, *Identities and Interactions*. New York: The Free Press, 1966.

McCroskey, James C., Carl E. Larson, and Mark L. Knapp, *An Introduction to Interpersonal Communication*. Englewood Cliffs, N. J.: Prentice Hall, 1971.

_____ **and Lawrence R. Wheeles**, *Introduction to Human Communication*. Boston: Allyn & Bacon, 1976.

McGuire, William J., "Attitude and Attitude Change," in *Handbook of Social Psychology*, vol. 2, 3rd ed., eds. Gardner Lindzey and Elliot Aronson. New York: Random House, 1985.

_____, "A Contextualist Theory of Knowledge: Its Implications for Innovation and Reform in Psychological Research," in *Advances in Experimental Social Psychology*, vol 16, ed. Leonard Berkowitz. New York: Academic, 1983.

McLaughlin, Margaret, *Conversation: How Talk is Organized*. Beverly Hills: Sage, 1984.

_____, **Michael J. Cody, and Nancy E. Rosenstein**, "Account Sequences in Conversations between Strangers," *Communication Monographs*, 50 (1983), 102–25.

Mead, George Herbert, *Mind, Self and Society*, ed. C. W. Morris. Chicago: University of Chicago Press, 1934.

Meehan, Eugene J., *Value Judgment and Social Science: Structures and Processes*. Homewood, Ill.: Dorsey, 1968.

Mehrabian, Albert, "Attitudes Inferred from Nonimmediacy of Verbal Communications," *Journal of Verbal Learning and Verbal Behavior*, 6 (1967), 294–95.

_____, "A Semantic Space for Nonverbal Behavior," *Journal of Counseling and Clinical Psychology*, 35 (1970), 248–57.

_____ **and Morton Wiener**, "Decoding of Inconsistent Communications," *Journal of Personality and Social Psychology*, 6 (1967), 109–14.

Meltzer, Bernard N., "Mead's Social Psychology," in *Symbolic Interaction: A Reader in Social Psychology*, 2nd ed. eds. Jerome G. Manis and Bernard Meltzer. Boston: Allyn & Bacon, 1972.

Metts, Sandra and William R. Cupach, "Situational Influence on the Use of Remedial Strategies in Embarrassing Predicaments," *Communication Monographs*, 56 (June 1989), 151–62.

Millar, Frank E. and L. Edna Rogers, "A Relational Approach to Interpersonal Communication," in Gerald R. Miller, *Explorations in Interpersonal Communication*. Beverly Hills: Sage, 1976.

Miller, Gerald R., "The Current Status of Theory and Research in Interpersonal Communication," *Human Communication Research*, 4 (1978), 164–78.

_____, *Explorations in Interpersonal Communication*. Beverly Hills: Sage, 1976.

_____ **and Michael Burgoon**, "Persuasion Research: Review and Commentary," *Communication Yearbook 2*, ed. Brent D. Ruben. New Brunswick, N. J.: Transaction Books, 1979.

_____ **and Mark Steinberg**, *Between People: A New Analysis of Interpersonal Communication*. Palo Alto, Calif: Science Research Associates, 1975.

_____ **and others**, "Compliance-Gaining Message Strategies: A Typology and Some Findings Concerning Effects of Situational Differences," *Communication Monographs*, 44 (1977), 37–51.

Mintzberg, Henry, Daru Raisinghani, and Andre Theoret, "The Structure of 'Unstructured' Decision Processes," *Administrative Science Quarterly*, 21 (1976), 246–75.

Monroe, Alan H. and Douglas Ehninger, *Principles and Types of Speech Communication*. Glenview, Ill.: Scott, Foresman, 1974.

Moreland, Richard L. and John M. Levine, "Socialization in Small Groups: Temporal Changes in Individual-Group Relations," in *Advances in Experimental Social Psychology*, vol. 15, ed. Leonard Berkowitz. New York: Academic, 1982.

Mortensen, C. David, "Communication Postulates," in *Contexts*, ed. Jean M. Civikly. New York: Holt, Rinehart & Winston, 1981.

_____, *Communication: The Study of Human Interaction*. New York: McGraw-Hill, 1972.

Muhlhausler, Peter and Rom Harre, *Pronouns and People: The Linguistic Construction of Social and Personal Identity*. Cambridge: Blackwell, 1990.

Newcomb, Theodore M., *The Acquaintance Process*. New York: Holt, Rinehart & Winston,, 1961.

_____, **Ralph H. Turner, and Philip E. Converse**, *Social Psychology: The Study of Human Interaction*. New York: McGraw-Hill, 1972.

Norton, Robert, *Communicator Style: Theory, Application, and Measures*. Beverly Hills: Sage, 1983.

O'Donnell-Trujillo, Nick, "Relational Communication: A Comparison of Coding Systems," *Communication Monographs*, 48 (1981), 91–105.

Park, Robert E., *Human Communities: The City and Human Ecology*, eds. Everett C. Hughes and others. New York: The Free Press, 1952.

Pearce, W. Barnett, "The Coordinated Management of Meaning: A Rules-Based Theory of Interpersonal Communication," in *Explorations in Interpersonal Communication*, ed. Gerald R. Miller. Beverly Hills: Sage, 1976.

_____ **and Forrest Conklin**, "A Model of Hierarchical Meanings in Coherent Conversaton and a Study of 'Indirect Responses,'" *Communication Monographs*, 46 (1979), 75–87.

_____ **and Vernon E. Cronen**, *Communication, Action and Meaning: The Creation of Social Realities*. New York: Holt, Rinehart & Winston, 1982.

_____, **Vernon E. Cronen, and Linda M. Harris**, "Methodological Considerations in Building Human Communication Theory," in *Human Communication Theory*, ed. Frank E. X. Dance. New York: Harper & Row, 1982.

_____ **and others**, "The Structure of Communication Rules and the Form of Conversation: An Experimental Simulation," *Western Journal of Speech Communication*, 44 (1980), 20–34.

Peirce, Charles Sanders, *Collected Papers*, eds. Charles Hartshorne, Paul Weiss, and Arthur W. Burks. Cambridge, Mass.: Harvard University Press, 1931, 1958.

Perloff, Richard M. and Timothy C. Brock, "'...And Thinking Makes it So': Cognitive Responses to Persuasion," in *Persuasion: New Directions in Theory and Research*, eds. Michael E. Roloff and Gerald R. Miller. Beverly Hills: Sage, 1980.

Pettit, Philip, *The Concept of Structuralism: A Critical Analysis*. Berkeley and Los Angeles: University of California Press, 1977.

Petty, Richard E., Thomas M. Ostrom, and Timothy C. Brock, "Historical Foundations of the Cognitive Response Approach to Attitudes and Persuasion," in *Cognitive Responses in Persuasion*, eds. Richard E. Petty, Thomas M. Ostrom, and Timothy C. Brock. Hillsdale, N. J.: Lawrence Erlbaum Associates, 1981.

Philipsen, Gerry, "Places for Speaking in Teamsterville," *The Quarterly Journal of Speech*, 62 (1976), 15–25.

_____,"Speaking 'Like a Man' in Teamsterville: Cultural Patterns of Role Enactment in an Urban Neighborhood," *Quarterly Journal of Speech*, 61 (1975), 13–22.

Piaget, Jean, *Biology and Knowledge*, trans. Beatrix Walsh. Chicago: University of Chicago Press, 1971.

_____, *The Construction of Reality in the Child*, trans. Margaret Cook. New York: Ballantine, 1971.

_____, *Piaget Sampler: An Introduction to Jean Piaget through his Own Words*, ed. Sarah Campbell. New York: John Wiley & Sons, 1976.

Pittinger, Robert Everett and others, *The First Five Minutes: A Sample of Microscopic Interview Analysis*. Ithaca, N. Y.: Paul Martineau, 1960.

Planalp, Sally and Karen Tracy, "Not to Change the Topic But...: A Cognitive Approach to the Study of Conversation," in *Communication Yearbook* 4, ed. Dan Nimmo. New Brunswick, N. J.: Transaction Books, 1980.

Poole, Marshall Scott, "Decision Development in Small Groups, II: A Study of Multiple Sequences in Group Development," *Communication Monographs*, 50 (1983), 206–32.

_____, "Decision Development in Small Groups, III: A Multiple Sequence Model of Group Decision Development," *Communication Monographs*, 50 (1983), 321–41.

Popper, Karl R., *The Logic of Scientific Discovery*, 2nd ed. New York: Harper Torchbooks, 1958.

Radway, Janice, "Identifying Ideological Seams: Mass Culture, Analytical Method, and Political Practice," *Communication*, 9 (1986), 93–123.

Rakow, Lana, "Feminist Studies: The Next Stage," *Critical Studies in Mass Communication*, 6 (June 1989), 209–14.

Rapoport, Anatol, "Foreword," in *Modern Systems Research for the Behavioral Scientist*, ed. Walter Buckley. Chicago: Aldine, 1968.

Reardon, Kathleen Kelley, *Persuasion: Theory and Context*. Beverly Hills: Sage, 1981.

Riccillo, Samuel C., "Modes of Speech as a Developmental Hierarchy: A Descriptive Study," *Western Journal of Speech Communication*, 47 (1983), 1–15.

Rogers, Carl, *Client-Centered Therapy*. Boston: Houghton Mifflin, 1951.

_____, *On Becoming a Person*. Boston: Houghton Mifflin, 1961.

Rogers, Everett M. and Rekha Agarwala-Rogers, *Communication in Organizations*. New York: The Free Press, 1976.

Rogers, L. Edna and Richard V. Farace, "Analysis of Relational Communication in Dyads: New Measurement Procedures," *Human Communication Research*, 1 (1975), 222–39.

Rogge, Edward and James C. Ching, *Advanced Public Speaking*. New York: Holt, Rinehart & Winston, 1966.

Rokeach, Milton, *Beliefs, Attitudes and Values*. San Francisco: Jossey-Bass, 1972.

_____, *The Nature of Human Values*. New York: The Free Press, 1973.

_____, "Value Theory and Communication Research: Review and Commentary," in *Communication Yearbook 3*, ed. Dan Nimmo. New Brunswick, N. J.: Transaction Books, 1979.

Roloff, Michael E. and Edwin F. Barnicott, "The Situational Use of Pro- and Anti-Social Compliance Gaining Strategies by High and Low Machiavellians," in *Communication Yearbook 2*, ed. Brent D. Ruben. New Brunswick, N. J.: Transaction Books, 1976.

Rosenthal, Robert and Ralph L. Rosnow, eds., *Artifact in Behavioral Research*. New York: Academic, 1969.

Rowland, Robert C., "On Limiting the Narrative Paradigm: Three Case Studies," *Communication Monographs*, 56 (March 1989), 39–54.

_____, "Narrative: Mode of Discourse or Paradigm?" *Communication Monographs*, 54 (September 1987), 264–75.

Sacks, H., E. Schegloff, and G. Jefferson, "A Simplest Systematic for the Organization of Turn-Taking for Conversation," in *Studies in the Organization of Conversational Interaction*, ed. J. Schenkein. New York: Academic, 1978.

Samter, Wendy and Brant R. Burleson, "Cognitive and Motivational Influences on Spontaneous Comforting Behavior," *Human Communication Research*, 11 (1984), 231–60.

Sarnoff, Irving, "Psychoanalytic Theory and Social Attitudes," *Public Opinion Quarterly*, 24 (1960), 251–79.

de Saussure, Ferdinand, *Course in General Linguistics*. New York: McGraw-Hill, 1966.

Scheflen, Albert E., *How Behavior Means*. Garden City, N. Y.: Doubleday, 1974.

Schenck-Hamlin, William J., Richard L. Wiseman, and G. N. Georgacarakos, "A Model of Properties of Compliance-Gaining Strategies," *Communication Quarterly*, 30 (1982), 92–100.

Schlenker, Barry R. and B. W. Darby, "The Use of Apologies in Social Predicaments," *Social Psychology Quarterly*, 44 (1981), 271–78.

Schneider, David L., Albert Hastorf, and Phoebe C. Ellsworth, *Person Perception*, 2nd ed. Reading, Mass.: Addison-Wesley, 1979.

Schonbach, P. A., "A Category System for Account Phases," *European Journal of Social Psychology*, 10 (1980), 195–200.

Schweder, Richard A. and Joan G. Miller, "The Social Construction of the Person: How Is It Possible?" in *The Social Construction of the Person*, eds. Kenneth J. Gergen and Keith E. Davis. New York: Springer-Verlag, 1985.

Schwichtenberg, Cathy, "Feminist Cultural Studies, " *Critical Studies in Mass Communication*, 6 (June 1989), 202–08.

Schutz, Alfred, "Concepts and Theory Formation in the Social Sciences," *Journal of Philosophy*, 51 (1954), 257–73.

Schutz, William, *Firo: A Three-Dimensional Theory of Interpersonal Behavior*. New York: Holt, Rinehart & Winston, 1958.

_____, *The Interpersonal Underworld*. Palo Alto, Calif.: Science and Behavior Books, 1966.

_____, "The Postulate of Interpersonal Needs," in *Messages*, 2nd ed., ed. Jean M. Civikly. New York: Random House, Inc., 1977.

Schwartz, Howard and Jerry Jacobs, *Qualitative Sociology: A Method to the Madness*. New York: The Free Press, 1979.

Scott, Marvin B. and Stanford M. Lyman, "Accounts," *American Sociological Review*, 33 (1968), 46–62.

Searle, John R., *Speech Acts: An Essay in the Philosophy of Language*. Cambridge: Cambridge University Press, 1969.

Secord, Paul, "Love, Misogyny, and Feminism in Selected Historical Periods: A Social-Psychological Explanation." in *Historical Social Psychology*, eds. Kenneth J. Gergen and Mary M. Gergen. Hillsdale, N. J.: Lawrence Erlbaum Associates, 1984.

_____ **and Carl W. Backman**, *Social Psychology*, 2nd ed. New York: McGraw-Hill, 1974.

Selltiz, Claire, Lawrence S. Wrightsman, and Stuart W. Cook, *Research Methods in Social Relations*, 3rd ed. New York: Holt, Rinehart & Winston, 1976.

Sereno, Kenneth K. and Edward M. Bodaken, *Trans-Per: Understanding Human Communication*. Boston: Houghton Mifflin, 1975.

Shannon, Claude E. and Warren Weaver, *The Mathematical Theory of Communication*. Urbana, Ill.: University of Illinois Press, 1949.

Shaw, Marvin E., *Group Dynamics: The Psychology of Small-Group Behavior*, 3rd ed. New York: McGraw-Hill, 1981.

Sheehy, Gail, *Passages: Predictable Crises of Adult Life*. New York: E. P. Dutton, 1976.

Sherif, Carolyn W., Muzafer Sherif, and Robert E. Nebergall, *Attitude and Attitude Change: The Social Judgment-Involvement Approach*. Philadelphia: W. B. Saunders, 1965.

Sherif, Muzafer, and Carl I. Hovland, *Social Judgment: Assimilation and Contrast Effects in Communication and Attitude Change*. New Haven: Yale University Press, 1961.

_____ **and Carolyn W. Sherif**, "Attitude as the Individual's Own Categories: The Social Judgment-Involvement Approach to Attitude and Attitude Change," in *Attitude, Ego-Involvement and Change*, eds. Carolyn W. Sherif and Muzafer Sherif. New York: John Wiley & Sons, 1967.

Shimanoff, Susan B., *Communication Rules: Theory and Research*. Beverly Hills: Sage, 1980.

Sieburg, Evelyn, "Dysfunctional Communication and Interpersonal Responsiveness in Small Groups. (Unpublished dissertation, University of Denver), 1969.

Sigman, Stuart J., "On Communication Rules from a Social Perspective," *Human Communication Research*, 7 (1980), 37–51.

_____, *A Perspective on Social Communication*. Lexington, Mass.: D. C. Heath, 1987.

Sillars, Alan J., "Attribution and Communication: Are People 'Naive Scientists' or Just Naive?" in *Social Cognition and Communication*, eds. Michael E. Roloff and Charles R. Berger. Beverly Hills: Sage, 1982.

_____, "Attributions and Communication in Roommate Conflict," *Communication Monographs*, 47 (1980), 180–200.

Slobin, Dan I., *Psycholinguistics*. Glenview, Ill.: Scott, Foresman, 1971.

Smith, Mary John, *Persuasion and Human Action: A Review and Critique of Social Influence Theories*. Belmont, Calif.: Wadsworth, 1982.

Spitzberg, Brian H. and Michael L. Hecht, "A Component Model of Relational Competence," *Human Communication Research*, 10 (1984), 575–99.

Stogdill, Ralph M., *Handbook of Leadership: A Survey of Theory and Research*. New York: The Free Press, 1974.

Stryker, Sheldon, "Social Psychology from the Standpoint of a Structural Symbolic Interactionism: Toward an Interdisciplinary Social Psychology," in *Advances in Experimental Social Psychology*, vol. 16, ed. Leonard Berkowitz. New York: Academic, 1983.

Stubbs, Michael, *Discourse Analysis: The Sociolinguistic Analysis of Natural Language*. Chicago: University of Chicago Press, 1983.

Sugarman, Leonie, *Life-Span Development: Concepts, Theories, and Interventions*. New York: Methuen, 1986.

Super, Donald E., "A Life-Span, Life-Space Approach to Career Development," *Journal of Vocational Behavior*, 16 (1980), 282–98.

Swanson, David L. and Jesse G. Delia, "The Nature of Human Communication," *Modules in Speech Communication*. Chicago: Science Research Associates, 1976.

Tannen, Deborah, *Conversational Style: Analyzing Talk Among Friends*. Norwood, N. J.: Ablex, 1984.

_____, *That's Not What I Meant!*. New York: William Morrow, 1986.

Tannenbaum, Percy H., "The Congruity Principle Revisited: Studies in the Reduction, Induction, and Generalization of Persuasion," in *Advances in Experimental Social Psychology*, vol. 3, ed. Leonard Berkowitz. New York: Academic, 1967.

Taylor, Shelley E. and Jennifer Crocker, "Schematic Bases of Social Information Processing," in *Social Cognition: The Ontario Symposium*, vol. 1, eds. E. Tory Higgins, C. Peter Herman, and Mark P. Zanna. Hillsdale, N. J.: Lawrence Erlbaum Associates, 1981.

Tedeschi, James T., ed., *Impression Management Theory and Social Psychology*. New York: Academic, 1981.

Thayer, Lee, "Communication: *Sine Qua Non* of the Behavioral Sciences," in *Interdisciplinary Approaches to Human Communication*, eds. Richard W. Budd and Brent D. Ruben. Rochelle Park, N. J.: Hayden, 1979.

Thibaut, John W. and Harold H. Kelley, *The Social Psychology of Groups*. New York: John Wiley & Sons, 1959.

Toulmin, Stephen, "Rules and Their Relevance of Understanding Human Behavior," in *Understanding Other Persons*, ed. Theodore Mischel. Oxford: Blackwell, 1974.

_____, *The Uses of Argument*. Cambridge: Cambridge University Press, 1958.

Trager, G. L., "Paralanguage: A First Approximation," *Studies in Linguistics*, 13 (1958), 1–12.

Treichler, Paul A. and Ellen Wartella, "Interventions: Feminist Theory and Communication Studies," *Communication*, 9 (1986), 1–18.

Trenholm, Sarah, *Persuasion and Social Influence*. Englewood Cliffs, N. J.: Prentice Hall, 1989.

Tuckman, Bruce, "Developmental Sequence in Small Groups," *Psychological Bulletin*, 63 (1965), 384–99.

Vetter, Harold J., *Language Behavior and Communication: An Introduction*. Itasca, Ill.: F. E. Peacock, 1969.

Vygotsky, Lev Semenovich, *Thought and Language*, eds. and trans. Eugenia Hanfmann and Gertrude Vakar. Cambridge, Mass.: MIT Press, 1962.

Watzlawick, Paul, Janet Beavin Bavelas, and Don D. Jackson, *Pragmatics of Human Communication*. New York: W. W. Norton, 1967.

Weaver, Richard M., "Some Rhetorical Aspects of Grammatical Categories," in *Methods of Rhetorical Criticism: A Twentieth Century Perspective*, 2nd ed., eds. Bernard L. Brock and Robert L. Scott. Detroit: Wayne State University Press, 1972.

Weaver, Warren, "The Mathematics of Communication," in *Basic Readings in Communication Theory*, 2nd ed., ed. C. David Mortensen. New York: Harper & Row, 1979.

Webb, Eugene J. and others, *Unobtrusive Measures: Nonreactive Research in the Social Sciences*. Chicago: Rand McNally, 1966.

Weick, Karl E., *The Social Psychology of Organizing*. Reading, Mass.: Addison-Wesley, 1969.

Weinstein, Eugene A., "The Development of Interpersonal Competence," in *Handbook of Socialization Theory and Research*, ed. David A. Goslin. Chicago: Rand McNally, 1969.

White, Hayden, "The Value of Narrativity in the Representation of Reality," in *On Narrative*, ed. W. J. T. Mitchell. Chicago: University of Chicago Press, 1984.

White, Ralph K. and Ronald Lippitt, "Leader Behavior and Member Reaction in Three 'Social Climates,'" in *Autocracy and Democracy*, eds. Ralph K. White and Ronald Lippitt. New York: Harper & Row, 1960.

Wiemann, John M., "Explication and Test of a Model of Communicative Competence," *Human Communication Research*, 3 (1977), 195–213.

_____, "Needed Research and Training in Speaking and Listening Literacy," *Communication Education*, 27 (1978), 310–15.

Wilder, Carol, "The Palo Alto Group: Difficulties and Direction of the Interactional View of Human Communication Research," *Human Communication Research*, 5 (1979), 171–86.

Wilder-Mott, C. and John H. Weakland, *Rigor and Imagination: Essays from the Legacy of Gregory Bateson*. New York: Holt, Rinehart & Winston, 1981.

Williams, Frederick, *Language and Speech: Introductory Perspectives*. Englewood Cliffs, N. J.: Prentice Hall, 1972.

Wilmot, William W., *Dyadic Communication*, 2nd ed. Reading, Mass.: Addison-Wesley, 1979.

Wilson, John F. and Carroll C. Arnold, *Public Speaking as a Liberal Art*, 3rd ed. Boston: Allyn & Bacon, 1974.

Wiseman, Richard L. and William J. Schenck-Hamlin, "A Multi-Dimensional Scaling Validation of an Inductively-Derived Set of Compliance-Gaining Strategies," *Communication Monographs*, 48 (1981), 251–70.

Wood, Barbara S., *Children and Communication: Verbal and Nonverbal Language Development*, 2nd ed. Englewood Cliffs, N. J.: Prentice Hall, 1981.

Wood, Julia T., "Communication and Relational Culture: Bases for the Study of Human Relationships," *Communication Quarterly*, 30 (1982), 75–82.

Zimbardo, Philip G., Ebbe B. Ebbesen, and Christina Maslach, *Influencing Attitudes and Changing Behaviors*, 2nd ed. Reading, Mass.: Addison-Wesley, 1977.

_____ **and others**, "Communicator Effectiveness in Producing Public Conformity and Private Attitude Change," *Journal of Personality*, 33 (1965), 233–55.

AUTHOR INDEX

SUBJECT INDEX